THE ANCIENT CENTRAL ANDES

"Quilter's text is a succinct and up to date account of the cultural history of the Central Andes. Period by period he cuts to the heart of the important developments, and provides students with a sense of the magnificence of ancient Andean civilization. His explanations and interpretations of past events are clear, yet nuanced and balanced."

Katharina Schreiber, *University of California, USA*

The Ancient Central Andes presents a general overview of the prehistoric peoples and cultures of the Central Andes, the region now encompassing most of Peru and significant parts of Ecuador, Bolivia, northern Chile, and northwestern Argentina. The book contextualizes past and modern scholarship and provides a balanced view of current research. Two opening chapters present the intellectual, political, and practical background and history of research in the Central Andes and the spatial, temporal, and formal dimensions of the study of its past. Chapters then proceed in chronological order from remote antiquity to the Spanish Conquest.

A number of important themes run through the book, including: the tension between those scholars who wish to study Peruvian antiquity on a comparative basis and those who take historicist approaches; the concept of "Lo Andino," commonly used by many specialists that assumes long-term, unchanging patterns of culture some of which are claimed to persist to the present; and culture change related to severe environmental events. Consensus opinions on interpretations are highlighted as are disputes among scholars regarding interpretations of the past.

The Ancient Central Andes provides an up-to-date, objective survey of the archaeology of the Central Andes that is much needed. Students and interested readers will benefit greatly from this introduction to a key period in South America's past.

Jeffrey Quilter is the William and Muriel Seabury Howells Director of the Peabody Museum of Archaeology and Ethnology at Harvard University, USA. He previously served as Director of the Pre-Columbian Studies Program and Curator of the Pre-Columbian Collection at Dumbarton Oaks, Washington DC and as a professor of Anthropology at Ripon College, Wisconsin. He has been involved in archaeological research particularly in Peru and Costa Rica. He has published numerous articles and books including *Life and Death at Paloma* (1989), *Cobble Circles and Standing Stones* (2004), *Treasures of the Andes* (2005), and *The Moche of Ancient Peru* (2011).

Routledge World Archaeology

Ancient Turkey, Antonio Sagona and Paul Zimansky
Prehistoric Britain, 2nd edition, Timothy C. Darvill

Forthcoming:

Ancient Iran, Roger Matthews and Hassan Fazeli
Ancient Crete, Jan Driessen
Formative Britain AD *400–1100*, Martin Carver
Ancient Southeast Asia, John Miksic and Goh Geok Yian
Prehistoric Italy, Robin Skeates

THE ANCIENT CENTRAL ANDES

Jeffrey Quilter

LONDON AND NEW YORK

First published 2014
by Routledge
2 Park Square, Milton Park, Abingdon, Oxon OX14 4RN

and by Routledge
711 Third Avenue, New York, NY 10017

Routledge is an imprint of the Taylor & Francis Group, an informa business

British Library Cataloguing in Publication Data
A catalogue record for this book is available from the British Library

Library of Congress Cataloging in Publication Data
Quilter, Jeffrey, 1949–
The ancient central Andes / Jeffrey Quilter.
pages cm. – (Routledge world archaeology)
Includes bibliographical references and index.
1. Indians of South America–Andes Region–Antiquities. 2. Indians of South America–Andes Region–History. 3. Indians of South America–Andes Region–Social life and customs.
4. Andes Region–Civilization. 5. Andes Region–Antiquities. I. Title.
F2229.Q55 2014
980'.01–dc23
2013025670

ISBN: 978-0-415-67309-9 (hbk)
ISBN: 978-0-415-67310-5 (pbk)
ISBN: 978-1-315-85794-7 (ebk)

Typeset in Sabon and Frutiger
by Saxon Graphics Ltd, Derby

Printed and bound in Great Britain by
TJ International Ltd, Padstow, Cornwall

CONTENTS

LIST OF FIGURES

ACKNOWLEDGMENTS

This book is an essay, an attempt to synthesize current knowledge of the prehistory of the Central Andes, the region once encompassed by the Inca Empire that includes parts of present day Colombia, Ecuador, Peru, Bolivia, Argentina, and Chile. I hope that the reader will find it informative and interesting in its presentation of the worlds of the ancient peoples of the Central Andes and some of the ideas that scholars have developed concerning them. I have certainly found writing this book informative, interesting, and exciting to research and write, even though I have spent almost half a century involved in the topics it covers. I learned much in investigating some issues with which I was relatively unfamiliar, and although my love for the subject has never flagged, I was reminded of why I became interested in the Andes in the first place.

Indeed, it is astounding to me how much new information is available, compared to when I first studied Andean prehistory a half-century ago, on everything from the major topics, such as the features of significant time periods and cultures, to small details about everyday life at various times and places. The pace of work and publication also has increased dramatically in recent years. Field, laboratory, and other investigations have been aided by more and better quality publications than ever before, and by new generations of scholars including world-class researchers in Europe, North America, Asia, and Latin America.

I have tried to present information as objectively as possible while being fully aware that complete objectivity is impossible to achieve in a work like this. I have included some topics and left others out, and in making those choices my own predilections and biases have influenced the contents of this book. As much as possible, however, I have tried to concentrate on major topics and issues with an occasional mention of a small detail that often speaks volumes. I have included topics that I believe most readers will want to know about, and tried to present differing views clearly without editorializing.

After two chapters in which I present background information, I proceed chronologically through prehistory from early to late times. The reader may note that I occasionally repeat statements. This is partly to emphasize key issues and themes and also because some readers may choose to read chapters separately. In the Afterword I also offer a summary thumbnail review of prehistory and my own perspective on some key issues and changing perspectives.

I take responsibility for all statements in this book on the prehistory and archaeology of the Central Andes. However, I have performed only a tiny amount of the research examined here; my job has been to present the work, ideas, and opinions of others. I hope that I have done so accurately and fairly. On occasion I will state my own opinion, but you, gentle reader, must make the final decision about the controversies you will learn about by reading the various publications in which arguments are set forth and which are referenced in my end notes. I also wish to note that there are many scholars conducting very fine work in the Central Andes whose contributions are not presented here. This is not because their work is unworthy of inclusion, but simply because the way I have structured the book demanded that I take certain paths which emphasized some issues more than others, even while I tried to be inclusive.

I thank the many institutions and people who helped me along the way in putting this book together. In many ways this book could not have been written without the many experiences that I have had in Andean countries throughout the years, but to list all of the institutions and people who have helped me during that time would be excessive for present purposes. In particular, many people and institutions have kindly helped in providing illustrations used in this book, or permission to use them. Other people in the last several years, and particularly in the past two years while I have been writing, have been very generous with their time and resources, and so I must thank them here.

I begin by thanking the staff at Routledge Publications, especially Matthew Gibbons who first invited me to write this book, and Amy Davis-Poynter and Kate Rosenberger who helped on many issues. Special thanks go to Rob Brown, Emma Hudson, and Louise Maskill the editors who helped to get my final manuscript into shape.

Sincere thanks also are rendered to Robert Batson, Brian Bauer, Robert Benfer, Sergio Chávez, Ryan Clasby, William Conklin, R. Alan Covey, Tom Cummins, Carlos Elera, Clark Erickson, Robert Feldman, Isabel Flores, César Gálvez, Christine Hastorf, William Isbell, John and Silvia Kembel, Alan Kolata, Michele Koons, George Lau, Steven LeBlanc, Ron Lippi. Don McClelland, Juan Antonio Murro, Bernadino Ojeda, Yoishio Onuki, O. Gabriel Prieto, Bruce Owen, Tom Patterson, Joanne Pillsbury, Kurt Rademaker, Scott Raymond, James B. Richardson III, John Rick, Mario Rivera, Matthew Robb, Lucy Salazar, Izumi Shimada, Helaine Silverman, Peter Stahl, Karen Stothert, John Topic, Santiago Uceda, Gary Urton, Rafael Eduardo Valdez, and Enrique Vergara. These people have shared ideas, information and illustrations that made their way into this book, and I am grateful to them for their aid. My life in Peru and my work there have been made much more pleasant, interesting, and productive by the generosity and friendship of Marco Aveggio and the support offered through the Fundación Wiese. Régulo Franco J. also has been a steadfast friend and colleague and I thank him for all of the support and friendship through the years. The same is true for the long-term collaborations and friendships with Luis Jaime Castillo B. and Santiago Uceda C. I thank them profoundly for their support, aid, and comfort.

I offer special thanks to a number of people who volunteered to read chapters of this book and give me advice on their contents. They are Ari Caramanica, R. Jeffrey Frost, Jennifer Ringberg, and Daniel H. Sandweiss. Kathryn Ness also rendered crucial and important services in helping with maps and radiocarbon dates, and Linda Ordogh performed the monumental task of compiling the final References Cited list. I thank them sincerely.

Whatever positive features this book may possess have been greatly improved by the enormous generosity of my friend of many years, Richard L. Burger. He read the manuscript in detail, provided illustrations, and offered a great number of suggestions and encouragement that all made for a better book. I have been lucky to know him not only because of his impressive knowledge of the Andes, past and present, and his generosity in sharing it with me, but also because of his steadfastness as a true friend.

I also once again acknowledge my parents, Joan and the late Thomas Quilter, for their support especially early in my career, and my children, Susanna and Elizabeth, for their support later in it. I cannot thank my wife, Sarah, enough for her patience with me, in general and especially while I was writing this book. Most of the text was written at our dining room table during evenings and weekends, and I appreciate her tolerance of me in this and other enterprises. I thank her, among many other reasons, for aid and comfort, wise council, and companionship in Peru, the US, and beyond. Although she has been included in the dedication of a previous book, this one is just for her.

IMAGE CREDITS

NOTES:

- Some photographs have been edited to remove blemishes or to increase the clarity of presentation.
- All objects not to scale unless otherwise indicated.
- The abbreviation PMAE is used for the Peabody Museum of Archaeology and Ethnology, Harvard University. Catalogue numbers of the objects are provided in parentheses.
- Every effort has been made to contact copyright holders. Please advise the publisher of any errors or omissions, and these will be corrected in subsequent editions.

1.1 Jeffrey Quilter and Routledge Press.
1.2 After Guamán Poma de Ayala, *circa* 1559.
1.3 Courtesy of Patrimono Nacional, Palacio Real, Madrid.
1.4 AMS Press, NY: 1973 reprint of the 1877 edition for the Peabody Museum.
2.1 Jeffrey Quilter and Routledge Press.
2.2 Jeffrey Quilter.
2.3 Richardson 1994: 13.
2.4 Jeffrey Quilter
3.1 Jeffrey Quilter and Routledge Press.
3.2 Jeffrey Quilter.
3.3 All by Daniel H. Sandweiss except upper right by Jeffrey Quilter.
3.4 All by Kurt Rademaker.
3.5 All photos by Jeffrey Quilter except Chinchorro mummy by Mario A. Rivera. Drawing of Paloma House by Bernadino Ojeda.
4.1 All by Scott Raymond except large stone plaque by Jim Zeidler and clay figurine from the collection of the Museo Antropológico y de Arte Contemporáneo, Guayaquil, Ecuador. The bowls were drawn by Anjan Bhatt.
4.2 Jeffrey Quilter and Routledge Press.

4.3 Aspero figurine drawing by Robert Feldman. Buena Vista sculpture: Robert Benfer. Huaca Prieta textiles (Left: Fabric 41.1/9826; Right: Fabric 41.2/1501), Courtesy of the Division of Anthropology, American Museum of Natural History. All others: Jeffrey Quilter.

4.4 Kotosh chambers after Izumi (1971: 65 [Fig. 12]). All others: Greider et al. 2012.

4.5 Engel 1963.

5.1 Jeffrey Quilter and Routledge Press.

5.2 Top row: Francisco Valdez. Center: After Villaba 1988: Fig. 15. Bottom: Ryan Clasby.

5.3 All courtesy Richard L. Burger, except top vista by Jeffrey Quilter.

5.4 All by Jeffrey Quilter except: Map of Huaca de los Reyes by William J Conklin. Temple model photographed in the Cerro Sechín Archaeological Museum. Stirrup-spout vessel: Amano Museum, Lima, Peru. Figurine: Ebnöther Collection (Inventory No. Eb 15988), Museum zu Allerheiligen, Schaffhausen, Switzerland.

5.5 All by Oscar Gabriel Prieto B.

6.1 John Kembel.

6.2 Gold objects © Dumbarton Oaks, Pre-Columbian Collection, Washington, DC. All images of sculpture by Richard L. Burger, except avian jaguar photo by Jeffrey Quilter.

6.3 After Elera 1994, Fig. 2.

6.4 Carhua textile © Dumbarton Oaks, Pre-Columbian Collection, Washington, DC. All others PMAE: Double-spout-and-bridge bottle (969-46-30/8656); Double-spout-and-bridge bottle 2 (58-51-30/8170); border 32-30-30/50; Embroidered figure: 32-75-30/F858.

6.5 Sergio Chávez and Karen M. Chávez.

7.1 Jeffrey Quilter and Routledge Press.

7.2 Yayno photo: George Lau. Sculpture photos: Jeffrey Quilter. Artifacts all PMAE: Pedestal bowl (42-29-30/4422), Kaolin house ceramic (46-77-30/5007), Man with camelid ceramic (09-3-30/75522) PMAE.

7.3 Sacrifice Ceremony drawing by Donna McClelland estate and Don McClelland. Temple model: Luis Jaime Castillo B. and the San José de Moro Project. Portrait bottle: PMAE 16-62-30/F729. Nose ornament and woman as Señora Museo de Cao/Fundación Wiese. Huaca de la Luna reconstruction: Santiago Uceda and the Huacas de Moche archaeological project.

7.4 Huaca Pucllana photos and vessel on right from site museum: Jeffrey Quilter. Fisherman vessel (Piece 35-1004; *Museo Nacional de Arqueología, Antropología e Historia del Perú*): Rafael Eduardo Valdez. Large vessel: Erik Maquera. Fish God ceremony from the Archive of the Museum of the Huaca Pucllana Site (*Archivo del Museo de Sitio Huaca Pucllana*).

7.5 PMAE ceramics: tall (09-3-30/75711), double-spout (09-3-30/75645), figurine (41-52-30/2924). Nasca Lines images by Gary Urton. Cahuachi map is a reworking and detail of Silverman 1993, Fig. 2.4.

7.6 PMAE. Pucara (45-9-30/11823.1.13.18.4), jar (39-101-30/2347), bowl (39-101-30/2352); incised stone (45-9-30-/11823.1.13.18.3).

8.1 Maps: Core of Tiahuanaco after Arellano L. 1991 (Fig 2). Akapana restoration picture Alan Kolata. Huari: William H. Isbell.

8.2 All Michele L. Koons.

8.3 Map by Jeffrey Quilter and Routledge Press. Top row artifacts all PMAE. Canteen (46-77-30/5405), Hat (42-12-30/3516), Kero (46-81-30/5485). Bottom textile detail © Dumbarton Oaks, Pre-Columbian Collection, Washington, DC.

8.4 Llamas: Jeffrey Quilter. Fields: Clark Erickson.

8.5 All Jeffrey Quilter except Marcahuamachuco by John Topic.

9.1 Map by Jeffrey Quilter and Routledge Press. Objects: PMAE: Manteño figurine (47-27-30/5626), feather fan (42-28-30/4586), and axe-money (46-77-30/5981). © Dumbarton Oaks, Pre-Columbian Collection, Washington, DC: Inlaid *Spondylus*, Chimú and shirt. Balsa illustration: Juan y Antonio de Ulloa 1784. *Spondylus* shell photo: Jeffrey Quilter.

9.2 Batán Grande photo: Jeffrey Quilter. Funerary Mask, © 2013 Metropolitan Museum of Art/Art Resource/Scala, Florence. Sicán Lord bottle: Oscar Gabriel Prieto B. Gourd detail: Enrique Vergara. Túcume photo: Daniel H. Sandweiss.

9.3 PMAE: Chan Chan aerial photo (2004.1.122.8.1), Chan Chan map: (2010.2.3.219), Litter back (52-30-30/7348). © Dumbarton Oaks, Pre-Columbian Collection, Washington, DC: silver disk and "glove." Frieze photo: Jeffrey Quilter.

9.4 Santiago Uceda and the Huacas de Moche Archaeological Project.

9.5 PMAE: Cuchimilco (41-52-30/2951); stacked pots vessel (968-14-30/8591); "Chancay Doll" (41-52-30/2951). Site photos by Jeffrey Quilter.

10.1 Map of Inca Cusco from Bauer 1998 (Map 1.2). All photos by Jeffrey Quilter.

10.2 All photos by Jeffrey Quilter. Interpretation of Quispiguanca by Robert Batson, originally published in Niles 1999 (Plate 2).

10.3 Original illustration by Guamán Poma for Martín de Murua. Image © The J. Paul Getty Museum.

10.4 Tunic © Dumbarton Oaks, Pre-Columbian Collection, Washington, DC. Illustrations after Guamán Poma *circa* 1599.

ON ORTHOGRAPHY AND DATING ISSUES

I take a relatively conservative approach to a number of issues that face anyone attempting to write a book such as this. These include orthography and dating systems in particular.

The language known as Inca or Quechua was not written down until after the arrival of the Spanish. Europeans therefore transliterated the spoken word; they wrote words in letters as they heard them, attempting to approximate sounds, some of which were not used in their own tongues, through the alphabets that they used for their own languages. The result was that written versions of words differed even within a single language system such as Spanish. As a consequence, different spelling systems for Quechua words have been developed over the years. Although variations were common in both English and Spanish, conventional spellings were well in place by the nineteenth century – such as *Huayna Capac*, one of the names of the last independent Inca emperor.

In this book I have generally chosen to follow conventional English spellings for terms that are widely known to the general public. Most of these words have long pedigrees in English usage and thus are as much English words as they are Peruvian or Inca, just as we use Germany for Deutschland and Peru instead of Perú for the countries that call themselves by those names. Thus, I write *Huayna Capac* and not *Whyna Capac*, and *quipu* rather than *khipu*.

I do follow some newer forms, however, because they quickly have become common usage among Andeanist scholars and they will help the reader to pronounce unfamiliar words. This is particularly true for accents such as Chavín and Chimú (sometimes accented in English publications, sometimes not). In Spanish, all syllables are commonly pronounced and words are usually accented on the penultimate syllable. Thus, Tahuantinsuyu is pronounced Tah-wan-teen-SOO-you. Accents are used to denote stress on syllables other than the penultimate one. Thus Chavín is sounded Cha-VEEN, and Chimú is Chee-MOO. Note that the "i" in each is soft and long. Another new trend is to differentiate geographic places from archaeological cultures. Thus, "Nazca" is geographic and "Nasca" is cultural. So too, "Huari" and "Tiahuanaco" are cities whereas "Wari" and "Tiwanaku" are the cultures in which those cities played important roles.

In a similar manner, I have mostly chosen to use the BC/AD system. While not universal, it is commonly in use in the English-speaking world and thus will be familiar to a great number of readers. The alternative is to use BP, signifying Before Present, or BCE and CE. The BP system is elegant and straightforward except for the problem of when the "present" is defined, an issue complicated by recent developments in radiocarbon dating. The BCE/CE terms signify Before Current Era and Current Era respectively – in other words, the same as the BC/AD system. For the earliest Andean eras, throughout Chapter 3 I use BP, and then I shift to the BC/AD system to discuss later times as I believe this will be easier for readers to understand and compare with their own knowledge of prehistory and history elsewhere.

Radiocarbon dates are not straightforward statements of specific dates in the past, and it would require several paragraphs to fully review this issue. Dates obtained through counting the amount of Carbon-14 in organic materials are presented as a time range, with greater confidence gained by accepting a wider time range. Further complications arise when determining dates by known variations in the amount of carbon isotopes in the atmosphere during different times in the past. These variations have been calculated and charted, and the dates obtained in laboratories must be calibrated to the variations in order to get the best calendar date possible. Old dates measured before calibrations became available used 1950 as the "present" from which both BP and BC/AD were calculated, but this has also changed more than half a century later.

Readers are warned that dates presented in this book are complicated by the fact that older studies relied upon rather straightforward interpretations of radiocarbon dates. More recently radiocarbon dates have been calibrated, as noted above. Because the calibrations vary depending on a number of factors, in some prehistoric periods differences between the "raw" radiocarbon date and the calibrated dates are significant, sometimes varying by more than 500 years. Fortunately this generally seems to be true for the remote past rather than recent times, when in general dates tend to be cited as broad ranges. Nevertheless, dates from radiocarbon analyses from the 1950s through the 1970s have often not be calibrated, while calibrations done in the 1980s and 1990s have often not been updated with new, more refined calibration systems. Another complication is that for many years Andeanist archaeologists did not rely much on radiocarbon dates, preferring to use relative dating systems such as changes in ceramic styles. As will be seen in the chapters that follow, some of these relative dating systems are now being revised. For general discussions I usually use BC/AD. In the chapters covering Periods and Horizons, I have chosen to use BP dates for the earliest phases of Andean prehistory, mostly in the Preceramic Period. I then switch to BC/AD for the later periods. Whenever I am sure that dates have been recently calibrated I note it with "cal." as an indicator. Extremely remote times, such as during the Ice Age, or general markers of periods are simply listed as "BP" while "circa" and "~" are both used to indicate a general time around the date specified. The reader should take the general dates of Periods and Horizons as generally agreed upon by most scholars. Dates for specific sites or events should be taken as likely to change as new research and dating takes place. General time ranges, such as those for the major Periods and Horizons, are still generally accepted as indicative of eras of significant cultural and social changes in the Central Andes.

1

BACKGROUNDS

AT CAJAMARCA

On the morning of November 15th, 1532, 260 Spanish soldiers of fortune surprised and captured Atahualpa Yupanqui, Emperor of Tawantinsuyu, in the highland city of Cajamarca, Peru, slaughtering and dispersing hundreds of his soldiers and retinue in the process. The event is often marked as the decisive moment of confrontation when Andeans and Europeans entered the modern era.[1] Vast regions and their peoples took chaotic, irreversible steps towards integration in global affairs in which both the Old World and the New were radically transformed. The Inca would have called it a *pachacuti*, an overturning, a term that refers to social revolutions as well as earthquakes.

Cajamarca is a story filled with drama: the Spanish struggle up the Andes in a race to beat the Inca to the city; the anxious hidden soldiers; the pomp and pageantry of the Inca retinue's grand entrance, unknowingly marching to its doom; the confrontation between a lone priest and an emperor in a vast plaza; the surprise attack; the desperate battle and slaughter; the capture of a king and a kingdom.

Everyone likes a good story and this is one of the best, whether viewed as a Spanish triumph or an Inca tragedy. However, the tale of the "Men of Cajamarca" is only one moment in a much longer and more complex narrative. The invasion of Peru by the Spaniards was years in the planning and had included scouting expeditions by Francisco Pizzaro, the chief conquistador. So too, Atahualpa's arrival in the plaza that fateful day was the result of a complicated chain of events.

In like manner the conquest of Peru was not done in a day's work, or even a generation's. The pivotal event in Cajamarca was followed by weeks, months, years, and centuries in which native and invader wrestled with each other and with new realities. Indeed, looking back at the years stretching to millennia prior to Cajamarca, both the Old and New Worlds had been enmeshed in complex cultural and social dynamics of their own. In general, however, most people educated in Western European institutions know considerably more about the ancient histories of Western Asia, the Mediterranean, and Europe than they do about the New World.

It is a sad state of affairs that many people in Europe, the United States, and even Latin American countries, when asked about the ancient New World can often barely muster the querulous response of, "the Aztecs in Mexico and the Incas in Peru?" That is roughly the equivalent of asking someone about Western European history and hearing "the Romans in Italy and the Vikings in Scandinavia?" or something similar. This is not the place to launch into a critique of the state of historical knowledge by populations in various parts of the world today. However, it is the purpose of this book to offer an easily read, comprehensive introduction to the ancient peoples and cultures of the Central Andes, the academic term for the region formerly incorporated by the Inca Empire (see Figure 1.1).

In this chapter I briefly review how Europeans interpreted the peoples of the Central Andes, from that first moment of contact in Cajamarca. Although the prehistory of the Central Andes is much more complex than they imagined—or, for the most part, were interested in—European concepts of the Inca and their subjects formed the basis of most subsequent understandings, as they still do today, for better and for worse. Better, because knowing about the Inca does offer a perspective from which to try and understand other, earlier societies; and worse, because by serving as a starting point, understandings of Inca society might predispose us to falsely interpret other societies that may have been quite different than that last prehispanic civilization.

Almost all of our understandings of the past are through Western European concepts. Even if we learn about Andean ways of knowledge, we interpret them through a Western lens. The tension between understanding different ways of thought while constricted by our own mental templates is a fundamental aspect of anthropology. Later in this book I will discuss this issue in greater depth. For now, we will follow the course of how different views of the ancient Andes developed, beginning with the Spanish arrival.

EARLY VIEWS

The Spaniards who came to the New World in the sixteenth century were not much interested in the distant past nor even in the customs of their New World contemporaries, excepting such knowledge as could help them gain gold and glory. With a few exceptions, the conquistadors were ill-educated and illiterate, and interpreted what they saw in terms of references already available to them. Thus they commonly referred to temples as "mosques" because many of them had been involved in wars against the Moors. Similarly they often referred to local lords as "caciques," a Caribbean term learned a generation before, while Andean people spoke of *curacas*.

Figure 1.1 Map of the Central Andes showing the extent of the Inca Empire, modern national boundaries, and some modern cities and towns mentioned in the text.

While for the most part the conquistadors were rapacious in their outlooks and intent, nevertheless there were a few among them who occasionally stopped and marveled at the civilizations into which they had stumbled or swaggered. Occasionally even the most heartless conquistadors stopped to wonder in awe at the people they were conquering and their handiworks. While their attentions were focused on gold and silver, they often could not help but appreciate other achievements. They sometimes saw the exquisite craftsmanship of gold ornaments but they also noted the intricacies of a beautiful textile or the engineering triumph of a temple with perfectly fitted stones. Some might have denied it, but others recognized that they were confronting highly organized societies with complex social systems and elaborate court rituals. They encountered landscapes completely transformed by human hands: the very word "Andes" derives from the Spanish *andenes*, referring to the hillsides the slopes of which had been converted into broad terraces for agriculture. It was not simply a "New World" but an entirely "Other World" that they encountered, a term employed by Columbus himself.[2] It is this complex, rich different way of living, with a deep historical past built on highly varied solutions to the basic human issues of survival, reproduction, and the search for meaning to life and the world, that intrigued conquistadors to various degrees, and which has certainly drawn subsequent explorers, scholars, tourists, and citizens into long-term pursuits concerned with studying the past.

Although the conquistadors generally did not have historical bents they wrote reports of what they saw and did, and these accounts are important for scholars because they describe indigenous politics and customs relatively unaffected by European influences. Granted, disease had swept ahead of the military men, throwing the Inca Empire into the turmoil of a civil war due to a disruption in royal dynastic succession, so that European influences were present long before face-to-face confrontations. Nevertheless, the eyewitness written accounts from the first Europeans in the New World are extremely valuable today because they provide a sense of what the independent indigenous societies had been like.

Different kinds of documents were made. Some were letters written close to the time of the events they discuss, such as those of Gonzalo Pizarro, brother to Francisco. Others are narratives written well after events had transpired, such as the account of Mansio Serra de Leguizamón, one of four of the last conquistadors whose testimonies were copied down 40 years after the conquest.[3] Still others are official documents written for various political purposes by Spanish authorities or individuals with their own agendas.

Extended narratives of the conquest of Peru with descriptions of native life as the Spanish saw it were mostly written by those who came after the first wave of invaders. One of the earliest is that of Pedro Cieza de León, who arrived in Peru in 1547 but did not publish the first volume of his account until 1553 when he had returned to Spain. The rest of his writings were only discovered and published in the late nineteenth and twentieth centuries.[4]

Another frequently cited chronicler is Garcilaso de la Vega, often known as "El Inca." Many conquistadors took Inca princesses as wives or concubines and Garcilaso was the product of such a union. He grew up in Cusco, the Inca capital, hearing stories from his native relatives about life before the conquest. By the age of twenty-one he was in Spain, but he did not publish his *Comentarios Reales de los Incas* until 1609, when he was seventy. While that volume and a later one, published posthumously in 1617, were extensive, Garcilaso was at pains to put the Inca in a good light, understandable given his background and his desire to have his Inca bloodline given equal status to that of European royalty.[5]

Felipe Guamán Poma de Ayala is another example of the diversity of voices that told of the past in the Colonial Period. He was the scion of a high-ranking native family from the southern highlands of Peru, and he learned Spanish as well as other native languages. At some time between 1600 and 1615 Guamán Poma wrote a thousand-page letter to the King of Spain complaining of the injustices and cruelties of the Spanish towards the Indians. He also took a swipe at a friar, Martin de Murúa, for whom he had worked as an illustrator on the cleric's own history of Peru. Gumán Poma's missive apparently never reached the Spanish King, and the document remained unknown until it was discovered in the Danish Royal Library in the first decade of the twentieth century. Since then, the almost 400 drawings the author created for his letter have become popular for posters and lecture slides among modern Andeanists and are widely known and appreciated in modern Andean countries, as along with the illustrations that Guamán Poma did on commission for Murúa which have only recently been discovered (see Figures 1.2 and 10.3).[6]

These various authors are but a few of many different accounts of the conquest of Peru, histories of the Inca Empire, and discussions of Andean life. There are many other writers, each with their own voice and agenda in taking quill in hand. In addition to letters and chronicles written to argue specific cases, many other documents were less consciously written for posterity. They include numerous court records and other legal documents. Court cases in which an indigenous community petitioned the Spanish authorities for rights to certain lands, frequently in conflict with other indigenous groups, often reveal numerous aspects of native society.

Historian Steve Stern states that the various ethnic, political, and linguistic groups in sixteenth century Peru did not perceive themselves as sharing a common identity until the 1560s when they were plotting to overthrow the Spanish.[7] The Inca gods were seen as having been defeated by the Spanish deity, so instead the old, pre-Inca gods, the *huacas*, were called upon to rise up and expel the Europeans. This is an important point to note for understanding prehistory. It is also emblematic of the highly unstable times of the Conquest Period, which lasted into the 1570s when Viceroy Toledo captured and executed the last Inca emperor in the line of the ancient kings, consolidated Spanish rule, and instituted administrative reforms. There were many revolts against the Spanish and such unstable times were not conducive to contemplations of the past; there was too much at stake in the present.

The eighteenth century brought the age of the Bourbons, and Enlightenment ideas and ideals made their way to Peru where colonial rule was firmly established. While there were still many injustices and revolutionary movements, the waves of violence and disease that had engulfed the Andes in the first two generations of the conquest had diminished. In the spirit of the Enlightenment the Archbishop of Trujillo, Martínez de Compañón, compiled an encyclopedic

Figure 1.2 Detail of an illustration by Guamán Poma (redrawn) of a *quipucamayoc*, a quipu-master, originally drawn *circa* 1559.

report on the North Coast of Peru for King Carlos III. Although most of the volumes have been lost, a tome of illustrations has been preserved that depicts ancient ruins, burial customs, and the daily lives and special celebrations of Peru's north coast peoples, often mixing old ways with new (see Figure 1.3).

Figure 1.3 Illustration by Martínez de Compañón of a North Coast woman weaving on a back-strap loom in the late eighteenth century.

The travels and writings of Alexander von Humboldt were extremely important in stimulating European interest in Latin America. Together with other scientists, his studies and writings about an expedition from 1799 to 1804 made important advances in a great variety of disciplines including biology, meteorology, and geology. It is for Humboldt that the cold water current off the coast of Peru is named, although recently it has more commonly been known as the Peru Current. The expedition did not specifically study antiquities but German scholars subsequently became interested in the ancient Andes, birthing a scholarly tradition that continues to the present day.[8]

It was not until the 1830s that an interest in archaeology resembling modern concerns began in the Andes. In the late 1830s through the 1840s the Swiss naturalist Johann Jakob von Tschudi and the Peruvian Francisco de Rivero traveled to visit various ruins and artifact collections, and in 1851 they published the first scholarly discussion of Peruvian antiquities: *Antegüedades Peruanas*. Their travels and studies were soon emulated by a number of other scholars who published the results of their own explorations and described ancient ruins and other remains.[9]

In the later nineteenth century German geologists Wilhelm Reiss and Mortiz Alphons Stübel continued the tradition established by Humboldt. In addition to their investigations of mountains and volcanoes they excavated burials at Ancón, a seaside resort near Lima, in 1874–75. Their large, lavishly illustrated volume on that excavation remains one of the great bibliographic triumphs of Andean studies.[10] At the same time Ephraim George Squier, who had formerly investigated ancient ruins in Ohio, was traveling in the region and soon published *Peru: Incidents of Travel and Exploration in the Land of the Incas* in 1877, gaining wide acclaim among English-reading audiences (see Figure 1.4).[11]

All of the studies and publications mentioned so far were carried out without the ability to make fine distinctions between different cultures and time periods in the past. The Incas had told the Spanish that before they brought their rule to their provinces people had lived in barbaric conditions, and generally the Europeans either believed them or did not think much about the issue. An appreciation of the great time depths of past cultures and the development of methods by which to construct chronologies of prehistoric events only began in the mid-nineteenth century. Thus an appreciation of pre-Inca cultures, and the possibility of the notion that complex societies had risen and fallen in the Andes long before the Inca, only slowly developed.

Max Uhle was a young German philologist whose family was friends with Alphons Stübel. Employed as a curator at the Dresden Museum, Uhle heard of Stübel's Peruvian travels and was encouraged by the older man to follow his interests there. In 1892 he traveled to Bolivia and conducted the first scientific excavations in the Central Andes at the large, impressive site of Tiahuanaco, later publishing his findings with Stübel. Uhle returned to Germany but went back to the Andes in 1896 for an extended stay, remaining there until 1900 sponsored by the American Exploration Society of Philadelphia and with the patronage of Mrs. Phoebe Hearst, mother of William Randolph Hearst the famous newspaper publisher. Uhle excavated in several different locales including Ica and Chincha on the South Coast, Pachacamac near Lima, and the Huacas de Moche, near the important colonial town of Trujillo.[12]

Figure 1.4 Illustration from Squier's *Incidents of Travel...* The author is likely pictured at left, gazing at architectural elements at Tiahuanaco, Bolivia.

Uhle's excavation techniques were of high standards for his day and he published well and thoroughly; much of what he did and wrote still stand as foundational work in Andean archaeology. Uhle was a pioneer in seeing groups of related artifacts through the concept of a "culture" that could be used as a methodological device for interpreting the past. He used this innovation in combination with the concept of a "horizon style" to great effect in developing the first archaeological chronology in the New World that explicitly conceived of prehistoric cultures as succeeding one another. In particular, by using new methods of identifying changes in pottery styles, Uhle was able to demonstrate that there were at least four different, successive prehistoric periods in the past, rather than simply an Inca period and pre-Inca barbarism. Thus, through Uhle's work the study of ancient Peru entered the modern era. Before turning to a review of more recent investigators and investigations, we will consider different ways of approaching our understanding of the past.

FRAMES OF REFERENCE

As is true for many other fields of inquiry, the ancient Andes has attracted and continues to attract a wide range of people bringing different perspectives and concerns to their investigations. Archaeologists are the most numerous investigators, but art historians, geographers, engineers, physicians, and many others have conducted research on ancient Andean topics at various times and to varying degrees. The investigations of scientists who are not studying ancient societies directly also can contribute to our knowledge of prehistory. For example, geologists and climatologists sometimes provide information on past environmental conditions that can be used for interpreting ancient societies by archaeologists, and in turn, archaeological data are often important for the research of other scientists and scholars. In addition, there are many people who are not scholars but who have a stake in archaeological sites, artifacts, and interpretations of prehistory. These include local, regional, and national politicians; guides, bus companies, and others in the tourist industry; and many others. In addition local people, often of meager means, who reside near sites often have their lives affected, for both good and bad, by the interests of strangers in their local ruins.

It is worth reviewing the most prominent kinds of scholars who have investigated the Andean past because who they are and what they do influences the understanding of prehistory among other researchers and the general public. The main academic disciplines are History, Art History, and Archaeology, and there are distinctive modes of carrying out studies within and sometimes across these fields of research that have considerable consequences for how the past is understood and presented.

Historians study the past using written records. Among the earliest historians interested in Peru was the Bostonian William H. Prescott (1796–1859). He never visited Latin America, but he wrote the *History of the Conquest of Mexico* (1843) and the *History of the Conquest of Peru* (1847) based on accounts written by Spanish conquistadors. Because they rely on documents, historians like Prescott have been drawn to the Incas. In addition to the accounts recorded by Spaniards who had been part of the conquest or who were descended from conquistadors, indigenous people were also sources of information. When the Spanish arrived in Peru there were still people in various places who remembered life before their communities were conquered or absorbed by the Inca. Many pre-Inca ways of life were still practiced in such locales. If history is written in the light and prehistory remains in the dark, then these remembered pasts and continuing practices are a kind of twilight or shadow. The study of historic records to understand life and events in pre-contact times is sometimes referred to as ethnohistory. Many archaeologists or art historians conduct ethnohistorical studies, but increasingly scholars in History Departments are also engaging in such work, and to them what they do is simply "History", with no "ethno" required.

Art Historians, by definition, study human creations that are referred to as "art." They investigate changes over time in art styles, aesthetics, symbolism, and other issues. What constitutes "art" is a difficult question to answer, and it has been the subject of much discussion by art historians themselves, as well as others. Many art historians whose areas of interest are in pre-contact societies, either in Latin America or elsewhere, are often more comfortable in talking to archaeologists than to some of their colleagues in their own departments. They tend to shun narrow definitions of "art" and prefer to consider their fields of interest as "visual culture" or "material culture," rather than becoming enmeshed in complex arguments about the nature of art that often have no clear resolution. These kinds of issues, which are sometimes as relevant for historians and archaeologists as they are for art historians, often have more to do with the dividing lines between academic departments and in universities or museums, and the resulting academic political battles, than they do with anything else.

Although it should be strongly emphasized that there are many exceptions to the general rule, it can be stated that art historians tend to spend their time with complete objects rather than fragments of pottery or stone tools, as many archaeologists do. They tend to be more interested in interpreting the symbolism of art, a field of investigation commonly referred to as "iconography," than in investigating other issues—subsistence economies, for example— although they may explore many other issues beyond "meaning" in ancient art.[13] Particularly in Andean studies, the interests of art historians are frequently quite wide-ranging and often overlap considerably with those of historians and archaeologists.

Archaeologists are the most numerous investigators of prehistory. They tend to look for and study the material remains of past human societies. Field archaeologists conduct surveys to find sites and often excavate them, but they may conduct other kinds of investigations as well, such as examining ancient astronomy or landscapes. Other archaeologists may not venture into the field at all, studying museum collections or conducting research in laboratories.

Those archaeologists who study the Inca may spend much more time with ethnohistorians than they do with archaeologists studying the earliest humans in Peru, who, in turn and depending on their interests, might spend more time working with geographers or geologists than with art historians. Thus, what any individual scholar does can be quite different from others in his or her department or in comparison with a similar scholar in the same kind of department at another university. To complicate matters even further, there are distinct schools of archaeology as well. There may be three or four archaeologists who excavate sites in the same Andean region, but their theoretical orientations, the methods employed, and the kinds of questions about the past that interest them may be quite different.[14]

An important school of Andean archaeology might be called "ideographic," "historical," or "civilizational." Archaeologists in this school tend to see themselves as Andeanists first and foremost, interested in understanding the rich and varied past of the prehistoric peoples and places of Western South America. In some ways this type of scholarship resembles that of researchers studying the ancient civilizations of Western Asia and the Mediterranean. Understanding what life was like in the distant past, how successive societies emerged, grew, and were eventually succeeded by others are ends in themselves. There is no need to justify such research because this kind of knowledge is desirable in and of itself, contributing to the understanding of the human condition, or with a narrower focus, contributing to the history of a people, place, or nation.

Scholars in this school of thought tend to follow traditions rooted in the Humanities even if they use research methods from the Sciences or Social Sciences. Self-identifying primarily as Andeanists means that the scholars of the civilizational school tend to emphasize the development of deep knowledge of all aspects of the Andes, both past and present. A professor with such an orientation encourages students to read the Spanish chroniclers, recent ethnographers, and other Andeanist archaeologists, even if the students' interests may be at the other end of the Andes or removed in time from the recommended works, in order to gain as much depth of knowledge as possible.

The exemplary model of such an Andeanist was John Howland Rowe (1918–2004), who spent his career in the Department of Anthropology at the University of California, Berkeley. While he was an archaeologist who conducted excavations in Cusco and its vicinity, Rowe was also highly knowledgeable about and published on a wide range of topics including linguistics, the chroniclers, art styles, and the like. Although he was aware of issues of anthropological theory and used them to advantage in some of his writings, his greatest interest and focus was on the description of the world of ancient Peru. He trained many graduate students who went on to enjoy important careers in the field. Indeed, his influence was and is still so pervasive that Andeanists often refer to the "Roweista" school of researchers.

Many archaeologists who are citizens of modern Andean nation states also follow the civilizational mode of investigation. This is largely due to a perception of the ancient past as part of a long national narrative. It is prehistory in the true sense of the term: the extension of the history of people—often conceived in terms of the citizens of contemporary nations— beyond the written record into remote antiquity. To complicate matters, however, from the 1960s through to the 1980s many archaeologists in Latin America were strongly influenced by Marxism, using its theories as means to understand the past as well as, in some cases, to contribute to social change in the present. One of the chief proponents of this approach is Luis G. Lumbreras of San Marcos National University in Lima, whose 1974 book *La Arqueología Como Cienca Social* (*Archaeology as a Social Science*) was widely read throughout Latin America and made him an archaeologist-intellectual of international repute. While Marxist theory is still followed by many archaeologists working in Latin America, not all of whom are from the region, scholars there have also followed other more recent trends as well.

Another major school of archaeology is Processualism, also sometimes known as the "New Archaeology." This was a movement in archaeology that was particularly strong in the United States during the 1960s and 1970s. It was part of a wider social trend that placed an emphasis on science, stimulated to a great degree by the US's competition with the Soviet Union, especially the "Space Race." To be "scientific" added legitimacy and raised the status of scholars, and perhaps more importantly gave them access to government research funds that were not available to those deemed not scientific enough.

There were different strains of Processualism, and some who might be labeled "processualists" or "new archaeologists" may not have even used the term themselves. Nevertheless, Lewis R. Binford, at the University of Mexico, and Kent V. Flannery and Joyce Marcus, at the University of Michigan, were in the vanguard of the new scientific approach to archaeology. The University of Michigan in particular retains its status as an archaeological program that is strongly scientific, and other universities, often populated with Michigan graduates who follow similar paths, include the University of California in Los Angeles, Northwestern University, and Arizona State University, among others.

The scientific or processual mode of investigation relied strongly on an interpretive framework of cultural evolution in which societies evolve from simple to complex. An important goal was to look at different societies throughout time and space, to generalize their characteristics as bands, tribes, chiefdoms, and states (the evolutionary progression), and conduct cross-cultural comparisons of their features and evolutionary development. Archaeologists with this focus were less interested in the details of particular cultures than in common, shared features. Indeed, many of those working in the Americas referred to the region as the "New World Laboratory", where models of cultural evolution developed in Mesopotamia and other Old World societies could be tested.

New Archaeology was a dominant mode of conducting research for more than two decades, and it had a strong influence on research. The largest, most extensive projects tended to be carried out by US archaeologists and the greatest source of funding was the National Science Foundation, which, as its name signals, funded research that was explicitly scientific in its theory and methodology. Many US archaeologists still work in this style, although they now tend to refer to themselves as "problem-oriented" rather than as processualists or scientists per se. Part of the reason for this shift is due to many criticisms that were leveled at New Archaeology, arising from the beginning but gathering momentum in the mid-1980s.

Another trend in archaeological theory is known as Post-Processualism, which developed in the 1980s and still has many adherents today. Unlike the New Archaeology, it tends not to have a single, coherent approach as to how to do archaeology. Rather, its adherents are united in their agreement as to what not to do: one must not oversimplify the past by using interpretive frameworks that over-generalize and ignore interesting and important differences between societies in different places and times. However, Post-Processualism as a kind of Critical Archaeology is consciously practiced by only a handful of archaeologists, and research has been continuing that asks basic questions about what happened in the past.

The Post-Processualist critique of the New Archaeology has been absorbed by most archaeologists to make them more careful about sweeping generalizations and glib comparisons between cultures such as may have been made in the past, and it has shifted many scholars towards research that resembles the civilizational school described above. The situation is complicated because many of the "lessons" of the New Archaeology about how to conduct research have become so ingrained in archaeological practice that they are no longer appreciated as having had a particular origin in the past, a situation that is perhaps surprising but nevertheless true for a group of people devoted to investigating past events. Furthermore, enough time has passed that some of the critiques of Post-Processualism have now become so widely accepted that those lessons too are not always recognized as having had their origins in a process of debate and discussion about how to do archaeology.

An example of these kinds of shifts in theory and method can be found in how scholars now approach ceramics, one of the basic sources of archaeological information. While earlier scholars may have occasionally recognized some of the difficulties involved in using ceramics to discuss the past, they often resorted to looking at different ceramic types as direct expressions of ancient cultures. In other words, ceramic styles were equated with social, political, or ethnic entities. Both the New Archaeology and Post-Processualism critiqued this view, pointing out that while ceramics can usefully serve to understand various aspects of ancient societies, the relationship between pottery styles and ancient social groups is much more complicated than has sometimes been assumed in the past, and therefore it must be approached with care and nuanced interpretations.

This new appreciation of the complexities of the material remains of the past has developed in parallel with a trend in history. Interpretation of the chroniclers is now carried out with an understanding that their writings were created with specific, often highly individualized agendas, and therefore the documents cannot be taken as simple facts. Rather, documents must be interpreted, keeping in mind the larger political, social, and even psychological dispositions of the authors and the intended audiences of the written works.

Most of the different modes of scholarship described above are devoted to the study of the past, in one way or another. Officially, however, the Processualists were dedicated to the larger mission of cross-cultural comparisons of cultures in order to understand large-scale patterns of human behavior, and not in the study of ancient societies for their own sakes. Archaeology was a method employed in the service of the larger project of anthropology. Although he is a geographer rather than an anthropologist, the popular writings of Jared Diamond are very much in this tradition, such as his book, *Guns, Germs, and Steel* (1997). It is important to note here that there were, and still are, many other academics and intellectuals who have drawn upon information on ancient societies in the Andes for their own purposes. This is particularly true of philosophers, political scientists and economists in relation to the Inca.

While the above discussion briefly describes different schools of research, it is also true that every scholar usually develops his or her own interests and modes of inquiry. A researcher trained in one theoretical school may have produced scholarship in the early stages of a career which is quite different from later works. Also, professors, museum curators, and other specialists often spend many years at specific sites or focusing on particular research questions, and their careers are subsequently defined by such long-term efforts. A brief look at the highlights from some leading Andeanists will be useful in understanding some of the research issues that will be discussed later in this book.

SOME NOTABLE ANDEANISTS

Max Uhle was the founder of modern archaeological research in the Central Andes, but the greatest name in the history of Andean studies is Julio C. Tello (1880–1947). A full-blooded native Peruvian *serrano*, a highlander, he was a true genius. Tello's work was so influential that he achieved international stature, gaining recognition from a wide variety of scholars and intellectuals around the world. In addition, Tello was prodigious in his fieldwork, scouring Peru to discover new sites or further explore known ones. In the 1960s and 1970s no greater compliment could be given to a young archaeologist than to hear an older hand say, "Even Tello didn't know about this site."

Tello's research and writings spanned a wide range of the Andean past. However, he is particularly noted for his excavations of mummy bundles from the Paracas Peninsula on the South Coast of Peru, and for his research at the site of Chavín de Huántar, in the central Peruvian highlands. In addition to establishing precedents in teaching, museums, publishing, and many other scholarly endeavors, Tello is noteworthy for his insights into the importance of Chavín.

Uhle had demonstrated that there were four major prehistoric periods, but Tello added a fifth. Based on changes in artifacts, especially ceramics, Uhle had identified what we now refer to as the Middle Horizon and periods before and after it. Tello demonstrated that there had been an earlier period of great civilization in Peru that had preceded Uhle's earliest phase, and that civilization was centered at the highland site of Chavín de Huántar. Consequently, by the late 1930s and early 1940s Peruvian prehistory was fairly well developed into several distinct and different time periods. Sites and artifacts could thus be ordered chronologically in relation to one another, a process known as relative dating. However, there was no means by which to determine a calendar date for those sites and artifacts, so it remained unclear exactly how ancient Chavín, or any other prehistoric cultures other than the very late ones, were related to one another.

Tello also saw Chavín as a "mother culture," establishing ideas and practices that continued into Inca times and beyond. However, while Tello was emphasizing the importance of Chavín another student of the past was arguing for the key role of coastal cultures in northern Peru. He was a gentleman scholar, but a very fine one, by the name of Rafael Larco Hoyle (1901–1966). The Larco family owned Chiclín, a large sugar plantation in the Chicama Valley north of the city of Trujillo, but Rafael did not spend all his youth there. He was educated in Maryland and then studied agricultural engineering at Cornell University. Something of a foreigner to his own country, when he returned to Peru he was impressed by the remains of the rich prehispanic past that were so prominent in ruins and intriguing artifacts on and near his family's hacienda.

Larco expanded an artifact collection started by his uncle and subsequently bought by his father, and also conducted excavations and other research. Building on the work of Max Uhle, he defined the Mochica culture and became an expert on the entire prehistory of his beloved North Coast. In 1946 he welcomed a team of archaeologists from the United States to work in the Virú Valley nearby. He invited one of them, Junius Bird, and his family to excavate at Huaca Prieta, a site on his property that was expected to be very early, and also hosted a conference of the entire Virú Valley team when their work was done. In addition to publishing many ground-breaking articles and books championing the North Coast as the place where Peruvian civilization began, Larco built a museum in Chiclín and then later moved his collection to a new museum in Lima that may still be visited today.

John H. Rowe (1918–2004) has already been mentioned as the foremost Andeanist scholar of his generation. His knowledge was wide-ranging and deep, and he made major contributions to linguistics, the history of anthropology and the study of prehistoric art, in addition to archaeology. Although there were precedents in the research of previous scholars, Rowe concentrated on building fine-grained chronologies of prehistory through the detailed analysis of ceramics. He, Dorothy Menzel, and Lawrence Dawson, all associated with the University of California, Berkeley, built a chronological system applicable to most of the Central Andes that is still in use today. While he wrote various articles on anthropological theory, he was primarily an empiricist who searched for the most accurate means to know and describe the past.

R. Tom Zuidema of the University of Illinois took another approach to the ancient Andes. Although, like Rowe, his scholarship has ranged over a wide range of subjects, he is most known for his research on the Inca. Whereas Rowe sifted through the chroniclers to determine which one was more reliable for his account of religion and which was better at discussing Inca political organization, Zuidema did not take these accounts at face value. Drawing upon Dutch structuralist anthropological theory, Zuidema interpreted the chronicles as distorted accounts of native dualistic concepts. In other words, the Spanish understood what they heard in terms of Western concepts of linear history, but the Inca were telling tales that followed different principles. Among his insights is the suggestion that the Inca king list was not a strict linear succession of rulers but may rather have represented pairs of rulers, shortening estimates of the length of their collective reigns considerably.

The rather different approaches of Rowe and Zuidema subsequently led to two different schools of thought on how to understand Inca history, religion, politics, and other matters. At the same time, however, John V. Murra (1916–2006) followed his interests along a completely different path. Born in the Ukraine, he fought on the Republican side in the Spanish Civil War and his interest in the Inca was a result of his politics. Starting in the sixteenth century, the peoples of the New World were frequently cited by European philosophers as examples of either uncivil barbarians or ideal utopians. These discussions became particularly pointed in the nineteenth century in the context of the rise of Marxism, and it is in this tradition that Murra conducted his studies. He was particularly interested in how a complex civilization run by an apparently all-powerful state could operate in the absence of money and markets. Again, as with the other scholars, he wrote many articles but is chiefly known for one that noted the importance of cloth as a medium of exchange and value, and another on economic organization based upon the distribution of different producers in the vertically stacked environmental zones of the Andes.

Donald W. Lathrap (1927–1990) was the founding father of a somewhat different school of modern Andean studies. Unlike Tello his research was not in the "heartland" of the ancient Andes, and unlike Rowe, Zuidema, and Murra he did not focus his studies on the Inca. Rather, his doctoral dissertation was on the Upper Amazon, the tropical forest region outside Inca control. Later work focused on Ecuador, an area that was incorporated into the Inca Empire relatively late and was, and often still is, thought to have participated very little in the affairs of the peoples of Peru to the south. Lathrap argued vigorously against this notion. Directly or through the work of his students he was able to demonstrate that peoples in the tropical lands on the peripheries of the Peruvian coastal desert and in the highlands were precocious in many cultural developments and continued to be actively and creatively involved with events that occurred in regions where complex civilizations arose. Lathrap saw patterns of culture of great antiquity that were widely shared throughout the ancient New World, such as deities of the lower waters, the terrestrial plane and the sky, all of whom were "masters of animals."

Although many more important scholars may be mentioned, our final example is Edward P. Lanning. Active in the field mostly in the 1960s, Lanning's great contribution was his recognition of the importance of the Preceramic Period in Peru. Although others had recognized the existence of a long period of complex cultural developments prior to the first use of pottery, Lanning developed a chronology to organize it into periods, especially for the Central Coast. He borrowed a great deal from a French expatriate living in Peru, Frédéric Andre Engel. Engel was a mostly self-trained archaeologist who was impressed by the writings of Vere Gordon Childe on the origins of agriculture in the Old World, and who wished to investigate the same issues in Peru. For a variety of reasons, however, Engel was never fully integrated into the community of Peruvianist archaeologists. Instead he worked alone, often in idiosyncratic ways.[15] Despite this he did recognize the importance of the Preceramic Period on the coast, just as his contemporary, Augusto Cardich, recognized the importance of the era in the highlands. However, it was Lanning who promulgated the importance of preceramic cultures in ways that gained attention from other scholars.

Lanning wrote a highly influential and long-lived introduction to Peruvian archaeology that was used as the best textbook in English for over two decades.[16] He also was a pioneer in examining changing environments in coastal Peru, realizing their importance in affecting culture change. He developed the basic notion of the importance of maritime resources as a foundation of complex societies, and his ideas were more fully developed by his student, Michael Moseley. Together, along with another of Lanning's students, Thomas Patterson, they published many important papers on the early cultures of the Central Coast of Peru that still remain relevant today.

There were and are many other notable scholars of the ancient Andes whose contributions have been profound and long-lasting. However, the seven mentioned above not only conducted seminal research and published widely read, influential articles and books; they also developed and often promoted new ways of thinking about the ancient Andes. Their ideas influenced and established schools of research through their graduate students and others, including scholars and professionals in fields far from anthropology. To take but one example, John Rowe's book-length article *Inca Culture at the Time of the Spanish Conquest* was published in 1946, but it is still essential reading for anyone interested in the subject and it remains among the most frequently cited articles on Andean archaeology.

Most of the scholars discussed above focused much of their attention on peoples and cultures that once existed in what is now the modern nation state of Peru. It is important to note, however, that in the other Andean countries there were archaeologists and other researchers who are considered today as the founding fathers and mothers of prehistorical research.

Knowledge gained in particular countries of the Central Andes commonly contributes to the understanding of processes in others. Modern national boundaries did not exist in the past, so that, particularly at certain times, the areas occupied by different archaeological cultures now cross modern frontiers. Furthermore, there are long-term trends for ties between large regions and the people in them which also cross modern boundaries, and sometimes mark greater distinctions between cultural regions within a modern country. However, most of Peru, western Bolivia, and southern Ecuador have continued to attract the greatest interest for prehistorians, partly because of the impressive accomplishments and our historical knowledge of the Inca.

AN ANDEANIST'S PERSPECTIVE

The observant reader will have noticed that three of the seven noted Andeanists discussed above were cited for their work on the Inca. However, this book will discuss societies thousands and hundreds of years before the Inca Empire. Why, then, is there such a concentration on Inca scholarship? Indeed, this book is being written by one Andeanist, so the reader might profit from understanding the author's particular orientation from the outset so that it might be taken into account while reading the chapters to follow.

I have presented a brief synopsis of how the Andean past has been recorded, different theoretical approaches, and notes on some notable Andeanists, so that by now the reader will understand that there is not one single version of the past which is necessarily more correct than another. However, this does not mean that any and all versions have equal merit. Rather, some scholars emphasize particular issues more than others, and some focus on details while others prefer to consider issues within the context of larger theoretical concerns. For much of the 150 years or so during which modern scholarship has occurred, the Inca have served as a touchstone by which almost all subsequent research on more remote antiquity has been carried out or evaluated. Simply put, many Andeanists have used what they know about the Inca to interpret the more distant past. This has sometimes been advantageous, but it can also inhibit understanding. An example will elucidate this point.

As noted above, John Murra was interested in what he saw as an Inca economic system in which markets did not exist. This stood in sharp contrast to the well-known market economies of Europe and even ancient Mexico. Murra saw the very different environmental zones of the Andes, stacked like the layers of a cake, as offering what he termed a "vertical archipelago," offering different resources in each "layer." Using various ethnohistoric and ethnographic examples, he suggested that people in the Andes occupied the different environmental zones, sending long-term colonists or short-term groups to gather resources and then exchanging the materials or products of these different zones among themselves without ever having to rely on the centralized locations typical of market economies. Murra urged archaeologists to investigate how long this distinctive economic system had been in existence.

Although a recent review of Murra's work has pointed out that originally he did not rule out the idea that markets or something like them may have existed in the ancient Andes, other scholars took up the notion, and Murra became more increasingly pointed in arguing that the vertical archipelago was *the* Andean economic system. It has now become something of a truism that there were no markets in the Andes, and therefore until recently no one has questioned the issue or looked to find archaeological sites that might have been or included areas for markets.[17]

The idea that there was a fundamental core of practices and beliefs of great antiquity throughout time and space in the Central Andes and which was unique and distinctive to the region—a form of "Andean Exceptionalism"—is sometimes referred to as "*Lo Andino*," which can be translated as "The Andean", as in "The Andean Way of Life." This concept is quite popular among both Andean peoples and many of those who study their past. It speaks to the concept of deep and long traditions, and furthermore there seems to be lots of evidence for it in the archaeological record.

Indeed, as far as we can tell there is ample evidence that there are long-standing and widespread traditions of belief and practice in the Andes, a pattern that does not exist in Europe and Western Asia. This probably has more to do with the Euro-Mediterranean region being different from the rest of the world than vice versa. Christianity and Islam both swept away many old beliefs in religious upheavals that appear not to have occurred (or at least, that we have not yet detected) in Amerindian societies—or, for that matter, in many places in Asia and Africa. Of course, the expansion of Western cultures across the globe through colonial enterprises did have profound effects on many non-Western societies, but these are relatively recent events in comparison to the deep history to be discussed in this book.

The problem with applying the concept of Lo Andino is that it doesn't explain anything, because it simply refers to the idea that things have always been the way they are, thereby implying a timeless state of being for Andean peoples and cultures. This is surely not the case. Even if there are longstanding Andean cultural patterns they had to start at some point in the past, even if that point is very remote in time. It is one of the tasks of archaeologists to investigate origins, and therefore we cannot simply assume that some cultural pattern or other always existed.

Ways of doing things or conceiving of the world can endure for many generations in some general features, but they can still be radically interpreted from one generation to the next. Examples abound. The theology and practice of Christianity in the third, eighth, eighteenth, and twentieth centuries all shared the same basic set of symbols, fundamental concepts, and rituals, and yet they were dramatically different in many ways. Also, those Christianities were further differentiated geographically and by various sects within some geographic regions. How much we might be able to separate out these differences in time and space using only archaeological data is a sobering issue to consider. The point is that this is exactly what archaeologists attempt to do.

The example of Christianity's variations is apt for comparison with the Andes in more ways than one. Much of what Andean archaeologists explore and discuss appears to be related to ancient religious systems. Archaeology makes order out of chaos, and one of the best ways to do this is through the building of chronologies based on changing artifact styles. As noted above, ceramics have traditionally been particularly important for archaeological investigations. Decorated pottery carries more information than undecorated pottery, so it is more easily placed into typologies. Undecorated pottery is commonly used for utilitarian purposes such as storage or cooking, and if subsistence economies and foodways do not change dramatically then the pots, pans, and storage bins will change little as well, making them less useful than decorated pottery in chronicling cultural changes. In the Andes, however, much of the decorated pottery seems to have been adorned with imagery that appears religious to us.

Interpreting the changes in the decorations and forms of fine ware ceramics, as they are known, is not an easy task, but when it is done well such work lays the foundation for highly useful chronologies as well as providing evidence for the spread of people and ideas, even though we have to be cautious in our interpretations. Nevertheless, ceramics are ubiquitous for much of prehistory and they have many characteristics that make them attractive for and useful in archaeological studies, with the consequence that they will always be relied upon to a great degree as a primary source of information about the past.

As already noted, there can be over-simplifications whereby changes in ceramics are assumed to have a one-to-one correlation with changes in culture overall, and this is sometimes disparagingly referred to as the "pots as people" tendency. Over-emphasis on ceramic changes can sometimes lead archaeologists to forget that other changes occurred as well, for example in technological or economic systems. Furthermore, changes in one medium, such as ceramics, may have occurred at different rates than changes in another, such as textiles, opening up the question of what such changes signify, either together or separately. These are all questions that archaeologists wrestle with, some with better results than others, but it is important to emphasize here that these issues do influence the way in which we understand the past.

This leads to two final and interrelated points. One is the issue of "reconstructing the past," and the other is the challenge to anthropology (and any historical science, ultimately) of searching for patterns in human behavior. An entire book could be written—indeed, many have been—on the fact that we cannot reconstruct the past for a variety of reasons. To put it succinctly, the past, like the present, is an infinite number of realities experienced and perceived differently by different people in it. Any attempt at "reconstruction" is highly selective, leaving many things out: there is no single "past" that can be pinned down and analyzed.

The second issue concerning searching for patterns also is a grand topic, but a germane point needs to be made for our present purposes, which is the tension that exists between trying to understand realities different from our own while at the same time looking for commonalities in the human experience. This has been one of the great intellectual traditions of anthropology: what are our shared human experiences and conditions, and what are those things that are radically different between peoples through time and space?

All humans are subject to "the thousand natural shocks that flesh is heir to," as Hamlet put it. They can only survive within a narrow range of temperatures. They need food and water, and to greater and lesser degrees they need clothing and shelter. There are strong impulses and motivations in most people to procreate, and beyond that humans are social animals and most desire social interactions with others like them.

Many people have developed similar ways to satisfy these needs and wants, resulting in similar patterns in similar environments. One style of anthropology, particularly when it is done in the scientific mode, is to look for similar patterns. Science seeks generalizations about the world, and anthropology, as a social science, does the same. However, in looking for common features the differences may be downplayed or ignored. Seeing the forest instead of the trees, as it were, has led to identifying (for example) bands, tribes, chiefdoms, and states in the scientific mode of anthropology and archaeology.

Anthropology's other goal is to identify unique human beliefs and practices. Some of those different practices may have had no effect on the future, others led to the demise of ancient societies, while still others were highly successful for long periods of time and knowledge about them may be of benefit (or at least be very interesting) to modern people. However, a difficulty in looking for uniqueness in the archaeological record is that humans understand the world through analogy, through using what they already know to comprehend new things and behaviors. This makes it quite difficult to identify practices that are outside of the experience or knowledge of those seeking them. Nevertheless we know that people behaved very differently in the past, and ignoring those differences inhibits our understanding of what happened. Meanwhile, attempting to reach an understanding that may come close to that of the people involved, who lived and thought differently from ourselves, will aid it.

Because the fundamental human needs to sustain life are shared by all, lying within a fairly narrow range of variation—we will all die after a few minutes without air, a few days without water, several weeks without food—basic ways and means by which to fulfill these needs seem to be quite similar throughout the world. Social relations tend to be more varied, but finding mates is such a strong motivation and so widely shared that there also are common relationship patterns in social systems.

However, what people believe about the meaning of life, the reasons why the world is the way it is, the gods, and other matters, can be highly varied, because these issues generally do not have an immediate effect on survival. Nevertheless it is interesting to consider that for many people issues of ideology or religion are often of overriding importance compared to those other more basic aspects of life. Once the fundamental needs for food, shelter, and so forth, are satisfied, then ideology seems to be in the forefront of people's minds, especially when that ideology is intimately tied up in politics—in determining who does or does not get the basic necessities of life, and also the things that make it pleasant or give people satisfaction.

One of the fundamental issues in the study of human societies is the degree to which ideas are the main engines of social and cultural change, versus the proposal that it is the basics of demographics, the mode and means of production and the like, that are the driving engines of history. These are complicated issues and they cannot be discussed in detail here, but they are important to consider before discussing the prehistory of the Central Andes. Especially for later periods of the past when the archaeological record is more extensive than for earlier eras, charting changes in religious systems and understanding how they were related to other aspects of life have been and remain important pursuits. How these relationships may be successfully interpreted, the difficulties they present for interpretation, and how to understand them in relation to other aspects of the archaeological record will be discussed at length as the story of the ancient Andes unfolds.

NOTES

1 For a well-written account of the first years of the conquest see MacQuarrie 2008. The very different Inca version of the events may be found in Legnani 2006.
2 Columbus on "Other World" Brinkbäumer and Höges 2006: 187.
3 Stirling 2000 offers a good account of the conquest focusing on this conquistador's life. Pillsbury 2008 offers an encyclopedic presentation of documentary sources for Andean studies.
4 There are a number of versions of Cieza de León in Spanish and English, one of which is Cieza de León 1998.
5 There are also many versions of Garcilaso. A recent abridged version is De la Vega 2006.
6 Again, many versions are available. See the abridged Guamán Poma de Ayala 2006. There are also writings *about* the chroniclers; Guamán Poma has had many works devoted to him. See Adorno 2000 for a start. The entire manuscript may be viewed in digital form at http://www.kb.dk/permalink/2006/poma/info/es/frontpage.htm.
7 Stern 1982.
8 Von Humboldt 2006.
9 De Rivero and de Tschudi 1851.
10 Reiss and Stübel 1880–1887.
11 Squier 1877.
12 Uhle's work will be cited in later chapters. On the man himself, see Kaulicke 1998 and Willey and Sabloff 1993: 89.
13 Many archaeologists who engage in the practice use the term "iconography" to refer to the study of the symbolic and social meanings of ancient art. In fact, however, the concepts of "iconography" and "iconology" as used in Art History are more complex than this.
14 Extensive citations will not be given in the following discussions of important archaeologists because their works will be cited in subsequent chapters.
15 Engel's publications (e.g. 1988) contain huge amounts of information but he used his own site designation system, ignoring the standardized systems in use by other archaeologists in Peru.
16 Lanning 1967.
17 Hirth and Pillsbury 2013.

2

SPACE, TIME, AND FORM IN THE CENTRAL ANDES

INTRODUCTION

We do not know how the ancient peoples of the Andes referred to themselves. None of the "cultures" in this book, except for those within the range of memories in the sixteenth century, are known by the names according to which their members identified themselves. Chavín, Moche, Nasca, Wari, and others are terms that refer to archaeological cultures. The concept of an archaeological culture was most clearly articulated by Vere Gordon Childe, an Australian who spent most of his career in the United Kingdom and who had a profound influence on archaeology. Childe defined an archaeological culture as a suite of artifacts and other remains that share a distinct style that existed in a geographical region for a length of time.[1]

Archaeologists have developed theories, methods, and terminology to identify and work with these space–time–form sets. Long-term trends in which many features seem to endure are sometimes referred to as "traditions." Because there usually aren't distinct geographical boundaries to patterns, a particular archaeological culture may be nested within increasingly larger groupings to eventually reach the concept of a "Culture Area," and the Central Andes is one such.

Consequently, "Moche" is a modern construct and "the Moche" never existed—or, at least, they never existed in exactly the way in which archaeologists conceive of them. The term refers to a recognized set of distinctive archaeological material remains found on the North Coast of Peru and coming from a given time period, generally agreed to be in the first centuries AD. The set of traits is first recognizable dating from a time roughly in the fourth century of our era, and it was no longer in existence by sometime in the ninth century. "No longer in existence" here means that the styles of artifacts and architecture identified as "Moche" either were no longer made, or else they had been transformed into new forms and

23

styles to such a point that they no longer appear to be part of a continuance of practice and belief from earlier times.

Thus, no one ever said, "I am a Moche," except for the residents of the modern town of Moche. How the people who used the artifacts and lived in the spaces that we identify as the Moche archaeological culture thought of themselves is unknown. This is important to remember because archaeologists themselves sometimes forget that archaeological cultures are not the same as ethnic or political groups. The concept of the Moche or any other archaeological culture is quite useful to enable us to study the past, but it only tells about the past in a particular kind of way and leaves much out.

The idea that archaeological cultures consist of a geographic region, a time span, and a set of objects is perfectly reasonable because the rest of our reality is stretched on the same three-dimensional framework. Space, time, and form are the dimensions of archaeology and of everyday, experienced existence itself. "Dimension" refers to something that requires its own measuring device.[2] Space is the distance between things as well as what they occupy. Linear, planar, and cubic units measure space. For linear measurements, for example, we use kilometers or miles as well as larger and smaller units as needed. Time is a measuring system that allows us to sequence events on various scales as well, from less than nanoseconds to millennia. Form is the manifestation of a physical entity. It is the perceived structure or shape of something, but it is also its color, roughness, size, and any other aspect of its existence that can be described. It is all those things that make an orange an orange and an apple an apple.

Because space, time, and form are so fundamental, we will consider some broad issues of the first two in particular with regard to the ancient Andes. We will then consider some issues of form and the relations between all three dimensions.

GEOGRAPHY

As noted at the beginning of this book, the Central Andes is a culture area defined as the geographic extent of the former Inca Empire. That entity stretched from a small area of southern Colombia through coastal and highland Ecuador and Peru, across the western half of Bolivia, through northwestern Argentina and northern Chile. The southern border of the region is commonly considered to be the Maule River, about 260 km (160 mi) south of Santiago, Chile's capital.

Following the coastal desert, the linear distance from the northernmost tip to the most southerly point of the Central Andes is close to 4,000 km (2,500 mi). The area covered by the region is roughly 1,631,000 square km (630,000 square mi). Charles Stanish has pointed out that if a map of the Inca Empire was laid over the Old World, the distance spanned would reach from London to Baghdad.[3] Like Eurasia, the range of different environments in that vast stretch of territory is also great and varied (see Figure 2.1).

Figure 2.1 Map of the Central Andes showing major geographical features and regions.

The relatively young Andes mountains, running roughly north to south close to the Pacific Ocean, form a continental divide at the extreme western edge of South America. This means that most of the continent, to the east of the Andes, is actually affected by meteorological events associated with the Atlantic Ocean. It also is the reason why the Amazon River is one of the longest flows in the world, because its headwaters lie on the eastern slopes of the Andes but the mouth of the river opens into the Atlantic 3,000 km (1,800 mi) away.

In gross terms, the geography of western South America consists of three broad zones running parallel to one another with the grain of the terrain running roughly northwest-southeast. These consist of a relatively narrow coastal plain, the Andes mountain range, and the tropical forest. There is desert on the coast and on the western flanks of the Andes, a range of temperate to cold and moist conditions in the mountains, and very wet tropical environments on the eastern Andean slopes. These differing regimes are due to the interactions of air masses and the land (see Figure 2.2).

From the east coast, wet air masses from the Atlantic Ocean travel westward across South America dropping rain throughout their journey, but their progress is blocked by the eastern slopes of the Andes. The altitudinal variations of the mountains produce different kinds of tropical vegetation at different elevations, providing different resources for human exploitation.

On the west coast the Humboldt Current, also sometimes referred to as the Peru Current, is a mass of cold water that swings up from the southern Pacific to run parallel with the shoreline of northern Chile and most of Peru. As the prevailing winds are from the west, clouds form when moisture-laden air crosses from the water to the land. In the austral summer (November to March) the reflection of solar radiation from the coastal desert warms the humid air so that it rises, passing over the western Andean foothills to cool at higher altitudes where the moisture falls as rain in the highlands. However, in the South American winter the heating effect of the sun on the desert coast is not as great so that in many places the wet air forms dense clouds that hang only a few hundred meters above the ground. In areas where the Andes foothills are relatively close to the ocean they are blanketed in these clouds, forming the dense fogs known in Peru as *garua*.

Minor variations in this pattern can have significant effects on plant, animal, and human life from place to place. For example, in the summer there are occasional short rain showers, especially on the north coast of Peru. Elsewhere, from time to time in the winter the *garua* can be thick and heavy enough that it extends well below its usual lower limit of 200 m (656 ft), while above 800 m (2,625 ft) skies are blue although there is a fog bank below one's feet. The conformation of the coast and mountains, especially in relation to the proximity of the Peru Current, also has an effect on local conditions. The coastal desert is driest in northern Chile and southern Peru, although in northern Peru the effects of the cold offshore waters are somewhat modified. The slightly moister conditions of the far north coast, especially from the Jequetepeque Valley northwards, support dry tropical forests in some river valleys. The exception to this regime is the large Sechura desert, the northernmost area where the Peru Current has any great influence before it swings westward back out to sea near the modern frontier of Ecuador and Peru. For millennia the Sechura has formed a frontier between the coastal desert of Peru and the tropical coast of Ecuador.

Figure 2.2 Major environmental zones. Top: Desert: Upraised beach, Chao Valley; Los Morteros huaca in middle distance. Center: Highlands: Tableland on the edge of the Urubamba Valley. Bottom: High tropical forest (*Ceja de Selva*): Lower Urubamba Valley near Machu Picchu.

MOUNTAINS

The Andes mountains are at their highest and most extensive in southern Peru and northern Chile, effectively blocking all moisture from traveling inland.[4] The great Altiplano plateau in Bolivia is thus a high, dry desert. Any rains that do fall in the region, along with ice melt-waters, make their way to Titicaca, one of the highest and largest lakes in the world, and this body of water was extremely important for ancient societies in the region. Another high altitude lake, Junín, is in the central highlands of Peru and also was regionally important.

Mountain rains and melt-waters from glaciers formed by Atlantic breezes combine to form rivers. In Peru, east of the continental divide the waters mostly head northwards. A series of important streams—the Mantaro, the Apurimac, the Vilcanota, and the Paucartambo in the southern highlands, the Huallaga and the Marañon in the north—eventually all connect to major tributaries of the Amazon. West of the continental divide the waters flow to the Pacific through relatively short valleys. The number of coastal valleys varies according to how various braided streams, dry branches, and other features are taken into account. However, in Peru alone there are between 30 and 40 such coastal valleys, depending on whether branches are counted separately or combined. They usually debouch perpendicular to the coast, although some twist and turn before their final run to the ocean.

The Andes are somewhat lower in Ecuador than in Peru, and they are also relatively irregular in their formation. The larger highland valleys were favored for habitation, such as that occupied by the modern-day capital city of Quito. Heading southwards the mountains form two parallel ranges in central Peru. The Cordillera Negra is the slightly lower western range, while the higher Cordillera Blanca has many snow-capped peaks. One of those peaks, Huascarán, is the highest mountain in Peru (6,768 m, 22,205 ft). The valley between the cordilleras, known as the *Callejon* ("big street") *de Huaylas*, carries the Santa, one of the longest rivers in highland and coastal Peru. It travels northwards for about 285 km (177 mi) and then swings westwards to the sea. It has been a corridor for travel and communication of great significance both in the past and the present.

Farther south the mountains are again relatively irregular with no distinct ranges. In the Bolivian Andes no mountains reach the height of Huascarán, but many come close such as Illimani (6,438 m, 21,122 ft). Furthermore, immense mountains ring the Altiplano, one of the highest habitable places on Earth. This vast, high plateau is larger than Britain, and at an average height of 4,000 m it lies above many snow-covered peaks in the rest of the Andes. Much of it is flat and featureless, a desert with no trees, little vegetation, piercingly cold nights, and hot days due to the intensity of the sun. The dry ghosts of ancient streams cut across the plains as well as the salty remains of desiccated lakes. The Uyuni Salt Lake, at 10,582 square km (4,085 square mi), is almost half again as large as the US state of Delaware, and it can be seen on the surface of the planet from a distance of more than 1,000 km (621 mi) in space.

The mountains and the Altiplano are the result of actions on the South American continent as it floats on plasma-like magma. The Nazca plate under the Pacific Ocean is subducting—that is, pushing downwards—underneath the South American continent. As it grinds downwards back into the earth's magma, it is tipping the western edge of South America upwards and crunching it, too. The downward thrust of the Nazca plate causes coastal uplift at the water's edge, and this upward force causes the rise of the Andes. The upward thrust of the high Andes mountains is so powerful that it results in smaller mountains and hills that stretch eastwards more than halfway across the continent.

Where the angle of subduction is steep, magma is pushed to the earth's surface in the form of volcanoes. Interestingly, while there are many active volcanoes in Ecuador and northern Chile, there are few in most of Peru except for in the south. There are 15 or 16 active volcanoes in southern Peru, depending on the cut-off date for "recent activity." One of the most famous Peruvian volcanoes is El Misti, looming over the city of Arequipa. However, there are no volcanoes north of the southern zone because the angle of subduction is relatively shallow.

From the perspective of human-based timescales, tectonics and the effects of the cold Peru Current and the dry coastal desert have both slow, long-term consequences and short, sharp ones. As a result of the slow-paced tectonics there is a gradual uplifting of the coast. Although it is barely perceptible over decades or centuries, such uplift can have dramatic effects on human abilities to exploit coastal resources. The uplifting process results in the raising of estuaries, so that they become beaches with fewer resources than the wetlands they once were. The uplift also strands agricultural fields above the level at which water can be delivered to them in irrigation canals and causes entrenchment or damage to the canals themselves.

The short-term, dramatic effects of Andean tectonics for most of the Central Andes are the earthquakes that are due to the thrust of the Nazca plate and farther south the Antarctica plate, underneath South America. Many of these are devastating, such as the 1970 destruction of the highland city of Huaraz in which half of the 30,000 inhabitants died and 90% of the buildings were destroyed. A total of 70,000 people in the region were killed, and the town of Yungay was completely annihilated in a matter of minutes by an avalanche following the quake. Such powerful earthquakes also occurred in prehistory, as evidenced in tilted walls and other signs of disruption at archaeological sites.

The severity of these earthquakes cannot be underestimated. In Colonial Period Peru, 51 significant quakes occurred between 1540 and 1799.[5] While indigenous people living in lightly-built, single storey structures may have been in less danger than colonial or recent populations living in tall adobe or concrete buildings, nevertheless earthquakes sometimes unleash huge avalanches of mud and loose, deadly gravel, as happened at Yungay. On the coast earthquakes often create tsunamis and also loosen huge amounts of soil that flow in rivers to the ocean, later returning to the land as sand dunes that inundate farm fields and towns.[6] In 1687 not a single building was left standing in Lima's chief port city of Callao, while in 1746 an earthquake left only 25 out of 3,000 houses standing in Lima and generated a 15 m (50 ft) tsunami that devastated Callao, killing thousands.[7]

EL NIÑO SOUTHERN OSCILLATION EVENTS

The cold waters of the Peru or Humboldt Current originate in the southern Pacific and flow along the shores of western South America from central Chile to the Peru–Ecuador border. The cold waters, welling up from great depths, are high in oxygen and nutrients, and they support the greatest maritime biome in the world. This rich source of easily harvested protein played a critical role in the origins of early complex societies in the Central Andes, and sustained later prehistoric cultures as well.

As noted above, the cold of the Humboldt Current interacts with the moist sea airs that pass over the desert coast to create rain in the highlands in the summer and roll in as low clouds when the temperature difference between water and land is less in the winter. Consequently, human populations both on the coast and in the highlands developed their cultures under these conditions. However, large masses of warmer ocean waters sometimes override the Humboldt Current. When this occurs the normal regime is disrupted, as are human lives. A repeating pattern of such events appears to have been established around 3800 BC, when the modern boundaries of the currents were established.[8]

The overriding of the Humboldt Current is known as the El Niño Southern Oscillation (ENSO), and the event and its meteorological consequences are commonly referred to jointly as El Niño, named after the Christ Child because it often arrives near Christmas.[9] The conventional wisdom of two or three decades ago was that El Niño occurred in a cycle of every seven years or so. Since then, however, intensive research on the ENSO phenomenon has revealed a much more complex picture. Even defining a "typical" El Niño event is not straightforward.[10] What can be stated, however, is that when severe El Niño events occurred, life would have become complicated for residents of the coast and the highlands.

On the coast, torrential rains and the resulting floods may have severely damaged the infrastructure of irrigation agriculture, such as canals, and inundated settlements. Fisherfolk saw the fish and seabird species with which they were most familiar disappear from the coast as they migrated with the colder waters. In the highlands the lack of rain would have meant drought for crops, camelid herds, and human populations.

These negatives would have been counter-balanced with opportunities. Rains in areas that were normally deserts resulted in the sudden blossoming of herbaceous plants. For people who did not have much investment in facilities susceptible to damage, such as foragers, shifting to exploit different resources could have been relatively easy, especially if communal knowledge preserved the lessons from previous El Niño experiences. The same held true for fisherfolk, while highland pastoralists could have moved their herds to lower elevations where new pasturage created by El Niño was available.

Except for cases in which floods harmed people or their means of making a living, the most critical issues in surviving El Niño events may have been how social groups adjusted their relations with one another under non-normal circumstances. For example, if highlanders held "rights" to pasture their camelids on the coast or had relatives there who would allow them pasturage, such shifts in subsistence strategies would have been easy to manage. However, we might expect that a fair amount of strife occurred when El Niño events were protracted and frequent, causing adaptive strategies to be stressed.

Another assumption that has undergone revision in the light of recent research is the view that El Niño events were uniformly destructive throughout the coast and adjacent highlands. New evidence suggests a much more complicated pattern. Although El Niños seem to have been more frequent on the North Coast of Peru, severe events impacted a greater geographical area reaching from the North Coast to the Central Coast. Even in strong events, however, the location of rainfall at any particular time and the degree of its intensity can vary greatly. One valley may experience devastating downpours and floods while its neighbor stays relatively dry.

The more complex picture of El Niño events that we now possess also complicates our views of past human behavior as a consequence. Although traces of El Niño rains and floods have been found at a number of sites from different time periods, how such events influenced the past is not always clear since there was a great degree of local variability in the effects of an ENSO event, as well as differences in the ways in which people may have responded to it. Another natural event that may have affected inhabitants of the ancient Andes is the occurrence of tsunamis; they can be hard to detect in the archaeological record and their effects are even more difficult to evaluate.

VERTICAL ZONES

The three major geographic zones—coast, highlands, and tropical forest—have many subdivisions that were and remain of great importance for human survival and prosperity. One set of subdivisions is the result of changing environmental zones due to altitude. Ecuador straddles and Peru is close to the equator which means that solar radiation is strong, but altitudinal effects play a critical role in plant communities. Nightly frosts may occur as many as 25 days per month during the highland winter at altitudes above 4,000 m, but areas below 3,000 m rarely drop below freezing. Altitudinal location is thus vital in determining resource potential and availability. In addition, the closely stacked vertical zones result in a landscape in which very different ecosystems can be reached within a relatively short distance by traveling up or down a mountain slope, but which extend horizontally over long stretches.

The Peruvian geographer Javier Pulgar Vidal has used the native nomenclature of Quechua speakers to refer to different environmental zones, and these terms are commonly used by a wide variety of people today.[11] Indeed, the term quechua itself refers to one of these zones, and the use of the term as a reference for a linguistic and cultural group likely came about because it referred to the people who lived in that particular environmental zone, showing how important the lands and the concepts associated with them are to the Andean peoples (see Figure 2.3).

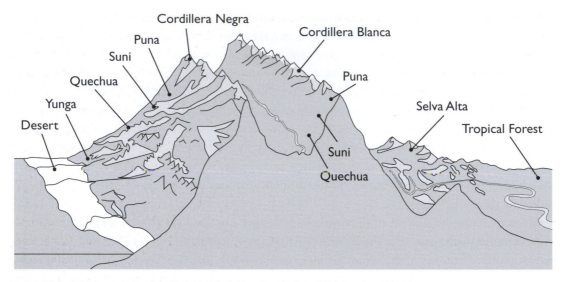

Figure 2.3 Environmental zones profile following Pulgar Vidal's classification.

The *chala* is the desert coast, from sea level to 1,000 meters (3,281 ft). The *yunga* refers to the warm lower valleys usually located between 1,000 and 2–3,000 meters (3,281 and 6,562–9,843 ft). This is the coastal area most commonly affected by *garua*, mentioned earlier. Both on the coast and on the eastern slopes of the Andes, the *yunga* zone is known for the production of highly valued tropical crops such as chili peppers (*ají*), coca, and various fruits.

The *quechua* is a mild zone, higher than the yunga, between 2,500 and 3,500 m (8,202–11,483 ft) above sea level. It consists mostly of low mountain valleys and was the area most prized for agriculture in the sierra, because it is frost-free and has good land to support the raising of a wide variety of plants including maize, squashes, cotton, and other fruits and vegetables.

The *suni*, between 3,000 and 3,500–4,000 m (9,843 and 11,483–13,123 ft) above sea level, is cold and damp. This zone receives the most rain of any of the zones, and the land is often steep. At these altitudes tubers (potatoes, *oca, ullucu, mashua*), chenopodiums (quinoa, *achis, caniwa*), lupines, and introduced grains (barley and wheat) are best grown.

The *puna* (3,500 to 3,800–4,800 m [11,483 and 12,467–15,748 ft]) is the highest zone consistently occupied by humans, and it is generally dry. Its high plains and rolling hills mainly support grass, making it the natural habitat of the wild camelids (vicuña and guanaco), deer, and waterfowl and fish in highland lakes. This is the region where pastoralism has been the best mode of survival since the herd animals were domesticated as early as 3500 BC. In northern Peru and Ecuador where the highest tablelands are less harsh than in southern Peru or Bolivia, the dry puna is replaced with a wetter regime of grasslands known as *páramo*, but interestingly camelid pastoralism arrived there relatively late, only about 2,000 years ago.[12] The highest Andean zone, the *janca* (between 4,800 and 6,768 m [15,748–22,205 ft] above sea level) does not sustain a consistent human presence.

On the eastern slopes of the Andes a high tropical forest, between 400 and 1,000 m (1,312–3,281 ft) above sea level, is composed of different habitats than the lower Amazon forest. In native terminology the higher zone is known as the *rupa-rupa*, but it is commonly referred to in Spanish as the *ceja de selva* (eyebrow of the jungle) or the *selva alta* (high jungle). The lower jungle (*selva baja*), between 80 and 400 m (262–1,312 ft) in altitude, is known as the *omagua* in Quechua.

The tropical forest has not received much attention in the foregoing discussion even though it is a vast area rich in plants, animals, and other resources. For the most part, tropical cultures are outside the realm of the Andean world in the sense that the peoples who lived there practiced very different lifestyles than those who lived on the coast or in the highlands. Nevertheless, there is abundant evidence that the tropical forest and its peoples had great influences on their neighbors. Although the Inca never conquered significant areas of the tropical lowlands, there were many points of contact. Powerful shamans who had special abilities to access the spirit world were thought to dwell in the jungle, and hallucinogenic plants that helped transport the shamans to supernatural realms, as well as the milder but highly important coca leaf, both came from the eastern lowlands.

In addition to our historical knowledge of Inca attitudes towards, and relations with, the tropical forest and its peoples, there is abundant archaeological evidence, starting in remote times and extending throughout prehistory, that there were strong ties between the coast, the highlands, and the jungle. Indeed, Carl Sauer and Donald Lathrap believed that New World agriculture started in the tropical forests, and the latter thought that many other cultural practices did as well.[13] As the Ecuadorian coast is unaffected by the Humboldt Current it is a tropical regime, and in this region the archaeological evidence points to very early domestication of important plants and the early emergence of social and cultural complexity. However, except for in western Ecuador archaeological research in the tropical lowlands has been far less intensive than in other areas of the Central Andes. Furthermore, the preservation of organic materials is poor in the humid conditions of the rainforest. Nevertheless, continuing research is demonstrating that the tropical forest was densely populated and that some areas supported ancient populations of great complexity, although much still remains to be learned.

Throughout these major environmental zones there are many specific habitats and resources that played crucial roles in the lives of Andean peoples. Outcrops of salt, obsidian, metal ores and various kinds of stones provided essential resources. Bogs, lagoons, and fog-nurtured hillside plant communities known as *lomas* offered distinct food resources and raw materials such as the stands of reeds essential for reed-boat construction at various spots on the coast. Rocky shores supported one kind of mollusk community, in contrast to sandy beaches. Humans were quick to exploit these and many more resources in a land that was at once harsh and bountiful.

TIME

Scholars in the different countries of the Central Andes culture area follow their own chronological systems for prehistory, and these are commonly based upon concerns of national identity and how it relates to prehistory. However, Peru plays a crucial role as the center of the area, so its chronology is of particular importance.

Several different chronological systems have been proposed since the end of World War II, at which time scholarship in the region increased dramatically. Two systems are most commonly used today, however. Peruvian archaeologist Luis Lumbreras developed one system and Americans John Rowe and Dorothy Menzel created the other.[14] Because they rely on the same data and similar inferences from them, the Lumbreras and Rowe-Menzel chronologies are quite similar in many ways. The Rowe-Menzel system was published first, so it will be discussed first here; the theoretical and practical reasons for how the system was developed are important to understand alongside the specifics of each chronological period.

In the mid-1960s radiocarbon dating was still relatively new in archaeology, and many archaeologists, including John Rowe, pointed out various problems with regard to relying on such dates to make inferences or assertions about prehistoric events and to build chronologies. Rowe and Menzel decided to use relative rather than chronometric dating for their chronological system. They picked the Ica Valley on the South Coast, which had one of the best ceramic sequences at the time, and they used it as a baseline for marking chronological change: when a change occurred in Ica it would be marked as a new time period, regardless of what may have been occurring in other areas of the Central Andes. This was done in order to create a distinct chronological system that took culture change into account but was not enslaved to it. This requires some further discussion in order to make the issue clear.

Consider the nineteenth century. We think of it in two senses, one chronological and the other cultural. The strict chronological definition of the period is the hundred-year span from the first day of 1801 to the last day of 1901 (not from 1800 to 1900, because the hundredth year must be completed for the period to span a century). Culturally, however, we think of the nineteenth century as characterized by ways of life and ideas that set it apart from the eighteenth century that preceded it and the twentieth century that followed. We have general notions of the nineteenth century that are associated with the rise of industrialism, romanticism, colonialism, and imperialism, even though these began before 1801 and continued after 1901. However, for better and for worse we tend to characterize the nineteenth century as a cultural period with its own distinct ways of doing things, qualitatively different from the centuries that came before and after it.

In some senses it could be argued that the nineteenth century as a cultural period began later than 1801, not starting until 1815 with the final defeat of Napoleon and the rise of Britain as a great world power. It could also be argued that it ended in 1914, when the start of World War I set events in motion that changed the world forever. Although the specifics of this proposal for conceptualizing different ways to consider the nineteenth century might be disputed, the general point is that cultural periods and chronological periods do not always coincide. This disjuncture between chronological periods and cultural periods can be applied to almost any other historical period in Western Europe or anywhere else. In discussing historical events we can often switch back and forth between referencing specific years or decades, and discussing cultural events that often occurred out of strict chronological order. However, this is not so easy to do in prehistory.

In working in prehistory, even with the more refined and numerous radiocarbon dates we currently have, we usually lack the finely delineated chronological resolution that would allow us to discuss events even with the span of a decade. While such resolution varies from place to place and from time to time, we usually have to discuss things in more coarse resolutions, referring to broader periods of time. However, we can't rely on the identification of major cultural changes as time markers. For example, if we wanted to use the first occurrence of pottery as a time marker, we would be confronted with two significant problems. The first is that the first use of pottery likely occurred at different times in different places within the Central Andes, so that it would be impossible to narrow the time to a tight enough period to serve as a date to mark cultural change. The second problem is that we would probably have to keep revising the date that marked the new time period as new research provided evidence to change the date, often to an earlier time.

Given these problems, it would be advantageous to have a fixed chronological system similar to the decades and centuries in history, against which we could place culture changes that may occur at different times in different places and that overlap the strict chronological times. This is what the Rowe-Menzel chronology does: it provides a set of chronological periods that are fixed in the same way that decades and centuries are fixed on a calendrical system, while also recognizing that particular cultural events may have occurred earlier or later in different parts of the Central Andes.

While the Rowe-Menzel chronology imposes a strict system on the past, it also recognizes significant large-scale events by using a system of Horizons in contrast to a set of Periods. Horizons are times during which there is evidence for widespread cultural influences throughout much of the Central Andes, while Periods are times when cultures were more regionally based. This is best understood by reviewing Horizons and Periods in detail (see Figure 2.4).

The Preceramic Period is the time from which no pottery is found at archaeological sites, and in the 1960s this era was not well known in the Ica Valley. It was clear, however, that the first ceramics were used in the valley around 1700 BC, so that date marks the beginning of the Initial Period. The term "initial" derives from the first use of ceramics. Around 800 BC, however, the decoration of ceramics in Ica starts to show influences from the ceremonial center of Chavín de Huántar in the highlands of Peru, and Chavín's influence was far and wide in other regions as well. Chavín influence waned in the ceramics of Ica at about 1 BC. This date thus marks the end of the Early Horizon. After this time, in the Early Intermediate Period, Ica ceramics revert to local styles not much found outside of the valley, a trend which continued between 0 and AD 650 At that later date, however, another highland power, Wari, once again influenced Ica ceramics so that this date marks the beginning of the Middle Horizon (AD 650 to 1000). Wari influence waned and local styles reemerged during the Late Intermediate Period from AD 1000 to 1450. Finally, Inca styles influenced Chincha ceramics during the Late Horizon between AD 1450 and 1550. The Spanish arrived in Peru in 1532, but it took some time for Inca influences to end in the Ica Valley.

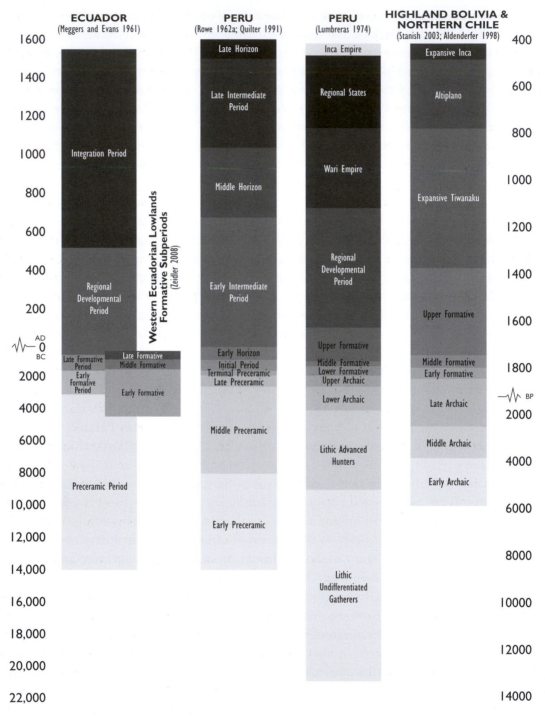

Figure 2.4 Chronological systems for the Central Andes. Dates for the Lumbreras system vary according to region. The dates shown are generalized.

It is worth emphasizing that the dates for these Periods and Horizons only refer to events in the Ica Valley, being arbitrary dates in relation to cultural events outside the valley in the same way that cultural events are often outside the parameters of European centuries. For example, the dates for the Middle Horizon do not mark the time of the rise of the Wari Empire, only the duration of Wari influence in Ica. It bears repeating that this is a chronological system, not a description of cultural events. Even some professional Andeanist archaeologists sometimes fail to grasp this rationale, complaining that the Rowe-Menzel system does not "work" for their culture region which may be far away from the Ica Valley and thus not "in step" with events there. However, the system works just as well as using European-derived centuries or decades to mark time periods in central Africa or East Asia.

The only significant modification of the Rowe-Menzel system to date has been the elaboration of the Preceramic Period into sub-periods. As previously noted this era was not well known when Rowe and Menzel developed their chronology, but Rowe's student Edward P. Lanning defined the Preceramic sub-periods through his work on the Central Coast. In order to have a more broadly applicable system, however, I have suggested that the use of Early (First Presence, *circa* 14,000 to 8000 BC), Middle (8000 to 4500 BC), Late (4500 to 3800 BC), and Terminal (3800 to 1500 BC) Preceramic Periods could be used throughout the Central Andes.[15] While this periodization is based on the Central Coast sequence, it is also generally applicable to the rest of the Central Andes.

The Peruvian archaeologist Luis G. Lumbreras developed the other major chronological system in use today. This system is based more strongly on cultural evolutionary theory than the Rowe-Menzel system. It begins with a Lithic Period (21,000 to 4000 BC), followed by the Archaic (4000 to 1300 BC) and Formative (1800 BC to AD 100) Periods. Lumbreras sees the Lithic Period as the time of the first peopling of the New World, followed by a sequence of increasingly more complex hunter–gatherer societies through time. The next period is divided into the Lower Archaic, when agriculture first appeared, and the Upper Archaic, which is when village horticultural communities became common and includes the time of the first large-scale ceremonial complexes of the Late Preceramic Period in the Rowe-Menzel system.

Lumbreras's Formative Period includes the Initial Period, the Early Horizon, and the early part of the Early Intermediate Period in the Rowe-Menzel sequence. It is based on a conception of the rise and influence of the site of Chavín de Huántar as an important phenomenon, so that the Lower Formative comprises the use of the first ceramics and new forms of temple architecture in ceremonial complexes. The Middle Formative is the time of the height of Chavín influence throughout Peru, and the Upper Formative is the time immediately after the collapse of Chavín when regional cultures began to form but were not as fully developed as they came to be in the Moche, Recuay, Lima, Huarpa, and Nasca cultures, among others.

The later Lumbreras periods are similar to those of the Rowe-Menzel system, with the Regional Developmental (AD 100 to 700), Wari Empire (AD 700 to 1100), Regional States (AD 1100 to 1470), and Tawantinsuyo Empire (AD 1430 to 1532) phases roughly equivalent to the Rowe-Menzel sequence from the Early Intermediate Period to the Late Horizon, although the time spans for each era are not the same in the two systems.

Today some archaeologists use the Rowe-Menzel system while others use the Lumbreras chronology. For most scholars there are no strong feelings about preferring one system over the other, and productive conversations commonly occur in which one speaker uses one system while the other party uses the other. Both the Rowe-Menzel and Lumbreras chronologies are prone to requiring adjustment, because when dates are revised for the first appearance of a new pottery style in Ica the beginning of the Rowe-Menzel Period or Horizon with which it is associated also would need to be revised, while the same is true for changes in the dates of the Wari Empire or any of the other time markers in the Lumbreras system.

It is only natural that as knowledge advances chronological and other systems used to discuss the past must be revised. Ideally, our discussions of prehistory should be done using dates that are as precise as possible, using either Before Present (BP) or BC/AD or the equivalent system, Before Common Era/Common Era (BCE/CE). Indeed, from the period stretching backward from about the fifth century of our era to the end of prehistory we can almost do this now for some Andean regions. However, for more remote times this ideal is still not possible. It is a goal to strive for that one day will probably be achieved for most of the prehistory of the Central Andes, except for the far distant past.

Because the purpose of this book is to present current knowledge of the Central Andes, no new system will be proposed here. Therefore this book is generally organized on the Rowe-Menzel system, but it will sometimes use others where appropriate, such as in Ecuador where the initial use of pottery occurred much earlier than in Peru. Lately the use of specific chronometric dates (e.g. BC/AD or BP) has been complicated by the varying calibrations of dates as produced by radiocarbon analyses in relation to adjustments due to the known fluctuations of carbon in the atmosphere. For most of the discussions in this book, however, these distinctions are usually not critical because the discussions are fairly generalized.

FORM

The formal features that make the Central Andes distinct from other culture areas are many, but at the same time they are not always exclusive to the region. For example, principles of social organization and religious ideas based on dualism are found among many traditions of indigenous peoples in the New World. It is less any one particular trait than the suite of beliefs, practices, and material culture that together add up to a distinctive Andean way.

As mentioned in the previous chapter, one problem in attempting to characterize an Andean way of doing things is that it leads to the concept of Lo Andino, which may be criticized as essentializing what was in reality a heterogeneous experience that was constantly changing and was different from place to place. However, while these are caveats well worth remembering, a goal of anthropological archaeology, as a social science, is generalization, which suggests that some consideration of what sets the Central Andes apart from other cultural phenomena is in order.

Before attempting to make some general statements, another issue must be raised. When culture areas for the New World were first developed more than a century ago, the level of detail known about various sub-regions was much less detailed than it is today, and so common features were easily seen. Since then, however, our information has become much more detailed, with the result that perceiving a cohesive unity to the region is somewhat harder to do. In 1948 Wendell Bennett defined the "Peruvian Co-Tradition" as a cohesive cultural unit within the Central Andes. Based on recent research, however, it could be argued that there are sub-regions of the Central Andes that in large measure were different enough that they might deserve consideration as separate culture areas in their own right.[16] One of these might be called the area of the South Andean Tradition, which would include the South Coast and Southern Highlands of Peru, western Bolivia, northwestern Argentina and northern Chile. Interactions in this region, not only within different environmental regimes but also between them, have great antiquity and are stronger than relations outside this large region. Similarly, a North Andean Tradition region could include the North Coast and adjacent highlands of Peru and even parts of Ecuador, especially at certain times in the past. A third sub-region would be the Central Peruvian Tradition (to distinguish it from the Central Andes). The peoples of the Central Coast and adjacent highlands had a distinct integrity in their ways of life and cultural practices for much of prehistory, as was the case for the other two areas previously described.

It is interesting to consider that these three areas, based on archaeology, are not too different from the four-fold division of the Inca Empire which called itself Tahuantinsuyu and which may be glossed as "the four parts taken as a whole." The four parts were: Chinchasuyu, comprising most of the Central and North Coasts and adjacent highlands; Cuntisuyu, the South Coast and adjacent highlands, Antisuyu, the tropical forest and adjacent highlands; and Collasuyu, comprising Bolivia, northwest Argentina and northern Chile. Each suyu was a semi-autonomous administrative unit with a governor directly responsible to the Inca emperor.[17]

From the perspective of making a living, the formal characteristics of the Central Andes include a reliance on domesticated plants including maize (*Zea mays*) at lower altitudes and hardier seed crops, roots, and tubers at higher altitudes. Quinoa (*Chenopodium quinoa*), once virtually unknown by Westerners but now appearing on our tables, was an important crop since it produces more protein per unit of cultivation than maize. One of the Andes' great gifts to the world is the potato (*Solanum tuberosum*). Thousands of varieties are known, varying according to size, shape, color, and texture. Ulluco (*Ullucus tuberosus*) and Oca (*Oxalis tuberosa*) follow close behind the potato as popular and important agricultural staples in the Andes. Along with manioc (*Manihot esculenta*), sweet potatoes (*Ipomoea batatas*) and squashes (*Cucurbita spp.*), they provided many different sources of starch. Lima beans (*Phaseolus lunatus*), common beans (*Phaseolus vulgaris*), and jack beans (*Canavalia sp.*) offered protein. Peanuts (*Arachis hypogaea*) were first cultivated in Peru, avocados (*Persea americana*) entered the diets of Andean peoples early on, and many fruits such as lucuma (*Pouteria lucuma*), chirimoya (*Annona cherimola*) and pacae (*Inga feuilleei*) added variety and sweetness to food culture. A wide variety of chili peppers (*Capsicum spp.*), also first domesticated in the Andes, added spice. On the coast, native wild cotton grew in different colors and was domesticated to produce one of the finest quality fabrics of its kind in the world.

For animal protein, transporting of goods, and wool for fabrics, the peoples of the area relied upon the Andean camelids, particularly the alpaca (*Vicugna pacos*) for wool and the llama (*Lama glama*) for transport, while the domesticated, rapidly reproducing guinea pig (*Cavia porcellus*) provided small but abundant bundles of reliable protein. Andean people also took advantage of wild food resources whenever possible, and these included a wide variety of plant foods as well as white-tailed deer (*Odocoileus virginianus*) and other game. At the same time and in a distinctively different way, the coast supported one of the great maritime traditions of the world. Large fish were both line-caught and speared, and netted sardines and anchovies provided great amounts of protein and fat while numerous shore birds, mollusks, and crustaceans also added to the diet. Whales were never deliberately hunted, as far as we know, and sea lions and seals also do not appear to have played major roles in diets except, perhaps, at some times and places early in prehistory.

Andean people not only raised a wide variety of crops and animals, many of which eventually spread throughout the world, but they also invented distinctive ways to process and preserve them. They invented freeze-drying. In the highlands, frost-resistant potatoes are exposed to freezing temperatures at night and intense solar radiation during the day. Trampling or otherwise squeezing excess moisture out of the potatoes during the day followed by repeated exposure to cold and heat produces a desiccated food that can last for a long period of time; *chuño*, freeze-dried potato, can last for months, even years. A similar process was carried out on llama meat. The result is *charqui*, from which the English word "jerky" is derived. Although other techniques for food preservation have not been explored extensively, there are various lines of evidence to suggest that Andean peoples were quite sophisticated in developing ways to keep their food palatable for long periods of time. Mollusk shells are found high in the Andes, which could have been brought there in wet seaweed, perhaps. Fish oil can also be preserved for a long period of time, needing only to be reheated to assure its quality. Inca storehouses are famed for the way in which their placement in the landscape, taking advantage of prevailing winds, and the ways in which they were constructed allowed for the drying and preservation of their contents.

Stimulants and narcotics were popular in the Central Andes. There is a long tradition of the brewing and consumption of an alcoholic beverage commonly known as *chicha*. This is a Caribbean word, an indication of the widespread use of the drink. The Quechua term is *awa*, although today the former term is in widespread use. Andean people made maize chicha, but occasionally they also used other plants such as *molle* (*Schinus molle*, the Peruvian pepper tree). The drinking of chicha was an important part of Andean rituals from a very early time.

Andean people also chewed the coca (*Ertyhroxylum coca*) leaf, and its popularity spread beyond the Central Andes to the Northern Andes and Southern Central America as well as southwards into Bolivia, Chile, and Argentina. The active cocaine alkaloid in the leaf is released through consuming lime in powder form, usually made from burnt limestone, shells, or plant ashes. Throughout much of South America, distinctive containers with sticks to withdraw and consume the lime often indicate that coca was chewed in prehistory, even when coca leaves are not recovered archaeologically.

The effects of the coca leaf are milder than highly concentrated cocaine, although it can be addictive and can produce a "high" if chewed in great quantities. The Inca controlled the substance, only allowing its use for rituals and celebrations and for workers undertaking strenuous tasks, such as long-distance travel in which coca could ease the burdens of the journey. Use of coca was likely to have been restricted in earlier times as well, although we do not have a great deal of information on this subject. Among indigenous people in the Andean countries today the plant is closely associated with national identity, used as offerings in rituals, and the leaves are read as a form of divination.

Tobacco was the most popular drug in the native New World but we do not have accurate information about its use, especially in South America, prior to about 1700. It was smoked and also snuffed, eaten, chewed, drunk, and licked. There is a distinct pattern according to which those peoples who favored coca chewing had little to no use for tobacco, so coastal and highland peoples in the Andes tended not to use it but tropical forest peoples did.[18]

There were many other mind-altering substances that were probably used in the ancient Andes. Some of these we know were definitely used, and others seem likely to have been used. For example, snuff tubes and trays are well known throughout the Central Andes but they seem to have been particularly popular in northern Chile. Powder found with them has been identified as the ground bean of the vilca tree (*Anandathera colubrina*).[19] Another mind-altering substance is the mescaline-rich San Pedro cactus (*Echinopsis pachanoi*). Numerous depictions of the distinctive cactus and its flowers are known from early times in Peru, and both vilca and San Pedro are still used in contemporary shamanic practices. Other psychotrophic plants that may have been used include yupa (*Pipitadenia spp.*) and ayahuasca (*Banisteriopsis spp.*). The latter is a Quechua word meaning "spirit vine" or "vine of the souls," and even though it is primarily a tropical plant it was used in the highlands. Much of prehistoric Andean religion appears to have included activities in which one or more people were brought into altered states of consciousness, whether through consumption of great quantities of alcohol in the form of chicha, or with stronger potions.

The various plants and animals of the Andes were raised using techniques that were established early and which appear to have changed little over the millennia. This is not a sign of any lack of innovation, but rather a testament to the people's strategy of finding solutions to making a living early and then refining them over the years. Irrigation agriculture developed at an early stage, first appearing during the Preceramic Period between 5,400 and 6,500 years ago.[20] Irrigation included not only the construction of canals and various systems for containing, slowing, and otherwise manipulating water, but also the terracing of hillsides.

When the Spanish entered Peru they were astonished at the way in which the landscape had been sculpted into vast systems of terraces. There were so many terraces that even today, in many valleys the extent of the ancient terraces is greater than the amount of land currently under cultivation. Terracing was not simply cutting into a hillside to change a slope into a platform; it also involved the engineering of the soil to improve its fertility and drainage. It can be confidently stated that the greatest amount of work and energy, and the most staggering monument to the industry of the ancient peoples of the Andes, lies not in the ruins of the great archaeological sites but in the vast terrace and irrigation systems that surround them.

Tools to work the fields were few but efficient. The Andean foot-plow is distinctive and was widely used. Andean peoples discovered metallurgy early, but they relied mostly upon hard woods and stone for their tools throughout the centuries, employing their metal craftsmen in making precious objects for rituals or adornment. By late antiquity, after about 1000 BC, metal tools had increased in use. It is hard to assess how widespread they were because metal is often worn away during use or re-melted and reworked to be used again. However, there are many examples of pins, needles, knives, axes, crow-bars, spear heads, and other tools and weapons to suggest that metal use was fairly widespread in late times.

Like all the peoples of the New World, Andean people made earthenwares—that is, ceramics fired at relatively low temperatures. Pottery was made without the use of the wheel. Many vessels were made using slabs of clay worked by hand. Some fancy ceramics were constructed using press-molds that allowed separate sections to be put together to complete a vessel, especially on the North Coast of Peru. Utilitarian cooking and storage vessels were well made but usually lacked adornment, but great attention was paid to pieces that were valued as prized objects to be used in ceremonies or buried in tombs. Most of the archaeological cultures to be discussed in this book are defined by fancy ceramics, commonly known as "finewares," made in distinctive styles. These range from monochromatic vessels with forms based on gourds or other plants and polished to a high, mirror-like gloss, through elaborate, composite modeled vessels in one or two colors, to distinctive works of art in a riot of different hues.

Many scholars like to emphasize textiles as *the* great art of the Andes.[21] It is commonly noted that the variety of textile techniques in the Andes was greater than that in the Western world in the first half of the twentieth century, before the advent of computer-assisted textile manufacturing. Weaving is still prized among people living traditional Andean lifestyles today, and one of the most prestigious gifts that could be given by the Inca ruler was *cumbi* cloth, the finest textile known, woven in seclusion by nun-like "chosen women." Textiles were not only prized for the great amount of artistry that they displayed but also because clothing was a mark of identity. Each community in the Inca Empire had its own distinctive style of dress, including headdresses. Some of these traditions remain today with local styles evolving in the half-millennium since the Spanish conquest.

Many other arts and crafts were practiced in the Andes as well as ceramics and textiles. Inca stonework is a marvel to behold, but so is the stone carving at Chavín de Huántar two millennia earlier, while small gem-like carvings in semi-precious stone and shell are known from Preceramic times onwards. Elaborate carvings in wood are known, although the general lack of wood in the Andes and the tendency for wood to decay makes such items relatively scarce in the archaeological record in many places. Today, travelers to Peru often buy gourds decorated by carving and carefully burning sections of the exterior of the fruit. Beyond the cheap versions made in a hurry and usually piled in baskets in the "Indian Markets," there are gourds that are artistic tours de force, and this tradition extends back to the Preceramic Period as well.

The Andes lacked draught animals but the llama can carry close to 45 kg (100 lb) comfortably, so camelid trains of many scores of animals carried goods throughout the region. The llama is a creature of high altitude, but a lowland variety, the *warizo*, was domesticated on the coast.[22] People also carried goods, as well as other people. High-ranking lords were carried in litters, at least in late prehistory, as shown in ceramics and sculptures. The Inca road system is famous and there is evidence that roads were built in earlier times as well, although the dates for the oldest roads are uncertain. Inca rope bridges are also well known, and again their antiquity is uncertain. A 6.7 m long by 2.9 m wide (22 ft by 9.5 ft) stone bridge at Chavín de Huántar was in use as late as 1945, in service for three millennia before it was destroyed in a landslide.[23]

There are virtually no navigable rivers in the highlands and coastal region of the Central Andes, so river travel played no role in ancient societies except in the tropical forest. Boats made of *totora* reeds came in large and small varieties and were used around the coasts as well as to traverse Lake Titicaca. Because the reeds become waterlogged and decay quickly, such vessels could not have made very long voyages. However, large rafts of balsa logs that included space for a cabin and storage areas on deck could make such trips. Westerners tend to think of rafts as rather flimsy, unreliable vessels, but these were highly seaworthy craft. The use of vertical boards as adjustable keels, as well as movable sails, allowed them to tack against the wind.[24] Pizarro encountered such a large balsa raft that was sailing from a southern part of the Peruvian coast to Ecuador on a trading mission, and such maritime trade likely had a long tradition.

Although Pizarro's ship encountered a raft on a trading mission, this kind of economic activity has generally been seen as an exception to the rule for Central Andean economic systems. Furthermore, Andean societies generally did not use money, they did not have banks, and the degree to which they conceived of wealth as residing in things is debatable at best. This issue of different economics is one of the key differences between many ancient societies and our own, and it is perhaps one of the hardest for modern people to comprehend. There is some evidence that at certain times there may have been units of exchange in the form of "proto-monies," especially late in prehistory. These could have facilitated the exchange of goods thanks to the standardization of the sizes or weights of the things that were being exchanged, such as ingots of metal. There appear to have been other standardized systems as well, such as units of weight or measurement like the "Preceramic Yard," which measured between 80 and 100 cm (31.5 to 39.4 in), but for the most part these have not been explored in depth.[25] Standardized units of weight or measurement can help to facilitate the exchange of goods, but the ways in which essential items and surplus materials and labor were utilized were very different in ancient societies than in the modern world.

In the last half of the twentieth century, anthropologist John V. Murra promulgated the idea that goods were distributed via the "vertical archipelago" of the Andean environment, without markets, as previously discussed. Because resource zones are stacked like layers in a cake, a system evolved in which the products of each zone were raised or collected by colonists or kinfolk, who then exchanged them with people in other zones without the need for the central place for redistribution which is an essential aspect of markets.[26] Many anthropologists, archaeologists, and other scholars accepted Murra's proposal. While Murra based his interpretation of Andean economics on Colonial Period documents describing the Inca, as well as on more recent practices in the Andes, the concept was used to interpret almost all ancient economies as well.

The trading vessel was an exception to verticality, but it was explained away as a distinctive practice of the people of Chincha on the coast, which the Inca tolerated because it was profitable to maintain. Other examples, such as evidence for the long-distance traders known as *mindalaes* in Ecuador, were also seen as exceptions.[27] Recently, however, some archaeologists have begun to question whether verticality was a uniquely evolved Andean system at all, suggesting rather that it was a distinct means of imperial control by the Inca state. Evidence is accruing that it is likely that there were markets in operation at various social and regional levels in the ancient Andes. This does not discount the possibility that the vertical archipelago system may have predated the Inca Empire; it merely enriches and further complicates our picture of the past, and is an example of how continuing research is needed to investigate such issues.[28]

SOCIAL, POLITICAL, AND RELIGIOUS SYSTEMS

The issue of whether past behaviors were unique or displayed common human patterns is, as noted previously, one of the key issues motivating our study of the past. In addition to struggling with this issue in terms of Andean economics, the same is true for society, politics, and religion. The issue is particularly salient for politics and economics because from very early times Europeans interpreted New World societies from their own perspectives and understandings. By the seventeenth century European *philosophes* had recognized that the Inca, in particular, were a highly ordered and regularized society. The result was that over the years the Inca have been characterized in extreme ways, from the ideal communist society to a fascist dictatorship. The authors of such claims usually knew few details about the Inca or their ancestors, and are working on the basis of highly romanticized, abstracted, and commonly wrong ideas.

Most scholarly or otherwise serious studies of Andean prehistory through the 1950s tried to simply understand what had happened in the past, relying on archaeological investigations as well as interpretations of the Inca and their contemporaries and immediate antecedents as reported by Spanish chroniclers.

In the 1960s, many archaeologists working on prehistoric cultures, especially those who were associated with the New Archaeology as mentioned in the previous chapter, adopted the theories of a group of anthropologists who had developed a more sophisticated version of cultural evolution than had been used when anthropology first developed as a discipline in the nineteenth century. Instead of seeing specific criteria by which societies advanced to reach a level of "civilization," the neoevolutionists of the late twentieth century saw multilinear evolution as progressing along multiple different pathways towards what they termed social or cultural "complexity." Instead of a checklist of traits, such as writing, metallurgy, and agriculture, that had to be present for a society, to reach "civilization" as conceived in the nineteenth century, the key criterion for "achieving" the highest levels of socio-cultural evolution became the attainment of a particular kind of political organization—the state.

Using this framework, the Inca could be recognized as a complex society because even though they didn't have writing they were clearly a state. The same is true of the Maya, who may have had writing but didn't have much in the way of metallurgy. They both manifested state-level political organization. While different cultures reach statehood in different ways, they can generally be classified in their earlier stages of development based on generalized political systems. The most common terms were derived from the writings of Morton Fried and Elman R. Service: bands, tribes, chiefdoms, and the state.[29]

Each step on the evolutionary ladder had distinctive features according to which socio-political systems, subsistence strategies, and even religions were linked together. This analytical system was attractive to archaeologists because they could link their archaeological data to behaviors assumed to be present in the socio-political categories.

A considerable amount of research has been carried out in the Central Andes, especially in Peru and Bolivia, in attempting to identify the first state. The Inca have long been seen as one of the great "civilizations" of the ancient world, but it seemed highly likely, based on the extensive ruins of earlier temple complexes and cities, that the Inca were not the first state. The question then became which culture was the first to develop state society, and various candidates have been proposed over the years.

At the same time that some scholars were searching for the first state, other archaeologists relied upon the concept of Lo Andino to project forms of political organization known at the time of the Spanish Conquest, and even in the contemporary Andes, into the remote past. The basic socio-political unit in the Andes is commonly said to be a corporate group known by the Quechua term *ayllu*. To complicate matters there is no easy definition of the ayllu that is agreed by all, but it may generally be defined as groups of extended families, which may also include non-related members, who work together in subsistence agriculture.[30]

When did ayllu organization start? How was it related to political systems above the local level? How easily would an interpretation of ancient socio-political organization based on the ayllu conform with concepts such as the "tribe" or "chiefdom?" Equally importantly, how can we recognize ayllu organization archaeologically? These are difficult questions to answer and they cannot be addressed here, but they are germane to the story of Andean prehistory.

Whether we can identify ancient ayllu organization or not, should we abandon attempts to compare indigenous Andean societies with other cultures from different times and places? Some

45

argue that the Andes should be studied on its own terms, while others maintain that comparative analyses are important for the larger mission of understanding the story of humankind, writ large.

Another contentious area of scholarship is religion, especially in its relation to politics. Both of these terms, "religion" and "politics," are Western European concepts that do not exist in any of the native languages of the Andes. Some scholars argue that while the concepts did not exist we can employ them analytically for our own purposes, while others argue that doing so obscures the very behaviors and ideas that we are trying to study and which are so different from our own.

Fancy ceramics, textiles, and stone carvings are some of the most informative materials that archaeologists may use to study the past, because they often carry a great amount of information via their decorations. Most of those decorations represent what appear to be religious ideas—gods, mythological heroes, and concepts about symmetry, balance, centeredness, and something approaching what Westerners call "aesthetics." Much of what happened in the Andes as defined by Periods and Horizons appears to have involved changes in belief systems and practices, and these also appear to have been tied to politics. Indeed, politics and religion appear to have been inseparable.

In the West we often think of politics and religion as two separate areas of human activity, even though Western history is filled with examples of how politics and religion or ideology are closely intertwined and often indistinguishable. The conflicts between Spain and England in the sixteenth century and the Thirty Years War in the seventeenth century pitched Catholics against Protestants. World War II was as much about ideology as it was about anything else, as was the Cold War, and there are many other examples as well.[31] How we can understand the ways in which what we call politics and religion were related, or how we can understand a phenomenon very different from our own experiences, are critical matters in trying to understand the ancient Andes.

One salient point that relates to the various issues discussed above concerning approaching the past, as well as the Lo Andino issue, is to keep in mind that it is our own tradition, that of Western Europe, that varies from the experiences of much of the rest of the world. In the West there was a dramatic break from early religious systems, first as a result of the coming of Christianity and later with Islam. Each of these systems drew upon the Jewish tradition of making the claim that its understanding of the sacred was the only truth and that no other interpretations were to be accepted, bringing about a gradual shift from "our god" to "the God." Among the results of this stance was a sharp break with the pagan traditions of the Mediterranean world and Classical Antiquity. Although there were continuities in beliefs and practices, the change from the world of the Greco-Roman pantheon or local pagan gods to Christian, and later in some places Muslim, religion was a sharp break with thousands of years of religious practice and belief.

The pre-Christian religions of the Old World were generally inclusive. Foreign gods were adopted into pantheons rather than excluded or persecuted. This kind of approach to religion, in which no claims are made that one religion has a monopoly on the truth, appears to have been more common, worldwide and through time, than the monopolistic monotheism that characterizes Western civilization today. There are many indications that this was the case in the Andes as well. Furthermore, as far as we can tell, there was no event that fundamentally broke with the past or that equated with the conversion of the Classical Mediterranean to Christianity. At most there were changes and conflicts, although these possibly were quite sharp and severe, but they resembled disputes between Catholics and Protestants within the Christian tradition. In other words, there may have been great upheavals and even wars between groups following different religions, but there were certain, fundamental tenets of belief and practice that were held in common.

Even in the Western European tradition "religion" can be defined in a great number of ways, and many archaeologists sometimes use the term "ideology" as a synonym. It is debatable whether this is useful or not, depending on how it is used. For present purposes we may define religion as a system of formulated ideas concerning relations between humans and other beings (deities, ancestors) and forces (e.g. "Nature"), expressed in rituals and other behavior that are held and practiced by groups of people. Although this definition could be critiqued in a number of ways, it provides an adequate account of most of what we can see archaeologically and which has analogies in human behavior.[32] Given this definition, we can state that different religions came and went in the ancient Andes, although there was much continuity too, as we shall see. In addition, there were those common understandings that underpinned the specific religions of any particular time and place.

People are sometimes organized into groups which consider themselves as constituting a distinct body of participants or believers in a particular religion. At other times and places, practices and beliefs are simply what people do as part of their sense of who they are. The German term *Weltanschauung* loosely translates as "world view." It is a way of understanding reality that is deeper than specific views on religion or politics; rather, it is a way of comprehending that is learned unconsciously, simply by being raised in a society in which people hold the same views about what constitutes reality. There are many indications that there was and is a distinctive Andean Weltanschauung (sometimes also known as a "cosmovision") that began very early in the distant past and is still in existence today among many Andean people.

The Andean worldview sees the world in movement and flux. There is an emphasis on asymmetric dualism: reality is comprised of states of being and forces that are different, but which need each other. Each is complementary to the other, completing it and necessary for it to be: one cannot survive without the other. The pair is thus the essential unit, not the atomistic individual.[33] Furthermore, one of the pair is slightly larger or more forceful than the other: up is literally and figuratively "higher" than down; male is bigger and stronger than female; the sun is stronger and brighter than the moon; and so on. It is this disparity between beings and forces that not only forms the nature of reality, but which also causes movement and makes things happen. The nearly equal partners in a pair are related by a central line, point, or axis. The near-pair can be subdivided or multiplied from a micro- to a macro-level. In many ways,

Andean worldviews were fractal in nature: the same basic structure existed at whatever scale one viewed reality.

Andean dualism is rooted in the concept of *ayni,* the "give-and-take" that circulates the energy of the universe in a pattern of continuous reciprocal interchanges.[34] The relationship into which this give-and-take process is formed is called *yanantin-masintin,* the first term referring to the relationship of near-equal, opposing but dependent entities and the second to the experiential manifestation of that relationship.[35]

Units of two are thus important in Andean thought, as are pairs of "twos," such as 4, 8, 16, and so on. Andean thought does not rest solely on dualistic concepts, however, as divisions into three are also known. The knotted string record keeping system used by the Inca, known as the *quipu* (or *khipu*), was organized on a ten-base system, and there is good evidence that the Moche also used a ten-base system as well.[36] The exploration of units of measurement and weight in Andean prehistory is in its infancy, but considerable information is also accumulating on Andean astronomy. It was quite sophisticated and different than the system with which we are familiar.[37]

Andean thought emphasizes a distribution of life force (*camay* in Quechua) across reality that does not make a sharp distinction between animate and inanimate, life and death, as is common in Western thought. Instead, camay is concentrated in greater or lesser degrees at certain times and places and in certain things. Camay is strong in wet things, with the waters of the mountains linked in a cycle to the waters of the oceans which return to the mountains as rain and snow falling from clouds. This bubbly, fluid energy is powerful, but so is the concentrated energy in dry things. The desiccated remains of human mummies and the dry mountain ranges that receive the water thus have different, complementary powers to young, squishy babies or the waters themselves.[38] Wet and dry, male and female, all are engaged in cycles of relations, as is time itself, so that history is not linear but instead repeats itself.

While dualism (and multiples of two) is a powerful concept and camay is everywhere, the sophistication of Andean cosmology allows it also to consider other patterns such as the importance of sets of three and the distribution of the life force in more complex arrangements than simple force fields. Energy may be *sami,* light and reined, or *hucha,* dense and heavy, a dual pairing of forces that flow between three levels of the Andean cosmos. *Hanaq pacha* is an "upper" world of celestial beings such as the sun, moon, and the ancestors; *kay pacha* is the middle world where humans live; and *ukhu pacha* is an "underworld" or "innerworld" in which the world of humans is inverted. Each of these worlds is often associated with a symbolic animal—in descending order, the condor, the puma, and the snake, a concept of "Masters of Animals" found throughout the New World. Maintaining balance and harmony between these various states of reality is the task of religious specialists, and illness as well as social and political disruptions occur when things fall out of balance in the ever-changing flow of relations.[39]

The Quechua term *huaca* is sometimes translated as "sacred thing," although its meaning encompasses not just the thing itself but the camay of the thing as well. We know from the writings of Spanish chroniclers that the Inca considered things that were somehow out of the ordinary or extraordinary to be huaca. This could be an unusually shaped potato or stone found in a field, an extraordinarily well-made artifact, or an exceptionally high mountain. Indeed, the tallest mountains were considered *apu*, great ancestors who had to be respected and appeased because they could, would, and did affect human lives. Huaca today is often used to refer to a large archaeological mound of stone or adobe bricks, and it is to the world of huacas and other artifacts that we now turn.

NOTES

1 Childe 1956.
2 Spaulding 1960.
3 Presented in a lecture in the Department of Anthropology, Harvard University, on May 5th, 2010: *Prehistoric State Formation in the Lake Titicaca Basin, Andean South America*.
4 Lamb 2006 provides an excellent discussion of the Andean mountains, especially in Bolivia.
5 Silgado Ferro 1978.
6 Sandweiss et al. 2009 on sediment cycling.
7 Silgado Ferro 1978. See Walker 2008 for details on the 1746 quake.
8 Rollins et al. 1986; Sandweiss et al. 1996; Andrus et al. 2008.
9 Details on ENSO and other climatic/geophysical events and their relations to ancient New World cultures may be found in Sandweiss and Quilter 2009.
10 Maasch 2008.
11 First published in 1938. See Pulgar Vidal 1987.
12 Miller and Gill 1990.
13 Sauer 1952 and Lathrap 1977 on the origins of agriculture (and more) in tropical America.
14 Lumbreras 1974b; Rowe 1962a.
15 Quilter 1991 on periodization of Preceramic Period.
16 See Bennett 1948 and Isbell and Silverman 2006 for a reappraisal of the Co-Tradition concept.
17 "Inca" refers to a culture, a political group, and an emperor. "Incas" is sometimes used to refer to all but the emperor, but this usage is not used here.
18 Cooper 1949.
19 Torres 2006.
20 Dillehay et al. 2005.
21 Murra 1962.
22 Bonavia 2009.
23 Burger 1992: 160.
24 Reported by Jorge Juan y Antonio Ulloa and cited in Urteaga 1978: 667.
25 Quilter 1991: 403 on the "Preceramic Yard."
26 See Murra 1972 and Hirth and Pillsbury 2013.
27 Salomon 1977 on *mindalaes*.
28 Hirth and Pillsbury (eds) 2013.
29 Fried 1967 and Service 1968.

30 The ayllu has a long and complex bibliography, and the concept itself has been questioned. See Weismantel 2006 for a critique and references source.

31 Many scholars contend that all ideological arguments mask more basic struggles about political/economic power, while others argue that ideology can act independently of those issues. This is too large a topic to tackle in these pages, and the reader is advised to consult the huge bibliography available on these issues.

32 For a good review of definitions of "ritual" see Bell 2009.

33 Burger and Salazar-Burger 1993.

34 Allen 2002.

35 Platt 1986; Webb 2012.

36 Donnan 2009 on Moche numbers and sets.

37 Urton 1988.

38 Salomon 1995.

39 Urton 1988; Platt 1986; Webb 2012.

3

THE EARLY AND MIDDLE PRECERAMIC PERIODS

ISSUES

The story of the first peoples of the Central Andes must begin with a global perspective, since it involves some of the most contentious contemporary issues in archaeology worldwide and views that have changed radically in less than 20 years (see Figure 3.1). For more than double that length of time there was a consensus among most archaeologists that the peoples of the New World all came from Asia, walking across Beringia, the 800-mile-wide "land bridge," at the end of the last Ice Age between 12,000 and 10,000 years ago.[1] The first people who entered the New World were part of a long-term migration that had started millennia earlier in Africa, the ancestral home of all humans. Most scholars believe that the evidence indicates that modern humans left Africa between 60,000 and 50,000 years ago, displacing and eventually succeeding populations of earlier migrants out of Africa and their descendants, such as the Neanderthals.[2] However, when and how people got to the New World are issues that remain uncertain, although research offers new ideas.

All of the evidence indicates a first occupation of the New World relatively late in prehistory, by people who were fully human and quite advanced in their abilities. How quickly people spread into the continent is hard to gauge, especially given the lack of comparable cases of entry into a pristine environment with regard to humans. They entered an environment where no human or near-human ancestor had ever trod, and in which animals had never been hunted except by other beasts. This means that, excepting Australia, there are virtually no analogies that we can use to compare the entry of humans into America, and given that America is one of the most distant lands from Africa, it is logical to assume that entry into the New World occurred relatively late.

Figure 3.1 Map of early sites in North and South America.

ICE, WATER, AND LAND

The Pleistocene, or Ice Age, began about 2.6 million years ago, probably due to shifts in the orbit of the earth from a circle to an ellipse (eccentricity), the tilt (obliquity) of the earth in its plane of travel, and the time of the year when the globe is closest and farthest from the sun (precession of the equinox).[3] There were about ten major periods of massive ice sheets, known as glaciations, with periods when the glaciers retreated, known as interglacials, of varying intensity.

It is only the last major stage, the Wisconsin, which bears directly on issues of human entry into the New World.[4] Authorities differ, but the Wisconsin is thought to have begun about 80,000 BP, diminished in intensity between 65,000 and 35,000 BP, and reached its maximum extent in the Late Wisconsin, between about 35,000 and 10,000 BP. A critical time period is *circa* 18,000 BP, the Late Glacial Maximum (LGM), when glaciers reached their maximum extents and sea levels were at their lowest because the waters of the oceans were incorporated into the ice sheets. Britain was connected to the European continent. The Chesapeake Bay was a river valley, and the East Coast of the United States was tens of miles further east than it is today. The lowering of the waters also exposed Beringia, that wide land between northeastern Asia and Alaska. It was a place in and of itself, not just a "bridge," although it is over this land that the immigrants to the New World are thought to have passed.

During the LGM there were two major ice sheets. The largest, the Laurentide ice sheet, extended as far south as the middle of Long Island, New York (resulting in a hilly North Shore and a flat South Shore), cutting across Georges Bank off Cape Cod, Massachusetts, to the east, and extending westward through northern New Jersey, Pennsylvania, and the southern Great Lakes states to Wisconsin, where it turned sharply northwards. The Cordilleran ice sheet was smaller and reached its southern limits in Montana, Idaho, and Washington. Each glacier moved at a different pace, but at their maxima they joined to form a single mass that blocked ice-free Beringia (including most of Alaska, except its southern coast) from the open lands south of the ice sheets. This issue is critical for inferring the arrival of humans south of the ice.

By 12,000 BP, in radiocarbon years as were used when these dates (earlier in calendar years) were first discussed, a corridor had opened up between the ice sheets, but it was likely impassable due to the swamps and debris left behind in the wake of the retreating ice. Only *circa* 11,500 BP was there probably a path clear enough for a feasible entry from Beringia. However, this possible date of entry is not proof of entry at that time, and this is the subject of many debates and discussions. Debates concerning the first people to enter the New World extend back to the first years when Europeans became aware of the continent. How those understandings were developed, rejected, or modified over the centuries, is a tale that would fill a large volume in itself, so only the key issues will be touched on here.

FIRST PEOPLES

By the 1950s archaeologists working in North America generally agreed that the distinct Clovis projectile point represented the earliest archaeological evidence for humans in the New World. The Clovis point and the slightly later Folsom point are comparatively large, with lanceolate (lance-like) forms, parallel edges, and a distinct channel or "flute" running up both sides of the blade, perhaps to haft it more securely to the shaft of a spear or the foreshaft of an atlatl (spear-thrower) dart.

Later points are often similar to Clovis and Folsom in shape, but they are not fluted. Fluted points are unique to the New World, so that this may be claimed as the first "American" invention. Archaeologists sometimes refer to Clovis and Folsom as individual archaeological cultures, or together (sometimes including some cultures represented by non-fluted points) they are referred to as "Paleoindians." Clovis points are found over a wide area of North America south of where the ice sheets were, although sites are few.

For many years it was thought that the Clovis people were specialized hunters who mostly preyed on the large Ice Age mammals, such as mammoths and mastadons, collectively known as megafauna, perhaps even causing their extinction.[5] However, continuing studies have suggested that Paleoindian diets were quite diverse and were not solely focused on hunted or scavenged meat, or on large animals of any kind.[6]

When the first discoveries of Paleoindian remains were made there was no easy way to date them. By the late 1950s, however, radiocarbon analyses were available and two decades or so later they had produced dates ranging from 11,570 BP to about 10,800 BP in radiocarbon years, now thought to be at their earliest 13,500 calendar years ago. This is relatively soon after the ice-free corridor between the northern glaciers became available for travel southwards from Beringia. Thus, it was concluded that the earliest people in the New World were those of the Clovis culture. On the surface this seemed an apparently straightforward piece of scientific progress, but there were some difficult issues that were not easily resolved.

One difficulty arose as the result of research conducted at the southern tip of South America by one of archaeology's most colorful, adventuresome, and brilliant practitioners, Junius B. Bird of the American Museum of Natural History. In 1934, he and his wife Peggy took a boat trip through the fjords of southern Chile searching for sites. Eventually they excavated at Palli Aike and Fell's Caves in the Straits of Magellan. Human remains in these caves were associated with the remains of native horses and giant ground sloths (mylodon). These alone demonstrated the great antiquity of human presence at the extreme southern tip of South America, and later radiocarbon dating confirmed human occupation there *circa* 11,000 BP, again, in radiocarbon years that were thought as the same as calendar years at the time.[7]

There had been speculation for many years that a "Paleolithic" era had existed in South America. Most of this was based on wishful thinking, however, and Czech-born Aleš Hrdličkca, the first curator of physical anthropology at the US National Museum of the Smithsonian Institution, had dominated scholarship in the late nineteenth and early twentieth centuries with his insistence that there was no sound evidence for an early human presence in the New World. Clovis and the other Paleoindian sites had changed that, however, and Bird's work showed that Ice Age era occupations were at the end point of migrations from Beringia.

The Straits of Magellan data confirmed that Paleoindians had been in southern South America, but they did not contribute much to the issue of when and how quickly humans got there. With no analogy to enable a comparison of the pace of migrations, it was thought possible that humans could have spread from Beringia to Patagonia in a few hundred years, a short enough time to be undetectable via the relatively coarse chronologies of radiocarbon dates. One of the results of Bird's work at Fell's Cave was the discovery of fishtail points, which are shaped as the name implies and also sometimes bear a flute-like channel flake on their bases (see Figure 3.4).[8] Further research demonstrated that there were no Clovis points in South America. Fishtail points are slightly later than Clovis points, but they are early enough to leave the question open as to whether or not they were derived from some earlier style.

The distributions of Clovis and fishtail points are usually defined as overlapping in Panama and Costa Rica, but otherwise they occupy two different mega-regions. It has been noted, however, that most of the projectile points claimed to be Clovis that have been found in Central or South America have only vague similarities to the classic forms seen in North America. They often do not have the distinctive parallel sides and the diagnostic "flutes," and the southern examples appear to be the remains of broad thinning flakes or laterally or basally-thinned stems of large triangular points.[9]

Many claims of evidence for early human occupations south of the United States have been shown to be later when re-dated using new techniques. In North America there have also been many claims for pre-Clovis sites. However, these too have often been shown to date later than originally thought, while others may be early but have not provided incontrovertible evidence for a pre-Clovis occupation. In the last two decades almost two dozen sites in North America have been claimed as pre-Clovis, in places ranging from Virginia to Florida to Wisconsin, and the evidence for pre-Clovis occupations at quite a few of these sites appears to be very strong.[10] At Paisley Cave, Oregon, human coprolites dated by two different radiocarbon laboratories produced dates of (cal.) 12,300 years ago—comfortably pre-Clovis—while DNA analysis of the samples concluded that the haplogroups (a broad category of similar DNA types) matched those of American Indians.[11] Further study also concluded that a stemmed form of projectile point at Paisley Cave likely pre-dates Clovis, which was a rather startling discovery.

Historical linguistics and genetics also have been employed to determine when and how the first people entered the New World, including some combined approaches in the mid-1980s.[12] The most recent genetic study confirms a previous proposal of three waves of immigrants. The majority of Native Americans are descendants of a population that reached the New World sometime before (cal.) 15,000 BP. An Eskimo-Aleut group and people related to Na-Dene and Chipewyan speakers arrived in later waves.

However, a radically new view of early colonization has developed as a result of work in Australia. Very early radiocarbon dates for the first humans there now support the view that humans were well established in Australia by (cal.) 50,000 BP, and that the only way they could have arrived from mainland Asia is via well-made boats that could travel out of sight of land.[13] Even though it has been a truism in prehistorical studies that anatomically fully modern humans had the same brain and other capabilities as citizens of modern states, the possibility of fairly sophisticated watercraft at such an early date was generally discounted and boats are notoriously scarce in the archaeological record because they aren't commonly preserved. However, the Australia case is impossible to ignore, which means that people could also have colonized the New World using fairly advanced watercraft.

It is highly unlikely that the peopling of the New World was by trans-Pacific routes across great stretches of ocean. Such travel was extremely difficult even in recent centuries. It is more likely that arrival in boats took place via shoreline travel with frequent stops, and in many cases settlement, along the way. Furthermore, the rough seas and cold climate of the northern Pacific mean that the people who traveled along a receding Beringian shoreline or down the coast of Alaska would have needed an elaborate material culture of clothing and gear to successfully make the passage.[14] However, although it is a cold and difficult passage, there is a rich "kelp highway" that stretches from Japan through the North Pacific down to California, and that rich oceanic system could have provided food for people as they made their way down the coast.[15] Much of this research is so new that further studies are likely to change our thinking or offer alternative theories in the very near future.

THE EARLY HUMAN PRESENCE IN SOUTH AMERICA

The pre-Clovis and Clovis eras began at the apogee of the southern extent of the glaciers and continued during their retreat northwards, a period known as the Terminal Pleistocene (~13,000 to 11,000 BP). Also known as the Younger Dryas, there was a re-advance of glaciers during this time after a warmer period (the Bolling-Allerod Interval), but the ice had retreated significantly and did not return to its earlier extent. The Holocene, in which we live now, is divided into Early (~11,000 to 9000 BP), Middle (~9000 to 3000 BP) and Late (~3000 BP to the present) phases, and during this period the climate and environment gradually warmed from the cold conditions of previous times, although there have been notable warmer and cooler periods within it. These different regimes have been important in making some regions of the Americas more or less attractive to prehistoric peoples, and such shifts were particularly important for the Central Andes.[16]

Today, the land is arid along the entire stretch of Peru's coast from Ecuador to Chile, although aridity increases from north to south and the frequency and intensity of El Niño events also diminishes in the same direction. However, several different studies indicate that prior to (cal.) 5800 BP, during the Middle Holocene, there was a relatively sharp difference in the regions north and south of the latitude line at 12° south. South of Lima was a zone of hyper-aridity in which stands of vegetation nurtured by coastal fogs, known as *lomas*, thrived (see Figure 3.2). These evolved in relative isolation so that today the plant community in any single lomas field is comprised of a different mix of species than its neighbors. North of Lima, however, lomas that are isolated today share many plants in common, leading to the conclusion that the fields were once continuous.[17] Similarly, as Daniel Sandweiss has pointed out, sites dating earlier than 5800 BP south of Lima tend to have soft tissues and other fragile organic materials preserved, while sites north of this line tend to not have such preservation.[18]

From the Terminal Pleistocene to the middle-Mid-Holocene, the coastal region north of the "Sandweiss Line" likely experienced seasonal rainfalls with relatively few ENSO events. Research at north coast sites confirms this pattern. Today the boundary between warm tropical waters and the cold Humboldt Current is further north, close to the Ecuador–Peru border. The Siches site lies in the Chira Valley which cuts through the extremely dry Sechura desert, but research there has indicated a mild climate in the early Holocene when the site was first occupied between (cal.) 8000 and 6900 BP, during the Siches Phase. Farther south the Ostra Base Camp, just north of the Santa River, was located next to the ocean and its occupants exploited warm water resources between (cal.) 10,750 and 10,250 BP. In addition, they carved incisions on the ends of small, flat ovoid pebbles, which may be the earliest portable art forms known in quantity in the New World since no practical use is known for these small stones (see Figure 3.3).

Figure 3.2 Lomas fields.

The northern coast of Peru was also probably wetter with more vegetation than is found there today. It is probably somewhere in this region, near the Santa Valley, that the boundary between the warm and cool waters existed in those early times. However, by the Honda Phase at Siches (cal. 6950 to 6350 BP) the cold-warm zone had shifted northwards and desertification had begun (see Figure 3.3).[19]

Another notable difference between different coastal regions is the varying effects of different rates of tectonic uplift. The Ostra Base Camp, noted above, was close to the beach when it was occupied but it is now more than a mile away from the ocean. Uplift is even greater south of Lima, especially south of Ica. Rivers are narrower and more deeply incised into the terrain than in the north, due to greater uplift. This has resulted in less agricultural land with fewer and more limited opportunities to expand fields through irrigation, as will be noted in discussions of the locations of large population centers in prehistory. Also, of course, the highlands and coast are subject to extreme tectonic uplifts in the form of earthquakes. All of these different environmental factors affected where and how humans inhabited different regions of the Central Andes, how sites were preserved, and where archaeologists have been able to find them.

In 1928 the remains of a mastodon were found in the Quebrada Chalán in the Punín Valley, near Riobamba in the Ecuadorian highlands. Franz Spillmann and Max Uhle were called in to examine the "Mastodon of Alangasí," and Spillmann noted that a projectile point was embedded in the ancient elephant's skull.[20] This is one of the best associations of Pleistocene megafauna and humans in South America, but the early date of the find and the paucity of follow-up study leave many details of the issue unresolved. Much later the La Cumbre rockshelter in the Moche Valley yielded the remains of mastodons and horses, but in a different stratum than the stone tools (Paiján points) also found there.[21]

Junius Bird searched for early humans in South America soon after they were identified in North America. Subsequently other archaeologists also looked for early sites and occasionally identified them. Edward P. Lanning, for example, found lithic quarries and workshops in the Chivateros and Oquendo hills in the Chillón Valley, not too far from the modern Lima airport. While some of the tools were likely from an early time, it has been hard to separate them from later visits to the quarries by people who continued to make similar basic tools.[22]

James B. Richardson III undertook the first systematic search for very early sites in Peru, investigating locations on the north coast where a narrow continental shelf was present. At such locations the Pleistocene and the modern shorelines are near each other, unlike in locales where shoreline sites on a wide continental shelf would now be under the water due to the rise in sea levels after the melting of the Ice Age glaciers.[23] In the early 1970s Richardson discovered the Amotape campsites that overlook the Talara Tar Seeps. The sites consisted mostly of surface scatters of stone tools and debris mixed with the shells of a mangrove-dwelling mollusk, *Anadara tuberculosa*. Thought to be very early at the time of discovery, calibrated dating on the shells now places the earliest occupation of Amotape (site PV-8-29) between (cal.) 12,800 and 12,580 BP. The tar seeps themselves were rich in Ice Age species including mastodons, other large mammals, birds and insects, and bones were radiocarbon dated to as early as (cal.) 16,700 BP,

Figure 3.3 Early coastal sites. Upper left: Quebrada Jaguay structure with postholes marked by balloons. Upper right: Ostra pebbles. Center: Ostra site. Bottom: Siches quebrada.

while a study of the birds present indicated that there had been seasonal precipitation during this time.[24] Unfortunately, however, there was no clear linkage between these very early remains in the tar seeps and the human presence at the nearby sites, and furthermore no stratified Amotape site has been found.

The first finds from Paleoindians in North America inspired Junius Bird's research in Tierra del Fuego, which in turn raised questions about North American archaeology. In more recent times, research in Chile has once again made North American archaeologists reconsider their data. Indeed, many of the closer examinations of previously found sites that were thought to be pre-Clovis, and the search for new ones in North America, are due to work at Monte Verde in south central Chile, carried out by Tom Dillehay and Mario Pino from the late 1970s into the 1980s.[25]

Monte Verde appears to have been a campsite for between 20 and 30 people dated to between (cal.) 14,800 and 13,800 BP. Preservation at the site was good due to the bog-like conditions of the banks of Chinchihuapi Creek. Finds included a 6 m long tent-like structure of poles, logs, and planks, covered with wood and animal hides and with internal divisions, possibly for separate living quarters. In addition to the worked wooden structural materials of the dwelling, cordage, wooden tools, and stone tools also were found, but no projectile points were recovered in association with the structures. Hearths, stone tools, and the remains of seeds, nuts, berries, and other plants, including a wild potato (*Solanum maglia*), also were identified.

The claims for Monte Verde resulted in considerable controversy at first. The site was far from regions where more archaeological research had been done, which made some scholars uneasy. The nearby site of Tagua Tagua had earlier been hailed as pre-Clovis, but there were a number of problems in supporting that claim. Some data seemed to be contradictory, such as pollen evidence in conflict with entomological data, suggesting that there may have been mixing of materials. Research suggests that some plants were likely brought to the site, however, and recently marine algae and seaweed that had to have been brought to Monte Verde have been radiocarbon dated to (cal.) 14,220 to 13,980 BP.

There were many other claims of very early sites in different parts of South America that later proved to be highly unlikely, such as Pedra Furada Cave in Brazil, for which no clear consensus has been reached on its antiquity.[26] With the new model of human entry probably via boats traveling down the Pacific shore, however, the possibility that there were very early occupations over wide areas of the continent is being reassessed.

Since the Monte Verde excavations there have been a number of sites in or near the Central Andes that have produced data that imply a very early occupation of the region. Also, in a drier regime in central Chile, Quebrada Santa Julia, a small lakeside camp, dates to (cal.) 13,000 BP, located about 175 km north of Santiago and 3.5 km from the Pacific. Projectile points claimed to be Clovis, though perhaps better described as exhibiting basal thinning, have been found there in association with the remains of extinct megafauna.[27] There is evidence that bones as well as lithic raw materials were brought to the site from locations 30 km outside the area. Other sites in the region, such as Quereo, appear to date to about the same time or slightly later.[28]

Piedra Museo, in the Deseado Department of Santa Cruz Province in Argentinian Patagonia, is an example of an old site that has been reappraised. It was discovered in 1910 but re-excavated in 1995 and radiocarbon dated to *circa* (cal.) 11,000 BP. Fishtail points found there were associated with the remains of mylodon (giant ground sloth) and hippidion (a small horse). Along with Casa de Minero and Cerro Tres Tetas, in the same era and region, these sites seem quite similar to the occupations found by Bird at Fell's Cave, and together they suggest that the southern cone of South America was fairly well occupied by humans at an early time.[29] While some areas of Argentina and Chile may have seen fairly intense human occupations by hunter-gatherer standards, other regions were lightly populated until quite late, such as the Central Sierra of Argentina that had relatively low occupation until after *circa* (cal.) 7000 BP.[30]

Several archaeological sites on the southern coast of Peru offer very early evidence for human coastal adaptations in the Central Andes, namely Quebrada Jaguay, the Ring Site, Quebrada Tacahuay, and Quebrada de los Burros.[31] Jaguay is located just north of the town of Camana, the Ring Site and Tacahuay near the town of Ilo, and Los Burros not far from the border with Chile. Tacahuay and Jaguay are Terminal Pleistocene in age with ephemeral and significant Early Holocene occupations respectively, while Burros and Ring are entirely Holocene occupations.[32]

Located only 7 or 8 km from the coast at the time, the occupants of Quebrada Jaguay had a relatively sophisticated and specialized maritime technology and adaptation that focused on clams (*Mesodesma sp.*), freshwater and marine crustaceans, and several species of drums (*Sciaenidae*) as well as mussels, anchovies, and various seabirds. Additionally, the remains of prickly pear cactus (*Opuntia* cf. *ficus-indica*) also were recovered, suggesting some interaction with higher elevations where the plant is found today.

It is likely that Quebrada Jaguay (cal. ~13,000 to 11,400 BP) was one stop in a seasonal round. Postholes from a rectangular structure were found in the earliest occupation phase, while a circular, semi-subterranean house was built in later times (see Figure 3.3). Many pieces of debitage from the production of both uni- and bi-facial tools were found at the site, including small quantities of obsidian from the Alca source between 145 and 225 km (90 to 140 mi) distant and substantial amounts of petrified wood from about 30 km (19 mi) inland.[33] Since the economy was entirely maritime oriented but did not include marine mammals there was apparently no need for projectile points, and none were found.

The Ring Site was a deep, well-stratified shell midden with a majority of faunal remains from maritime food resources, indicating that marine subsistence economies were already well developed during its occupation and probably at its beginning; it has a single basal date of (cal.) ~12,040 to 11,430 BP. No plant remains were preserved and research at the site was brief, consisting only of test excavations before it was bulldozed for road construction.[34]

Investigations at Quebrada Tacahuay also suggest a complete coastal adaptation but no Alca obsidian was found, suggesting a lack of trade with interior peoples or the absence of a seasonal round. There is evidence of catastrophic floods and debris flows at Quebrada Tacahuay, and an increase in the frequency and intensity of El Niño events throughout the region may have encouraged the site's abandonment until much later in prehistory, when a reoccupation occurred.

In northern coastal Chile 13 Huentelauquén Complex sites date to between (cal.) 11,700 and 9500 BP. There was a strong emphasis on fish and mollusks in the diet, augmented by sea mammals and birds.[35] Further down the coast the Quero site has an early occupation (Quero I) between (cal.) 13,800 and 13,000 BP and a later phase (Quero II) between (cal.) 13,000 and 10,600 BP. The site appears to have been a butchering location for deer and ancestral camelids as well as sloth, horse, and mastodon. Butchering tools were few and expediently made, and no projectile points were found in either occupation.[36]

Other intriguing cases for very early occupation of South America are found in the Amazon Basin near the town of Monte Alegre, in the Brazilian state of Roraima. Caverna da Pedra Pintada, overlooking the Amazon floodplain, is a painted cave as its name indicates.[37] While such decorations are notoriously difficult to date, pigment chunks and paint drops were found in layers and on early stone artifacts, suggesting that some of the paintings are early and others late. Wood charcoal, plants (palm nuts, legume seeds, brazil nuts, various fruit pits), and animal remains (small and large fish, shellfish, turtles, tortoises, lizards, medium-sized rodents, and birds) were found in the deposits, and studies suggest that the local habitat was already tropical forest. Lithic remains consisted of flakes, unifacial scrapers, blade-like flakes, a graver, and triangular projectile points, some of which were stemmed.

Radiocarbon, thermoluminescence, and optically stimulated luminescence were all used to date Caverna da Pedra Pintada to between *circa* (cal.) 10,500 BP. Anna Roosevelt and her colleagues suggest that the site occupants were well adapted to life in the tropical forest, following a "broad spectrum" subsistence strategy with a stone tool tradition completely different from that of Clovis, but contemporary with it. Furthermore, while Caverna da Pedra Pintada is the most carefully studied early site in the Amazon, numerous other sites and individual large, triangular projectile points the same as or similar to those found in the cave have been discovered throughout the region, further testifying to a substantial, widespread human population.

A credible claim for Terminal Pleistocene/Early Holocene sites comes from northern Peru, on and near the Pampa de Paiján, the largest stretch of desert north of Chile.[38] Paiján points are distinctive and often have long needle-like shapes. Apparent Paiján hunting camps dating to between (cal.) 12,800–11,400 BP are 15 km or more inland and were almost double that distance from the coast during the Ice Age since the continental shelf in this area is wide. Thus, any Paiján shoreline sites are now under water. A survey of the *quebrada* (small valley) of Santa Maria, north of the town of Ascope in the Chicama Valley, found 45 concentrations of stone tools. Of these, two had fishtail points while the rest were associated with the Paiján tradition. In this same area, more than two dozen artifact concentrations were found on a terrace at site PV23-130. Whether the fishtail and Paiján points found in these concentrations were used simultaneously or represent different groups or eras is not yet known.

It has been assumed for some time that during the era of Paiján occupation, environmental conditions were more humid than they are today. The identification of numerous Paiján sites in the Quebrada Santa Maria is another indicator of wetter conditions because the intensity of occupation is greater than could be sustained today when the area is so dry. Indeed, two large sites were equidistant from a spring that has been dry within historic memory, but which was reactivated after the El Niño event of 1999.

The unusual, needle-nose shapes of some Paiján points have been interpreted as being specialized weapons for spearing fish. The food remains at some of the Quebrada Santa Maria sites include land snails, some fish and marine shells, and also deer. However, as noted, many sites were far inland. It may be that the Paiján "points" were knives, not spearheads, and that their narrow shapes came from resharpening their edges, while fishtail points served as the tips of projectile weapons. Then again, as lizards appear to be the main food source judging from remains at Paiján sites, perhaps the points were designed to hunt them. The presence of some chert lithic remains among assemblages mostly consisting of local rock crystal and quartz suggests long-distance exchanges or mobile hunting groups.[39]

Paiján has been difficult to date. Until relatively recently most sites were found on the coast and near the desert, such as the alluvial terrace known as the Pampa de los Fósiles. No structures have been located with certainty, but about a dozen burials have been reported.[40] The remains are often in very poor states of preservation, but they exhibit general mortuary practices that include flexed body position, hands placed near the face, and wrapping in a reed mat. Skulls were missing in many cases, although in those that have been found there is some evidence for possible cranial modification. All of these practices are also known to occur in later periods. Dating of remains from Tomb 2 at site PV22-13 produced a radiocarbon date of 10,200 +/− 180 BP.[41]

The most-studied early archaeological culture of the Central Andes is Las Vegas, on the Santa Elena Peninsula in southern Ecuador, the focus of work directed by Karen E. Stothert. More than 30 sites are known and extensive research was carried out at site OGSE-80. While the Vegas culture shares many features with Middle Preceramic sites in Peru, a pre-Vegas occupation dates to between (cal.) 13,000 and 11,400 BP, at which time site occupants were exploiting wild cucurbits and likely domesticating them. The local tool kit did not include projectile points or bifacial tools, and a broad-spectrum subsistence economy was followed in the tropical-maritime environment.[42]

It is interesting to consider that evidence suggests that the very early sites for humans in South America are coastal. This is a radically different view of the past compared to three decades ago when research focused in the highlands, such as the large-scale project directed by Richard MacNeish in the Ayacucho Basin.[43] Although early sites were found there, they mostly date to the early Middle Preceramic. The trend for early coastal sites continues at Huaca Prieta, at the edge of the sea in the Chicama Valley, where by Tom Dillehay and other archaeologists have produced very early dates that would make Huaca Prieta one of the earliest known sites in the New World, *circa* (cal.) 14,200 to 13,300 BP.[44]

Indeed, although much research was carried out from the 1960s through to the 1980s looking for very early sites in highland areas, most caves and rock shelters in the sierra and altiplano tend to be slightly later than the earliest of the coastal Peruvian sites. However, Kurt Rademaker found and excavated the Cuncaicha rock shelter in the Pucuncho Basin, a large, highland depression with grasslands and wetland surrounded by volcanoes.[45] Bone beads, quartz crystals, obsidian, human remains and those of plants and animals also were recovered. Two fragments of fishtail points were found, as well as triangular, stemmed points. At 4,480 m above sea level and dating to *circa* (cal.) 12,000 BP, it is the highest Ice Age site in South America and perhaps the entire New World. Other potential occupations have also been found in the region, as well as isolated artifact finds. Even if this was a temporary base camp in a seasonal round of movement, the Cuncaicha rock shelter is remarkable in demonstrating that people quickly exploited a wide range of environmental zones from very early times in the Central Andes (see Figure 3.4)

When these various sites are considered together it is not hard to conclude that humans were in South America before Clovis times, and that they had already diversified to take advantage of different resources by mid-Early Preceramic times. However, people certainly were not plentiful, their possessions were few, and they were more mobile compared to humans of later times. Although the coastal migration route from Asia into the New World has received more support in recent years, the earliest South American sites are found over a wide range of environments including occupations well inland. Thus, the issue of exactly when and how the earliest humans arrived in the Americas remains an ongoing subject of study.

THE MIDDLE PRECERAMIC

The Preceramic Period is divided into Early, Middle, and Late phases.[46] The Early Preceramic dates from the entry of humans into the New World, at sometime between (cal.) 16,000 and 14,000 BP, to the beginning of the establishment of modern environmental conditions *circa* 9000 BP. The Middle Preceramic lasted between (cal.) 9000 and 5000 BP, when archaeological cultures that stretch beyond just a few sites indicate that population sizes and adaptations to local environments had reached quantitatively and qualitatively different levels than before. The Late Preceramic, from (cal.) 5000 to 3600 BP, was the time which provides the first evidence of substantial reliance on domesticated plants and animals, and of many practices that become important in later times such as irrigation technology. In addition, it was when ceremonial complexes that required the organization of labor beyond small groups of people appeared in many parts of the Central Andes.

The humans who entered the New World were already fairly sophisticated, carrying many useful ideas and practices with them. The first immigrants to the New World were not primitive people groping their way across Beringia, but highly specialized hunter-gatherer-foragers. Dogs and the bottle gourd (*Laganeria siceraria*) were almost certainly domesticated in Asia and came to the New World in early human migrations.[47] In fact, evidence now indicates that gourds were brought to the New World with the first inhabitants or soon after, once again suggesting that the immigrants at this time were already more than specialized big game hunters.

Figure 3.4 The Cuncaicha rock shelter. Top: Vista of the Pucuncho Basin, 4,480 m (14,698 ft) above sea level. Center (L to R): Two triangular stemmed points, broken fishtail point, side and dorsal view of biface (roughly to scale). Bottom: The Cuncaicha rock shelter.

However, although early New World immigrants may have brought some domesticates with them, it is in the Middle Preceramic Period that we can identify people focusing on relatively local resources and beginning the domestication of them. This can be seen in many of the highland sites, from Ecuador through Peru and Bolivia to Chile and Argentina. In each region, as modern environmental conditions were established, different subsistence strategies developed.

With a slightly moister environment, high altitude *paramo* grasslands became established in Ecuador rather than the short-grass *puna* farther south. Chobshi rock shelter was a base camp located at an elevation of about 2,500 m (8,202 ft) which was occupied between *circa* (cal.) 7500 and 6000 BP. The earliest deposits contain the remains of pudu deer, hare, agouti, tapir and tinaous (partridge), indicating an exploitation of a range of altitudinal zones. Some of the projectile point styles in this southern Ecuadorian locale show similarities with points at sites to the north, such as El Inga and Cublán, while others are similar to Paiján points and others found at cave sites in Peru, such as Guitarrero Cave and points in the Ayampitín tradition. A broad-based subsistence strategy seems to have been followed in Ecuador which changed little until about 4000 BP, when farming villages began to occur in highland basins and valleys.[48]

Many Middle Preceramic sites were investigated in the 1970s and the 1980s in the Central Highlands of Peru. These include sites in the upper Santa Valley, such as Guitarrero Cave and Lauricocha, and on the puna around Lake Junín, such as the caves of Pachamachay, Uchcumachay, Panalauca, and Telemarchay. A large-scale project also was conducted in the Ayacucho Basin under the direction of Richard MacNeish, famed for his discovery of early maize in Mexico. Studies of the Archaic Period in Bolivia and adjacent highland areas of Chile and Argentina have been fewer in number, and have tended to suggest a continuation of Early Preceramic lifestyles into later times.[49]

The same is true for the coast. Middle Preceramic practices were elaborations of patterns set down in earlier times. Only in areas where environmental change was considerable did lifestyles change dramatically. Thus, Paiján was adapted to an environmental regime that changed by the Middle Preceramic. The Las Vegas sites in Ecuador, however, were oriented at a very early time to a littoral subsistence economy in a tropical environment that did not change radically during the occupation of the site. The same can be said for some Peruvian south coast sites and lifestyles, such as at Paracas Village 96 and Paracas 514, so these are also interpreted as Middle Preceramic. In addition, in various places there appear to be unusual, somewhat precocious developments. These include the Zaña Valley on Peru's north coast and the Chinchorro culture of the northern desert of Chile. Before looking at these exceptional cases, however, it is worth considering the relationships between settlement and subsistence systems that become clear for this time period in the archaeological record.

SETTLEMENT AND SUBSISTENCE STRATEGIES

From the late 1950s through to the mid-1970s much archaeological research in the Central Andes focused on questions of plant and animal domestication, especially in trying to determine if there were large-scale, uniform patterns that pertained over widespread regions in the Central Andes. An example of the search for patterns is a debate that developed in Central Peruvian highland research regarding the mobility of earlier peoples there. Most scholars agreed that people first practiced a mixed deer-camelid hunting strategy, and then gradually focused on camelids (llama, alpaca, guanaco, and vicuña) and eventually domesticated the llama and the alpaca.

Danièle Lavallée maintained that people exploited resources at slightly different elevations as they moved seasonally within the puna zone. However, John Rick, following ideas previously presented by Augusto Cardich, argued that there was a more focused and specialized pattern of permanent occupation due to the year-round availability of camelids and wild plants, with early, specialized vicuña hunting leading to year-round occupation of the puna.[50] This early specialization resulted not only in early puna sedentism but also in a separation of high valley people and puna folk who did not enter the lower environmental zone. Rick pointed to the fact that marine shells were found in some of the high valley sites, indicating some contact with the coast, whereas the puna sites lacked such shells and had restricted distributions of obsidian suggesting that the region was relatively closed off from the outside.

Thomas Lynch proposed a Central Andean Archaic Tradition to include the Upper Santa Valley, Lake Junín, and the Húanaco region where Lauricocha Cave is located. The shared tradition was defined based mostly on technology, but with an inferred wide-ranging subsistence strategy for Middle Preceramic hunters in general.[51] Lynch championed the idea of transhumance, the regularized, seasonal movement of peoples from highlands to lowlands—in this case, the Peruvian coast. Tres Ventanas Cave, at the headwaters of the Chilca Valley at 3,700 m altitude with a long occupation beginning around (cal.) 11,940 to 11,260 BP, contained the remains of some marine shells, and similar finds, including sea fish bones, have been found at early sites in Chile at 1,500 m altitude and 100 km inland. These were thought to be examples of transhumance.[52]

It is likely that close, long-term association of people with camelids led to the animals' domestication, although it is difficult to distinguish between the bones of wild and domesticated animals and there is a great range of variability within camelid anatomy. However, when camelids are domesticated they are penned up rather than roaming freely, resulting in many newborn deaths due to crowded conditions in corrals. Jane Wheeler studied the percentages of camelids dying young at different sites and noted an abrupt increase in newborn mortality rates starting at *circa* 6000 BP, suggesting this date as the beginning of a domestication that took centuries to complete.[53]

There was likely great variability in the rate of domestication. In the area around Lake Junín it occurred between (cal.) 8000 and 4000 BP, and the same generally holds true for Ayacucho, 500 km (310 mi) to the south, with domestication occurring in the Cachi Phase, *circa* cal. 5000 BP.[54] Five hundred kilometers to the north of Lake Junín, however, at the site of Huaricoto, deer continued to be the main source of meat throughout the Preceramic Period and were only replaced by camelids in the Early Horizon *circa* (cal.) 2500 BP.[55]

Both puna and high valley dwellers seem to have practiced similar lifestyles. They used rock shelters or caves as base camps, where they built small round houses that were occupied for more or less time depending on resource procurement strategies. In the Middle Preceramic Period residential mobility was high where there were "gaps" between utilizable resource zones, such as in the dry upper valleys of the Peruvian coast or where resources were spread thin relative to the human population. At other locales people moved shorter distances, or sometimes not at all when food was within easy reach from one place.

In the Cusco Valley there was a succession of (locally defined) Early Archaic (*circa* cal. 11,500 to 9000 BP), Middle Archaic (*circa* cal. 9000 to 7000 BP) and Late Archaic (*circa* cal. 7000 to 4200 BP) hunters.[56] Changes between these cultures are mostly marked by different projectile point styles, with spine-shouldered and diamond-shaped-with-rounded-base types being the earliest, followed by more varied forms. Middle Archaic groups in the region apparently occupied lower altitude sites (3,650 to 3,450 m, 11,975 to 11,319 ft) than earlier peoples, perhaps due to a period of high aridity in the southern highlands of Peru and adjacent Bolivia which may have forced people to lower altitudes.

Middle Archaic groups in the Cusco area moved in a seasonal round hunting camelid, deer, and small mammals such as wild guinea pigs. At the Kasapata site postholes of a small, circular Late Archaic structure with a possible hearth were found, but such dwellings were likely used earlier, too.

In the Late Archaic the climate shifted to become more like that of today and by the end of the period some groups were semi-sedentary, practicing incipient horticulture and animal domestication. The Kasapata site covered 4,000 square meters (around 1 acre) and had a dense deposit of middens. There was an early, short-term residency period and a later, longer one, as indicated by more middens and more diverse tools. In the later period there are fewer deer remains, while camelids continued to be hunted and the increased presence of guinea pig remains suggests that they were in the process of being domesticated.

Human skeletons at Kasapata indicate high infant mortality and high rates of infectious diseases. Studies of human remains indicate that carbohydrates dominated the diet, and there is evidence for the practice of cranial deformation. Burial practices included the disposal of pre- and perinatal remains informally, perhaps in trash dumps, with greater care in the burial of older infants, children, and adults. One older infant burial had red ocher applied to it, while another was buried with a string of beads carved from a fox humerus. Two adults were buried under cairns of heated rocks.

From the Titicaca Basin to the Pacific coast and into Chile, Early and Middle Archaic projectile point styles were quite similar. This suggests that population density was light and that people probably moved through large regions over long periods of time. Since the coastal sites date much earlier than the highlands, Cynthia Klink and Mark Aldenderfer suggest that the initial Titicaca populations came from lower valleys to the west.[57] At the same time there are general stylistic similarities between projectile points from Titicaca, the South Coast, and the central highlands, such as unstemmed, unshouldered foliate points. As sites increase in number through time, however, so does the diversity of projectile point styles. By the Late Archaic the ties between Titicaca and the central highlands had ended, although links between the latter region and the coast continued. These patterns may be reflections of some interactions becoming more focused within smaller regions than before.

The Asana site, at an altitude of 3,435 m (11,270 ft), is located next to a small quebrada of the same name in the Osmore drainage in Peru's southern highlands. It was a base camp for mobile hunter-gatherers between 10,500 and 3500 BP.[58] Although conditions may have been more humid early in its occupation, the region is dry with scrubby cactus predominating in a rocky landscape. Asana was visited over hundreds of years with people spending longer periods there over time. Towards the end of its occupation, prepared floors outlined by posts suggest that ceremonial activities took place there.

In the Titicaca Basin early research found few Archaic sites near the lake. However, when studies were carried out near fresh water sources in upland puna areas, sites from very early times were found with occupations beginning between (cal.) 10,000 and 8000 BP.[59] The upland locations of open-air sites suggest that the first peoples were mobile hunters of wild camelids who came to drink or camp at water holes and other water sources. There is a dramatic increase in the number of sites for the Late Archaic Period and a concurrent increase in the number of styles of projectile points. This suggests that at this time populations had become dense enough in relation to resources that social differentiation and subsistence strategies increased in variability. However, hunting and gathering lasted well into the Late Preceramic Period in the Titicaca Basin, at the same time as some coastal peoples were fully agricultural and building large ceremonial architectural complexes.

COASTAL CULTURES

In Ecuador the term "Formative" is used consistently instead of "Preceramic." The Ecuadorian Formative is divided into three sub-periods and known for three significant archaeological cultures: the Early Formative (cal. 6400 to 3450 BP) and the Valdivia Culture; the Middle Formative (cal. 3430 to 2830 BP) and the Machalilla Culture; and the Late Formative (cal. 3300 to 2300 BP) and the Chorrera culture. The Ecuadorian Formative spans several periods of Peruvian prehistory, and discussion of them will correspond with those eras in subsequent chapters, therefore covering early Ecuadorian ceramics in the Late Preceramic Period while bearing in mind that this is a time period not a cultural phase.[60]

Much of our knowledge of Formative Ecuador is based on studies carried out in the southwest of the country, particularly in the Santa Elena Peninsula and the nearby Chanduy Valley, comprising an area of less than 200 square km (77 square mi). The Las Vegas culture continued from earlier times, although most sites consist of small, dense, lithic scatters at a variety of littoral settings and low interior hills. Although these sites are on the coast, terrestrial animals and near- and offshore fish are more prevalent than shellfish and other coastal resources in comparison with later occupations in the region. *Algarrobo* (*Prosopis sp.* [mesquite]) seeds were an important gathered food as well.

Maize phytoliths—microcrystals found in leaves and other plant parts which are distinctive for different species—were found at Vegas and are believed to be present at the site and in the region by (cal.) 7000 BP.[61] However, the importance of maize as a foodstuff is not clear, and even if it was grown at Vegas culture sites it does not appear to have been a crucial part of diets. The issue of maize and plant domestication in general will be addressed in more detail in the next chapter.[62]

All the Vegas sites are within 6 km of one another, and a wide variety of resource localities could have been exploited from a single place. Today the peninsula experiences a distinct dry season and droughts that can last several years. Presuming similar conditions, Vegas populations therefore likely had fairly flexible settlement strategies. Although it may have been temporarily vacated from time to time, the Vegas Site forms the largest settlement in the region, occupied more or less continuously from about 10,000 to 6600 BP and probably serving as a base camp from which people went to the smaller sites to extract resources.[63]

No human remains were found at other sites on the peninsula, but 192 burials were found at Vegas. Grave goods included spoons and ornaments of shell, polished stone axes, red ocher, and round stones. The site may have been an exceptionally large base camp, or perhaps an early ceremonial center that was only visited sporadically for the burial of the dead. A small structure only 1.5 m. in diameter was found there, which may have been used only for sleeping or as a retreat from inclement weather.

The Cementerio de Nanchoc is on a low hill in a dry side canyon by the Nanchoc River, a tributary of the Zaña River, some 80 km inland from the Pacific on Peru's north coast and in an ecotone between a semi-arid thorn forest and the river flood plain.[64] Conditions were likely similar during the Pircas phase (*circa* cal. 9700 to 7800 BP) and the Tierra Blanca phase (*circa* cal. 7800 to 5000 BP), when the region was fairly well populated by early farmers who grew squash, quinoa, cassava, peanuts, and other crops in small household plots on alluvial fans, although they also still foraged and hunted for food. Their diets appear to have been mostly focused on plants and they maintained a unificial tool industry producing flakes, choppers, gravers, and scrapers to process these foods.

In the Pircas phase the Nanchoc folk lived in quite small (2 m [6.5 ft] diameter) houses of adobes, rocks, and grasses or sedges, but by the subsequent Tierra Blanca phase at least one rectangular house with rounded corners is known. Gardening systems may have improved from earlier to later times and two non-residential mound structures appear to have been used in the Pircas phase. These two structures are on either side of a small arroyo, and together they cover about 2 hectares (5 acres). The eastern mound is in the modern cemetery of Nanchoc from which the site derives its name. Use of the modern graveyard limited archaeological study of this structure, but it was judged to be roughly oval in shape and about 30 m in maximum dimension. The western mound was roughly triangular in shape, 30 m long with a 20 m base (98 ft by 66 ft), with three levels conforming to the rise of the hill and demarcated by lines of stones to form terraces. Tom Dillehay and his team found evidence of lime production in this space, feasible due to the abundance of travertine and calcite deposits in the region. The lime could have been produced as a dietary supplement or for coca chewing; this is suggested by coca leaves found at Nanchoc from slightly later periods than the time when the structure was in use.

Nanchoc funeral customs included primary burials in flexed positions covered with rocks, a pattern seen over a wide area of the Andes in these early times. However, a practice of secondary burial also seems to have been followed, since stacked, cut human long bones were encountered. Cannibalism has been suggested, although the removal of flesh from bones is often part of the processing of human remains to create secondary burials. Quartz crystals, copper ore, and malachite were found at some domestic sites. The latter two materials suggest the possibility of early metallurgy, although no direct evidence of this has been found. The recovery of a seashell and a fragment of a Paiján point indicate some contact with the coast.

Unlike in other areas, on the Central Coast of Peru the proximity of hills and ocean provided for closely packed resource zones and allowed for short-distance mobility and early sedentism.[65] The Paloma site in the Chilca Valley was ideally located to exploit the three major resource zones: the lomas, the river valley, and the shore (see Figure 3.5).[66] It was a short-term camp in its earliest occupation *circa* (cal.) 7700 BP. By about 5500 BP Paloma may have been inhabited year-round, except in high summer, but by 2800 BP it may no longer have been occupied at all as new settlement systems were adopted. People built round huts, 2 to 3 m in diameter, of wooden poles stuffed with grass for insulation and covered with reed mats, at the lower edge of a fog-fed lomas field. The field was probably green most of the year at first, because as trees and large bushes became established they trapped more fog moisture that also provided drinking water, condensing in pits dug for the purpose. The lomas would have been pleasant to live in and provided a variety of plants and animals for food, fiber, and other uses (see Figure 3.5).

Paloma is a little over 7 km (4.4 mi) from the Chilca River, close enough for people to easily gather resources there, such as crayfish and reeds for fibers to be used in mats, cordage, and clothing. The Pacific, only 4 km (2.5 mi) distant, provided maritime resources that were more important than riverine ones. The Palomans were skilled fisher folk venturing into relatively deep waters. They also gathered mollusks, some of which they hauled all the way back to the site, presumably for medium-term storage in their shells. Although they primarily lived off the land and the sea, they raised bottle gourds for bowls and net floats and there is some evidence that they may have encouraged the growth of a wild begonia native to the lomas, harvesting the edible bulb for food.[67]

It is likely that only five or six families of several individuals each resided at Paloma at any one time. Similar lomas or riverine base camps, like the one at the nearby Chilca I site, were established when resource zones were close. Elsewhere, where the coastal hills were further from the shore or the river, people practiced more mobile settlement systems.

Far to the south of Paloma, villages on the Paracas Peninsula in southern Peru showed similar ways of life. Rio Grande de Nazca 49 was much like Chilca I, situated on a terrace bordering a

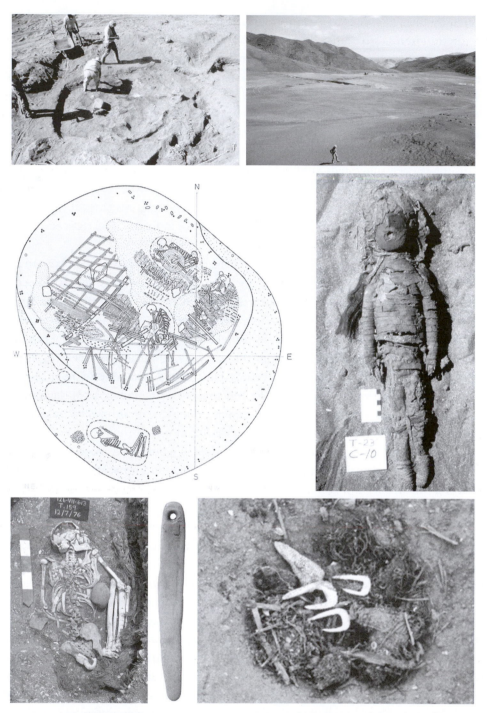

Figure 3.5 Clockwise from upper right: The Paloma site, once in lomas, now in desert; Chinchorro mummy; Paloma fishhooks in subfloor pit; textile tool; Burial 159, the young shark victim; Drawing of House 100/101 with burials; House 100/101 under excavation.

stream. The Paracas 514 and 96 sites (*circa* cal. 6000 BP) were close to each other. At the latter site there were circular huts about 4 m (13 ft) in diameter, with the dead wrapped in mats, clothing (including leather and looped fiber caps), and in one case a vicuña fur robe.[68]

Thus, from southern Ecuador to southern Peru village life was beginning between 8,000 and 6,000 years ago. Most people were still fairly mobile, but in many places where it was possible to do so, people stayed in one place for fairly long periods of time and the domestication of plants and animals was under way. Although there were still large regions where human population was low, people were successfully adapting to local environmental conditions. However, their relatively simple modes of survival nevertheless supported rich spiritual and ceremonial lives.

EARLY BELIEFS AND RITUALS

We know a considerable amount about the spiritual and ritual worlds of early Andean peoples, mostly through their art and mortuary practices, although the earliest hunters and foragers produced little in the way of art or ornamentation that has survived. Like highly mobile people in other places and at different times, skill and care likely was invested in finely crafted tools for making a living, and few non-utilitarian objects were made due to the need to travel light. Even many of the utilitarian items were made of perishable materials, such as net bags and clothing. However, there are many examples of mundane to spectacular rock art throughout the Andes; they are difficult to date, but Middle Preceramic peoples or even earlier folk likely made petroglyphs (engravings) and pictographs (paintings).

At Paloma a few textiles, pendants, beads, and other small items that carried some meaning or value were more commonly found in the graves of children than in adult burials, and a few other sites have shown similar results. These patterns, including the use of flexed positions for the dead, apply to sites on the coast and in the highlands.

A sense that Paloma was thought of as "home" is shown by the fact that site residents buried their dead below the floors of their huts or immediately outside them. Flexed bodies, wrapped in reed mats, often had their hands placed near the face or between the thighs. Men appear to have been buried in the eastern sectors of houses, women in the west, and children on an imaginary northwest line that separated the adults.

A few everyday items such as clothing, in the form of "bikini" type briefs for the men and short rush skirts for the women, sometimes accompanied the dead, as did the occasional bone tool used in making textiles from wild plants. The fact that these tools were worn as pendants and taken to the grave underscores the importance of textile making in early Peru. Mussel valves were sometimes filled with small items, such as red ocher pigment (perhaps for body paint), and these as well as cut shell discs and crescents also were placed in burials.

Bioarchaeological studies of the human remains found at Paloma suggest that life was difficult and short. People suffered sprains and broken bones in their feet and hands. Tooth infections could be lethal, and arthritis took its toll in the damp winters of coastal Peru. There were probably many other illnesses and diseases that the Palomans suffered which did not leave marks on bones. Few individuals lived into their forties, and death in childbirth was common. The many infant and neonatal burials found at the site, often buried with more apparent care and more grave goods than older folk, seem poignant, suggesting that the young were treasured, seen as essential to the continuance of society and greatly mourned when they died. A special mortuary facility for the burial of the very young was constructed in the form of a square hut.

It is sobering to consider that if puberty began between 14 and 17 and death could be expected from the late twenties into the thirties, the Palomans were able to reproduce themselves and raise their children to the age of puberty just as the parental generation was dying off. Life was harsh, and yet the Palomans survived and reproduced. However, it is no wonder that they gave special attention to the burial of infants, suggesting that they recognized how close to the margin the continuation of their society was. Robert Benfer has traced the health of Palomans through time and found that they did gradually get healthier and live a little longer. A few more years of life may have made a great difference in supporting cultural continuity between the generations.

Other burials also demonstrate the care and concern expressed by members of the families that occupied the site. A young, twenty-something man and an older one in his forties were buried together in a loving embrace, accompanied by quartz crystals, a split mano (a hand grinding stone), and a long staff, suggesting that they may have been seers or shamans based on ethnographic analogies with later people. A 17-year-old young man is perhaps the world's earliest known shark victim. A shark bit his arm and took off his leg, as revealed by distinctive teeth marks. He was a highly valued member of his community because his body was brought all the way back to the site from the shore, where he was buried in a grave much more elaborate than typical ones.

A specially built ossuary containing the remains of a man, two women, and a young teenaged boy was also found at Paloma. The use of special burial facilities such as this one, as well as the infant mortuary house, is another very early pattern found in Peru, which seems to presage the development of more elaborate facilities in later times and the cult of the veneration of ancestors. Similarly, there is evidence suggesting that burials were covered in salt, perhaps to preserve the remains and possibly to preserve the dead.[69] Fires were sometimes made on graves, an early practice also found elsewhere in the Andes, such as at Kasapata.

Chilca I is only 8 km (5 mi) from Paloma, on the bank of the river after which it is named. The site was not excavated or studied to the same extent as Paloma, but it was occupied between 5700 and 3600 BP, at roughly the same time as Paloma's main occupation.[70] Huts very like those at Paloma were also found at Chilca I and burial practices were similar, including special attention devoted to child burials. Unlike its neighbor, however, at Chilca there was a separate cemetery area. Stones were sometimes found on top of burials at Paloma and also at Chilca I. At the latter site, however, some women were found with as many as five stakes nailed through different parts of their bodies, although whether this was done before or after their demise is unknown. There also was an ossuary (House 6) at Chilca I containing eight flexed burials, hands at their faces, oriented with heads to north and placed side-by-side with a large whale vertebra placed on top of them.

In addition to the ossuaries at Paloma and Chilca I, several other Middle Preceramic sites have revealed ossuaries or cemetery-like arrangements of the dead. At Bandurria, occupied into the Late Preceramic, many burials were placed around a large stone monolith. These early practices are examples of a great concern with the dead and their roles as ancestors that find later prehistoric expression in the elaborate mummies created by the Inca.

One of the most striking and distinctive Middle Preceramic burial customs is that of the Chinchorro archaeological culture who lived in far northern coastal Chile and neighboring southern Peru.[71] Dating as early as *circa* 7000 BP, Chinchorro has been claimed to be the earliest culture to practice mummification if the term is understood to mean a deliberate attempt to preserve the physical remains of the dead by manipulation of the cadaver (see Figure 3.5).

In the earliest period (*circa* 7000 to 5000 BP), a Black Mummy technique was followed for adults, children, and even fetuses, in which the internal organs were removed and the body disassembled. The remains were then heat-dried, and then sticks were inserted and tied together to reinforce the skeletal structure as it was reassembled. Then the cavities were filled with vegetal matter or animal hair and the skin was replaced, sometimes wrapped in strips and sometimes whole. In some cases animal skins were used, or else a layer of white ash was plastered over the form to resemble skin. Then the entire mummy was painted in manganese, giving it a black color. A later (*circa* 4500 to 4000 BP) Red Mummy technique did not disarticulate the dead, instead using incisions to remove the organs, but otherwise it followed similar steps except that a red ocher paint was used for the body with the face painted black, often with the addition of a human hair wig dressed in tassels. A short two-century pattern at the very end of the tradition was to simply coat the dead in mud. The reasons for these elaborate treatments are not known, but the mummies may have been exposed to public display for some period of time, for worship or even for joint participation in ceremonies and fiestas.

Less elaborate burial customs have been well documented at many other sites. Some of the similarities are quite striking. For example, wigs appear to have been made and placed on some of the Paloma dead. The use of fire in or on graves is quite widespread, as are group burials or ossuaries. These practices suggest that people came to the New World with a common set of practices, which then diversified but retained some key features such as the use of fire in mortuary rites. Another possibility is that there were ideas and practices that developed and then were shared very early in the occupation of the Andes. It is quite possible that both processes occurred, with old ideas being maintained and new ones developed and then shared. At present we do not have sufficient evidence to decide between these possibilities, however.

THE MIDDLE PRECERAMIC TO LATE PRECERAMIC TRANSITION

The Middle Preceramic Period was a time when people in the Central Andes began to fully and successfully integrate themselves into regional and local ecosystems. It was the time when the landscape began to fill with people, although more so in some areas than in others. Plant and animal domestication had barely begun at the start of the period, but it was fully under way by its end.

From some theoretical perspectives these cultural changes could be interpreted as part of the process of what Gordon Childe termed the "Neolithic Revolution," the change from human reliance on wild foods to agriculture and cultivated resources. However, current evidence suggests that there was no "Neolithic Revolution" in the Central Andes; rather, there was a "Neolithic Evolution" which was already under way when humans first entered the New World. As previously noted, the earliest people in the Americas likely grew gourds and raised their own dogs. Many plants were likely "managed" for quite some time before they were fully domesticated, such as the Paloma wild begonias. In the highlands hunting and foraging probably lasted until quite late in prehistory in some areas, while in others domestication was already under way.

The process of domestication was ragged, occurring in some places and not in others for reasons that are still unclear. We have already seen that camelid domestication appears to have occurred in one highland area although it was apparently not practiced relatively close by. The same seems to hold true for guinea pigs, those convenient little bundles of meat that are easy to care for and which reproduce rapidly. The earliest *cuy* remains date to the Piki/Chihua Phases at Preceramic sites in Ayacucho (*circa* cal. 6100 to 4000 BP) and at Guitarrero Cave (Complex IV). By the Late Preceramic cuy remains are abundant at the site of Kotosh, but cuy seem to not be common on the coast until much later in prehistory.[72] So too, as already noted, maize may have been present early but did not assume an important role in diets until late in prehistory, and even then its popularity seems to have been highly variable, perhaps having more to do with brewing chicha for ritual fiestas than serving as a food staple.

We do not have many details about the causes of these changes or associated behavior occurring alongside them. As is the case with so many other aspects of life in remote times, we do not have much knowledge of the social stresses that may have been experienced as a result of warfare and raiding. Not only are toolkits small, lightweight, and perishable, but the same kinds of weapons that were used for the hunt were probably also used for fighting. None of the burials previously discussed show clear features that could be indisputably interpreted as the result of human violence. However, on the far South Coast of Peru, at the Villa del Mar site near the mouth of the Ilo River, a young man of the Chinchorro culture aged 17 to 20 years met a violent end.[73] His skeleton was found with six projectile points in it, most in his upper body and one in his pelvis. The piercing of the bones indicates that the points entered the man's body with force and came from behind him. The excavators noted that while he died violently, he was buried in a standard way, although he was not treated to the elaborate mummification process found in some Chinchorro burials. The contrast between violent death and "normal" burial made the excavators hesitate between considering the man's death to be a case of homicide or an instance of sacrifice. In either case it is one of the earliest examples of violent death in the Andes, and underscores the fact that hunter-gatherer lives were not necessarily peaceful. The stakes in the female burials at Chilca I are hard to interpret, but they suggest that fear or anger was expressed through this act.

Evidence from the Vegas site in Ecuador, numerous sites in Peru, and the Chinchorro mummies of Chile, all suggest that Middle Preceramic cultures show clear signs of shared general attitudes towards the dead. They were treated in more or less elaborate ways in these various places, but in all of them bodies of the deceased were given considerable attention and we can infer that these activities served as a form of religious practice and associated social bonding. While it seems that almost all members of communities were interred with respect—even the stakes and stones at Paloma and Chilca I (perhaps to keep the dead from wandering?) were features of planned burials—the special attention given to the young is a pattern that was set early, and which continued to and beyond the Inca. The practice of mummification is not seen everywhere, but there is a suggestion in the salt-coated, bewigged Palomans and particularly in the mummification practices of the Chinchorro that the people were preserving the physical remains of the dead in order that some aspect of their existence might continue. Such practices and facilities—including ossuaries and dance floors—suggest that conceptions of infants and children as sources of fertility and the older dead as ancestors, which are known with certainty in late prehistory, began at a very early time. It is likely that there is a direct link between Middle Preceramic practices and elaborations of them in the Late Preceramic.

Environmental change may have played an important role in some of the Middle to Late Preceramic changes of residential location, variation in ways of making a living, and evolution of socio-political systems. The best case study we currently have for this notion concerns the lomas vegetation of the Central Coast of Peru. A mature lomas field includes trees that help trap moisture to support lower storey shrubs and herbaceous plants. Cutting the trees eliminates the trapping system: the moisture is no longer held low to the ground, leading to a breakdown in the ecology. Whereas a mature lomas may remain fairly moist and green during the austral summer, albeit contracting and dying back to some degree, once the trees are gone the lomas may disappear completely during the summer and consist only of light vegetation in the winter months with the heaviest fogs.

At Paloma, Robert Benfer studied the nature and dimensions of fuel sources in hearths at the site over time.[74] He found that wood decreased and poor quality fuel sources, such as the bromeliad *Tillandsia*, increased in use. In addition, the sizes of wood sources decreased over time, with an increase in the use of smaller twigs. This study suggests that the lomas were indeed under stress, shrinking over time. How much this was due to natural forces or to human ones is uncertain, but human over-exploitation is a strong possibility. If this pattern of lomas reduction was fairly widespread on the Central Coast, it could have played a role in pushing people into river valleys and forcing them to rely more on horticulture than they had done previously. If this were the case it would fit a model of culture change that has been proposed for the processes that led to the domestication of plants and animals, or at least to an increased reliance on them. In this model, change is not due to a deliberate choice for "progress" but rather to attempts to maintain existing socio-cultural systems in the face of stress. Despite such attempts, however, modifications of everyday practice that may seem to be relatively minor in fact result in rather dramatic long-term alterations in lifestyle. Whatever the cause, dramatic changes did occur in the Late Preceramic Period.

NOTES

1 See Dillehay 2008 and Meltzer 2009 for overviews of issues on initial peopling of the New World.
2 However, tools associated with early Homo sapiens have been found at Jebel Faya, in the eastern Arabian Peninsula, and they date to 125,000 years ago. Thus, the issue of the first dispersal from Africa is open to question. See Armitage et al. 2011.
3 See http://www.quaternary.stratigraphy.org.uk/charts/ for definitions of geologic periods.
4 Meltzer 2009 covers much of the following in detail.
5 Paul Martin (1984) was a strong proponent of human agency in megafauna extinctions. See the Discussion section of Surovell and Grund 2012 for references to various theories on the issue.
6 Meltzer 2009, p. 254 and pp. 259–260.
7 Bird 1988.
8 Whether the channels on fishtail points are true examples of "fluting" or not is a matter of debate that is unsettled and largely unpublished.
9 Ranere and Cooke 1991 and Gruhn and Bryan 1977 on Clovis in Panama. Roosevelt et al. 2002 on Clovis not in South America.
10 On Page-Ladson: Webb 2005.
11 Gilbert et al. 2008.
12 Greenberg et al. 1986 on linguistics and genetics. Reich et al. 2012 on recent genetic studies.
13 See O'Connell and Allen 2004; Mellars et al. 2007.
14 Davidson 2013, who also provides a general comparison of the early colonization of Australia and America.
15 Erlandson et al. 2007.
16 A thorough review of early Andean coastal sites may be found in Sandweiss (in press).
17 Rundel and Dillon 1998 and Rundel et al. 1991.
18 Sandweiss 2003.
19 Andrus et al. 2008.
20 Reinoso Hermida 1973.
21 Ossa and Moseley 1971, listed as 1971 in bibliography on La Cumbre.
22 Chauchat 1988 covers views on coastal sites. See Quilter 1986 for a reassessment of the Chivateros and Oquendo complexes, however. A more recent review of early coastal sites is found in Sandweiss 2008.
23 Richardson 1978 and 1981.
24 Campbell 1982.
25 Dillehay 1989 on Monte Verde.
26 Guidon and Delibrias 1986.

27 Jackson et al. 2007 on Santa Julia. "Basal thinning" refers to flakes taken off the lower portion of the tool, but not the distinctive "flutes" of Clovis and Folsom.

28 Núñez et al. 1994.

29 Miotti 1999 and Miotti and Salemme 2004 on Piedra Museo. Paunero et al. 2007 on Casa de Minero.

30 Rivero 2012.

31 Sandweiss (in press).

32 Keefer et al. 1998 on Quebrada Tacahuay. Sandweiss et al. 1998 on Quebrada Jaguay.

33 Rademaker et al. 2012 on the distance of the Alca source from Jaguay.

34 Sandweiss et al. 1989.

35 Llagostera et al. 2000.

36 Núñez et al. 1994.

37 Roosevelt et al. 2002 and Roosevelt et al. 1996.

38 Chauchat 1988; Chauchat et al. 1992.

39 Briceño Rosario 1999; Gálvez Mora 1999.

40 Briceño Rosario 1999; Gálvez Mora 1999.

41 Chauchat and Lacombre 1984.

42 Piperno and Stothert 2003 on squashes in pre-Vegas. Stothert 1985 on Vegas in general.

43 MacNeish et al. 1983.

44 Dillehay et. al 2012. See Rademaker et al. 2012 for an up-to-date review of early dates.

45 Rademaker et al. 2012.

46 Quilter 1991.

47 Wayne et al. 2006 on early dogs. Erickson et al. on early gourds.

48 Discussions of the sites in this paragraph may be found in Stothert and Quilter 1991.

49 Lynch 1980 on Guitarrero. Cardich 1958, 1964, and 1980 on Lauricocha. Rick 1980 on Pachamachay. Kaulicke 1999 on Uchcumachay. Matos 1975 on Panalauca. Lavallée et al. 1985 and et al. 1982 on Telemarchay. MacNeish et al. 1983 on the Ayacucho Project.

50 Lavallée et al. 1985; Rick 1980.

51 Lynch 1980.

52 Engel 1969, 1970; Meighan and True 1980; Rademaker et al. (in press).

53 Wheeler 1985, 1999.

54 Wheeler 1984. On camelid domestication in general see Bonavia 2009 and Megoni Goñalons and Yacobaccio 2006.

55 Burger 1985: 532.

56 Bauer 2007.

57 Klink and Aldenderfer 2005: 50.

58 Aldenderfer 1998.

59 Cipolla 2005.

60 Ziedler 2008 on Chorerra etc. The considerable overlapping of dates for the Middle and Late Formative in Ecuador is symptomatic of a mixing of time periods and cultural phases, which remains an issue that needs resolution.

61 Pearsall and Piperno 1990 on Vegas maize. Thompson 2006 on issues of phytoliths and dating maize domestication in Central and South America. Bonavia and Grobman 1999 on claims for early maize in coastal Peru.

62 Pearsall 1992 for a somewhat dated but still very comprehensive overview of plant domestication in South America. Gourds now appear to have entered the New World with the first people.

63 Raymond 2003: 38–39.

64 Dillehay et al. 1997.

65 Lanning and Patterson 1964; Patterson 1971.

66 Benfer 1999; Quilter 1989.
67 Benfer 1990.
68 Engel 1976: 89.
69 Benfer 1999: 233.
70 Donnan 1964; Engel 1976.
71 Arriaza 1995. It is unclear if the dates cited are calibrated. Calibrations would provide a range of 6000 to 4000 BP in calendar years.
72 Cuy at Ayacucho in MacNeish et al. 1983: 9. At Guitarrero Cave in Lynch 1980: 314. At Kostosh in Wing 1972.
73 Guillén and Carpio 1999.
74 Benfer 1986.

4

THE LATE PRECERAMIC PERIOD

EMERGING COMPLEXITY

Although differences between coastal, highland, and tropical cultures are clear in earlier times, it was in the Late Preceramic Period that regional distinctions came into sharp focus as different sectors of the Central Andes took somewhat divergent paths in their economies, political systems, and religious practices. Our understanding of this divergence is partly due to the availability of more archaeological data from later periods, but it is also likely due to greater numbers of people who fine-tuned their adaptations to local environments and differentiated themselves from their neighbors. Defining the differences and similarities, and explaining how and why they came about, are pursuits that have preoccupied scholars for a considerable amount of time.

Herbert J. Spinden (1879–1967) served in the leading US museums of his day and was a grand theorist. During his lifetime enough research had been done that some strikingly similar patterns were identified in early prehistoric cultures throughout a wide region of the Americas, especially from Mexico through the Central Andes. Spinden suggested that there was a "hearth" in the tropical forests of northwestern South America where many cultural patterns developed, and it was from there that they spread, or diffused to use the terminology of the times, to the Andes in the south, Mesoamerica in the north, and perhaps beyond.

In the next generation of archaeologists, Donald W. Lathrap championed Spinden's general ideas. His field research was in the tropical forest, especially in Ecuador, and he made many forceful claims that this tropical region was "precocious" in its cultural development, adopting agriculture, ceramics, and other practices well before they developed in Peru.

Working in the tropical forest is difficult especially for scholars raised in temperate climes, even though it may have been a bountiful land for preindustrial people. It is an uncomfortable and often dangerous place, particularly the region east of the Andes. The humid and wet conditions do not preserve organic materials as does the climate on the desert coast or even in the sierra, and the dense vegetation makes survey, excavation, and travel difficult. Because of these factors, archaeological research in tropical forest regions has been less extensive than elsewhere. Nevertheless, the work that has been carried out there suggests that the region supported dense populations of people whose activities were highly important for developments in the sierra and at the coast. One macro-region where these events have been chronicled is Ecuador.

PRECOCIOUS ECUADOR

While the eastern foothills of the Andes and the Amazon Basin are far from urban centers, the west coast of Ecuador is less isolated although it is still a tropical region. Furthermore, because the Humboldt Current swings away from the coast close to the modern Peru–Ecuador border, western Ecuador is a tropical land. There are coastal hills and river valleys, but the high mountains are further from the shore than in Peru. Instead of the roughly parallel river valleys of coastal Peru, the Guayas Basin dominates the region running from north to south, debouching into the Gulf of Guayaquil. The terrain is thus varied enough to foster the growth of local cultures, but not so formidable as to prevent relatively easy communication between them. Variations in topography and altitude and the availability of plentiful fresh water and maritime resources offered abundant resources for human use, in distinctive micro-environments that ranged from zones as dry as the Peruvian deserts to fog-covered hills and tropical wetlands.[1]

The Vegas culture was succeeded by the Valdivia culture in southwestern Ecuador (see Figure 4.1). Valdivia was actually known well before Vegas because of its ceramics, which were once considered the earliest in the New World. They are still on the list of very early ceramics, but it is the larger picture of Valdivia life that makes this culture particularly interesting as an example of the precociousness of prehistoric Ecuadorian cultures.[2]

The Valdivia site that has received the most attention is Real Alto, in the Chanduy Valley.[3] The first occupation there occurred in the Terminal Archaic (*circa* 4800 to 4000 BC), comfortably in the range of the Middle Preceramic Period of Peru. The culture of this early occupation was quite similar to the Vegas culture previously described. However, the next phase saw the establishment of the Real Alto village that was occupied for over two millennia.

The first Real Alto village, established around 3900 BC, was a hamlet of between a dozen to fifteen elliptical pole-and-thatch huts clustered in a circular or U-shaped pattern. It was home to between 50 and 60 people, and the dead were buried next to houses in a manner generally similar to the pattern at Paloma. By 2500 BC the site had expanded to four times its previous size, eventually covering almost 12.5 hectares (31 acres), and the population may have reached 1200 people. There were as many as a hundred sturdy houses arranged in a rectangular pattern around a central plaza which was open at one end, with four irregularly shaped mounds in the

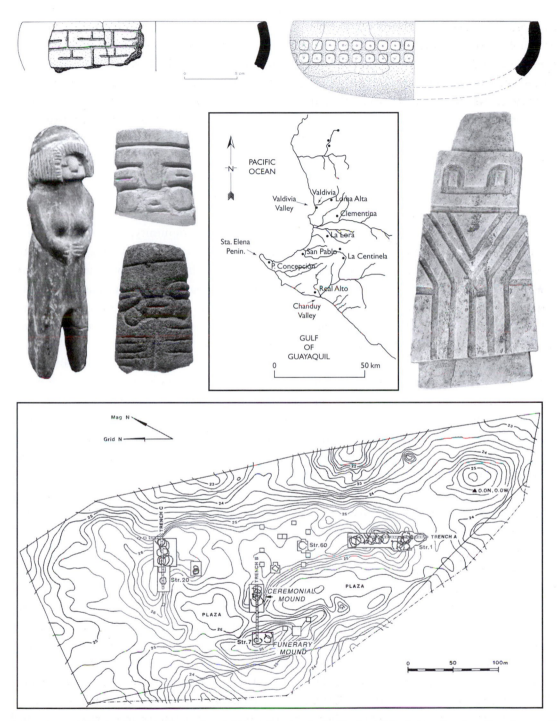

Figure 4.1 Valdivia: Top: Two early Valdivia bowls. Left: Red polished female clay figurine and fragments of two stone figurines. Center: Map of early coastal Valdivia sites. Right: Stone plaque idol. Bottom: Map of Real Alto.

central plaza with structures for communal use. The two largest of these were the Fiesta House Mound, containing evidence of feasting, and the Charnel House Mound holding burials, presumably of high-ranking villagers. Real Alto may have served as some kind of regional center at this time, a role more clearly in evidence by the next and last phase of occupation *circa* 1800 BC when outlying hamlets are found.

Valdivia thus became a fully sedentary, horticultural society with increasing social distinctions and long-range contacts. Beans (*Canavalia plagiosperma*), cotton (*Gossypium spp.*), manioc (*Manihot sp.*), and maize (*Zea mays*) were all being grown at Valdivia sites perhaps as early as 3300 BC and likely no later than 1500 BC, at Valdivia's end.[4] By at least Middle Valdivia times watercraft had reached La Plata and La Puná islands, both far from land. Trade by water was accompanied in late Valdivia times by exchanges of Quito Basin obsidian.[5]

Real Alto and Loma Alta, the other well known Valdivia community, have been compared to recent Gê-Bororo villages of the Amazon Basin. The village plan defines social groupings and symbolically replicates relations between them. In addition, the village plan mimics that of a single house, implying that concepts of micro and macro relations were in operation. James Zeidler has suggested that increasing population density in resource-rich coastal Ecuador helped to stimulate social competition and the intensification of prestige goods and structures, with resulting social rankings becoming established.[6]

Variability in house size and the location of residences near or close to the ceremonial centers of villages may have been expressions of the relative ranking of the residents, with higher ranking families closer to the village center. The "house" may have been a physical, social, and metaphorical primary unit in Valdivian communities. Despite the rich resources of the region and the growth of villages, however, there was a slight drop in overall health from Vegas times, a common pattern when people shift from being fairly mobile to being sedentary, and there was a high incidence of bone trauma, suggesting either domestic violence or intergroup warfare, probably raiding.[7]

Late Valdivia populations expanded north and south of their Guayas Province heartland, settling at the San Isidro site in the Jama Valley (Piquigua Phase) and the La Emerenciana site in El Oro Province respectively, as well as establishing new centers farther inland in Guayas, such as at Peñon del Río. All of these have relatively large-scale public architecture, while in the old Valdivia area no such sites exist, and instead populations were dispersed.[8] The causes of the failure of Real Alto to capitalize on its importance of earlier times are unclear.

There were impressive long-distance exchange systems in Formative Ecuador that traded in a wide variety of items. Charged with symbolism, they included natural products such as *Spondylus* and *Strombus galeatus* shells from tropical waters, while stone mortars were made at specific places and in styles that were probably used in regional religious and social movements. Many of these goods were contemporaneously or soon to be developed in or introduced to Peru.

Thus there is a growing body of evidence from Ecuador and elsewhere in northwestern South America that people there had villages, domesticated plants, long-distance exchange systems, and rich ritual lives at very early times.[9] However, people in other areas of the Andes were also engaged in similar activities. Were the tropical forest peoples truly precocious, or is this view partly due to the variable nature of the archaeological record in different areas of the Andes? Archaeological research in Ecuador has tended to focus particularly on early cultures such as Vegas and Valdivia, so that the data available for the interpretation of early cultures is rich, but is the view of Ecuadorian precociousness a consequence of the way archaeology has been carried out there? A review of the evidence for Peru will offer some issues to consider.

PERU

As noted in the previous chapter, in the Middle Preceramic Period there were widely shared customs with distinct local variations over great areas in terms of the treatment of the dead, most clearly visible at present in the coastal regions of Peru and Ecuador. Over time there was an increase in the effort expended in formalizing burial places, such as at Paloma, where the ossuaries in reed and mat-covered huts of the Middle Preceramic Period were replaced by rectangular, semi-subterranean structures in the Late Preceramic. Elsewhere, transitions *in situ*, such as can be seen at Paloma, are not always clear. Eventually, however, a standard pattern of sunken, semi-subterranean plazas or chambers became a common form of ceremonial space in the core of the Central Andes. At some sites these chambers alone were sufficient for rituals, while at others a circular plaza was paired with a rectangular building, often terraced with a central staircase.

Early large-scale architecture worldwide tended to consist of solid constructions that grew in size through time. A small burial mound or ceremonial platform was often first built. After a period of use, another layer of architecture was built on top of it. Uses may have changed through time, and while previous structures may have contained rooms they were often filled in or buried in order to provide a solid foundation for the next construction stage. In Preceramic Peru, reed net-bags filled with rocks, called *shicra*, were commonly employed as fill. Thus, buildings grew in size over time, but the increase in the amount of usable space was not as great as might be expected judging by the size of the building alone.

Currently the oldest known such structure in Peru is at Sechín Bajo, in the Casma Valley, with radiocarbon dates at (cal.) 5500 BP and the structure continuing in use to the later Initial Period.[10] If the dating for this site is correct it would place it well within the Middle Preceramic Period, but for now it can be seen to express patterns more typical of the Late Preceramic. It consists of a circular sunken plaza, between 10 and 12 m (33 to 39 ft) in diameter made of rocks and adobe bricks.

Huaca Prieta is a single, large mound that was built up like a Middle Eastern tell, although it may have been reconfigured for ceremonial purposes during its use (see Figure 4.2).[11] The site is famous for its historic status as the first Preceramic site to be intentionally excavated and studied by Junius Bird (after his Patagonian studies), and it has recently gained attention as a result of research by Tom Dillehay and his team which indicates that it was occupied at a very early date. The meticulous study of the early textiles there, done by Bird and his assistant, Milica Dimitrijevic Skinner, still stands as a landmark in Andean archaeology (see Figure 4.3). In the Chao Valley the Los Morteros Site, named for the great number of stone mortar fragments found on its summit, is another candidate for the earliest mound, located at the edge of an old shoreline (see Figure 2.2).[12]

Further down the coast, about 105 km (65 mi) north of Lima, Río Seco is a large site complex with many mounds, most of which appear to have been platforms, possibly the bases of dwellings.[13] However, two of these are larger than the rest. Excavations in one of them showed five to six interconnected rooms at the basal level. That structure was filled with boulders brought from the bed of the Río Seco a mile away. New rooms were built on top of this infill, and were later themselves filled in to make way for new construction. The final work was to cover the entire mound with sand and place several large vertical blocks of stone on its summit. The second pyramid seems to have undergone the same general sequence. For several hundred yards around the bases of the pyramids there is a layer of shell deposits on the surface of the ground, with many ceremonial caches or offerings deposited in holes. These consist of bundles of sticks, leaves, sedges, and other plant parts, gourds, shellfish, and body parts or bones of birds and sea lions.

The overall impression given by the research at Río Seco is of a relatively simple society, the members of which nevertheless had a considerable amount of free time to devote to mound construction and ritual activities as represented by the numerous offerings there. Although the archaeological evidence may be deceptive because we have a foreshortened view of activities that likely took place over many generations, it appears that the local inhabitants were doing fairly well within a relatively simple subsistence economy. Whether the river ever held water after the Pleistocene is unknown, but the site is next to the ocean, and of course shellfish and other marine resources were in great abundance. Equally importantly, Río Seco is very close to the Lomas Lachay, a large stretch of coastal hills that stay green all year round even today and were probably as rich or richer in the past, thereby offering an important resource zone for exploitation.

At least 20 ceremonial sites in the Supe Valley, most of them quite large, all date to the Late Preceramic Period. These sites, especially Caral, have probably had more financial and human resources devoted to their study than all the other coastal Preceramic sites combined, so we know a fair amount about them. At the same time, however, our understanding of these sites is elusive because they often yield very few artifacts, which means that architectural features are the primary means by which we infer information about these large, imposing complexes.

One of the early Supe temple complexes is Aspero, located near the ocean at the mouth of the valley (see Figure 4.3).[14] There are 17 mounds spread over about 13 hectares (32 acres), built from a mix of adobes, stones, and mud mortar. Six of the mounds appear to be temple structures; Robert Feldman excavated three of them and a Peruvian team continues to excavate at the site in 2013. There is no clear patterning of the various sized mounds in relation to one another, although they are built on the slopes of coastal hills to aid in adding height to the structures. The slopes of many of the hills were artificially terraced as well, often with stone facings.

Figure 4.2 Map of Late Preceramic sites in Peru and Ecuador.

Figure 4.3 Late Preceramic Peru. Top: Two designs of Huaca Prieta textiles. Middle: Stone huaca from El Paraíso. Two views of biconvex, double-holed, red stone bead. Miniature *schicra* bag found with El Paraíso stone huaca. Drawing of figurine from Aspero wearing necklace of biconvex beads. Lower: Frowning Disc sculpture from Buena Vista. Huaca de los Idolos, Aspero.

Two major structures were investigated by Robert Feldman. The Huaca de los Idolos was a truncated pyramid with a central stairway leading to interconnected rooms, probably shrines, at the top of the structure and dating between (cal.) 2900 and 1970 BC. A cache of 13 unbaked clay figurines (5 to 14 cm tall) in a collection of baskets, mats, and plant and animal fur (possibly llama or guinea pig) was found in one of the many rooms on the huaca summit. Most of the figurines portray humans, although many are only fragments. The better preserved examples show figures with elaborate turbans and hairstyles, and some wear necklaces of distinctive, large, flat beads (see Figure 4.3).

The Huaca de los Sacrifícios also contained a series of rooms at its summit. Two burials, a two-month old infant and an (un-sexed) adult, were found in the floor of one room and are among the earliest known examples of Andean human sacrifice (or, at least, dedicatory burials). The adult was not well preserved, but the infant was elaborately interred in a basket with a beaded cap on its head, multiple wrappings of cotton textiles and reed mats, and with a large, four-legged grinding stone placed on top of the burial.

The site complex at Caral consists of 20 structures covering over 60 hectares (150 acres), some 14 km (9 mi) up the valley from Aspero and the coast.[15] Six large stone-built structures, ziggurat-like in form, cover the central part of the site. In most of them, a single chamber or set of small rooms is commonly at the top of the stairs and a circular, sunken plaza is often at the bottom. Unlike at Aspero there is clear site organization at Caral, with most of the main pyramids oriented around an empty space that could have served as a ceremonial plaza. Large standing stones, known in later times as *huancas* in Quechua, are in plazas oriented in relation to the temples, and one temple appears to have had a large fire pit that may have been a key component in rituals carried out there.

The Major Pyramid (*Pirámide Mayor*) is more than 1.6 hectares (4 acres) in area and 18 m (60 ft) high. The inference that festivals and ceremonies took place in these spaces was confirmed by the discovery of 32 condor and pelican bone flutes and 37 deer and llama bone cornets, incised with designs that appear to represent monkeys and birds. Unbaked clay figurines of people with elaborate hairstyles and hats, similar to those found at Aspero, have also been discovered.

While there are many early sites on the Central Coast of Peru, on the North Coast Ventarrón in the Lambayeque Valley is of particular interest due to its early murals.[16] The first temple there consisted of a large rectangular solid with curved corners, with a lower platform and access stairs at one of its narrow ends. At the top of the higher platform and to its rear, a rectangular, walled compound contained a two-tier platform at the back with the upper section apparently forming an altar-like area. At each side of the upper platform, short projecting walls narrowed the space seen from below. On these walls were murals of a deer caught in a net, imagery that was still popular in the region during the time of the Lambayeque culture, which depicted a similar scene on ceramics 3,000 years after Ventarrón.

The exterior of the compound walls was painted in broad stripes of red and white (coincidentally the colors of the flag of Peru), giving the structure its current name of the Red and White Temple (*Templo Rojo-Blanco*). A large hearth near the interior platforms was likely used in rituals carried out in these spaces. Skeletons of a monkey and a parrot at the site indicate contact with tropical regions, or else a more tropical environment for the local area at the time the site was occupied.

A second phase of construction increased the temple's area to 2,500 square m (27,000 square ft). This, the Green Temple (*Templo Verde*), consisted of three tiered platforms. Access to the rectangular temple at the top, built to a similar plan to that of the Red and White Temple, was by a side stairway to the first platform and then via central stairs to the upper level on one of the short sides. The upper platform was built with distinctive conical buttresses surrounding it, a unique design feature.

The Ventarrón site, while remarkable, stands alone in the Lambayeque Valley as a Late Preceramic temple; indeed, our knowledge of large cultural processes in the region is inhibited by a lack of comparison of the site with others on the North Coast. On the Central Coast, however, knowledge of many sites allows us to consider such issues.

The Late Preceramic site complex that has received the greatest attention on the Central Coast is El Paraíso on the old Chuquitanta hacienda in the lower Chillón Valley (see Figure 4.3).[17] Depending on how one counts, there are 9 or 10 major structures at the site. The two largest structures, each more than 300 m (984 ft) in length and 75 to 100 m (246 to 328 ft) in width, are parallel to each other, while additional structures form a U-pattern around a large space that could have served as a plaza.

Unit I is relatively small compared to many other structures, but it may have had an important role due to its location at the center of the base of the U-shape. Its upper floor plan was organized into two relatively separate sections, one that may have consisted of residential or administrative rooms and another suite of ceremonial spaces. The main ceremonial chamber in Unit I had a rectangular sunken pit with a fire-reddened floor and a large, charcoal-filled, circular pit at each corner. A niche in a wall in a nearby room held a large stone resembling a human torso and painted red. This, an early example of a small *huaca*, was accompanied by gourd bowls filled with various plants as well as a small version of a *shicra* bag filled not with stones but rather with cakes of lime wrapped in leaves (see Figure 4.3).

There are many other Late Preceramic monumental complexes in the Chillón and other Central Coast valleys. Some show the U-shaped arrangement, such as Salamanquejo, just a few kilometers inland from El Paraíso, while others do not take this form, such as Buena Vista further up the valley.[18] The latter site is remarkable for a large adobe sculpture of what appears to be one of those yellow Happy Faces turned very grouchy, flanked by two mythological deer-like creatures. This Menacing God appears to have been the main deity of Buena Vista, and its shrine, as well as the site in general, was oriented towards various astronomical events, as were others among these Late Preceramic complexes. In addition, the site was "decommissioned" by ceremonial burial, a practice also seen in the sand covering at Río Seco and one that was continued in later prehistory as well.[19]

There were probably many different gods at these various centers. In contrast to the Menacing God of Buena Vista, a large beast that some have interpreted as a stylized feline was modeled on the central stairs of a temple at Punkurí in the Nepeña Valley.[20] The remnants of this temple are relatively small, only 3,000 square m in area and 8 m high. However, the feline and other temple features such as columns and walls were all painted in bright colors and with both natural motifs, such as crabs, as well as supernatural ones. Dated to (cal.) 2200 to 1800 BC, many of its construction and decorative techniques appear to have continued in the subsequent Initial Period in the nearby Casma Valley.

There are many other Late Preceramic monumental site complexes throughout Peru. It is interesting to consider that while we have the remains of what appear to be deities in murals and sculpture at some sites, at others they are entirely absent. This may be partly the result of better preservation at one site than another, or it may be that the gods of some sites were in the form of statues or other objects that were removed when the site was decommissioned. While the deities appear to have taken different forms and thus probably represented local gods, there is a surprisingly similar form of architecture over wide areas, although with notable exceptions such as the rather unique (for now) constructions at Ventarrón.

The concentration of large Late Preceramic architectural complexes on the Central and North coasts of Peru is also noteworthy. This appears to be more than simply the product of where research has been concentrated. For example, there are very few such sites on the South Coast even though that region has been the subject of intensive archaeological study for many years. While the tropical forest, especially western Ecuador, may have been "precocious" in the early phases of the Late Preceramic, the Central and North coasts of Peru were especially busy places soon after. The reasons for this have been the subject of a considerable amount of discussion for some time.

CULTURAL DYNAMICS IN THE LATE PRECERAMIC ANDES: THE MARITIME FOUNDATIONS OF ANDEAN CIVILIZATION

In 1975 Michael E. Moseley published a small book, the thesis of which is still being discussed today.[21] He claimed that the great ceremonial centers built along the Central Coast of Peru in the Late Preceramic Period, and the societies that built them, were founded on the rich maritime resources of the coast of Peru and not on maize agriculture. This was quite a startling proposition for two reasons. First, grain agriculture was thought to have been the key to early civilizations in the Old World and in Mexico, so a maritime foundation in Peru would seem to run counter to this general pattern. Second, Moseley did not claim that it was some other kind of agriculture that helped to produce Andean civilization, but that it was resources completely provided by nature—gathered and fished—that served as the foundations of civilization. The food offered by the Humboldt Current and the Pacific shoreline was so abundant and so dependable that it was sufficient to support highly complex societies with great amounts of leisure time to build huge ceremonial centers. This was quite a challenge to prevailing notions of the origins of civilization.

Considerable debate followed Moseley's presentation of his thesis, and there were slight changes in the arguments made by both sides over the following decade as the discussions continued. For example, Moseley shifted his emphasis from shellfish and seafood in general to the great quantities of food available in the form of small fish such as anchovies and sardines. On the other side, some scholars insisted that maize must have been crucial to support Late Preceramic societies, while others suggested that it must have been other terrestrial foods or their combination with maritime resources that were critical. In fact, very little research had been done on subsistence economies around the large Late Preceramic ceremonial complexes when the debate began, although the controversy did stir archaeologists to investigate the issue more fully and carefully.

Much of the early debate on the relative importance of marine versus terrestrial resources was based on the assumption that the key land-based food was maize or corn, because it was known to have been so important in Mesoamerican civilizations and was grown in quantity by the Inca when the Spanish arrived in the sixteenth century. The search for the earliest maize has thus taken on a special status in the Andes. As noted in the previous chapter, maize phytoliths were found at the Vegas Site in Ecuador. While there were concerns that they may have migrated into early deposits through the soil, further studies supported the interpretation that the phytoliths were indeed valid indicators of domesticated maize at the site.[22] Recently, however, even earlier evidence for maize in the Central Andes has been found at Huaca Prieta, and a Preceramic component at the nearby site of Paredones has yielded radiocarbon dates indicating that a popcorn variety was in use there (cal .) *circa* 8800 to 8500 BP.[23] Another project identified pollen and starch grains in soil samples, tool residues, and coprolite contents at Late Preceramic (*circa* 3000 to 1800 BC) sites in the Fortaleza Valley, leading researchers to suggest that maize was widely grown and constituted a main component of the diet throughout the period.[24] However, no plant parts have been found in any excavations associated with the samples from which the microfossil remains were recovered.

Current evidence suggests that maize was present in Ecuador and Peru at a fairly early time, but that it was not a major component of diets. If it had been important it would be in evidence in many forms with cobs, stems, and leaves in abundance, but it simply is not. Maize did not become a staple crop in the Central Andes until well after Chavín, and at present it is only clearly a major dietary component in parts of the Inca Empire.[25] Irrigation and monument building in Peru and other regions thus developed without maize as an essential or even an important ingredient.

It is worth noting that the discussion of the "foundations" of Andean civilization is part of a long-standing debate in Peruvian archaeology between the relative importance of the coast and the highlands. In the 1930s and 1940s the *serrano* (highlander) Julio C. Tello argued for the priority of ancient mountain cultures, while Rafael Larco Hoyle argued in favor of coastal cultures. This kind of thinking still exists today in arguments about the "first" site that yields evidence for the earliest known use of one or more kinds of agriculture, irrigation, large-scale construction, and so forth. The "first" evidence, however, is less important than is the first point at which there is good evidence of the fairly *widespread* use of the item or practice in question, because only then can such new ways of doing things be seen as having had an effect on cultures in general.

After much research, Moseley's general argument has been supported in that the rich marine resources did seem to provide abundant and reliable food allowing the elaboration of other cultural expressions. While marine resources at the coast were a foundation, however, it was the eventual addition of agricultural resources that guaranteed a culture's success. So too, the coast or highlands—or, as we have seen, the tropical forest—might have become socially or politically complex without the need for contact with the other major region, but it was the combination of them that was crucial to the eventual development of the dazzling cultures of the ancient Central Andes later in prehistory.

The "Maritime Debate" tended to focus on issues of protein sources, since these are often in short supply for foragers.[26] However, coastal Peru differs from other regions in that fish and mollusks provide great amounts of protein and are relatively easily procured. When the first studies were done, starches seemed to be rare in the Preceramic larder. Beans, squashes, and a few examples of the remains of some tubers and roots were found at a few sites, but otherwise fruits (*lucuma* [*Pouteria lucuma*], *pacae* [*Inga feuillei*]) were the most easily identifiable carbohydrate sources, largely because they could be identified through pits, rinds, and other non-edible residues.[27] Thus, the amount of carbohydrates in Preceramic diets was hard to estimate, while it was recognized that tubers and roots would usually have been consumed completely and therefore left few to no remains.

New techniques are able to identify microscopic starch grains that are preserved over long periods of time. A team of scholars working at Buena Vista in the Chillón Valley have used this technique, scraping the interiors of bowls made from gourds and squashes and identifying arrowroot (*Maranta arundinacea*), manioc (*Manihot esculenta*), chili peppers (*Capsicum sp.*) and possibly potato (*Soalnum sp.*).[28] Although manioc and chili peppers were already known to be part of Late Preceramic diets, the study suggests that they and the other plants were domesticated and locally grown. A similar study has been carried out for the succeeding Initial Period that also demonstrates that agriculture was complex and well developed at a very early time on the coast.[29]

Thus, if the "precocity" of coastal Peru was due to rich maritime resources, that foundation must be seen as having been laid in the Middle Preceramic or even earlier, because by the Late Preceramic high protein seafood was already fully complemented by a well developed agricultural system. That subsistence base included plants grown not only for food, but also for clothing and technology.

Cotton was an extremely important agricultural product on the coast. Michael Moseley pointed out that two of the earliest domesticated plants were "industrial" products—cotton for making fish nets and lines, and gourds for net floats—while the third, chili pepper, was a seasoning that is still an important ingredient in the classic Peruvian dish of *ceviche*, marinated, uncooked fish. Cotton was not only used for nets but also for textiles, thereby serving as a conveyor of symbolism according to religious and social values.

Once thought to have been first domesticated in the Old World, research by James Vreeland has demonstrated conclusively that cotton is native to Peru and that small-scale farmers on the North Coast have maintained a 5,000-year-old tradition of growing native cotton there.[30] However, the earliest archaeologically discovered cotton is from Ecuador, not Peru, found at Real Alto and dated to between 3500 and 2500 BC.[31] Although Ecuador has the earliest cotton, however, the earliest textiles are from coastal Peru where preservation is better.

Gossypium barbadense L. S. sp. peruvianum grows as a large bush or small tree up to 3 m (10 ft) high, and it produces cotton for as long as five years. The fibers are not only white, but also come in shades of cream, tan, dark brown, a light lilac, and even a shade of green. Cotton is so important that a few archaeologists refer to some sites as dating to the "Cotton Preceramic Period" rather than Late Preceramic Peru. While this is a handy way to distinguish certain sites from others, Junius Bird warned long ago that because cotton was used at different times in different places the term lacks precision, and so it will not be used here.[32]

Huaca Prieta was one of the first sites excavated with the intent to understand the Preceramic Period.[33] Among the most important discoveries made there in 1946–47 by Bird was the recovery of decorated cotton textiles and two decorated gourds found in burials associated with an apparent residential occupation (see Figure 4.3). Careful analysis of the patterns of twining revealed that some of the elements composing the textiles had been colored and manipulated to produce geometric designs as well as striking images. The latter included a snake in the belly of a condor that probably expressed a myth, while another showed a pair of crabs arranged in a design motif that was used late into prehistory. The Huaca Prieta gourds were small containers that were carved in designs that are quite similar to imagery found on Valdivia ceramics, and for many years it was suggested that this indicated long-distance contact between the coast of Peru and Ecuador. More recent studies suggest that there was a widespread art style that was common from the North Coast of Peru to Ecuador, as expressed in textiles and gourds at several sites including La Galgada, Huaca Prieta, and Valdivia occupations (see Figure 4.2).[34]

With regard to gourds, while evidence now suggests that Paleoindians may have come to the New World already knowing about gourd domestication, gourd growing remained important. The Peruvian archaeologist Gabriel Prieto believes that Preceramic peoples used methods to influence the final shapes to suit their own needs as gourds were growing, probably by binding them in forms of some sort.[35]

Early reports by the Spanish noted that communities on the coast were highly specialized. There were fisher-folk living close to the shore who offered maritime and coastal resources to people living further up the valleys, who would exchange agricultural produce with the coastal populations. Could a similar division into specialties have been in place five millennia or so earlier? Suggestions have been made that an important reason for the location of the large Late Preceramic architectural complexes close to river floodplains or easily irrigated lands was to grow cotton, which could be then exchanged with specialized fisher-folk on the coast and perhaps traded up-valley to the highlands. Indeed, this may have been a key reason why large Late Preceramic architectural complexes were developed.[36] However, Prieto has found that cotton can be grown within a stone's throw of the beach by tapping into the relatively high fresh water table, at least on the North Coast.[37] This means that fishing communities could have been self-sufficient in growing their own cotton—and other plants as well, for that matter.

If cotton was an important product of the architectural complexes, then perhaps it was specifically raised to trade with highland communities. Like most large, important places, the grand architectural centers of coastal Peru were probably built and prospered through a combination of economic advantage and the prestige gained through their renown as important cultural places. In ancient societies, that prestige often took the form of religious symbolism and ceremony.

THE KOTOSH RELIGIOUS TRADITION

La Galgada is an architectural complex in the Tablachaca canyon, on a tributary of the Santa River. Research there led by Terence Grieder and Alberto Bueno Mendoza revealed much about Late Preceramic societies (see Figure 4.4).[38] The La Galgada complex consisted of two main structures apparently of the same form, although one was slightly larger than the other. In addition, a circular sunken court was constructed at the bottom of the stairway belonging to the larger structure.

Research was concentrated mostly in the larger mound. The edifice consisted of a series of stacked terraces with rounded corners and a central staircase, with small buildings at the summit. Extensive excavations in this complex found that the architecture was built up over time, as ceremonial chambers were converted into tombs with new ceremonial rooms built on top of them (see Figure 4.4).

The burials in these chambers are among the most elaborate Preceramic interments ever encountered, but they do not suggest that the social system at La Galgada was highly stratified. Both men and women were wrapped in various textiles and buried with their personal jewelry. The latter mostly consisted of large bone pins that look like precursors to the *tupus* of later times, which were used to pin shawls together. They had large, flat, circular ends often inlaid with green stone (chrysacola or sodalite). Large, flat, double-holed, biconvex beads of the kind shown on the Aspero figurines, made of a distinct red stone—a compacted ferruginous diatomite—were found with the burials, as well as beads of the same form made of *Spondylus princeps,* the red shell from Ecuadorian waters. In addition, small square, blue stone beads like those found on a hat from one of the Aspero burials were also discovered at La Galgada.

Small carved stone bowls, carved shell pendants and beads, and small wooden tools were among the other La Galgada grave goods. Cotton textiles were similar to those found at Huaca Prieta, showing similar design motifs. The age range of the individuals and the fact that both men and women were buried in the chambers suggests that La Galgada society was organized on the basis of extended families, rather than on a highly organized system separate from family ties.

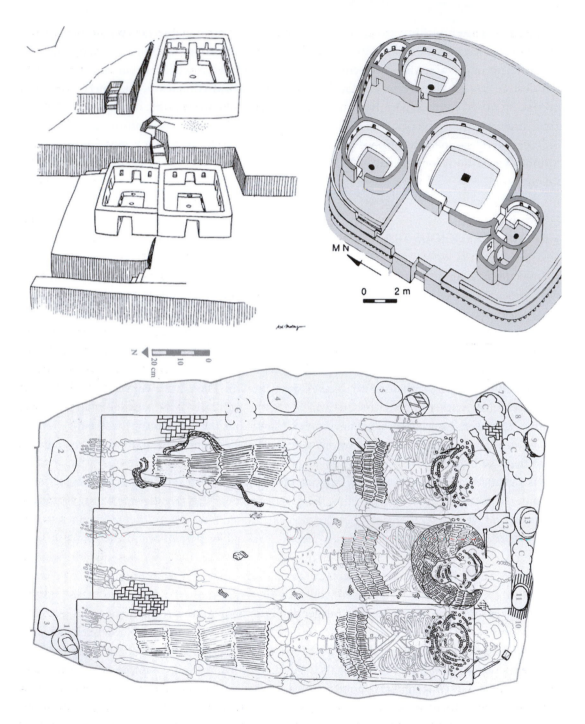

Figure 4.4 The Kotosh religious tradition. Top left: Artist's interpretation of chambers at Kotosh. Top right: Artist's interpretation of Kotosh-style chambers at La Galgada. Bottom: La Galgada high status burials.

The La Galgada researchers suggest that the site location attracted settlers because conditions allowed for extensive irrigation agriculture. The area was also important in exchange systems between the coast and the highlands, and a local mountain peak may have had sacred significance. The profile of the mountain today can be viewed as a recumbent female form, probably making it an *apu*, an ancestor mountain, perhaps representing *Pachamama* (Mother Earth).

A survey of the middle section of the canyon found 11 sites in a 10 km (6 mi) wide section that was well suited for irrigation agriculture. The sites were of various sizes and were also probably of different functions. More than one of the sites was likely a ceremonial center similar to La Galgada, with many residential occupations nearby as well. The researchers note that many of these sites were occupied into the Initial Period, as was La Galgada. In the subsequent Early Horizon, however, the major center of the area shifted to the site of Castillo de Cocabal, in the smaller but highly fertile Ancos River Valley, a tributary of the Tablachaca.

Small chambers like the ones at La Galgada were first identified at Kotosh, from which the concept of the Kotosh Religious Tradition gets its name (see Figure 4.4). The Kotosh site is high on the eastern slopes of the Andes in the Huallaga River Basin, and a University of Tokyo expedition conducting research there discovered a particularly striking chamber that included not only a sunken pit with a central fire, but also niches above the surrounding bench (see Figure 4.4).[39] In the Temple of the Crossed Hands (*Templo de Las Manos Cruzados*) crossed arms modeled in plaster were made underneath niches flanking an entryway, with one set exhibiting right-arm-over-left-arm and the other left-over-right, interpreted as male and female respectively and expressing concepts of dualism.

Huaricoto, near Huaraz in the Central Highlands of Peru, is yet another site with layers of chambers built one over the other through time, as in the aforementioned cases.[40] The reasons why old chambers were abandoned and new chambers built are not clear. Since there is no evidence that the rooms lost their functionality it is more likely that some social force was at work—perhaps the end of a family line that had maintained a particular chamber over the generations. At Huaricoto chambers were first built in the Late Preceramic Period, but new ones continued to be constructed there through the Early Horizon.

The many sites with similar ritual chambers on the eastern and western slopes of the Andes and in the Central Highlands of Peru indicate that the religious system that used these structures was widespread. According to Richard Burger and Lucy Salazar, this Kotosh Religious Tradition was a religious system followed by ordinary people, existing outside the large temple complexes such as Caral and El Paraíso.[41]

A particular social unit, whether a family or a sodality (i.e. a "club"), probably built, maintained, and used an individual chamber. The round-to-square interiors of these kiva-like structures suggest that the people who participated in the rituals were of relatively equal status, since there would be little in the seating arrangement to distinguish between high or low ranking members. The niches may simply have been handy places to keep items used in ceremonies; at Kotosh seeds and clay figurines were found in them, and some niches may have held cult statues.

The plaster hands in the Temple of the Crossed Hands seem to suggest there may have been something like heads in the niches above them.

At the center of every Kotosh Religious Tradition chamber is a small hearth with an elaborate sub-floor ventilation system that kept air flowing to the pit. The Kotosh Religious Tradition thus involved a ritual that focused on a central fire in an enclosed room. Grouped together in the confines of a small chamber, rituals around the central hearth would certainly have promoted a sense of group solidarity.

While it may have been a separate "Little Tradition" practiced by common folk, the fact that the buildings of the Kotosh Religious Tradition shared architectural features with larger sites suggests that the "Great Traditions" of the large ceremonial centers partook of similar ideas and practices.[42] For example, it is interesting that the terraces of the main temple at La Galgada replicate the rounded corners of the small ritual chambers contained within the terrace platforms themselves, an expression of a continuity between the micro- and the macro-scales. This is another Andean concept that is seen repeatedly in later prehistory.

Of course, this micro–macro relationship is not unique to the Andes. Furthermore, it is also common that in many cultures the large temples and pyramids of the élite represent elaborations of religious concepts and practices that had their origins in egalitarian societies. In this recurring combination of various ideas and practices, some of which are shared by many other cultures and others that are quite specific to the Andes, we can see a distinct form of Andean civilization.

In summary, in the Late Preceramic Period there was a shared set of common architectural features consisting of terraced buildings with central staircases, often with sunken circular plazas at the bottom, existing over a wide area of the Central Coast of Peru.[43] Furthermore, these sites were built using similar construction techniques, such as the employment of shicra fill and building with stone masonry without the use of mortar.

There were local and regional variations in how the basic building blocks of ceremonial architecture were configured. The degree to which these variations represent differences in religious, social, or political systems is hard to assess. The chief differences between sites and regions seem to be less in the forms of buildings than in the way in which they were laid out in relation to one another. We cannot at present assess whether these differences were due to deliberate planning of ceremonial centers, or whether they simply grew through time. For example, the early site complex of Aspero seems to have been built to make the most of the local hills to give height to the structures, and formal relationships between the temples appear to have been a low priority. However, Caral appears to have been built according to the concept of a central plaza-like space surrounded by temples on a quadrangular plan. El Paraíso is based on a similar pattern to Caral, with the exception that no circular sunken plazas have yet been identified at the site. Also, one end of El Paraíso's rectangular plan is open, suggesting that it was a precursor to the U-shaped temple complexes of the Initial Period.

The terraces-and-sunken-plaza arrangement of the Central Coast seems to have been less popular further north. Although we do not have many examples of early North Coast architecture, Ventarrón consists of a single large massive block as a temple, and it is built of local clays rather than stone. Are these differences due to different sized supporting populations, or do they represent distinct architectural (and therefore religious) traditions? Central staircases and sunken plazas (although they are not circular) point to an underlying shared concept of what a temple should be, despite differences in the details, but only further research will clarify this issue.

At the same time that large ceremonial centers were being built, the Kotosh Religious Tradition was also practiced at less impressive sites. Such simpler structures can be found near the Paloma Site as noted in the previous chapter, at Huaynuná, close to the Casma Valley, and scattered at or near numerous small habitation sites throughout the coastal region, including on the South Coast where large-scale Late Preceramic architectural complexes are absent.[44] Elsewhere or at different times many large sites may not have followed the Kotosh Religious Tradition at all. Río Seco, already mentioned, consists of two large pyramids and many relatively small platform constructions with refuse surrounding them, suggesting that the site was mostly residential. Las Haldas, just south of the Casma Valley, also differs from the Central Coast complexes: it consists of a linear arrangement of large rectangular platforms and plazas with quadrangular sunken courts. Once thought to be mostly Late Preceramic, the site is now considered to be mostly Initial Period but it is likely that its basic format was established in the Preceramic era.[45]

SOCIETY AND POLITICS IN THE LATE PRECERAMIC PERIOD

What were the social roles of these massive architectural complexes? Ruth Shady, the director of research at Caral, has suggested that the site represents the world's first state, city, and civilization. Caral and other Late Preceramic architectural complexes certainly represent a considerable marshaling of human resources to build and maintain them. Such sites probably drew many people to them for religious festivals, and these same people may have contributed their labor to help build the massive structures. The number of possible domestic structures at Caral is far fewer than the number of people needed to erect the structures, and thus the construction could be interpreted to imply the existence of a hierarchical society. We can consider the socio-political roles of the architectural complexes by focusing on how the sites may have been used and the distribution of the sites on the landscape, and by considering the regional styles of the complexes.

Four large sites that have been studied in detail—Ventarrón, Caral, Río Seco, and El Paraíso—offer opportunities for comparisons. At Ventarrón and Caral, where excavation projects have been large and long-term, all the major constructions can reasonably be interpreted as ceremonial spaces and temples. At El Paraíso, Unit I, the most extensively studied structure, contains ceremonial rooms and a section that could have combined ceremony, residence, and possibly some kind of administrative function. Tracing the pattern of walls and corridors in the largest constructions at El Paraíso revealed rooms that may have been residential, but minimal excavation in them means that they cannot be conclusively interpreted as such.[46] At Caral, some small rooms next to the bottom of the terrace temples have been interpreted as residences, perhaps for priests or similar officials, and these are somewhat analogous to similar rooms found in the western sector of Unit I at El Paraíso.

Few studies have been carried out to determine if there were residences outside the core of the ceremonial centers, in locales where we might expect to find the support personnel for the priests who lived within the stone-built complexes. There also is very little information on domestic sites outside the ceremonial centers. Small fishing villages along the shores of the Lurín-Rímac-Chillón valleys, studied by Lanning, Patterson, and Moseley, in research that led to the Maritime Hypothesis, are among the few examples of populations outside the central locations, but these are not particularly impressive as towns; at best they are more like small hamlets.

Estimating population sizes at the large ceremonial centers is difficult because we cannot easily determine how much space was devoted to residences and how much to ceremonial activities. In one of the few attempts to determine population size Wendt estimated that between 2,500 and 3,000 people had been buried around the platforms at Río Seco.[47] However, the overall impression is that populations at large centers and in the outlying communities associated with them greatly increased between the time of the Middle and Late Preceramic Periods.[48]

The best example we have of a medium-sized Late Preceramic community is the Asia I site in the Omas Valley, about 100 km (62 mi) south of Lima (see Figure 4.5).[49] Asia I is on the north bank of the river among a cluster of other mounds, some of which are also Late Preceramic in date. Unit I was a low, circular mound, in which Frédéric Engel's excavations uncovered a 12 × 12.5 m (39 × 41 ft) stone-and-adobe-walled compound with interior rooms. Forty sub-floor graves were found in the structure. In many ways, burial customs were quite similar to those in Paloma: bodies were flexed, wrapped in one or more reed mats, and accompanied by a few goods probably used in life such as clothing (belts, mantles, ropes), gourd bowls, baskets, and miscellaneous items such as textile bags, pins, sticks, bone spatulas, bead necklaces and pendants. However, there was enough deterioration of organic materials that clothing on skeletons did not preserve well, although there was evidence that skull deformation and trephination (cutting sections out of the skull) were practiced.

Overall, there were more items of material culture found at Asia I than at earlier sites probably because the people living at Asia I formed a more sedentary community. Preserved items included wooden spears, fiber slings, a spear-thrower, and wooden trays. Two small tablets, one of baked and the other of unbaked clay, were decorated with beads and the insertion of pyrite in their centers. These served as mirrors, not to look into but to reflect light, and they were probably used in religious rites as may have been the case for quartz crystals found at Paloma. Long-distance exchange is indicated by the presence of obsidian, occurring naturally only in the distant highlands, although there were only a few examples of this volcanic stone found at Asia I.

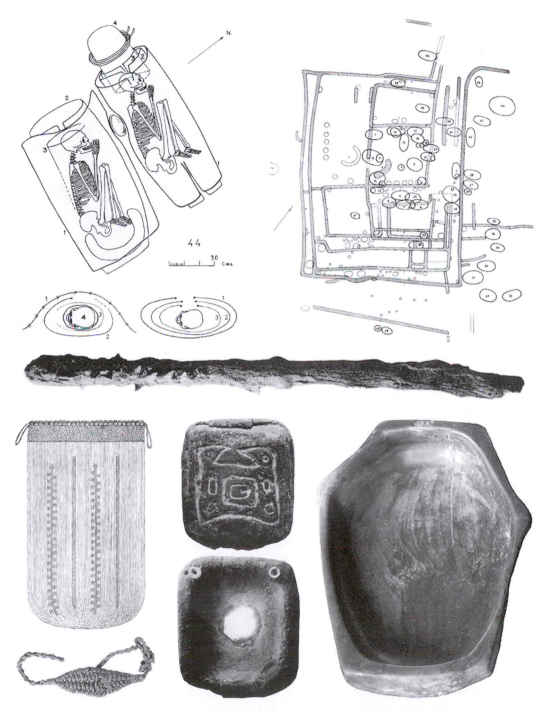

Figure 4.5 Asia I. Top left: Burials with multiple wrappings. Top right: Map of main structure showing location of burials and pits (ovals). Center: Fish-tooth-studded club. Lower left: Bag, sling, baked clay with pyrite mirror (lower) and incised birds (upper) on back, wooden tray.

The Asia I inhabitants had a wide-ranging subsistence economy that included horticulture, with the most calories probably coming from beans and fruits, although starch studies like those recently carried out for Buena Vista are not available. Various grass seeds were collected, as well as many varieties of shellfish. Fish caught by hook (*Corvina* [sea bass], *Sciaena gilberti*) and net (*Engraulis ringens*, anchovies) were important foods. The most common mammal bones were from sea lions (*Arctocephalus australis* or *Otaria flavescens*), with only a few bones recovered from deer or camelids.

The lives of the people of Asia I were not entirely peaceful. In addition to projectile points, slings, and spears, a stout stick with fish (possibly shark) teeth embedded in its distal end was likely used for fighting, not for hunting (see Figure 4.5). Two burials lacked heads, suggesting that they had been lost in fights, the earliest evidence of trophy-head taking, while four pits with one or more mat-wrapped heads without bodies were found, as were several "burials" that included mats and offerings but no bodies. These remains suggest that there was inter-communal violence in the Late Preceramic Period. The degree of violence is hard to assess and would require a detailed study of the rest of the skeletons to search for evidence of wounds.

Some of the other mounds in the vicinity of Asia I may cover ceremonial structures, but there is no large-scale, monumental architecture like that at sites from Lima northwards; the Omas Valley is in the region, previously described, where coastal uplift and entrenching of rivers is more severe than to the north.

However, the size of the monumental complexes implies that there must have been fairly large populations in the valleys where they are located. There are a number of issues as yet unresolved with regard to this. First, the large sites grew over time and many of them were occupied for centuries. A relatively small number of people could have added new floors or even significantly remodeled an entire structure within a single generation. The same is true for the astounding number of ceremonial sites known for some areas, such as the Supe Valley. The great numbers of sites may be due to the palimpsest effect of sites being used and then abandoned over hundreds of years in the Late Preceramic and Initial Periods.

Another consideration is the way in which people tend to use the land in the Andes. It is a long-standing pattern that at least in relatively peaceful times, settlements were established just off the edge of irrigated fields. Non-irrigated lands in the Late Preceramic Period, where people probably lived, may have been swept away or buried by later, larger canal systems and the fields that they watered. Whatever the case, the number of known Late Preceramic domestic communities is far smaller than we would expect given the number and nature of the large ceremonial complexes on the Central and North Central coasts. Lack of data on such settlements frustrates attempts to estimate population density and to identify the presence or absence of different kinds of sites—or site hierarchies—that could help to determine the nature of socio-political systems.

One of the most explicit signs of socio-political organization is mortuary data. All of the relatively few Late Preceramic burials suggest comparatively low degrees of political and social hierarchy. The few burials that we have from the period suggest that power was distributed among families or possibly sodalities, rather than concentrated in the hands of a few chiefs or nobles. The best and largest example of this is at La Galgada. None of the burials there could be considered to represent a single locus of power such as a paramount chief. All the archaeological sites discussed to this point were relatively egalitarian communities in which status and power were, for the most part, achieved rather than ascribed.

The numerous kiva-like chambers of the Kotosh Religious Tradition, as seen at sites such as Kotosh, Huaricoto, and La Galgada, indicate that there were multiple groups who participated in rituals at such centers, eventually burying some of their dead at them by converting their ceremonial chambers into tombs. The fact that there are many chamber-tombs at such sites, and that none seem to stand out from the others in terms of their size, elaboration, or contents, is further evidence to suggest a relatively egalitarian socio-political system.

We do not have a clear understanding of whether the people buried in these tombs lived close by or were brought from somewhere in the surrounding region for burial at a Kotosh Religious Tradition center. It seems most likely that the areal distribution of participants was fairly wide simply because we must assume that domestic sites would have been widely dispersed, situated near agricultural fields, on beaches, and at other places where the people made their living. Perhaps only a few members of communities were buried in the central chambers, with the rest of the dead being interred in more modest graves closer to home. Those individuals who were honored with burial at a temple site may have been the heads of family groups, or, as mentioned earlier, they may have been members of religious or club-like organizations that cut across family ties. Genetic or dental studies of the occupants of chambers could aid in clarifying this issue, but to date no such analyses have been undertaken.

If the people who were buried at the Kotosh centers were brought from various outlying communities to be interred at them, it follows that while the chambers were operating as ceremonial rooms those same people came from afar to participate in rituals there. Some complexes, such as Huaricoto, remained relatively small, while others, like La Galgada, grew into large, important centers with elaborate and impressive architecture. At present it can only be speculated as to why centers were established at one place and not others, and why some prospered while others did not. Central nodes in regional systems usually serve multiple purposes and successful ones serve those purposes well. La Galgada, for example, was probably a link in long-distance exchange systems. A combination of population growth, trade and prosperity among the regional supporting communities, and success in religious activities at the center (which probably included economic exchanges) likely resulted in the growth of centers like Kotosh or La Galgada.

If the Late Preceramic architectural complexes were not cities or states and if political systems were not hierarchical, then how might we conceive of the ways in which society was organized and the roles these complexes played in their own times? Rather than consider the centers as nodes in a political system from which power flowed outwards, we might consider them as loci that pulled people and resources towards them. In other words, these ceremonial complexes may have been the result of the efforts of pilgrims, traders, and others who came to them with their devotions, labors, and goods, as well as local populations living nearby who felt an allegiance to their local ceremonial center.

While there may have been relatively low levels of socio-political hierarchy in the Late Preceramic Period and most politics were locally based, nevertheless there was incipient hierarchy in the making. There was a common value system for certain prestige items. The most distinctive of these are the tabular, biconvex, double-holed beads made of either red diatomite or red *Spondylus princeps* shell (see Figure 4.3). Beads made of the red stone are more common than those of shell, and we may speculate that the overwhelming popularity of the mollusk in later prehistory was not shared in the Late Preceramic, and that it only replaced diatomite in value as time passed. Sources of the stone remain to be discovered.

As noted previously, the distinctive double-holed beads are known at several sites: Aspero, Badurria, Río Seco, and La Galgada. That they were highly valued and may have circulated among an emerging élite is supported by the depiction of necklaces of these beads on Aspero figurines. Small blue-green beads of sodalite or chrysacola, a relative of turquoise, may also have been prestige goods.

How widespread and how longlasting the biconvex bead interaction sphere may have been is unknown. Known sites that have yielded beads cluster between the Chancay and the Santa valleys, a linear distance of 250 km (155 mi) along the coast. The architectural formats of the sites in question are generally similar, suggesting that a common plan was followed at each site, although with local variations incorporated. The degree to which this system stretched beyond the known region cannot be estimated at present, mostly because research at most Late Preceramic sites has always been on a small scale, especially given their large sizes. Thus, for example, we cannot determine whether or not El Paraíso lacks these beads and was outside the interaction sphere. Were the beads and other items part of the paraphernalia of the Kotosh Religious Tradition, or part of a related but separate religious system, or did they transcend regions? This and many other issues remain to be investigated in future research.

Among other items that may have been used to denote special status are inlaid bone needles, stone mortars, pestles, and cups, and the ever-important textiles. The hats or headdresses and skirts on figurines as well as the presence of fancy textiles in the La Galgada tombs, and similar figurines found at Caral, all suggest that decorated textiles were markers of high status in the Late Preceramic Period. The most complete Aspero figurine that displays a necklace of biconvex beads also exhibits a large belt, or possibly a rolled top of a skirt (see Figure 4.3). This style may have demonstrated that the wearer had a great quantity of textiles at his or her disposal, and it would have been another sign of status.

Presumably there must have been a contingent of resident priests and other officials to maintain the ceremonial sites from day to day, but they appear not to have had social roles that gave them power over those who came to use such centers. Perhaps they were more like the staff at a country club than powerful priests at a church. Power appears to have stayed in the hands of the people who came to use the facilities and not in the hands of those who hosted them. Of course, we must expect that there was considerable variation in how these social roles developed and changed in particular places over time. There were variations in the expression of the Kotosh Religious Tradition to such an extent that in some places it may have developed into quite a different system altogether, much like Protestantism developed out of Catholicism. El Paraíso may be one such example of this, and perhaps Caral became a much more complex system than others, as its excavator Ruth Shady claims. In general, however, the picture we have of Late Preceramic Peru is one of large ceremonial complexes with relatively simple societies building and supporting them.

ASSESSING THE LATE PRECERAMIC CENTRAL ANDES

The Central Andes between 2500 and 1500 BC was a highly complex world in which an abundance of natural resources coupled with the energies of many people resulted in a rich cultural landscape. However, a full appreciation of that world is constrained by the great length of time that separates it from our own era, the subsequent erasure of many of its achievements, and the relatively tiny amount of research that has exposed some of that richness.

We have comparatively detailed views of certain regions, while some of the more extreme environments appear to have been relatively under populated at this early time. The intense amount of work that has been carried out in southwestern Ecuador, for example, reveals a steady growth in population, the adoption or invention of many practices or things, and the expression of beliefs that were or which became widespread and of long duration. However, it is unlikely that this part of the continent was exceptional. Rather, it is probably characteristic of successful adaptations to varying local conditions throughout the tropical forest region. On the coast of Peru, the rich waters of the Humboldt Current provided different resources in kind and quantity than the tropical forest, but the river valleys, especially on the North and Central Coasts, probably did not differ greatly in the resources they provided in comparison with the more forested regions of Ecuador and the Amazon.

Within western South America the marginal zones—high altitude punas and deserts with small or few river valleys—were not densely occupied, and consequently sedentism, domestication, and temple building began later. These late-developing areas are mostly in the southern Central Andes, the Bolivian Altiplano, the Atacama Desert, and other places that had similar extreme environments. This perspective must be tempered with the understanding that some regions that might appear to us as marginal may not have been thought so by ancient Andean people. A prime example of this is intermontane valleys with altitudes of 3,000 m (around 10,000 ft) or so. These places are not considered as particularly high by *serranos* today, even though they are challenging to lowlanders, and this view likely pertained in the remote past also.

James B. Richardson III and Daniel Sandweiss posed a question as to the timing of the emergence of the Late Preceramic monumental architectural complexes on the Central Coast of Peru.[50] If maritime resources were critical to the rise of such systems and the resources were always there, why didn't earlier fisher-folk build big temple mounds? Although data are relatively scarce, the evidence suggests that from about (cal.) 8800 to 5800 BP, during the Middle Preceramic Period, El Niño events were absent or extremely rare. From about (cal.) 5800 to 3200 BP, El Niño events occurred infrequently, probably every 50 to 100 years. As described earlier, this happened when the boundary between the environmental regime fostered by the Humboldt Current and the warmer waters of the Panamanian system shifted northwards, from near Ostra and Almejas, to the modern boundary near Siches.[51] In other words, the change occurred when modern environmental conditions were established with the Humboldt Current running parallel to most of the coast of Peru.

The biotic change that came with the Humboldt Current was the increase in the number of small schooling fish, the anchovies and sardines that occupy lower trophic levels than the fish associated with warmer waters. The fact that these fish came with the Humboldt and its associated El Niño events starting around (cal.) 5800 BP thus appears to be a critical factor not only in why coastal Peru achieved such complexity, but also in the timing of the area's development, and it serves to support Michael Moseley's "Maritime Hypothesis."

However, it is likely that the appearance of abundant, small schooling fish was not the only factor in the development of complexity on the Peruvian coast. The availability of other resources and the development of irrigation farming that allowed for the raising of crops, providing raw materials for fishing equipment as well as carbohydrates to accompany the proteins and fats gained from fish, also were very important. If the fish played such a critical role in the development of ceremonial centers, this fact may also explain why political hierarchies did not emerge with great strength. Fish resources were a gift of the sea, of *Mamacocha*, to use the Inca term for the sea goddess, and they could not be controlled in the same way as the agricultural fields or the irrigation waters that fed them. Any claims by temple priests to appease or convince the gods to bring or to keep the fish in abundance were probably weak and only partly convincing bases for political power, unlike the command of irrigation canals in later times.

Many cultural patterns that would persist to the time of the arrival of Europeans and beyond were already in place in the Late Preceramic Period. The great South American maritime tradition and irrigation agriculture provided abundant resources. Many, though not all, foodstuffs and materials that remained important were already being raised, and camelids and guinea pigs were well on the way to domestication by the end of the era.

The organization of space, and inferentially of people and of the cosmos, according to generally dualistic principles can be seen in architecture and other material culture. Whether or not the ceremonial centers were urban centers is a matter of definition. It can be said, however, that there was certainly a diversity in the kinds and sizes of communities across much of the Central Andes. Political organization was the same as social organization and based on kin relationships. Linkages beyond local communities were established and maintained by some people, probably the heads of families, who travelled to participate in rituals at ceremonial centers and in the exchange of prestige goods. At the same time, some incipient socio-political hierarchy was developing as priest-leaders at temple sites probably exchanged certain precious goods that only they could own, as well as sacred knowledge of rituals and other religious "quasi-commodities."

It is likely that there was a conception of the world as permeated with energy flows which were concentrated in particular things and locations, and with perceived continuities between microcosmic and macrocosmic objects and events. Certain standing stones and smaller objects appear to be expressions of things later known as *huancas* and *huacas* respectively. Large archaeological sites were oriented to celestial events that included solstices, equinoxes, the Pleiades, and the Milky Way, and thus human affairs were seen as synchronous with or identical to what we refer to as natural forces.

In summary, late in the third millennium BC societies had reached impressive levels of complexity in the Central Andes. At present, the region that stands out as exceptional in this zone stretches from the Central Coast of Peru northwards along the shore into Ecuador. However, it is likely that large-scale monumental architecture, ceramics, plant domestication, and many other practices were already in use in other areas of the tropical forest, especially in the area of northern Peru and eastern Ecuador, but we do not have good evidence for this at present. Although it is possible that similar developments were taking place in the highlands, evidence there is also generally lacking. Highland Ecuador has yielded evidence of early, dense occupations, as will be seen in the next chapter, but there is little similar evidence in Peru or Bolivia. Especially in the latter case, the "Formative" is not much in evidence until about 1500 BC when the first ceramics and towns appear in the archaeological record.

The Central-North coast of Peru and the tropical regions of Ecuador share rich resource zones packed in close proximity, whereas the high altitude zones are relatively poorer in resources. In highland Bolivia, resources were spread thin and were mobile, mostly in the form of wild camelid herds. In the Late Preceramic Period some people in the region were living in pithouses for at least part of the year. They were probably still relatively mobile and depended mostly on hunted and gathered resources. At Jiskairumoko (*circa* [cal.] 2100 to 1900 BC), in the Ilave River drainage, burials in pit houses suggest that the structures were thought of as homes, with which people identified and to which they returned after hunting expeditions.[52] Burials were simple, but an (unsexed) adult was adorned with a necklace of coarse greenstone beads interspersed with nine tubular gold beads. This is the earliest known evidence for metalworking in South America. The hammering of nuggets or grains of gold into sheets—cold working—is a much more complicated procedure than it may seem to be, and so this discovery suggests a fairly advanced metalworking technology at quite an early time.

We must therefore conclude that the cultural precocity of the coastal Peru–Ecuador zone is due to the greater quantity and quality of the resources the areas provided. However, power centers shifted in later times, as we will see in forthcoming chapters. It is important to emphasize the fact that prodigious efforts were marshaled to build large complexes, but material wealth and social hierarchy were at low levels compared with other times and places. This is because the principles that underpinned these efforts were very different than the ones we live by today, and they did not emphasize the accumulation of material wealth or the marking of sharp social distinctions between people. This was true throughout the Central Andes for long periods of time, but by the end of the Late Preceramic Period Ecuador and North-to-Central Coastal Peru had begun to diverge in different directions. Although these two regions might be judged the most "advanced" of their time, the peoples of coastal Peru became entangled in or embraced increasing social complexity, incorporating into that process many of the material items first documented in Ecuador. In Ecuador itself, however, the pathway to complexity seems to have been deliberately avoided in favor of maintaining relatively independent communities, which consequently undermined the growth of social differentiation.

NOTES

1 Damp 1984.
2 See Lathrap et al. 1975 for a general introduction to the idea of "Precocious" Formative Ecuador.
3 Lathrap et al. 1977.
4 Damp et al. 1981 on beans, Damp and Pearsall 1994 on cotton, Isendahl 2011 on manioc. See the following discussion of maize.
5 Zeidler 2008: 464.
6 Zeidler 2008.
7 Ubelaker 2003.
8 Zeidler 2008: 464; Zeidler and Pearsall 1994 on Guaya and Jama. Staller 1991 and 2001 on La Emernciana. Marcos 2003 on Peñon del Río.
9 Damp 1984.
10 Fuchs et al. 2006.
11 Dillehay personal communication, June 2012.
12 On the Sechín complex, see Pozorski and Pozorski 1987.
13 Wendt 1964; Lanning 1967: 69–70.
14 Feldman 1980.
15 Shady et al. 2001; Shady and Kleihege 2010.
16 At the time of writing, information regarding Ventarrón is based solely on the author's visit to the site.
17 Quilter 1985.
18 Benfer: web.
19 cf. Duncan et al. 2009.
20 Samaniengo 2011.
21 Moseley 1975.
22 Pearsall 1992 cites evidence for accepting the phytolith data, as well as publications that critiqued it.
23 Grobman et al. 2011.
24 Haas et al. 2013.
25 The bibliography on the maize debate is extensive. See Burger 2012a.
26 "The Maritime Debate" bibliography is extensive. See Sandweiss (in press).
27 See, for example, Quilter et al. 1991, a study carried out before current micro-analyses were feasible.
28 Duncan et al. 2009.
29 Burger et al. 2012.
30 Vreeland 1993.
31 Damp and Pearsall 1994.

32 Bird, personal communication, *circa* 1985.
33 Bird and Hyslop 1985.
34 Bischof 2000.
35 Gabriel Prieto, personal communication, November, 2012.
36 Quilter 1992.
37 Gabriel Prieto, personal communication, November, 2012.
38 Grieder et al. 2012.
39 Seiichi 1971; Seiichi and Terada 1972.
40 Burger 1992: 45–53; Burger and Salazar-Burger 1985, 1986.
41 Elizabeth Bonnier (1997) has termed the architectural format of small chambers the "Mito Tradition," distinguishing it from the religious practice of the Kotosh Tradition.
42 The concept of the Great and Little Traditions was first developed by Robert Redfield (1956).
43 There is much discussion of the sites in the Chico Norte, such as Caral, as being exceptional. However, while the region had a great density of sites in the Late Preceramic it nevertheless generally conforms to a general "Central Coast" pattern.
44 Huaynuná: Pozorski and Pozorski 1987.
45 Las Haldas: Engel 1970; Pozorski and Pozorski 1987.
46 Quilter 1985.
47 Wendt 1964.
48 Burger 1992: 33.
49 Engel 1963.
50 Richardson and Sandweiss 2008.
51 Andrus et al. 2008.
52 Aldenderfer et al. 2008.

5

THE INITIAL PERIOD

TEXTILES AND POTTERY

There were many continuities from the Late Preceramic through into the Initial Period, but nevertheless significant changes do appear to have occurred. Many Late Preceramic temple sites were abandoned and new ceremonial complexes arose (see Figure 5.1). However, ceramics were adopted in many regions where they had not previously been used, and the heddle loom was now employed to make textiles—the two hallmarks of Initial Period culture. The widespread adoption of these technologies is a sign that new social relations were being formed, and they also provide archaeologists with more data by which to investigate the past.

Preceramic Period textiles are impressive in the variety of designs and styles produced using very simple techniques, including the elaborate designs seen at Huaca Prieta and La Galgada in particular. Knotting was used extensively but the predominant method was twining, the manipulation of fibers by hand. In twining, each element is interwoven among others by use of the fingers or by a large, needle-like device (a bodkin) that moves the yarn back and forth between parallel rows of other elements held still by pegs in the ground or by some other means.

True weaving uses a heddle that keeps groups of warp threads separated and stationary, thus allowing the rapid passing of weft threads back and forth between them. By employing more than one heddle or by using fingers different groups of warp threads can be raised and lowered, allowing for the production of different designs in the finished product. In the Andes, as well as throughout most of ancient America, various kinds of looms were used including upright structures as well as the backstrap loom, in which the tension on the warps is controlled by a belt passing around the weaver's waist (see Figure 1.3). The grid-like arrangement of warps and wefts lends itself to the production of geometrical designs, but the relative fineness of the

110

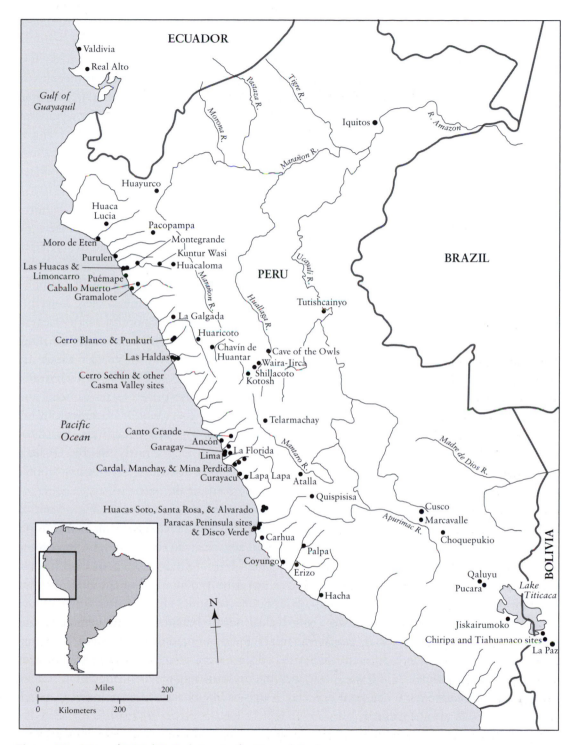

Figure 5.1 Map of Initial Period sites in the Central Andes.

weave can reduce or increase the geometric quality of the motifs. A great number of other techniques, such as embroidery or painting directly on cloth, can also vary the appearance of a textile.

Textiles are often claimed to have been the pre-eminent art form of the Ancient Andes.[1] It is clear that cloth occupied a very high place in the value systems of ancient Andeans from an early time, and it continued to be valued into late prehistory and beyond to the present day. As noted in Chapter 2, one of the most prestigious items that could be given as a gift by the Inca emperor to his subjects was a finely-woven garment of cloth referred to as *qompi* or *cumbi*. The range of techniques and styles in use at the time of the Spanish arrival was so great as to rival those known and produced by computer-aided industrial weaving today. Indeed, some techniques were so elaborate that they cannot be done except by human hands.

The study of ancient Andean textiles is a scholarly discipline in itself since it requires knowledge of the many different aspects of fabric production, from the technology of weaving systems and the chemistry of dyes to the social uses of clothing and the symbolism expressed in and by textiles. Because of factors of preservation, most of the ancient Andean textiles available for study come from the coast where cotton was the predominant material, although examples of woolen textiles, either from the highlands or in sierra styles, are often found there as well.

The majority of archaeologists in the world depend on the study of pottery as an essential tool in understanding ancient societies. Ceramic vessels are strong but not tough, breaking easily but generally retaining much information in fragmentary form, the bits of which are commonly known as shards (in Britain) or sherds (in the United States). Because pottery vessels were used for food storage, preparation, and consumption but also prized as status items and sometimes were decorated to convey religious or other ideas, the study of ceramics can tell archaeologists much about ancient societies. Furthermore, because of the relatively short lives of ceramic vessels, pottery fragments enter the archaeological record fairly rapidly. Of little value to their ancient owners, the piles or scatters of fragments of discarded cooking and storage vessels become extremely valuable to archaeologists as records of the past.

Presumably, weaving was invented and spread throughout the Andes because it permitted textiles to be produced more quickly and in more elaborate and interesting forms and patterns than twining. Weaving can be seen as a kind of logical advancement in textile arts, proceeding directly from twining. Pottery can also be seen as an extension of the previous gourd technology, and it has been noted that cutting a gourd in various ways produces all of the basic ceramic vessel forms. As with weaving's relationship with twining, ceramics allow greater opportunities for decoration than gourds. Gourds were embellished mostly by cutting and burning designs into them, and occasionally also by employing inlays and painting on their surfaces. However, ceramics can be formed into different shapes that depart from gourd-derived forms. Designs can be made in clay while it is still wet, using incision, excision, appliqué, and stamping, among other "plastic" treatments. When semi-dry, clay vessels can be burnished or polished to a high shine and they can also be painted.

In the Andes, as throughout the New World, for most of prehistory all ceramics were earthenwares, requiring relatively low firing temperatures. Pottery was mostly hand-crafted or mold-made. The former technique usually consists of adding slabs of clay to one another, while in the latter technique piece-molds are used to make vessel sections which are then stuck together using clay slurry. Both these techniques were widespread, but certain methods were more favored at different times and in different places.

As noted in the previous chapter, ceramics were used for several hundred years in Ecuador before people further south adopted pottery. Indeed, the stirrup-spout bottle that is ubiquitous across great areas and through centuries in Peru first appears in late Valdivia contexts in southern Ecuador *circa* (cal.) 2200 to 2300 BC, in Jelí Phase ceramics that include some of the earliest single- and stirrup-spout bottles in the Central Andes from the La Emerenciana site in El Oro Province.[2] People in northern Peru were in contact with Ecuadorians at least by the Late Preceramic Period, as shown by the Huaca Prieta gourds as well as trade items such as distinctive T-shaped stone axes. However, although Peruvians almost certainly knew of Ecuadorian ceramics, they did not adopt the technology until generations later. Why? Presumably Peruvians did not see a need for ceramics—in the same way, perhaps, that people who use forks don't see a need to use chopsticks and vice versa.

Ceramics can be used for two things that cannot be done with gourds. They can be used to cook foods for long periods of time and obtain the maximum amount of nutrition, thus allowing for the exploitation of some resources that might have been under-utilized previously. Small shellfish and tiny crabs could be cooked slowly, and starchy vegetables could be boiled into soups and stews. Quite significantly, fruits could also be heated and then fermented into alcoholic brews. Thus there was a technological reason for adopting ceramics, but there were other social and ideological reasons as well. How and why pottery was first used is therefore a question of great significance, which is tied to understanding many different aspects of ancient life.

THE EARLIEST CERAMICS

Very early ceramics dating to between (cal.) 18,300 and 15,430 BP have been identified in China, although pottery seems to first appear in three regions, Japan, China, and far eastern Russia, at about the same time, *circa* (cal.) 13,700 to 13,000 BP.[3] This leads to the possibility that the first humans to enter the New World could have brought ceramics with them. Given that the evidence for the first human populations in the New World is scarce, however, addressing this question is difficult. It is possible that ceramics did not travel with highly mobile first settlers, or that knowledge of pottery making was subsequently lost in the millennia between early colonization and later times.

Currently the earliest ceramics found in the New World were discovered in Colombia at the San Jacinto 1 site.[4] San Jacinto is located near the Caribbean coast in the Lower Magdalena Valley, and is therefore outside the Central Andes. The earliest uncalibrated dates for the ceramics are between 5940 and 5190 BP, calibrated between 4000 and 3700 BC. This pottery is fiber-tempered, a technique found widely in very early ceramics throughout the world, such as in the southeastern United States and in Brazil, although it is generally not found in the Central Andes. Fiber-temper refers to the inclusion of fragments of plant material, such as palmetto leaves, sometimes burnt, in the clay to give it strength and durability. The pottery was apparently made by hunter-gatherers who lived at a base camp and also used special-purpose locales, such as San Jacinto 1, in exploiting a wide range of resource zones. Pottery vessels may have been used on a short-term basis to prepare a fermented beverage from seeds that were seasonally abundant nearby.

Early ceramics are found throughout the north Pacific coastal lowlands of Colombia; Monsú pottery dates to *circa* 3500 BC and Puerto Hormiga ceramics to about 3000 BC. Early pottery is also found in Ecuador, and as previously noted, the most studied variety is Valdivia, with sites distributed from the central coast into the Guayas Basin. The earliest known Valdivia ceramics were found at the very bottom of the Loma Alta site, dating to between (cal.) 4400 and 3300 BC, some 15 km up the valley from the mouth of the Valdivia River.[5] These ceramics are technically developed and are found in several distinctive shape categories, suggesting that they are not the first of their kind. There is also another ceramic style, San Pedro, which is earlier but not apparently related to the better-known Valdivia tradition, which may indicate that both are derived from still earlier styles.

From the start, Valdivia ceramics were both technologically and stylistically well developed (see Figure 4.1). Different clay and temper mixtures were used for utilitarian wares, to reduce the effects of thermal shock, and for prestige wares, to carry enhanced decorations.[6] Decorative motifs became more elaborate through time, but even in Early Valdivia drinking and feasting vessel forms were highly standardized, as noted by many scholars.[7]

Jars and bowls were decorated differently, with the former adorned with combing, finger decoration, embossing, and corrugation and the latter with incised or excised geometric designs on polished red slips. These included hachured triangles, interlocking fret bands, spaced lattice or net-like elements, and zigzag or wavy lines. Peter Stahl has suggested that these designs were inspired by hallucinogenic visions that were probably part of the drinking festivities for which these bowls likely were used, conforming to known practices among Amazonian groups.[8]

Valdivia is also well known for distinctive human figurines (see Figure 4.1). The earliest ones are small, no more than 12 cm (5 in) in height, and are usually made of soft stone such as gypsum. These often display both male and female attributes. Later figurines, emblematic of the Valdivia culture, were made with two cylinders of clay molded together to produce a solid upper body with separated legs and no feet. The overwhelming majority of the figurines depict women, often with prominent breasts, curvaceous hips, and elaborate hairstyles or combinations of elaborate hair and headdresses. These figurines have been found in various locations such as on floors, near hearths, and in food preparation areas, and they are sometimes broken. If these areas were more commonly the domains of girls and women, then the figurines may also have been part of the world of females rather than males. In Late Valdivia times impressive, large incised stone tablets also were made, although their uses are uncertain.

For many years large early sites have been known outside the Valdivia region, but only recently have any been studied in detail. Santa Ana-La Florida is one such locale, covering slightly over a hectare on the Valladolid River at the low altitude of 1,000 m (3,280 ft), in the Ecuadorian *ceja de montaña,* the hilly, tropical terrain above the true tropical forest (see Figure 5.2).[9] Situated on an alluvial terrace, the site revealed two distinct Formative occupations from 3000 to 200 BC. The lowest component had long sets of curvilinear walls that ended in a spiral pattern, apparently marking the center of the site. There, a stone-lined hearth 80 cm in diameter was associated with a ceremonial offering that included a rich assortment of semi-precious stone masks, pendants, and a bowl. Nearby and deeper, a stone-lined tomb held human remains, stone and marine shell ornaments, stone bowls and mortars, and stirrup-spout vessels. The dating of this feature is (cal.) 2270 to 2260 BC, which seems quite early and technically places it in the Late Preceramic Period of Peru.

The elaborateness and richness of the grave goods, the architecture and other labor investments at Santa Ana-La Florida are much greater than any that have been documented for the better known Valdivia cultures of the coast, while many of the motifs on the carved stone objects, such as avian and snake designs, are identical to those found on textiles from contemporary sites in Peru. In addition, the ceramics at the site are highly developed and elaborate even though pottery was not adopted in Peru until centuries later. The excavator, Francisco Valdez, has suggested that the Santa Ana-La Florida site is a manifestation of what he has defined as the Mayo-Chinchipe Culture, and many more similar sites are likely waiting to be found.[10]

The Santa Ana-La Florida site is located in an ideal place for long-distance exchange, since it is near rivers that head to both the Pacific and the Amazon. Meanwhile Huayurco in Peru, low in the Chinchipe Valley, is in the orbit of the North Peruvian-Ecuadorian *ceja de selva* regime. This site has been known for some time for decorated stone mortars and vessels, which it traded. Furthermore, Cerro Narrio in Ecuador, known for even longer, was another important node in long-distance exchanges.[11]

Some scholars see the earliest ceramics in Peru as having little in common with those from other regions, while others note similarities. Richard Burger has pointed out that early ceramic assemblages over a wide area of the coast share basic features, but they differ from some of the more elaborate pottery from the tropical forest.[12]

Pottery from Erizo in Ica, on the South Coast, Ancón Bay, and the La Florida U-shaped ceremonial center on the Central Coast, and Huaca Negra in the Virú Valley, are all technologically primitive with eggshell-thin walls and only a few forms, mostly restricted to neck vessels and open, shallow bowls. While technologically similar, however, decorations vary. La Florida and Ancón ceramics are relatively similar, but the former has broad, shallow incisions while in the latter black painting is more common (see Figure 5.3).

Many of the early pottery styles in Peru and Ecuador share common technology and motifs. In terms of forms, deep, in-curved bowls, known as "neckless ollas," or sometimes simply as "ollas," are widespread, as are wide, shallow, often flat-bottomed bowls such as those found at

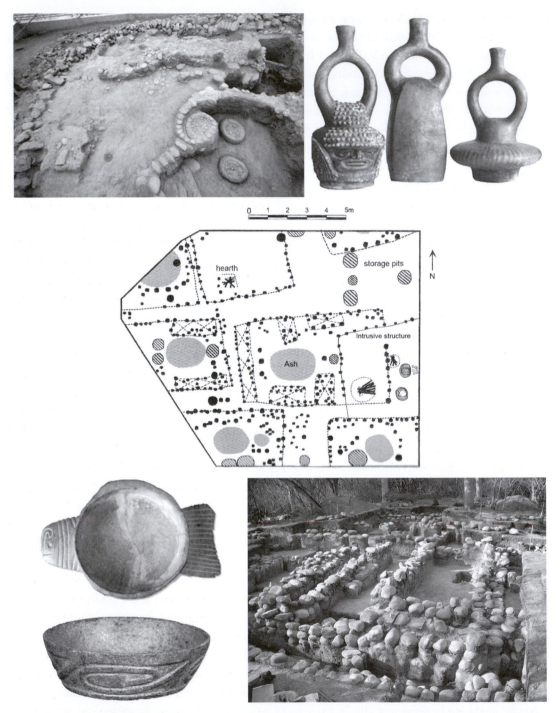

Figure 5.2 The Initial Period and Late Formative in Northern Peru and Ecuador. Top: Spiral structure and ceramics from Santa Ana-La Florida, Ecuador. Center: Map of houses and features at Cotocollao, Ecuador. Bottom: Stone bowls and excavations at Huayurco.

Gramalote in the Moche Valley (see Figure 5.5). The latter have straight, slightly flaring, or slightly in-curving sides. Such ceramics have been found at Huaca La Florida, where a single-spout bottle was also recovered, and in the Toril assemblage at Huaricoto, a Kotosh Religious Tradition center in the Central Peruvian Highlands that went through the Preceramic–Initial Period transition.[13] Decoration on these early ceramics tends to be plastic. The simplest forms are incisions on relatively unmodified surfaces. Other vessels may be smoothed, burnished, fine-combed, punctated, or incised with groups of parallel lines. The use of appliqué nubbins, often round, and often also punctuated, is also quite distinctive.

A favored decorative technique for many early ceramics was the use of nicked appliqué strips of clay on vessel bodies. These strips were commonly impressed to create either a corrugated effect separate squares, or pillow-like forms. The impressed strips often were used in multiples, sometimes as parallel elements or sometimes arranged to create squares or other designs.

Ceramics with nicked appliqué strips include early Jambelí, in southwestern Ecuador, and Guañape, found on the Peru North Coast (and one of the first early ceramics identified), and they have been also found at La Galgada. They also occur in the northern highlands such as in the Cajamarca region, at Huacaloma, and at Huaricoto. Similar ceramics are found, in the highlands and at Bagua on the lower eastern slopes of the Andes, although another, local and highly decorative Bagua style also is present at the site.[14]

The widespread occurrence of ceramics with similar forms and decorations is evidence that peoples of the coast, highland, and tropical forest regions were all in contact with one another in the early Initial Period and likely even earlier. While ceramics seem to appear almost simultaneously throughout a broad swath stretching from Ecuador to Central Peru, there are consistently somewhat earlier dates for pottery from tropical forest regions, especially, as noted above, in regions contiguous with but outside the Central Andes. Many of the earliest pottery forms are relatively simple and crude, such as those found in the central highlands and on the coast of Peru, while there appear to have been fancier ceramics either contemporaneously or rapidly succeeding the simpler styles in tropical areas. The Chambira style, dating to 2000 to 1000 BC, is from a tributary of the Marañon and has yielded the first examples of double spout-and-bridge bottles, a style that was to become widely popular in later times, as well as figurines exhibiting elaborate jewelry and head deformation.[15]

Given the apparent precocity of tropical forest peoples, Daniel Morales has suggested that early ceramics, architectural forms, and indeed a suite of ideas and practices originated in the Amazon and were then brought to the Andean regions by people who migrated there. He cites the onset of a period of cooler and more arid weather—the Andean Neo-Glacial, according to Augusto Cardich, *circa* 2500 to 1000 BC—that reduced tropical forest, increased savannas and encouraged people to migrate out of the region, bringing their objects and practices with them.[16] Many of the earliest ceramics in Colombia and Ecuador are earlier than the Andean Neo-Glacial, so this theory does not explain the origins of pottery in general, but it could partly serve as an explanation for the movement of people and styles from tropical regions into the highlands and coast, and therefore explain the spread of ceramics in the Initial Period.

Another example of elaborate ceramics coeval with or quickly succeeding earlier, simpler styles are Waira-jirca ceramics, which have bands with interior hatching filled with post-fired red, white, and yellow mineral pigments. Their tropical forest origin seems without question since examples have been found at the Cave of the Owls in the *ceja de selva* at only 500 m (1,600 ft) above sea level. Many Waira-jirca features are also in evidence in Early and Late Tutishcanyo pottery from the tropical Central Ucayali River. The tropical version was made in elaborate forms that used carination and basal and labial flanges, although some simpler forms are known on the Peruvian coast. The style succeeded earlier Toril pottery at Huaricoto and Kotosh, and apparent trade sherds of tropical forest styles have been found at these two Húanaco sites.

The apparent strong connections between tropical forest ceramics and some of the early potteries found in the highlands and coast encouraged Warren DeBoer to consider the distribution of ceramic forms in the Formative using the historically documented vessel categories of the Shipibo, who live by the Ucayali River in the Upper Amazon, not too far removed from the eastern Andean foothills.[17] The Shipibo have two major categories of ceramics: cooking pots, and vessels for storage/eating/drinking. The cooking vessels are not decorated and include pots in very large sizes for preparing great quantities of chicha. There are also large and small vessels for everyday cooking, and a very small version for either cooking small batches of medicine or for use by travelers. Non-cooking pots consist of jars and bowls. These include the equivalent of beer kegs for parties, medium-sized vessels for everyday storage of water or beer, and the smallest which are used as canteens by travelers. Bowls follow a similar pattern in their different sizes. These non-cooking vessels all tend to be elaborately decorated.

Taken as a whole, the early prehistoric ceramic assemblages in the Central Andes have ollas, which are equated with cooking, bowls, associated with eating, and jars that held liquids including drinking vessels. DeBoer discerned that Early Valdivia collections and the ceramics of the highland site of Cotocollao had relatively balanced assemblages, suggesting a range of domestic activities. However, the majority of the early Peruvian assemblages are dominated by neckless ollas used for cooking with very few jars, and a few have many jars but little else.

DeBoer also discovered that almost all of the early vessels throughout Ecuador and Peru were well below feasting size. This suggests that the feasting practice known for the Shipibo and for later Peruvian assemblages was not in operation, or that feasting was practiced differently with three or four medium-sized vessels for party guests to drink from rather than the extra-large bowls of later times. In some places gourd bowls could have been used as drinking or serving/eating vessels, and these would only have been preserved in exceptional circumstances.

During the early historic period when people mostly still moved without the aid of modern transportation, an interaction sphere on the eastern side of the Andes stretched throughout all of the major tributaries of the Amazon, an area 1,200 km in length and 600 km at its maximum width (746 × 373 mi). In addition there were sub-regions, such as one in which asymmetric double spout-and-bridge bottles were a favored form. The same kinds of interaction spheres likely existed in prehistory.

VILLAGES AND CEREMONIAL CENTERS

Ecuadorian precociousness in pottery is paired with evidence of developed farming communities, as seen in the Santa Elena Peninsula and adjoining regions. In the northern Ecuadorian highlands the site of Cotocollao, just north of Quito, is seen as emblematic of cultural developments in the sierra, although few other sites have been studied in detail and most of its occupation dates from late in the Formative. The site was excavated as a salvage project so some details are lacking, but nevertheless considerable information was retrieved (see Figure 5.2).

Cotocollao was a large village occupied between (cal.) 1800 to 400 BC. Even in the earliest occupation the village was well organized into closely spaced rectangular houses made of wooden beams and wattle-and-daub walls; the dimensions of a completely excavated structure were 8 m by 5 m (8 × 16 ft). No public architecture is known, but a large, central cemetery area may have been the focus of ceremonial life.[18] The village subsistence economy was fully agricultural and included maize, potatoes, achira, oca, quinoa, and beans. White-tailed deer and rabbit were hunted, but many other animals were also identified as probable food as well.[19] Camelids are notably absent.

At Cotocollao there were more than 34 classes of pottery vessels and a wide range of stone artifacts, which included obsidian flaked tools, a suite of axes, and containers including elaborate stone bowls and mortars. Obsidian was prominent at the site because it is near a major source of the volcanic glass, and it is likely that the prosperity of the village was tied to trade in this material. Cotocollao was not alone and probably not unique since more than 70 other sites resembling it have been identified in valleys to the east.

Sometime between 752 and 192 BC, probably around 500 BC, the Pululahua volcano erupted, blowing five to six cubic km of formerly compacted material into the air to a height between 28 and 33 km (17 to 21 mi). It was one of the greatest volcanic explosions in the last 10,000 years, placed in the 99th percentile of eruptions; the caldera it left behind measures 3 km (around 2 mi) in diameter.[20] The tephra, or airborne material, blanketed the highlands and coast for an area of more than 40,000 square km (15,000 square mi). The thickness of the deposit varied depending on the proximity to the blast.

Cotocollao, its neighboring sites, and the greater part of the western flanks of the Andes and the Ecuadorian coast were affected, and they were subsequently abandoned. Fleeing the area did not occur immediately, but it appears to have happened within months, probably after farmers realized that they could not effectively work their fields in the bottomlands that were the primary areas for cultivation and which were also the most severely affected by tephra deposits.[21] The entire region was not repopulated for some 500 years.

We may infer that this catastrophic event also had dramatic effects on the cultural history of Ecuador and perhaps beyond. For example, obsidian trade routes out of the Quito basin were disrupted and reconfigured in the wake of the eruption. Zeidler and Isaacson suggest that people fleeing the affected zone would have entered relatively unpopulated regions to the north and gone into the region of the sparse populations of the coastal Chorrera archaeological culture to the south.[22] This influx of displaced people would surely have influenced subsequent events, although these effects are hard to assess.

THE MANCHAY CULTURE OF THE CENTRAL COAST OF PERU

On the coast of Peru, many of the Late Preceramic ceremonial centers continued to grow and expand in the Initial Period. These include La Galgada, Huaricoto, Las Haldas, Piruru, Punkurí, the Casma Valley sites, and many more. However, other architectural complexes were abandoned, such as Ventarrón, Aspero, Caral, and El Paraíso.[23] We do not know if the variable successes and failures of different centers should be understood as collective expressions of major cultural changes, or if the continuities and endings were simply the results of the kinds of variable successes we should expect of large, complex centers that vied with one another for followers. El Paraíso was occupied until quite late, well into the time period when ceramics were in use, and yet no ceramics have been found at the site to date. It is unlikely that it was the technological aspects of ceramics per se which made other centers prosper, but rather a suite of activities of which pottery was one element.

Another possibility is that natural disasters, over-exploitation of the environment, or a combination of these things, as well as socio-political factors, contributed to the demise of the Late Preceramic centers that did not continue into the Initial Period. While the Supe or Chillón valleys may have supported large populations in later times (although reports are meager), they never again appear to have been at the forefront of cultural developments or to have sustained large ceremonial centers as they did in the Late Preceramic Period. We might assume that if the demise of these centers was strictly due to socio-political influences, the valley would have rebounded at least at some point in the following millennia. No evidence suggests that this was the case, however, raising the possibility that some significant event, such as soil salinization, geological uplift, the encroaching of dunes into farmland, or another catastrophe or gradual processes may have been involved in such apparently dramatic changes.

Many new centers were built, and it was in the Initial Period that distinct U-shaped ceremonial centers come into prominence on the Central Coast of Peru. Some of the Late Preceramic centers may have grown into U-shaped centers, but not enough excavation has been carried out in these complexes to reach the earliest constructions. At La Galgada, Kotosh Religious Tradition chambers had been filled with burials and then new chambers were built above them. The excavators noted that one of the latest building efforts in the North Mound was a local compromise between the old Kotosh chambers and the emerging U-shaped temples.[24] In this phase a fire pit was retained in a white floor, but the space was enlarged into an open courtyard with elevated platforms on three sides in a recognizable U-shape. Similar modifications of old architecture to new religious patterns probably also occurred elsewhere, but a detailed study of which sites were new and which were Preceramic centers that continued to prosper remains to be carried out.

Richard Burger has conducted the most detailed research on three of these complexes, Mina Perdida, Cardal, and Manchay Bajo, all in the Lurín Valley just south of Lima (see Figure 5.3).[25] The sequence of construction places Mina Perdida as the earliest, followed by Cardal and then Manchay Bajo, although occupation at the sites overlapped between 1200 and 900 BC. The greatest amount of research has been focused on Cardal, 14 km (8.7 mi) inland from the shore and covering 20 hectares (49 acres) (see Figure 5.3).

The term "U-shaped" is a misnomer. These sites are often more J-shaped than U-shaped, and a broken "J" at that. From the air the complexes usually exhibit a long central mound, a long right arm and a short left arm. On closer inspection, the short left arm is not connected to the base; instead, there is a gap between them. At Cardal this gap was 75 m (246 ft) wide and served as an entryway into the complex since an elevated road or causeway was found passing through it. The Cardal central platform measures 145 by 60 m (475 × 196 ft) and is 17 m (56 ft) in height. The long, right (eastern) arm is 300 by 90 m (984 × 295 ft) and 12 m (39 ft) high, while the partly destroyed left arm is 120 by 55 m (394 × 180 ft) and 8 m (26 ft) high.

Cardal was designed to impress the people entering it. The unequal arms of the U-shaped centers expressed asymmetrical dualism, a concept that is clearly in evidence later in prehistory: the yanantin-masintin pairing of unequal but complementary entities discussed in Chapter 2. A long central avenue or causeway ran from the exterior, perpendicular to the central platform at the base of the complex. Along the way the central plaza was divided into large, wide terraces with small structures on them. The causeway or street became a staircase ascending to the central platform arriving at an atrium decorated with a mural, in clay bas relief, of a huge fanged mouth painted in cream, yellow, red, and black. Each fang was about a meter long, with the mural band raised above the atrium floor so that it could be seen from the plaza below. Thus, the site was made to resemble a living monster god, with the priests entering and leaving the atrium literally moving in and out of the maw of the god.

The excavators found a series of superimposed structures on top of the central platform. One group of rooms may have been residences in a later phase of use. Nearby was a building with a suite of small rooms and narrow passageways. Two central rectangular rooms were at the center of this complex. Each room had a three-level altar resembling a small staircase, and these were set back-to-back against a shared wall that appeared to have had a window in it: dualism is clearly in evidence here too. The staircase-style altar remained popular throughout prehistory (see Figure 7.3).

A row of four circular depressions were observed along the outside margin of the right arm of the complex. These varied in size, between 9 and 13 m (29 to 43 ft) in diameter, and all had clean floors indicating that they were ceremonial chambers. One room had the skull of a child left as an offering, while another had a central stone-lined hearth. No evidence of domestic or craft activities were found in any of the other excavations carried out in this wing of the complex.

Another stairway led down from the top of the central platform to ground level behind the U, where there was a dispersed group of adobe houses with interior rooms and large patios. Evidence of cooking areas and storage facilities were found in association with the houses. All

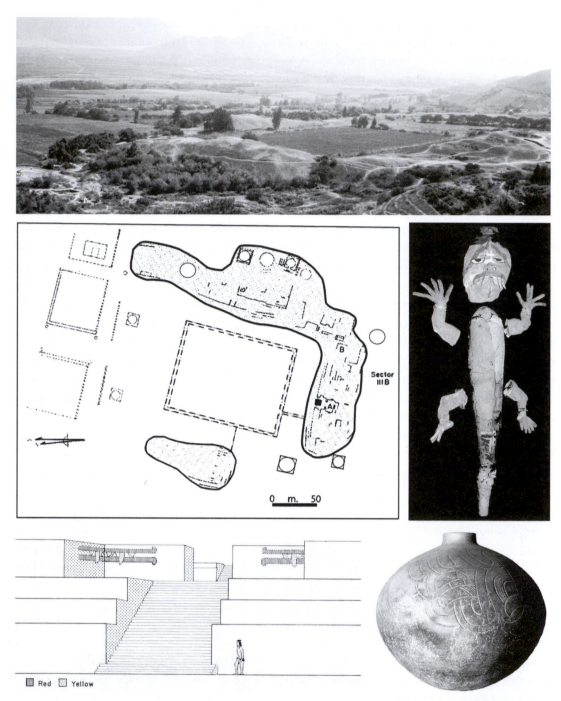

Figure 5.3 Manchay culture: Top: Cardal vista seen from southeast of the corner of the right arm and central mound. Middle left: Map of Cardal. Middle right: Puppet idol from Mina Perdida. Bottom left: Sketch of the mouth band mural at Cardal. Bottom right: Manchay Culture ceramic from Ancón.

of the major food crops were grown and found in and around the dwellings. Cotton was grown nearby or brought to the site since signs of the processing and spinning of raw cotton were found. Burials were discovered under the floors of the houses and at the same levels outside them. This appears to be the only residential area at Cardal. Extrapolating from excavations in the domestic area behind the central platform, the residential population behind it probably consisted of nuclear families or slightly larger social units totaling no more than about 300 people.

There was a minimum of three major construction phases on the central platform, including the building of new stairs and the renovation of the atrium. When the Middle Temple was closed before remodeling, *circa* 850 BC, sixteen burials were placed in the atrium floor along the centerline of the space and the site in general. The burials consist of individuals of a broad range of ages, and both males and females. The dead were wrapped in simple cloth and fiber mats, sometimes with red pigments applied to their heads. Burial goods of everyday items or personal adornments accompanied the dead, including crude spindle whorls, cooking pots, and perforated stones.

One burial stood out among the others. This was of an adult male who was interred wearing red-painted ear spools and a necklace of 13 large canines. He was also holding a painted bone tool. The teeth are likely those of male sea lions and the ear spools were made from sea mammal bone, possibly whale or dolphin. There were no signs of violence done to this individual or any of the other skeletons. If these people were sacrifices, they were killed in ways that left no traces. It is more likely, however, that they were honored people who were buried in a sacred place.

The small size of the domestic area of Cardal, the modest houses with their equally modest burials, artifacts, and food remains, and the relatively simple burials in the atrium, all suggest that the social group in charge of the ceremonial complex was not markedly different from the people who came to participate in rituals. In fact, analysis of the atrium burials revealed that these individuals had been in poorer health than the people of Paloma, exhibiting many nutritional problems as well as other issues. Lack of surveys, as well as the difficulties of finding early sites in an intensely used landscape, makes it difficult to estimate overall population sizes or the nature of settlement patterns. However, the likelihood is that populations were spread throughout the valley, in farmsteads or hamlets on land just outside the margins of the irrigated fields.

The Lurín Valley is small, and even under the best environmental conditions it could never have produced enough irrigated crops to support a large number of people. Despite this, however, there are eight Initial Period ceremonial centers in the valley, four of which were in view of one another or nearly so. Similarly, there are substantial amounts of fish and shellfish remains in the domestic area and in the space between the left and central mounds at Cardal. There are so many anchovy and mussel remains mixed with broken serving vessels in the latter space that they inevitably suggest feasting activities there or nearby. However, no fishing equipment of any kind was found at the site, so the marine resources must have been brought 14 km (8.7 mi) inland by coastal dwellers. The distance is not great, and so it is not unreasonable to expect seafood at Cardal. Nevertheless, the lack of fishing gear suggests that community economic specializations were already present in Peru during this early time period.

Pottery serves as one line of evidence for communication within the larger world of the U-shaped centers. The 100 km (62 mi) stretch from Ancón Bay, north of Lima, to Curayacu south of Lurín exhibits somewhat different ceramic styles at different locations along the shore. The Chira style consists of pottery with incised and punctate decorations; this style is known at Ancón Bay, to the north. La Florida ceramics with their deeply incised designs are named after a U-shaped complex at the Rimac Valley neck. Curayacu has long been known for the discovery of a remarkably large, painted human figurine, and its ceramic style generally emphasizes painting.

Whether these sub-regional distinctions in ceramic styles, defined more than four decades ago, will endure in the light of further research remains to be seen.[26] At Cardal the range of ceramic forms is relatively small, and this is also generally true elsewhere. Single-necked bottles with flaring rims, convex or straight-sided bowls with rounded bottoms, and undecorated neckless ollas are the basic forms, and all appear to have been used in food storage or preparation (see Figure 5.5).

Small annular-based cups decorated with incised rectilinear geometric designs were a distinctive form at Cardal. A bottle found smashed in the center of one of the circular plazas was also highly decorated. It had an annular base, two spouts, and incised, interlocking, bicephalic snakes with punctate decorations. This design, albeit in more geometric form, is also known from Late Preceramic textiles. The rest of the pottery at Cardal is usually plain, but when it is decorated the patterns consist of small, stamped circles irregularly arrayed on bowls, or zoned punctuation on bowl and bottle exteriors.

Four sherds with Cardal-like stamped circles have been found at Curayacu, site some 20 km distant, while examples of Curayacu and Ancón styles were found at Cardal.[27] This strongly suggests that there were ongoing interactions between people at different sites within the sphere of the U-shaped architectural complexes. Cardal was thus a local center drawing people to it from the mid- to lower valley, rather than an urban complex that sent people outwards. It was a place designed to hold more people than those who lived there. While they may be interpreted in a number of ways, the separate, different-sized circular sunken plazas on the right arm are reminiscent of similar structures dating from the Late Preceramic Period. Each one could have served a separate social unit. This would seem to be a natural progression, from the separate chambers of the Kotosh Religious Tradition at Huaricoto and La Galgada to a somewhat more formally arranged system of separate ceremonial chambers for social groups at Cardal.

The fact that Cardal was close to other U-shaped centers with overlapping dates suggests that there was competition among them, probably for people to come and support one center as opposed to another. When we consider the events that occurred at these places it is important to remember that the concept of "religion" does not fully describe the kinds of experiences that people had there. It was more a combination of religion and entertainment, including the direct participation of the pilgrims who came to the ceremonial sites. At the nearby Mina Perdida

U-shaped complex, a large, colorfully painted puppet-like figure made of gourd and string gives a hint of the kinds of spectacles that took place there (see Figure 5.3).

There are at least 40 U-shaped temple complexes on the Central Coast between the Lurín and Supe Valleys. Most of these have received little research attention, but all show generally similar patterns. Noteworthy sites include La Florida in the upper Rimac Valley and Garagay in a lower portion of the same valley. The Garagay atrium has received special attention for its boldly painted bas-relief clay friezes of various monster-gods. Similarities in construction techniques, architectural patterns, ceramic styles, and subsistence patterns are so standardized among these centers that they can be considered as part of a single archaeological culture, which Richard Burger has termed Manchay.

The Manchay Archaeological Culture refers to the Initial Period U-shaped centers from the Lurín Valley to the Chancay Valley, along with a shared set of artifacts and practices. The architectural features include flat-topped, U-shaped platform complexes decorated by painted, unbaked clay friezes, oriented north-northeast and with an open space between at least one of the asymmetric arms of the U and a central platform. The central platform has an inset atrium, fronted by a wide staircase rising from a large, rectangular central plaza. Manchay culture sites and ceremonial artifacts share a common iconographic style, and contain simple pit burials with few grave goods.[28]

Why the Manchay culture's range stretched from Lurín to Chancay is uncertain. South of Lurín there are large stretches of desert, and as previously noted, river valleys are small. Factors of travel, links with differing highland regions, and the continuation of earlier patterns from the Late Preceramic Period may have played roles in delimiting the Manchay culture area from a different tradition on the North Coast.

CASMA VALLEY INITIAL PERIOD SITES

The Casma Valley and its vicinity contains one of the greatest concentrations of Late Preceramic through Initial Period architectural complexes on the coast of Peru.[29] Not in the valley itself but likely within its cultural orbit, the Las Haldas complex is 20 km (12 mi.) south of the Casma but only 100 m (328 ft) from the ocean. The main part of the site consists of a long series of platforms and plazas stretching 400 m (1,312 ft) in length. Ancillary buildings on either side of the southern end of the complex (where construction is greatest) cover an area 200 m (656 ft) in length, and the entire site covers more than 40 hectares (99 acres). Construction continued from the Late Preceramic Period through the Initial Period and into the Early Horizon, although the site's apogee was during the Initial Period. Pre-temple Initial Period refuse has yielded ceramics with incision, punctation, and zoned punctation decorations on their exteriors. Zoned red slip and zoned black graphite sherds were rare, but they seem to be among the earliest fancy decorated ceramics in the region. Neckless ollas were common and a few narrow-necked bottles and jars were also recovered.

In the Casma Valley itself, Late Preceramic culture appears to have carried on with no sharp break from the past. Cerro Sechín, 13 km (8 mi) from the Pacific, has attracted a great deal of attention due to the impressive art there. A 50 square m (538 square ft) building has received considerable attention, although it sits within a larger site complex that has had minimal study. The square building with rounded corners consists of two structures, one within the other. The earliest construction may date to the Late Preceramic Period while the latest dates to the Initial Period.[30] The inner, earlier, structure was built with conical adobes and may have had three building phases, while the outer one is the latest and is distinctive for its carved monoliths (see Figure 5.4).

The perimeter wall around Cerro Sechín has attracted the most attention of any construction in the complex. This wall consists of large, irregular stone monoliths interspersed with smaller but still impressively-sized blocks. Originally there were probably 400 stones, each carved with humans who had been killed in various ways, or else showing body parts such as heads, arms, intestines, and vertebrae. There are many depictions of human heads with eyes shut and with blood or vessels flowing or dangling from them, while some sculptures show victims cut in two with their intestines spilling downward. Stacked heads are carved on another monolith, victorious warriors elsewhere, and carvings of two elaborate banners on flagstaffs flank the main entrance.

Two kilometers upstream from Cerro Sechín, the main mound of Sechín Alto is so large that for many years people, including archaeologists, thought that it was a hill. The main temple is immense with a base of 300 by 250 m (984 × 820 ft) and a height of 35 m (114 ft). Covering an area of 7 hectares (17 acres) it contains an estimated two million cubic meters of fill. It was built partly of conical adobes, a hallmark of Initial Period and Early Horizon architecture, with later use of granite blocks some of which weighed over two tons. It had massive central stairs and numerous rooms on its summit, some of the earliest painted in bright yellow, black, red, and white, and an adobe frieze on its exterior, now mostly vanished.

Most of Sechín Alto dates from the early to the middle Initial Period. At its height it was probably the largest architectural complex in the New World. It vies with the later Huaca del Sol in the Moche Valley as the largest mound construction in the ancient New World. Three of the major secondary temple complexes alone would be large structures anywhere else, and there were many smaller buildings as well. In front of the main temple structure, a series of plazas that included at least three circular courts stretched for more than a kilometer.

A third complex, sometimes known as Pampa de la Llamas-Moxeke, is located in the desert close to a southern tributary of the Casma River and covers at least 1.5 square km (0.6 square mi).[31] The complex consists of two main buildings, oriented towards each other on the same axis and 1.35 km (0.8 mi) apart. The western building is Moxeke, a 30 m (98 ft) high tiered pyramid, 160 by 170 m (524 × 557 ft) on its sides. It was constructed using conical adobes with stone revetment walls. In niches in the atrium and around the sides of the building, massive adobe sculptures of the upper bodies and heads of anthropomorphs painted in bright colors confronted pilgrims when the temple was in use.[32]

Figure 5.4 Cupisnique culture. Top left: The central mound and nearby lateral structures (noted by white lines) at Huaca de los Reyes, Caballo Muerto Complex. Top right: Map of Huaca de los Reyes. Center left: "Classic" black, polished Cupisnique stirrup-spout vessel. Center: Artist's model of Sechín Alto main temple. Center right: Tembladera-style figurine of double flute player. Bottom left: Cerro Sechín from the rear, with Sechín Alto in the far distance. Bottom right: Carved monolith in wall at Cerro Sechín, of person with spilling entrails.

More than a kilometer east of Moxeke is Huaca A, a 140 m (459 ft) square, 9 m (30 ft) high building made mostly of unworked stones in clay mortar, set in a rectangular plaza that includes a sunken circular court on one end. The building is divided into three sections. The central section has a large square court in the middle with two large round-cornered chambers flanking it. On each side of this central section are many small sub-rectangular rooms of varying sizes and with many niches in their interiors.

All the rooms so far examined in Huaca A have high thresholds and doorways built to hold wooden poles to block entry into them. Julio C. Tello, who first explored the Casma complexes, and the Pozorskis who conducted research at Moxeke in the 1980s, all came to the same conclusion that Huaca A was a public storehouse. Excavation found most of the chambers empty of artifacts, containing only a few beads, an anthracite mirror, a few textiles and the like. What seemed to be an unusually great number of small rodent bones strongly suggested that storage of foodstuffs might have occurred in these spaces. However, communication between rooms would have been quite awkward if the entire complex was a storage facility, and it is quite possible that Huaca A was a ceremonial complex in which goods were stored as part of worshippers' offerings, or that the use of the facility for storage occurred in later times.

One or more large rectangular plazas were located between Moxeke and Huaca A. To the south and especially to the north of the central ceremonial area there are over 70 orderly ranked rectangular platforms. Some of these were never finished, but those that are complete have an atrium in front of a small room. These appear to have been some sort of public or ritual chambers, not residences.

Two other large site complexes are in the same valley. Taukachi-Konkan is close to Sechín Alto and is visible from the summit of its main mound. This site covers an area of 1,250 by 500 m (4,100 × 1,640 ft). The main mound is U-shaped, similar to the form of the La Galgada northern mound late in its history, and it has lateral plazas and rooms as well as plazas and circular courts fronting it, but information on the mounds at the site lacks detail because structures are obscured by later occupation of the area. The other site, Huerequeque, is 21 km (13 mi) from Cerro Sechín and consists of a large central mound with rooms at its top and a lower plaza complex, together covering about 35 hectares (87 acres) on a sloping hillside. It has also suffered from later prehistoric activities, but sherds date its occupation to the Initial Period.

The Casma Valley sites are close to one another. Sechín Alto is 2 km (1.2 mi) from Cerro Sechín, and Moxeke is about a 5 km (3 mi) walk away from the ruins of Sechín Alto as they are currently visible, shorter if one crosses the coastal hills. We do not know whether two or more of these temple complexes were in operation at the same time, but it seems likely that they were, at least for a while. Also, the dating of the Casma Valley complexes in general is a difficult task. As noted above, there may be Late Preceramic continuities at some sites that would place the earliest structures in the late third or the very early centuries of the second millennium BC in. The main mounds seem to have been in operation *circa* 1800 to 1700 BC. Sheila and Thomas Pozorski believe that construction halted *circa* 1400 BC, while Richard Burger believes that building continued through to about 1000 BC.[33]

CABALLO MUERTO IN THE MOCHE VALLEY

The Caballo Muerto complex consists of eight unaligned large mounds covering an area of over 2 square km (0.8 square mi) in the Moche Valley. It is associated with the Cupisnique archaeological culture (see Figure 5.4).[34] The site complex has been known for a long time and received some previous study, mostly at Huaca de los Reyes, famous for its anthropomorphic adobe friezes in Cupisnique style.[35] Huaca de los Reyes consists of a two-tiered, terraced platform 6 m (around 20 ft) high, flanked on either side by two platforms with three aligned rectangular plazas (see Figure 5.4). There is strong bilateral symmetry in the organization of the site with matching buildings and sets of colonnades on either side of two of the plazas, and this general architectural format, with variations, is also common in the other complexes.

Recent excavations by Jason Nesbitt have added substantially to our knowledge of the Caballo Muerto site complex and the Cupisnique culture.[36] Although temple complexes on the Central Coast northwards shared many common features, such as the use of raised temples, plazas, and sunken courts, specific forms distinguish different cultural traditions. Thus, while the Manchay culture favored J-shaped temples, a more symmetrical U-shape was typical of Cupisnique complexes. A square-room format, noted by Tom and Sheila Pozorski and seen in "sub-rectangular" rooms from at least as early as the Kotosh Religious Tradition, is common in Cupisnique sites, but it was not used by the Manchay culture although both traditions favored central staircases in their temples. As in many other Initial Period sites, there are hints that there may have been Late Preceramic temples at Caballo Muerto, but there appears to have been rapid development of the area in the Initial Period starting at about 1600 BC.

The largest single mound at the site is the Huaca Herederos Grande measuring 120 by 100 m (394 × 328 ft) and originally standing over 20 m (66 ft) high. The most recent study has been concentrated on Huaca de la Cruz, Huaca Cortada, Huaca Guavalito, and Huaca Curaca, all of impressive sizes. Nesbitt has identified four phases through this work (Cortijo, 1600 to 1100 BC; San Lorenzo, 1100 to 800 BC; Laredo, 800 to 700 BC; and Curaca, 700 to 200 BC). The last of these was the era of the ascendency and influence of Chavín de Huantar, during the Early Horizon.

These sites were built on the Moche Valley floodplain, suggesting that population density was relatively low in the region since good farmland was used for temple construction. There is strong evidence that probably since the earliest Initial Period occupation there were residences and special function buildings in the areas between the main temples, such as an enigmatic structure known as the Hall of the Niches. The local residents lived on a mix of seafood, lomas resources, and the full range of Andean coastal agricultural crops including beans, peanuts, manioc, maize, potatoes, and various other vegetables and fruits—another piece of evidence that coastal agriculture was well developed at an early time.

The earliest construction techniques at Caballo Muerto show strong continuities with earlier patterns. At Huaca de la Cruz, for example, large quarried stone uprights were spaced along the main façade and interspersed with flat, small stones. This huaca was also built using the modular square rooms with rounded corners known at Casma Valley sites. All the complexes used combinations of terraced platforms with aligned plazas, commonly with bilaterally organized adjacent platforms. When temple tops are preserved, they usually reveal suites of small rooms when excavated. Patios or chambers with colonnades, like those seen at Huaca de los Reyes, are also one of the distinct features of Cupisnique architecture.

Architectural complexes underwent changes as they were remodeled. At least five building phases, with radical changes in the final three, took place at Huaca de la Cruz as the structure was reworked into a symmetrical U-shaped format like that at Huaca de los Reyes. When Huaca Cortada was constructed a U-shape was followed, but corners were angled, not rounded, suggesting that the era of the square room modular forms had passed or that it had been associated with a particular social group or religious practice.

The Huacas de la Cruz, Cortada and Herederos Chica and the Hall of the Niches all were functioning during the Cortijo Phase. In the San Lorenzo Phase the last work on Cortada occurred, and there is evidence for domestic areas around it. This period also saw the construction of Huaca de los Reyes and Huaca Herederos Grande. The Laredo Phase is short and mostly related to changes in stirrup-spout vessel forms, but the era did see the last occupation of Huaca Cortada. Thus, when Chavín influence arrived at Caballo Muerto some temples were no longer in operation.

Some specific discoveries by Nesbitt deserve special mention here for the insights they provide about Andean culture in general. One of these is the fact that during a major building phase at Huaca de la Cruz, alternating bands of yellow-brown sand and gray sand were poured over the earlier architecture to create a foundation for the new construction. This is a case of "temple burial" as seen at the Late Preceramic site of Buena Vista. The alternating colors were employed for religious purposes, not practical ones, and this underscores a concern with symbolic acts, that were important even when they couldn't be seen. This is a ritual pattern that began early and continued throughout Andean prehistory and beyond.

Another example of an early but enduring cultural pattern is the incorporation of a natural, bedrock feature into the architecture of Plaza II at Huaca de la Cruz. This is the earliest known example of this practice, best known among the Inca who extensively incorporated either completely natural or modified natural rock formations into highly formalized architecture. The feature at Huaca de la Cruz was not only incorporated in the Initial Period; it appears to have been re-excavated in the Middle Horizon (or perhaps it was exposed all the time), when it was given a sacrificed human as an offering. The bedrock feature was likely an expression of the sacred character of the earth on which the huaca was built, and perhaps at the same time it served to "naturalize" the religion of Huaca de la Cruz. The incorporation of natural features and carved ones in temple architecture implies that there is a seamless continuity between Pachamama (the "Mother Earth" of the Incas) and the priests or rulers in charge of the buildings that grow out of her.

Food remains in refuse on the north platform at Huaca de la Cruz provide evidence that feasting was an important activity at these temples. We have already noted the importance of drinking chicha, probably occurring from a very early time in the Central Andes, and it is logical to assume that feasting occurred from the remotest times forwards. Human remains were also present in the feasting refuse at Huaca de la Cruz. Nesbitt suggests that this was a form of "endo-cannibalism" in which the remains of the beloved departed were eaten in reverence to absorb some of their essence into living communicants; this is a practice known for the Amazon.

THE WORLD OF THE INITIAL PERIOD

The world of the Initial Period was more than ceremonial centers in river or mountain valleys. Geological and human activities have erased much of the larger cultural landscape, but some traces do remain. Canto Grande is a side canyon between the Rimac and Chillón rivers with a fairly wide plain.[37] As late as the 1980s there were many "desert markings" there, mostly parallel straight lines and trapezoids stretching for hundreds of meters. These appear to date to at least the Initial Period and were oriented towards astronomical events. They are the earliest known desert markings in Peru, but there were many others, the most famous of which are the Nazca lines of later times on the South Coast.

We lack information about what was occurring in many areas of the Central Andes. For example, we currently know very little about Initial Period ceremonial centers on the South Coast of Peru. Work there has tended to concentrate on ceramics and textiles, with little study of large-scale architectural complexes or settlements. South of the Lurín Valley few architectural complexes are known except for the Chincha Valley, where there are at least 11 large pyramid-like mounds with about the same number of smaller mounds, all in the mid- to lower valley and all thought to date from the Initial Period. Some of these have been mapped to a greater or lesser extent, and by combining these maps with aerial photographs the general plans of the complexes have been outlined. Surface collections of sherds offer possible dates for some of the sites, but such determinations are always tentative since excavation often reveals sites to be earlier.

Initial Period large-scale architecture is virtually absent in the South Coast region which was later occupied by the Paracas culture and then the Nasca. Similarly, the first large-scale public architecture occurs relatively late in Bolivia compared to other areas of the Central Andes, and therefore it will be discussed in the next chapter. By the late Initial Period, *circa* 1200 BC, camelid hunters had become camelid herders. In Bolivia, north of Lake Poopó, the Wankarani culture passed through a long period of slow development from about 2000 BC through the Initial Period and the Early Horizon (locally termed the Early through Middle Formative). Their mixed pastoral and agrarian economy (based on quinoa and potatoes) allowed a degree of sedentism also expressed in crude pottery and copper metallurgy.

Wankarani villages consisted of many round, thatched adobe houses with walls painted red on the outside and yellow inside. Some communities may have held as many as 4,000 people. These were apparently autonomous villages with nested groups of houses, probably reflecting similarly nested social units. At the La Barca site, however, some groups had better quality cuts of camelid meat and had access to better quality obsidian and basalt for tools, imported from long distances, than others in the same community.[38] Simple carvings of camelid heads may have been used in household rituals or perhaps were inserted into walls in poorly known ceremonial structures, thereby foreshadowing later practices.[39] Between 1500 and 800 BC small, autonomous settlements with sunken enclosures appear in the early Chiripa culture, the first permanent architecture along the shore of Lake Titicaca.[40] However, this culture emerges more strongly in later times.

If the number and sizes of temple complexes are used as general indicators of cultural, economic, and political complexity, then the Peruvian coast from the Lurín Valley northwards was where the greatest social complexity occurred during the Central Andean Initial Period. Within this region there are perhaps three different cultural traditions identified by different architectural and artifactual patterns. The first are the "J-shaped" temples of the Central Coast, from the Lurín to the Chancay valleys, built by the Manchay archaeological culture.

The Norte Chico culture that was so prominent in the Late Preceramic Period does not appear to be represented by significant Initial Period monumental complexes in the mid- to lower valleys. The Nepeña-Casma Valley region had a cultural tradition definitely different from the Manchay culture, although some very general traits were shared such as the ways in which sunken plazas and platforms were arranged, the use of murals, and some general similarities in ceramics. Nepeña-Casma also shares general traits but has more in common with Cupisnique, to its north, than Manchay to its south.[41] For example, sub-rectangular rooms with niches are found from Casma northwards. However, the Nepeña-Casma zone also has its own distinct traditions such as favoring the use of large, painted adobe figures of anthropomorphic or zoomorphic deities, as seen not only at Moxeke but also at Punkurí and Cerro Blanco in Nepeña.[42] The arrangement of sites in long linear sets of temples and plazas, as seen at both Las Haldas and Sechín Alto, also seems to be a Nepeña-Casma feature.

Particularly in the case of early time periods, any generalizations, especially with regard to settlement patterns and the distribution of temple types, must be made with caution because early structures may have been buried by later constructions. This is the case at San Juanito in the Santa Valley. What appeared to be an Early Intermediate Period temple had been built over the top of an Initial Period structure with wall friezes in Cupisnique style.[43] As at Lurín, there were multiple temples overlapping in date in the Santa Valley, suggesting competing pilgrimage centers there.

The Cupisnique culture stretched from the Chao Valley northwards. Nesbitt distinguishes a southern variant, covering the area from Chao to Chicama, and a northern variety common mostly in the Jequetepeque Valley. Throughout this region many traits were shared in common, such as a high value placed on beautifully-made large stone mortars and general artistic styles. From at least Nepeña to the Chicama Valley a common ceramic style was also followed, named the Guañape style during early research in the Virú Valley. North of the Pampa de Paiján, however, there are notable differences in Cupisnique styles.

The site of Purulén, in the Zaña Vally, is the largest Initial Period complex in the northern Cupisnique region. The largest mound measures 80 by 50 m (262 × 164 ft) and is 8 m (26 ft) high. It is one of a total of 15 mounds surrounded by at least 50 hectares (124 acres) of apparently domestic structures.[44] Elsewhere in the region there are clustered settlements with multiple, low platform mounds around a rectangular plaza that seem to be Initial Period sites. In the Jequetepeque Valley these were located in the middle valley, as revealed by a survey in the late 1970s that identified 52 sites before the region was flooded by a dam.[45] Two large sites also followed this pattern. Las Huacas (Site J24.I) was built on a narrow plateau, covered 4.6 hectares (11 acres), and contained ceramics that resembled those found at Huacaloma, in the Cajamarca region in the adjacent highlands. Montegrande was even larger at 13 hectares (32 acres) with aligned platforms surrounded by a dense, highly organized residential sector. While sharing the trait of sub-rectangular rooms, these mid-valley sites used cylindrical burial towers that were generally similar to a form later known as *chullpas*, but which are not found elsewhere in the Initial Period.

Although the Jequetepeque ceramics shared similarities with Huacaloma and distinctive, different Cupisnique fancy wares were found in different regions, all the early Initial Period ceramics in the greater region resembled long-necked bottles with simple incisions and incised appliqué bands for decoration. New ceramic styles become popular in the late Initial Period (*circa* 1100 to 800 BC) when Huaca de los Reyes was founded at Caballo Muerto. The first appearance of very dark colored, highly polished and modeled ceramics that often are considered typical of the Cupisnique style were produced at this time, as well as the first stirrup-spout bottles in Peru. This was a form that remained popular for over two millennia.

The new ceramic styles of the late Initial Period were part of many other changes that indicate major cultural shifts in Peru. In addition to the founding of Huaca de los Reyes in the Moche Valley, the U-shaped center of Limoncarro was established in the Jequetepeque.[46] Near the town of Tembladera in a branch of the Jequetepeque Valley, new platforms were built with square plazas that resemble Kuntur Wasi, a highland temple complex that later reorganized itself as a result of Chavín influence. Further up the valley the Cajamarca area has a good sequence of Initial Period ceramics and architecture, but the patterns are clearest in the later period when Chavín de Huántar began to exert its influence.

POLITICS AND RELIGION IN ANCIENT PERU

Today, Westerners are familiar with churches and temples as places where religious specialists hold highly organized services. However, Andean temples were probably more like contemporary Hindu temple complexes where services are held by priests but a variety of other activities occur as well, with many different devotions towards images of the gods and other acts of veneration at shrines within the complexes. Numerous festivals occur throughout the year so that there is almost always a reason to make a pilgrimage to such a center. Hindu temples are peopled by priests, but also by a great number of other staff members who manage the place as well as the pilgrims who come there. One of the wealthiest Hindu temples today is the temple of Vishnu at Tirumala. Six thousand staff members serve at Tirumala and an average of 30,000 pilgrims visit each day, with the temple earning $165 million a year.[47]

Hindu temples have distinct regional styles due to various factors including the local popularity of particular gods, ethnic or linguistic differences, and historical circumstances. However, they all consider themselves Hindu temples, whether they are dedicated to Shiva, Vishnu or other deities. They can be contrasted with Christian churches, Muslim mosques, Jewish synagogues and so forth, and yet they are quite different from one another among devotees. The differences or similarities become important depending on what level of analysis one deems important.

The examples of Hindu temples and Christian churches serve as cautionary tales in considering the ceremonial complexes of ancient Peru, particularly the Preceramic and Initial Period temples already discussed although the same caution should be applied to later ones as well. We cannot be certain about the extent to which the different architectural patterns reflect differences in religious practices and beliefs and the social fields in which they were embedded, and to what degree the differences are relatively minor, suggesting that a generally similar religious system was practiced throughout great areas of the Central Andes. Broadly speaking it appears that religious practice was relatively uniform over large areas from an early time, and these centers do not appear to have been in control of outlying communities.

We have few examples of what life was like in small communities away from the large ceremonial centers, but a notable exception is Gramalote, on the edge of the beach at Huanchaquito in the Moche Valley (see Figure 5.5). There, Gabriel Prieto uncovered eight houses with separate rooms for sleeping and storage, constructed of beach stones, mud mortar, and with reed mats for roofs.

Gramalote's residents used ceramics for cooking, but they also made small vessels to contain red ochre paint that they produced and used in quantity, perhaps for body decorations or trade. They grew a variety of crops including cotton, and they hunted sharks, taking advantage of vulnerable females when they came close to shore to give birth.

Gramalote was a sizable community, with perhaps 50 houses at its height during the middle of its occupation between 1550 and 1200 BC. This would have been securely within the early phases of the development of the Caballo Muerto ceremonial complex, and yet there is no evidence in the various remains at Gramalote of any kind of control of the site by Caballo Muerto. The Gramalote villagers constructed their own ceremonial structure, estimated to be between 1,000 and 1,200 square m (10,764 to 12,917 square ft) in area. Little in the way of art or fancy ceramics were in evidence at the site. The red paint, small amulets, and other remains suggest that religious practices were local and "shamanistic" and not particularly tied to rites at the large ceremonial centers.

Figure 5.5 Gramalote. Top right: Artist's interpretation of a house (note bed) with excavated houses below. Top left: Gourd ladle and bowl. Center row: Three varieties of neckless ollas. Bottom row: Punctate and incised sherds (not correlated with olla types).

At San Juanito in the Santa Valley, a woman of advanced age, about 60, was buried under a stairway with adjoining walls covered in Cupisnique murals, noted above.[48] She was covered in seven layers of textiles and buried with a headdress of cotton, fibers, furs, and human hair, a small anthropomorphic wooden statue, eight gourds, and a necklace of *paucash* (*Cervantesia tomentosa*) fruits. Above the burial a large, engraved stone mortar and pestle were found; the impression is that this was an honored person, not a sacrifice. Although Initial Period burials are relatively rare, when the San Juanito burial and the burials at Cardal are considered and compared with earlier ones, such as those at Late Preceramic La Galgada, the continuity suggests that socio-political ranking systems were not radically different despite the passage of a number of centuries.

In the north, on the coast and in the highlands, some Initial Period centers appear to have grown directly out of Late Preceramic precedents in their formats. All of the Initial Period centers, including the U-shaped ones, seem to have drawn on basic concepts, such as dualism, and certain architectural formats, such as the construction of a sunken chamber inside another room. On the north coast there was a continuation of the Late Preceramic practice of combining circular sunken courts with terraced, flat-topped pyramids and the popularity of sub-rectangular (i.e. round-cornered) structures, perhaps derived from the Kotosh Religious Tradition, although these features are found in innovative arrangements in many places.

While it may have started in the Late Preceramic, the Kotosh Religious Tradition is mostly a phenomenon of the Initial Period and we may even speculate that its development may have had something to do with the demise of some of the Late Preceramic centers. The small-scale nature of practice in enclosed chambers organized to emphasize community and relative equality among participants, and the separateness of chambers, each by itself within a larger collection of them, contrasts with the large, imposing Late Preceramic ceremonial complexes.

The Late Preceramic use of *huancas* (standing stones), seen particularly in the Supe Valley sites such as Bandurria and Caral, ran counter to the tenets of the Kotosh Religious Tradition with its enclosed, secluded chambers. Single, isolated, standing stones disappear from the coast of Peru in the Initial Period and never regain their popularity or status, even though they remained important in the highlands and the altiplano. Taken together, these patterns suggest that the Kotosh Religious Tradition may have been a "Little Tradition" that developed in opposition to the Late Preceramic ceremonial centers and the attempts of the centralized priests and other leaders to consolidate political power. Some of the similarities in architectural formats between the large Late Preceramic sites and the Kotosh Religious Tradition chambers, such as sunken courts with fire pits as at El Paraíso, may belie social differences among practitioners in different settings.

Whatever the climatic or other reasons that influenced the changes seen in the transition between the Late Preceramic and the Initial Period, it is likely that social and political events, often inextricably related to religion, were probably occurring. Some centers and regions failed, such as El Paraíso and the Supe Valley sites, while others survived and even profited from these changes, such as La Galgada and the sites of the Casma Valley.

All these complex cultural developments were accomplished via subsistence economies that do not appear to be fundamentally different from those of the Late Preceramic Period—except, perhaps, that a greater variety of foods was available and technologies such as irrigation agriculture had advanced in complexity. However, coastal sites continued to find their animal protein primarily in the ocean and on the shore, while their carbohydrates came from irrigation agriculture that produced a wide range of crops. Starch grain analyses from pottery recovered from Cardal, Mina Perdida and Manchay Bajo, in Lurín, revealed that the most common remains were of manioc and potato, with achira and maize being prepared and consumed in lesser quantities.[49]

As with Late Preceramic monumental centers, many Initial Period ceremonial sites were abandoned at the end of the period. At Sechín Alto the construction of a wing on the north side of the main mound appears to have been halted suddenly. People of the Early Horizon later squatted on the site and dug into the top of the mound. This sudden abandonment of construction activities suggests that some kind of dramatic event might have taken place and caused activities there to come to an abrupt halt, but whether this was generally true is unknown.

The degree to which natural or social forces resulted in these changes are hard to assess. At Manchay Bajo, the last of the Manchay Culture sites to be abandoned in the Lurín Valley, a large perimeter wall was built around the main structure apparently to protect against landslides from nearby hills caused by El Niño rains.[50] Such an action suggests that natural events may have triggered cultural change, but it also highlights how humans can adapt to them. While a series of natural disasters, and perhaps other stresses on society such as pressure from overpopulation, may have been at work, there is also rather strong evidence that the rise of a large and powerful ceremonial center in the central highlands of Peru played an important role in realigning the religious and social world of the Central Andes. That center is known today as Chavín de Huántar.

NOTES

1 Murra 1962.
2 See Staller 2001 on Jelí Phase ceramics. Dates based on Staller and Thompson 2002.
3 Boaretto et al. 2009; Yaroslav 2006.
4 Oyuela-Caycedo and Bonzani 2005.
5 Zeidler 2003.
6 Marcos 2003: 21.
7 Damp 1982; Lathrap et al. 1975; Raymond 2003; Stahl 1985.
8 Stahl 1985.
9 Valdez et al. 2005; Valdez 2008.
10 Zeidler 2003: 480 and Valdez 2008: 880, 878 on comparisons.
11 Zeidler 1988 on Huayurco; Braun 1982; Bruhns 1989; Collier and Murra 1943 on Cerro Narrio.
12 Burger 1992: 58–59.
13 Patterson 1985: 64, Figure 5d on La Florida; Burger 1985 on comparisons of other ceramics.

14 Shady 1975.
15 Morales Chocano 1998.
16 Cardich 1980; see also Meggers 1981.
17 DeBoer 2003.
18 Villalba 1988: 108.
19 Pearsall 2003.
20 Simkin et al. 1981, cited in Zeidler and Isaacson 2003: 104.
21 Zeidler and Isaacson 2003: 89.
22 Zeidler and Isaacson 2003: 109.
23 Some of these sites, such as El Paraíso and Caral, show succeeding occupations, although they were apparently very light.
24 Grieder et al. 1988: 43.
25 Burger 1987; Burger and Salazar-Burger 1991.
26 Lumbreras 1974.
27 Burger 1987: 371.
28 Burger and Salazar 2008; Williams 1985.
29 T. Pozorski and S. Pozorski 1987; S. Pozorski and T. Pozorski 2011.
30 Bischof 1994, 2008; Samaniego et al. 1985.
31 The site is sometimes known as Pampas de Las Llamas-Moxeke, but it is a single complex.
32 The statues and murals were preserved at the time of Julio C. Tello's work at the site in the 1920s. They may have been destroyed in a subsequent earthquake since they are no longer visible.
33 See S. Pozorski and T. Pozorski 1987, 2011. Burger: personal communication.
34 Comparisons between complexes are difficult to make because of sub-surface features in different valleys and the issue of contemporaneous uses of temples that may or may not have been investigated in one valley or another. The Casma Valley complex thus may have been as large or larger than Caballo Muerto, but we do not have comparative data available to make this assessment.
35 T. Pozorski 1980; Moseley and Watanabe 1974.
36 Nesbitt 2012.
37 Rosselló Truel 1997.
38 Rose 2001; Janusek 2008: 69–72.
39 Capriles Flores 2011.
40 Hastorf 1999, 2008.
41 If Initial Period sites are identified in the Norte Chico it will be interesting to see how they relate to Manchay in the south and Nepeña-Casma in the north, or whether it is different from both.
42 Samaniego 2011; Shibata 2011.
43 Chapdelaine and Pimentel 2008.
44 Alva 1986.
45 Ravines 1985.
46 Sahai and Martinez 2010.
47 Templenet.com. For a discussion of how contemporary Hindu temples are tied to political and economic affairs, see Halpern 2012.
48 Chapdelaine and Pimentel 2008.
49 Burger et al. 2012.
50 Burger and Salazar 2008.

6

THE EARLY HORIZON

CHAVÍN DE HUÁNTAR

Even though more than two thousand years of social complexity preceded it, Chavín de Huántar is often the first topic discussed in depth in archaeology and art history books on the ancient Andes. This is less because it was the first pan-regional art style than because it is so captivating and powerful to modern eyes. At the same time, however, the Chavín de Huántar site and the archaeological culture of which it is symbolic are hardly known in the way that other great art styles and sites are recognized throughout the world, although this is beginning to change thanks to museum exhibits and the development of the site for tourism.

Chavín de Huántar was one of the earliest archaeological sites to be described in Peru. The sixteenth century conquistador and chronicler Pedro Cieza de León was so impressed that he claimed it was built by a race of giants, marvelling at the finely carved monuments he saw there.[1] Others followed him, including the Italo-Peruvian Antonio Raimondi (1826–1890), famed as a naturalist and for his role in founding the medical school and the department of analytical chemistry at the University of San Marcos, Lima. He retrieved a remarkable highly polished and engraved slab of granite from the site that is now housed in the National Museum of Archaeology, Lima and which bears his name, being known as the Raimondi Stone (see Figure 6.2).

What has astounded visitors over the centuries is the sheer size of Chavín's architecture and the quality of its stone carvings. The ingenuity of the site's engineering, the superb craftsmanship in the buildings' execution, and the visions expressed in Chavín stone carvings were never exceeded, only matched, in later prehistory. In the 1940s Julio C. Tello laid the foundations of all future research at Chavín de Huántar through his extensive excavations and publications. Subsequently John H. Rowe interpreted major construction periods and correlated them with his sequence of stone carving styles, among other important contributions. In addition to his excavations and studies on art and architecture, Rowe also focused on the role of Chavín as a "Horizon" during which it spread its influence throughout a large portion of modern Peru. This interpretation has shaped subsequent thinking about the site and stimulated debate concerning it. Luis G. Lumbreras undertook field research in the mid-1960s, as did Richard L. Burger in the mid-1970s, and Lumbreras and John W. Rick, with substantial contributions by Silvia R. Kembel, in the 2000s.[2]

Chavín de Huántar lies at an elevation of 3,180 m (10,430 ft) in the upper end of the Conchucos Valley at the junction of the Mosna and Wacheqsa rivers. At this relatively low elevation the site was well placed for contact with the tropical forest, the sierra, and the coast. The Mosna and Wacheqsa form the Marañon River, a tributary to the Amazon, and Chavín also is located on a pass from the Conchucos to the Callejón de Huaylas, the large north-south trending valley that holds the Santa River which eventually turns and debouches into the Pacific. Closer at hand, Chavín's location also offered hot springs nearby, easy access to high quality building stone, and deep, rich sediments for agriculture.

Chavín de Huántar consists of a large ceremonial complex and an adjacent town (see Figure 6.1). The ceremonial center visible today is the end product of several hundred years of construction, remodeling, and additions. The most visible large-scale constructions at the site, not all of which have been explored, cover an area of 10 hectares (24.7 acres) with a total site area of 50 hectares (123.6 acres). Within this complex the most important edifice was a U-shaped structure facing eastwards. Rowe called this structure the Old Temple. Similar to U-shaped temples on the coast, it was asymmetric with a total width of slightly more than 100 m (328 ft) and about 14 m (46 ft) high. Nestled within the arms of the U was a sunken circular plaza 21 m (69 ft) in diameter. According to Richard Burger the time of the Old Temple is associated with a ceramic assemblage known as Urrubarriu, followed by a brief Chakinani phase.[3]

As the site grew in importance the old right arm of the U-shaped structure was expanded with the addition of about 45 m (147 ft) of wall length. This first shifted the asymmetry of the temple complex from a dominant left arm to a dominant right arm. The plazas in front of the complex then were completely reoriented towards a new entrance, now known as the Black and White Portal, distinctive in its contrasting use of black and white stone steps, with dualism further emphasized by carvings on the pillars around the entrance. This New Temple is sometimes referred to as the Castillo (castle). It was used at the height of Chavín's influence and is associated with Janabarriu-style pottery.

A large patio fronts the Castillo and runs around a large rectangular plaza measuring 105 by 85 m, (344 × 279 ft), within which is a square sunken court 20 m (66 ft) on a side. A set of black-and-white stone steps, similar to the steps of the portal to the temple, is on the main access route from the Castillo, while other stairs descend to the rectangular plaza on at least one side with more steps into the sunken plaza on each of its other sides. The great abundance of stairways suggests that many people gathered in these spaces and that movement on vertical and horizontal planes was an important part of the experience of being at the temple. This feature was a continuation of Late Preceramic and Initial Period ceremonial centers.

Figure 6.1 View of the core of the Chavín de Huántar temple complex from a nearby hill. The Castillo is the darker structure at left, with its upper left corner touching the road.

Although the New Temple may have been an expression of new socio-political and economic forces, there appears to have been continuity in religious practice at the site. Both the Circular Plaza and the New Temple are oriented towards a modified hill over which the sun rose on the summer solstice. Also, a 20-ton stone altar on the edge of the principal plaza has circular depressions in it that may represent the stars of the Pleiades.[4] The times of the rising and setting of this constellation were considered important in marking changes of seasons throughout the ancient Andes and the New World in general.

The amount of thought, labor, and resources devoted to constructing Chavín de Huántar must have impressed ancient visitors to the site as much or more than modern tourists and researchers. Even more impressive is the fact that extra effort was given to aspects of construction that many visitors never saw. Much of the fine stonework was painted, so that the high quality work was for religious purposes, not to please mortals. Some finely polished lintels and carvings may or may not have been visible, but the discerning eye might have noticed the immensity of the long, single blocks of limestone that form the steps to a sunken plaza. More startling were the large rectangular-facing stones (ashlars) with elaborate images, as well as three-dimensional sculptures designed to dazzle and disorient.

The Mosna River was artificially diverted to provide more room for the plazas and surrounding structures to the east of the New Temple. A complex series of stone-lined drains was built under the temple to prevent erosion, and other shafts were constructed to allow air to enter rooms deep within the New Temple. The bulk of the temple was solid with relatively small interior passageways and rooms. The main construction technique was to build parallel walls or chambers and then fill them in. On the coast this method also had been followed in the Preceramic and Initial Periods, with piles of shicra or adobes serving to fill up the spaces. At Chavín, however, the fill consisted of carefully laid stone. This was then covered with fine masonry, meaning that the fill was never seen once the construction was complete. The great amount of extra time and trouble it took to use laid fill was likely due to a conception of the construction of the temple as a sacred act. Again, similar practices are known from earlier times, such as the extra effort required to fill Huaca de la Cruz with layered colored sands when it was decommissioned.

The skill and care shown in the construction techniques was matched by the ingenuity with which architecture was designed to awe visitors. The people who came to Chavín de Huántar were pilgrims who probably traveled great distances to reach this sacred place that was the home of gods. The rank of a person likely determined how deeply he or she was allowed to enter into the sacred precincts. The large, more distant plazas were probably more accessible than smaller patios closer to the main temple, while entry into the Castillo may have been reserved for specially chosen ones or those of the highest rank.

ART AND RITUAL AT CHAVÍN DE HUÁNTAR

Chavín sculptural art was a unique invention with no precedents or descendants. The art is basically representational, but it is done in a style and convention that idealized natural phenomena, especially animals, and transformed them into supernatural beings. Thus a jaguar was shown in its elemental form, but was rendered supernatural through the manner by which it was presented and by elaborations of features that no natural jaguar has. The art style included the use of modular width and bilateral symmetry, the juxtaposition of profile faces to be read as a third full face, an architectural conception of design such as the employment of modular units, and the use of visual metaphors. The Raimondi Stone employs many of these traits. It can be "read" upside down, even though the likelihood of prehistoric acrobatics for such a purpose seems relatively low. Rather, these kinds of readings were subconsciously registered, creating awe in the viewers (see Figure 6.2).

Many of the sculptural elements can only be seen in detail when the viewer is relatively close to the temple buildings. From a distance, however, the temple would have still presented powerful, mysterious imagery. On the sides and back of the main temple larger-than-life heads appeared to jut out of the temple walls some 10 m (33 ft) above the ground. These tenon head sculptures grimace with fangs and nasal mucus, and they are arranged so

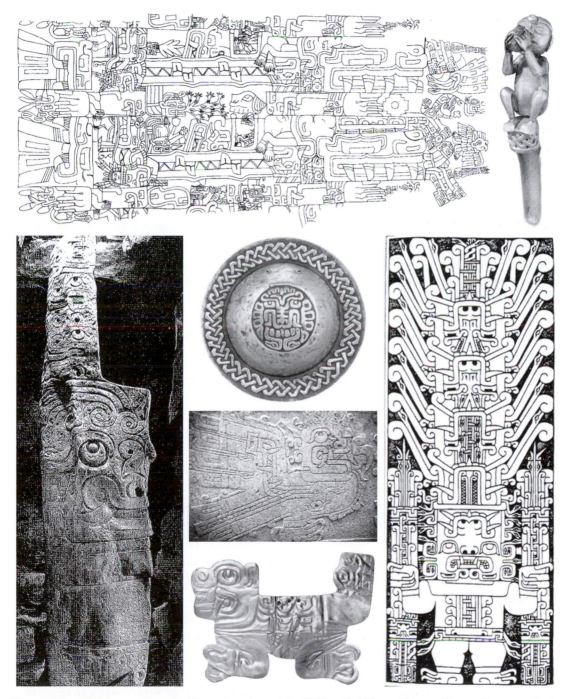

Figure 6.2 Chavín art. Top: Roll-out drawing of the Tello Obelisk and bimetallic snuff spoon. Left: View of the right side of the upper portion of the Lanzón. Center: Chavín goldwork and (center) stone carving of winged jaguar. Right: Roll-out drawing of the Raimondi Stone.

that in sequence they represent priests or gods transforming from human to supernatural forms.

On the summit of the Castillo there was a 2 m (6.6 ft) high platform with a matching pair of two-room buildings. The face of the temple was flat with two rectangular openings containing short stairways 6 m (20 ft) above the ground, creating "negative balconies" from which priests would have seemed to mysteriously emerge to the crowd below.[5] This feature is a good example of Chavín innovation. Whereas coastal U-shaped temples highlighted central stairways that served as performance spaces for priests and others to ascend towards and descend from the holy of holies, at Chavín the priests' and gods' movements were mysterious, proceeding from the inside out with priests confronting crowds below, rather than carried out via central stairs with clear routes from the plaza floors to the holiest shrines on temple summits.

The music of blaring trumpets, smoke, the swirling of fantastic imagery, and the performances of priests and their attendants must have created a powerful sacred environment. Indeed, studies have suggested that the canals that ran through the temple for the practical purpose of preventing erosion may have been deliberately constructed to create a powerful, pulsating sound so that the temple or the gods within it could be heard roaring.

Those who were allowed to enter the temple were led through a maze-like series of passageways that are still intact. These passageways, known collectively as the labyrinth, lead into small chambers called galleries. People from different regions of Peru deposited pottery and other items in the Ofrendas (Offerings) Gallery as offerings to the great god of Chavín de Huántar. Pottery found here came from the Central Coast, the Casma and Jequetepeque Valleys, the Cajamarca region in the northern highlands, and the region of Kotosh in the *ceja de selva*.

The great god of Chavín has been in place for three millennia, at a cruciform intersection in the labyrinth at the center of the Old Temple on an axis with the center of the Sunken Circular Plaza outside. The statue is known as the Lanzón (Big Lance) because of its blade-like shape (see Figure 6.2). The god has a monster-like head on an anthropomorphic body, with one hand raised and the other down as if to balance the forces of the universe.[6] Nearby, a hidden chamber has remarkable acoustic properties so that words spoken in mid-tones boom around the nearby Lanzón. This indicates that the supreme deity of Chavín de Huántar, as represented in this sculpture, was an oracle probably visited by a very few specially selected pilgrims or priests. The god was also worshipped with sacrifices; human finger bones incised with Chavín designs were found on the Lanzón's head.[7]

The select few who were admitted to the inner precincts of the temple were probably prepared to meet the god not only by the sensory overload of the complex carvings, the incongruous architecture, the labyrinth, the clouds of incense, and the blaring sounds, but also through the use of psychoactive drugs. One of the sculptures at Chavín shows a supernatural figure carrying a long section of San Pedro cactus (*Echinopsis pachanoi*), the flesh of which is rich in mescaline and which is still used in shamanic practices today. The nasal mucus depicted on some of the tenon heads around the temple walls reflects the experience of inhaling powdered *vilca* (*Anadenanthera colubrina*), another powerful hallucinogenic snuff made from the beans of a tree common to the *ceja de selva* and tropical forest.[8] A beautiful bimetallic spoon in Chavín style and numerous examples of elaborate stone mortars and pestles were likely used to prepare and inhale this drug (see Figure 6.2).[9] The less powerful but still effective chicha alcoholic beverage was also probably consumed. Like earlier ceremonial centers and also at later ones throughout prehistory, temple sites such as Chavín combined activities that we might separate into "religion," "entertainment," "performance," and "celebration", integrating them into a seamless experience.

There are many sculptures at Chavín that appear to depict the principal deity of the Lanzón. One carving is known as the "Medusa" because it shows the god with snakes for hair, holding two shells from tropical waters, a *Strombus galeatus* and a *Spondylus*, in each hand. The god on the Raimondi Stone has an elaborate headdress and is often referred to as the Staff God because of the long objects he holds in each hand, although these may be torches or some other object, not necessarily staffs.[10] Although he is depicted somewhat differently, all of these images seem to refer to the same deity.

The Tello Obelisk, named after its discoverer, deserves special attention partly because it does not appear to depict the principal deity (see Figure 6.2). Like the Lanzón, it is a single shaft of stone with a prismatic cross section and a notch at its top. Unlike the Lanzón, however, the original location of the Tello Obelisk is unknown, but it is generally considered to have had a very important role in the temple. While the Lanzón depicts a relatively straightforward image of an anthropomorphic god, the Tello Obelisk is carved with relatively fine-line complex imagery portraying two supernatural black caymans, the large crocodiles of tropical rivers.

Donald Lathrap carried out an extensive, detailed study of the imagery of plants, animals, and beings sprouting out of the supernatural caymans' bodies, including peanuts, chili peppers, manioc, bottle gourds, and two kinds of marine shells. The imagery of the supernatural caymans can thus be interpreted as an origin myth related to lowland domesticated plants, as known in recent Amazonian mythology, expressed in a dualistic mode. Following this interpretation, Gary Urton draws upon Inca and tropical forest myths to suggest that each of the two depicted beasts is an *amaru*, the Quechua term for a dragon or giant serpent, and thus not a cayman but rather a composite beast that symbolically mediates between different ontological states, such as male/female, domestic/wild, and natural/cultural.[11]

The references to plants and animals domesticated from the tropical forest combined with symbols from the highlands and coast are what made (and continue to make) Chavín art so distinctive. Located in the highlands but close to the tropical forest and not too far from the coast, it was the meshing of the symbolism of these different environmental zones that made Chavín so powerful and enchanting. As Richard Burger has pointed out, Chavín seems to have been a synthesis of Initial Period religious traditions, perhaps the expression of a revitalization movement in which something entirely new was created that nevertheless drew upon old ways and ideas.[12]

THE CHAVÍN HORIZON

The support staff who ran the religious center, crafted luxury cult items, and hosted pilgrims were likely the main occupants of the town outside the Chavín temple complex. The community expanded significantly from its beginnings in the Urabarriu phase as a small settlement to the north of the temple with a probable population of no more than 500 people. They had already diverted the Huachecsa River, however, and built the 6 m (around 20 ft) stone bridge across it that was still used into the twentieth century. By the Janabarriu phase, at Chavín's apogee, the town was twenty times larger. The population may have grown not only as a result of wealth contributed by temple visitors, but also by expanding terraced land for potato and root crop agriculture, and by integrating high altitude camelid pastoralists into the economy. The subsistence base was expanded rather than radically transformed; throughout Chavín's history maize does not appear to have played an important role in the diet, even though it was cultivated and consumed.[13]

Chavín's cult spread throughout much of Peru. Some old Initial Period centers, such as Pacopampa and Kuntur Wasi in the northern highlands, accepted the new religion, rearranging sacred spaces, carving stone monuments and adopting ceramic, metalwork, and other artifact styles in the Chavín style. In many places, rather than undergoing a wholesale conversion to an entirely new religion Chavín elements were added to local traditions that continued. Chavín was highly effective in drawing upon widespread existing ideas, reformulating them, and then sending them back to be re-absorbed by the ceremonial centers and regions from whence many ideas had originated in the first place.

There is an almost complete absence of military themes in Chavín art and artifact assemblages, suggesting that Chavín's spread was peaceful, although the link between art and politics is often tenuous. The Chavín religion included a suite of specialized ritual and high-status "luxury" goods that appear to have been standardized, and it is by these items that the spread of the religion can be documented.

Gold jewelry, stone spoons and mortars, and carved bone and shell, including ornaments and *Strombus galeatus* shell trumpets, were made at Chavín and then sent to various sites. The shells were imported from the coast, including from the warm waters of Ecuador, brought to Chavín, worked, and then redistributed. Several engraved *Strombus galeatus* shells that may have been used for generations before being buried as offerings were found in the *Galeria de los Caracolas* (Gallery of the Conch Shells) within the labyrinth of the temple.

Obsidian, the volcanic glass highly valued for its cutting properties, was procured from the Quispisisa source 450 km (280 mi) to the south of Chavín in the Vilcashuaman area of Ayacucho.[14] Eventually it replaced the local chert at Chavín de Huántar, a clear indication of the prestige and power of the ceremonial center which probably distributed the obsidian to many of the other Chavín-influenced sites.

In both Ayacucho and Huancavelica no examples of ceremonial centers are known prior to the Atalla site, 450 km (280 mi) south of Chavín. Its residents emulated Chavín ceramics and cut stone masonry while maintaining local traits such as circular dwellings and burials in or near them. Fifteen kilometers west of Atalla is the largest deposit of mercury known in Latin America, occurring in the form of cinnabar (mercuric sulfide), a bright red mineral that was greatly valued as a pigment by many ancient peoples. Chavín thus appears to have controlled one of the major cinnabar sources in Peru.[15]

One of the most striking examples of Chavín's influence in the Central Andes is the role of metal objects that served as powerful conveyors of religious ideology. It is only with Chavín that metal objects come to be known in abundance in Peru (see Figure 6.2). Whether this is due to technological breakthroughs or the degree to which Chavín religious leaders deliberately and fully exploited known technologies cannot be currently assessed. The majority of objects are made of gold alloys formed into items for adornment or ritual use. These include crowns, ear ornaments, pectorals, bangles, beads, trumpets, and snuff spoons, all probably used by priests. They were made from sheets of metal, bent or folded and joined through the use of tabs and slots as well as by sweat welding and soldering. The sheets were decorated by chasing or repoussé and by cutting out spaces and then filling them in again with bangles hung by rings. Distinctive gold Chavín paraphernalia is found throughout the region in which the center had influence. While there is a recognizable style there is variability in the metallurgy, so the issue of the degree to which Chavín de Huántar controlled the production of goods associated with its religion remains somewhat uncertain. We could expect that through time the center's monopoly over the religious system and its paraphernalia may have changed.

Chavín-style ceramics and the pottery influenced by it are the most widespread and indicative signs of the religious center's influence. Bowls with incised decorations around the rims and single- and stirrup-spout bottles dominate assemblages, with an increase in the use of jars in the Janabarriu phase when Chavín was in its ascendency. "Classic" Janabarriu-style fine vessels usually had very dark gray surfaces due to firing in an oxygen-reduced environment, with surfaces often further blackened by superficial reduction or smudging. Decorative techniques emphasized highly polished surfaces that reflected light. Stamping, brushing, and seal impressing were common techniques employed for the relatively quick production of some high quality ceramics, with the finest pieces sculpted or modeled while the clay was still plastic. Some of the finest pieces from Chavín de Huántar were bowls and single-spout bottles carved in heavy relief with motifs similar to stone carvings, but with even more elaborate interlinking of decorative elements than in the less yielding stone.

The Cupisnique style of the Chicama-Jequetepeque region, the Tembladera style in the middle Jequetepeque Valley, and the Chongoyape style in the Lambayeque Valley are quite distinct, but they all share some common features that identify them as Chavín-influenced. These similarities, combined with the styles of other objects, show that Chavín's relations varied across the landscape. It probably had peer-polity interactions with centers such as Pacopampa and Kuntur Wasi to the north. Indeed, the exact relationship of north coast Cupisnique centers such as Huaca Lucia and Huaca de los Reyes with Chavín de Huántar is not entirely clear, although in general the evidence points to the highland center as pre-eminent in its time.

To the south, Chavín may have established religious centers itself, perhaps similar to the way in which "daughter" oracles were established during Inca times. In some places Chavín influence was less direct, such as in the high grasslands of the central highlands of Junín and Pasco where camelids abounded. In such places Chavín influence is often apparent in the use of stamps on ceramics, in the form of concentric circles that appear to be symbolic references to jaguar spots. Elsewhere, such as at Atalla, Chavín may have had a much more direct influence on local events.

The tropical forest references in Chavín art were due to direct knowledge of jungle regions rather than simply the portrayal of exotic animals, like the lions on coats of arms in Medieval Europe. Recent research in the Jaén district, a low tropical region now in far northern Peru, demonstrates Chavín's long reach. Ryan Clasby and Jorge Meneses B. found that the site of Huayurco was occupied from the Late Initial Period through the Early Horizon into the Early Intermediate Period.[16] It had fairly extensive architecture, exotic ceramics, marine shell jewelry and many other items indicating that it prospered greatly during Chavín times. Trade in fancy stone bowls that had begun centuries before continued at Huayurco, which apparently served as an intermediary site in their distribution. It was linked via river courses to Ecuadorian sites to the north as well as Peruvian highland regions to the south.

The basis of Chavín's power appears to have been its ability to attract pilgrims, with significant benefits from the gifts they brought to the temple. Social distinctions are in evidence within the urban complex surrounding the ceremonial center as well as throughout the nearby region. More gold jewelry, cinnabar, exotic ceramics, and foods are found in the urban area to the west of the temple than in the town area to its east. People living in nearby high altitude villages sent only the select cuts of llama meat to the urban zone and used local chert for cutting tools, while townspeople used knives of imported obsidian. Evidence suggests that the meat was freeze-dried into *charqui*.[17] All the residents of the town ate great amounts of llama meat and thus dined well, but the residents of the western town area ate younger, more succulent animals than those in the eastern, lower status zone.[18]

While the priests at Chavín de Huántar were developing more pronounced social hierarchies than in previous times through their creation of secret rituals, specialized ceremonial goods, and élite jewelry, there still remained strong local traditions throughout much of the Central Andes. An example of this is found on the north coast of Peru at the site of Morro de Eten on the coast of the Lambayeque Valley, which flourished in the late Initial Period when Chavín was rising to pre-eminence.[19] There, a very tall man, almost two meters (6 ft) in height, died at about the age of 60—an extremely advanced age for the time—and was buried in the ground, extended on his back (see Figure 6.3). He was placed on a fish (a pilchard [*Sardinops sagax sagax*]) oriented in the same direction as the burial with the head to the northeast, and large rocks were placed on top of the grave.

The man's head and long bones were covered in red hematite. There were no ceramic grave goods, but offerings included two deer bone spatulas, an anthracite mirror, two pieces of worked slate, and 16 cut and polished mussel shells (*Choromytilus chorus*) of different

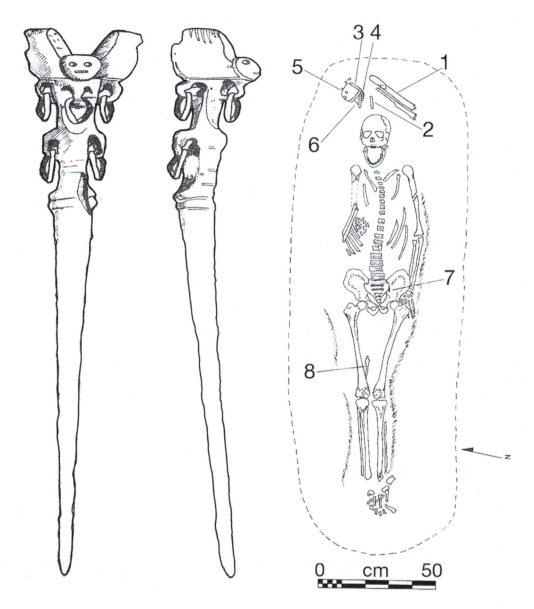

Figure 6.3 The Morro de Eten Burial. Right: The burial with artifacts (1. Deer bone "spatulas", 2. Worked slate, 3. Polished mussel shells, 4. Lumps of yellow ochre, 5. Anthracite mirror, 6. Worked slate, 7. Fish bones, 8. The wand.) Left: Front (left) and side (right) view of the wand.

sizes, stacked together. There were traces of textile on some of the shells; they may have been wrapped in fabric or contained in a bag. Textile imprints also were found on one of the slate pieces. The most striking artifact was a carved deer bone, close to 21 cm (8.5 in) in length. One end was carved into a human-like face between two outstretched "wings," while below a series of loops probably held small metal or shell objects that jangled when they were shaken. Most of the rest of this object was smooth, tapering to a dull point at the distal end.

The cause of the man's death is unknown. He had been in relatively good health all his life, with two exceptions. First, there was evidence of micro-traumas and inflammation in his knees, indicating that they had experienced much stress. Second, his right femur (thigh bone) was much larger than his left and also appeared to have experienced inflammation and trauma. This is the same area in which the carved artifact was found, and when it was analyzed trace amounts of human tissue were found on it. The association of the femur and the artifact led the investigators to conclude that the artifact had been carried in the living tissue of the man's right leg. Over time the muscle formed an interior scab around the long hole into which the object was inserted on the rear of his leg, but the creation of this sheath of human muscle took a long time and was a painful process that included sporadic infections.

This man was a religious specialist of the kind generally referred to as a shaman.[20] The carved deer bone kept in his leg may have been a wand, and was certainly a rattle-like device. Perhaps the leg sheath was designed to allow him to magically produce the item during shamanic sessions related to mystical flight, as represented in the finial showing a face with wings. The spatulas were likely used for ingesting a psychotropic substance to produce a trance state in himself or his patients, while the mirror reflected light on objects or people, a very common practice in shamanic activities. The thin, flat pieces of slate had numerous lines on their surfaces suggesting that something had been sharpened on them, but their specific uses are hard to assess. The same is true for the mussel shells; a guess might be that they were cast to scry or predict the future.

The creation of the leg sheath probably began at early age. However, if the shaman had suffered because of keeping his wand in his leg, he nevertheless walked great distances, perhaps to pilgrimage centers, or else he danced for long periods of time in ecstatic trances. He may have been feared and respected by his local community judging by the rocks on his grave, perhaps placed there to make sure that he stayed in place. As in the case of interments at Gramalote, this burial suggests that local religion was key to everyday life in the Initial Period.

The greater the distance from Chavín de Huántar, the less it controlled or influenced local populations. The Huamachuco-Quirovilca-Cajamarca area of the northern highlands and the lower reaches of the Casma-Nepeña-Santa Valleys on the northern Central Coast appear to have deliberately avoided or resisted being drawn into Chavín's orbit of influence. These regions are also places where there is the clearest evidence of organized warfare during the Early Horizon. Many years ago the idea of a *Pax Chavinensis* was proposed—the notion that the religious cult created a common community of people living in relative peace with one another over large areas of Peru. The idea still holds and Chavín does appear to be a horizon—a cultural phenomenon that spread throughout many different regions for a long period of time, although, apparently, there were some areas that did not fall under Chavín hegemony.[21]

RISE AND COLLAPSE

As previously noted, Richard Burger has suggested that Chavín may have been a revitalization movement in which the old ideas of Initial Period centers were reformulated into something new.[22] Chavín reworked long-established cultural concepts of reciprocity, dualism, and the value of labor and materials as expressions of fundamental ontological principles. While Chavín's innovations in art, architecture, and religion drew more and more people into its orbit, its resourcefulness and energy in controlling long-distance exchange systems in precious goods probably secured its pre-eminence.

A different perspective from Burger's view of Chavín's rise, but one which does not completely conflict with it, is taken by scholars interested in ancient climate. They point out that towards the end of the Initial Period the frequency of major El Niño events increased dramatically, shifting from once every two or three generations to one a decade, with events often spaced closely together.[23] Devastating floods on the coast could have undermined the authority of the religious leaders in the ceremonial centers there, which appear to have ceased to function well before Chavín's collapse.[24] In this context, the cause of Chavín's rise as a crisis cult or revitalization movement may have been an increase in severe El Niño events. Paul Roscoe observes that the locations of Chavín and the other large Early Horizon centers are all in the mid- to northern highlands, directly to the east of those areas of the coast that would have been most strongly affected by severe El Niños, and in areas where drought in the highlands might have encouraged the rise of leaders and centers who claimed access to divine intervention.[25]

A team of archaeologists led by John Rick has spent more than a decade engaged in extensive excavations within the main temple precinct and nearby areas at Chavín de Huántar. Many specific finds are noteworthy, such as the identification of a great number of building episodes and vertical additions to the temple. However, it is their interpretation of the chronology of the site that has caused the most controversy. In their perspective, Chavín began much earlier in the Initial Period and thus was less a revitalization movement than one of a number of Initial Period centers that competed with one another to attract pilgrims and adherents.[26] The implication is that Chavín was not so much a force that spread its doctrine and art style throughout great regions of Peru, but rather a particularly successful Initial Period center. This view fits with the perspective of some Peruvian archaeologists such as Luis G. Lumbreras who think in terms of a "Formative Period," rather than the Rowe-Menzel perspective of an Initial Period succeeded by a Early Horizon as supported by Richard Burger.

The issue, if extrapolated to its full extent, is not simply a question of terminology. Did the elaborate gold work found at places such as Kuntur Wasi come from Chavín de Huántar, or was it locally made? Are ceramics with circle-and-dot motifs resembling Janabarriu pottery the result of influence from Chavín de Huántar, or was the style more generally shared rather than disseminated from the premier ceremonial center? From a theoretical perspective, "demoting" Chavín de Huántar to a highly successful Initial Period center but not a dominant force would not simply require abandoning the concept of the Early Horizon and perhaps the Rowe-Menzel chronological system in favor of the Lumbreras model. It would also favor a cultural evolutionary perspective of a steady growth through time in the complexity of ancient Andean cultures, rather than the model of eras of broad unification followed by widespread collapses. These are the kinds of issues that remain to be resolved in the issue of Chavín de Huántar's chronology and the relevance of its role.

While chronological concerns are always important, the weight of evidence strongly suggests that Chavín de Huántar was more than just one of a number of Initial Period temples. The site itself is exceptional, and there is no other contemporary ceremonial center that even approximates the amount of labor and craftsmanship that was lavished on the Chavín ceremonial complex. Furthermore, new studies are beginning to demonstrate how Chavín transformed many local regions. For example, in the Upper Huallaga Basin, where Kotosh is located, there was a direct continuity in the location of Late Preceramic temples through the Initial Period. However, in the Kotosh Chavín Period (*circa* 600 to 250 BC) a great number of old sites were abandoned and new ones built. These changes appear to have been due to ideology rather than practical matters. For instance, the Initial Period Waira-jirca temple complex was abandoned, but a new temple, Sajar-patac, was built on the opposite bank of the Huallaga River. Along with the changes in settlement, old ceramic styles were also forsaken in favor of new, Chavín related pottery.[27] These major shifts in terms of temple abandonment and the establishment of new ones suggest that Chavín did indeed have a powerful influence on local peoples in many places in ancient Peru, and it was not simply a first among equals.

THE SOUTH-CENTRAL ANDEAN INTERACTION SPHERE

As previously noted, the South Coast of Peru is extremely arid. The Chilca, Mala, and Omas valleys have small floodplains and irrigable land. Cañete, Chincha, and Pisco are richer environments, but there is a long section of coastal desert stretching 160 km (102 mi) from the mouth of the Pisco River to the mouth of the Ica River. Individual streams are often seasonally ephemeral, and river courses are cut deep. Two more small streams, the Acarí and the Yauca, complete the list of South Coast valleys. Beyond them lies the Far South Coast.

Most research on the South Coast has focused on the region associated with the Nasca Culture of the Early Intermediate Period. This includes the Ica River that flows more north-south than east-west, and the dendritic cluster of streams that merge to form the Rio Grande de Nazca. These tributaries consist of two groups, a set that converges near the modern town of Palpa and a group to the south. These are sometimes distinguished as the Northern and Southern Nazca regions respectively.[28]

These features of terrain and water had a strong influence on human settlement. The southern Central Coast valleys from Chilca to Cañete probably reached relatively high population densities early, but the total number of people in them was small in relation to the larger valleys to the north and south. In the Chilca Valley, for example, large sites such as Anitval and

Huarangal are not well dated but they appear to have been occupied early and probably abandoned and reoccupied throughout prehistory. There were large fishing villages on the coast, such as Curayacu and Santa Maria, which show Chavín influence in their ceramics. So too, in Chilca, the Lapa Lapa site covers 10 hectares (25 acres). Here, houses were made of adobe bricks as well as wattle-and-daub, known as *quincha* in Peru, and were placed on terraces built into a hillside in the lower mid-valley. The site complex included a fortified granary on a high slope, defensive walls, and a temple on a trapezoidal mound.[29] This site is also poorly dated, but it likely dates to the late Early Horizon. Many such settlements existed throughout the Central Andes. Most have not been studied in detail, but their presence indicates the success of early farmers in the region.

All coastal peoples in Peru maintained contacts with highlanders, whether as kin, friends, or foe, but this is especially clear along the South Coast. The finger-like system of South Coast river valleys reached upriver deep into the highlands. Populations in the more northerly of the South Coast valleys were closely tied to people in the modern Peruvian Departments of Huancavelica and Ayacucho, while further south there were ties to Apurimac and Cusco. Exchanges and influences between all these regions were continuous throughout the past in a South-Central Andean Interaction Sphere that sometimes included the Titicaca Basin and northern Chile. This was in many ways a world apart from the regions to the north, although the forces of history variously brought peoples together into greater or lesser contact throughout the centuries.

Although the extreme aridity of the South Coast has provided archaeologists with evidence of very early occupation there, population density was light during the Preceramic Period. A broad-based subsistence strategy with fairly high mobility was probably practiced by relatively few people for long periods of time. The site of Pernil Alto (PAP 226), in the Río Grande Valley, had multiple occupation phases dating to *circa* 3800 to 3000 BC, and there is evidence of an early occupation at the Nasca ceremonial center of Cahuachi. Flexed burials in pits inside houses at the former site were quite similar to those found at Paloma and Chilca on the Central Coast, and it is likely that general cultural patterns were also similar.[30]

The archaeological picture of prehistory becomes clearer with the first use of ceramics. In general, the ceramics of the South Coast are distinct from other regions except for their close relations to the southern highlands. They also serve as the backbone of a regional chronology, but at the same time the region is also well known for magnificent early textiles, mummy bundles, trephination, and the famous Nazca Lines. However, although the ceramics of the region share general features, there are distinct sub-regional styles.

Issues of unity and diversity are complicated by the history of research in the region. In 1925 Julio C. Tello, Toribio Mejía Xesspe, and their colleagues were alarmed by the appearance on the art market of spectacular textiles, which were being looted from sites on the Paracas Peninsula. Thus alerted, they mounted an expedition to the peninsula and uncovered spectacular mummy bundles at a number of sites on different sides of a hill known as Cerro Colorado.

Tello identified two occupation phases from this work, based on two sites (see Figure 6.4). Paracas Cavernas had simple funerary bundles in pits or bottle-shaped tombs, with textiles showing linear embroidered designs and distinctive ceramics with incised, post-fired paint also using linear motifs (see Figure 6.4). The other style is known as Paracas Necropolis, found at the site of Wari Kayán. The Paracas Necropolis style succeeds Cavernas with large, elaborate funerary bundles buried in groups, sometimes in old Cavernas period structures. Ceramics found with these burials are in a style known as Topará, consisting of finely made, polished monochrome wares often in the shapes of fruits.

The two Paracas terms were used to refer to archaeological cultures, textile styles, and ceramic styles, resulting in considerable confusion when subsequent research demonstrated that the three were not strictly sequential.[31] The attempt to work out ceramic chronologies was both aided and complicated by other research, such as that of Alfred Kroeber who worked with Tello on the Paracas Peninsula. The master ceramic chronology for local use, which also serves as the basis for the chronology of Peru in general, was developed by Dorothy Menzel, John Rowe, and Lawrence Dawson using the ceramics of the Ica Valley.[32] The Ocucaje style—also known as the "Paracas Pottery of Ica"—sequence was divided into ten phases, and with some modifications it still holds today.[33]

As far as can be determined, the people of the region lived relatively simple lives based on agriculture, and yet they produced striking ceramics and remarkable textiles. The most elaborate Paracas Cavernas ceramics were decorated in four or five colors using a resin-based paint after vessels were fired, which is a hallmark of Paracas pottery. Painted surfaces, often outlined by incisions, were thus unstable and easily damaged, suggesting that these vessels were made strictly as funerary items or for very limited uses.

Unlike on the North Coast where first single-spout bottles and then stirrup spouts came to be favored, Paracas ceramics and South Coast potteries in general expressed dualism through the use of the double-spout-and-bridge design that remained regionally popular throughout prehistory (see Figure 6.4). Double-spout-and-bridge bottles tend to resemble enclosed bowls rather than tall containers. There are occasional examples of vessels shaped in figural forms, such as a double-headed serpent, while in late Paracas times spectacular pottery masks, panpipes, and trumpets also were made in this style.

The designs were executed by incising parallel bands around large panels containing curvilinear depictions of stylized animals. In some double-spout-and-bridge bottles the vessel was mostly left plain. The highly burnished surface was sometimes contrasted by isolated designs or a band of incised, repeating, geometric motifs. One of the two spouts could be modified into the head of an animal, a humanoid, or a supernatural.

Among the most striking Paracas design motifs are highly abstracted Chavín-like images (see Figure 6.4). In these, the form of an animal—a feline, for example—was treated in an extreme rectilinear manner with head, body, and tail all rendered as rectangles. The creature's image was sometimes wrapped around the side of a bowl so that if it was viewed from the side lacking the head, the image might appear completely abstract to someone unfamiliar with the canons of the art style.

Figure 6.4 Early Horizon on the South Coast: Paracas Culture. Top: Fragment of a Carhua textile. Center: Paracas embroidered textile border and cut-out embroidered figure. Bottom: Paracas (Ocucaje) double-spout-and-bridge bottles with incised and (right) negative paint decoration.

Playing with depictions that trick the eye of the viewer is something that was shared with Chavín sculpture, and it was later to be used in textiles of the Middle Horizon Wari and Tiwanaku cultures of the south central highlands and the Bolivian Altiplano. In addition to jaguars, caymans and other exotic jungle creatures were also depicted such as those at Chavín, although the habitats of these animals were even further away from the South Coast than from the Central Highlands. The nature of the imagery, the use and style of incision, and the juxtaposition of body parts and elements all seem to relate to stone carving styles at Chavín de Huántar.[34] However, post-fired painting in zones on an otherwise plain, burnished or polished surface is not a style associated with Chavín de Huántar, identified rather with the Tembladera style of the North Coast of Peru. Similarly, "negative painting" on ceramics is also only found on the South Coast and the North Coast in the region of Tembladera in the Jequetepeque Valley.[35] These similarities strongly suggest that there was point-to-point contact between the North and South Coasts in the Initial Period and the Early Horizon, perhaps via coastal oceanic travel.[36]

Direct influence from Chavín de Huántar may also be in evidence in a series of textiles found on the South Coast, especially from the site of Carhua (aka Karwa) (see Figure 6.4). These weavings include technical innovations such as the creation of designs by the introduction of threads that played no role in the basic structure of the textile (suprastructural construction) and warp wrapping in which colored fibers were wrapped onto warps to produce a block color design that was later held together by using a needle to insert wefts.[37]

Many Carhua and related textiles consist of strips of plain cotton sewn together to produce wide square or rectangular panels. Designs were then painted on the panels in black outline, with the motifs within them highlighted in solid black or white. The outline quality of the textile designs has suggested that some of the images may have been based on carvings at Chavín de Huántar. Indeed, it has been suggested that highland missionaries may have used such textiles as a convenient medium by which to proselytize the Chavín religion. Many of the designs do appear to have been derived from sculpture while others appear local, such as supernaturals associated with cotton, a distinctly coastal crop. The use of painted textiles appears to be a South Coast tradition that experienced a distinct phase in which there were strong Chavín influences, although textiles continued to be painted afterwards. The designs have greater similarities to Chavín sculptures than do ceramics at Chavín itself.[38] Some images appear to replicate Chavín temple gods while others, such as a cotton deity, are either adaptations of highland religious ideas or local deities. Some of these cloths are so large that it is hard to imagine them as wall hangings since they would likely tear. William Conklin has suggested that they may have been used as portable ceremonial spaces.

Despite apparent strong ties to Chavín cultures far away, South Coast peoples were also relatively independent and did not align their fortunes tightly with Chavín de Huántar or its nearer cult centers, so that when the religion finally collapsed it did not also destabilize the south. In general, the ceramic and textile traditions of the South Coast and the funerary practices in which they are represented continued into the Early Intermediate Period with no dramatic interruptions, until the Nasca archaeological culture emerged as a distinct expression of local ideas and identities.

An example of the continuity of life on the South Coast is the treatment of the Paracas Necropolis-style mummy bundles.[39] Bodies were preserved by first drying them, then packing cotton or leaves around them, and then wrapping them in multiple layers of fabrics. Over 400 burials excavated by Tello and his colleagues are legendary in the richness of the textiles, both in terms of the designs and colors, and the complexities of the weaving and embroidery employed to make and ornament them (see Figure 6.4).

Large "mantles" may have been made expressly as funeral offerings, while other textiles were probably clothing worn in life.[40] The innermost wrappings were the most complex, with extensive embroidered designs of several kinds including "linear" and "block" styles. The earlier, linear style often depicts supernatural animals similar to those seen on Cavernas pottery, with a special significance given to felines. The later Necropolis style includes anthropomorphs that often appear to be flying and are sometimes shown with human trophy heads or various kinds of plants sprouting from them. Both of these motifs are linked to ideas of fertility, and they remained as powerful symbols through Nasca culture times.

Many Paracas Necropolis bundles bear evidence of having been opened with new textiles and other offerings placed in them. The mixture of different styles of materials in a single bundle was a factor in the confusion in attempts to date them by archaeologists and art historians, as well as the fact that the tradition of burying high status people at Wari Kayán continued through many generations and across numerous social and cultural changes. The burials at Wari Kayán were probably leaders of societies from elsewhere in the region, whose remains were brought to the desolate but sacred peninsula for burial in an élite necropolis.[41] They exhibited high rates of cranial deformation, a practice that varies in its popularity as well as the degree to which it was common among élites and commoners at various times in the ancient Andes.

SOUTH COAST SETTLEMENTS

There are a number of large architectural complexes on the South Coast that may have been founded in the Initial Period and occupied into the Early Horizon. Most of these have not been extensively studied. Some of these huacas appear to have followed architectural canons not found elsewhere, such as a series of rectangular courts that link a tall, relatively narrow and high pyramidal form to create a long, rectangular complex. This can be seen at the Huaca Soto, the Huaca Santa Rosa, and the Huaca Alvarado. These are large complexes as impressive as any seen elsewhere. For example, Huaca Santa Rosa is 430 m in length, 170 m at its maximum width, and 25 m in height (1,411 × 558 × 82 ft).[42] La Cumbe follows a completely different format, since it is almost square with sides measuring 180 by 150 m (591 × 492 ft).[43] These are impressive monuments, and when they are eventually investigated it is likely that they will add much to our understanding of early cultures in the region. Further south, in the Ica Valley, no large monuments are known for the Initial Period and populations appear to have been relatively light.

Populations were concentrated in the river valleys where they first relied on floodplain agriculture and later on irrigation. The date of the first use of the latter is still uncertain. The nature of the hydrology of the South Coast is such that the most attractive places to live in river valleys were far from the coast, and thus maritime resources played relatively small roles in diets except at sites located directly on the shore.[44]

Among the few settlements of significant size that have been investigated, Hacha dates to between 1700 and 1000 BC, covering 16 hectares (40 acres) and containing both adobe and quincha houses.[45] Small projectile points, animal bones, fish, and shellfish remains were relatively common, while vegetal remains (cotton, gourds, Lima beans, squash, peanuts, achira, and maize) were relatively rare, although stone hoes were frequently found. There were two major occupation phases at Hacha. The earliest, Hacha 1, produces ceramics of soft paste in rectangular forms with no surface decoration. The second, Hacha 2, is associated with the architecture and finds include neckless ollas, various styles of bowls, and bottles with early versions of the double-spout-and-bridge form. A few sherds also exhibit post-fired resin painting and incised designs. The ceramic sequence at the site thus appears to represent the earliest pottery of the region, although there are issues surrounding the dating of both phases.[46]

Disco Verde is perhaps one of the best known early sites in the region, located near the village of Puerto Nuevo de Paracas and overlooking the water. It was deeply stratified and showed a long sequence of occupation during the excavation of its midden. Frédéric Engel identified pre-Chavín influenced ceramics there, including resist-decorated ceramics ("negative painting") like those also found at Hacha 2 and on the far South Coast at La Ramada. Later in the sequence, Paracas style ceramics are found. Stamped circular dots on these wares are another sign of Chavín influence, and these trends also occurred at Puerto Nuevo.[47]

Investigation of funeral chambers at site BRiG 3117, situated on a spur overlooking the Rio Grande de Nazca Valley, has clarified many issues concerning the Late Formative or Early Horizon occupation of the South Coast in general.[48] In a region of the valley known as Coyungo, the site lies 14 km from the ocean and had been looted, but investigations still recovered much information. Four funeral chambers were probably cemeteries for local people. Biological analyses suggest that the burials were of people whose genetic make-up showed intermarriage between valley peoples and those of the Andean foothills to the east or north. Many of the recovered textiles were in the Carhua styles, while the use of camelid fibers showed contact with highland populations. Pottery included not only negative painted wares resembling those of the North Coast, but also northern forms including the bottle and *florero* (flowerpot-shaped) wares. Both post-fired painted ceramics and pyroengraved gourd fragments exhibited Chavín motifs as well. Clinching the Chavín influence, radiocarbon dates placed the use of the funeral structures comfortably in the range between 800 and 500 BC when Chavín de Huántar's influence was at its apogee.

One of the few large sites to have been investigated extensively, Cerrillos consists of six terraces built into the side of a hill 112 km (70 mi) from the sea, where the Ica River turns southwards.[49] Originally thought to have been domestic in nature, more recent work suggests that Cerrillos was a ceremonial complex during the Formative with a later occupation as well. The site was occupied for a long period of time, from 850 to 50 BC, and the complete Ocucaje style ceramic sequence of the Ica Valley is in evidence. In addition, during the Formative occupation pottery with Chavín and North Coast influences and also pottery from the Central Coast and highlands were found, while crucibles indicate that metalworking took place at the site.

The people of the Paracas culture were short. In a studied sample, the average heights of males and females in the Archaic Period were 165.88 cm (5 ft 5 in) and 155.17 cm (5 ft 1 in) respectively. In the Paracas Period these dropped to 154.4 cm (5 ft 1 in) and 142.9 cm (4 ft 8 in), but then heights increased in the succeeding Nasca culture to 158.7 cm (5 ft 2 in) and 148.0 cm (4 ft 10 in). Taken together, the biological information suggests that the Paracas population was hard pressed to survive.[50] The mortality of 12- to 15-year-olds in Paracas was higher than in other studied populations, both locally and in prehistory in general. Spongiosclerosis— abnormal bone growth due to anemia—was also high among Paracas populations. Life was not only hard; it was also dangerous. There were many depressive fractures on skulls, and an adult male burial was found with an obsidian point between its ribs, its head missing, and cut marks on the axis (the vertebra that supports the skull)—indisputable evidence of the practice of taking "trophy heads" that became very popular on the South Coast in later prehistory.

HIGHLANDS AND ALTIPLANO

In the region that eventually became the heartland of the Inca, village life is first evident in the archaeological record in the Middle Formative (*circa* 1500 to 500 BC). However, the earliest known ceramic style in the Cusco Valley, Marcavalle, was already well developed by this point, suggesting the existence of antecedents that are still poorly known.[51] Agriculture and camelid herding were practiced by at least the middle of the period, and obsidian trade was underway, with sources in the Colca Valley and near Qoatahuaci.[52] The southern highlands supported similar villages elsewhere, such as at Minaspata in the Lucre Basin.[53] Social organization was probably based on kin affiliations within local communities, with links to neighbors and beyond through marriage and descent. Populations apparently grew steadily under this regime, leading to increased social complexity in later times.

By the Late Formative (500 BC to AD 200) the archaeological culture known as Chanapata, from the distinct ceramics identified by John H. Rowe in 1944, was dominant in the Cusco region. As with many other early ceramics, decoration consisted mostly of incision, punctation, burnishing and other surface treatments, while there is a shift over time from black to red wares dominating within assemblages.

There had been a great increase in population in the region from earlier times, so that of the 80 Formative Period sites known, most date to the Late Formative.[54] By this time sites are located close to prime agricultural lands, and the archaeological record clearly shows that quinoa, beans, and maize were grown. Furthermore, sites range in size from single homesteads and hamlets, through villages, to what appear to be dominant regional sites at Wimpillay and Muyu Orco, the former on a broad terrace of the Huatanay River and the latter on a steeply rounded hill next to it. These sites are not only the largest in the Cusco Valley and the adjacent Oropesa Basin, but they also yielded the finest quality pottery.

Brian Bauer believes that these various lines of evidence suggest that simple chiefdoms were present in the Cusco region, very likely centered at Wimpillay.[55] Such societies probably existed throughout the southern sierra, perhaps centered in different river basins; the site of Chokepukio in the Lucre Basin may be another example, and polities may also have existed in the Chusichaca area and in the Cuyo Basin. These kinds of communities, and the social processes that they were experiencing, seem quite similar to what was taking place on the Altiplano.[56]

At 3,800 m (12,500 ft) Lake Titicaca is the world's highest commercially navigable lake and the largest lake, by volume, in South America. Five major rivers feed into it, while a small stream, the Rio Desaguadero, flows out. Lake Titicaca is at the northern end of the Altiplano, which has the same average height as the lake. The high, treeless plain is a harsh environment with a distant horizon often punctuated by one or more snow-capped Andean peaks. The Andes here are at their most massive in their entire South American range, and the widest, driest stretch of the Atacama Desert is to the southwest. Only by traveling far to the north and east are warm, moist lowlands eventually reached.

Despite the severe conditions of the region, the Altiplano was the home of some of the most innovative cultures in South America. Charles Stanish and Amanda Cohen note that if the Titicaca Basin is defined by its hydrology alone, it is twice the size of the country of Belize.[57] Taking into account the span of the influence of Titicaca cultures at their height, during the era of Tiwanaku, the region covered 720,000 square km (278,000 square mi), a region larger than California and Nevada put together, or the Netherlands, Belgium, France, and Switzerland combined.

The earliest sedentary communities are relatively poorly understood, although Early Formative (1500 to 800 BC) settlements have been found along the Titicaca lakeshore. Domestic structures were ephemeral, but there is evidence of surface level and sunken court ritual enclosures oriented to high mountain peaks that seem to be precedents for the better known sites of the Middle (800 to 250 BC) and Late (250 BC to AD 475) Formative.[58]

Our knowledge of early Titicaca archaeology began in 1933–34 when Wendell C. Bennett excavated at the site of Chiripa at the southern end of Lake Titicaca; this remains the most fully excavated pre-Tiwanaku site in the region (see Figure 6.5).[59] The Chiripa site and its ceramics came to typify the first complex societies of the southern end of the lake, while Pucara holds that position on the northern end. Pucara dates somewhat later, however, and northern ceramics contemporary with Early Chiripa are known as Qaluyu. Early Chiripa and Qaluyu ceramics were soon joined by Kalasasaya, Taraco, and Pucara wares. Vessels were made in a wide variety of forms and with different manufacturing techniques. Related pottery styles include Huaricani in the middle Moquegua Valley, Faldas el Moro in the lower Azapa drainage, and Wankarani in the Lake Poopó highlands.[60] There is a preference for painted decoration in Chiripa wares, as opposed to incision and polychrome decoration in Pucara and Kalasasaya. The use of incision, practiced in Chiripa ceramics early on, perhaps due to ties with the South Coast, was abandoned throughout the region over time in favor of painted decorations.[61]

Research since Bennett's work at Chiripa has demonstrated that a consistent architectural pattern was followed for early temples throughout the lake basin (see Figure 6.5). They were usually built on the tops of high hills, on artificial mounds at lake level, or at the bases of impressive cliffs. The most important feature was an open, sunken court, nearly square with an off-center stairway entrance. The courts were about 15 m (50 ft) on a side and 2 m (6 ft) or more in depth. The sunken plaza walls were faced with large stones, sometimes interrupted with tall slabs or pillars. It is uncertain whether these surfaces were covered with plaster or not. A series of separate structures, or sometimes a single architectural complex divided into rooms, ringed the sunken court at ground level. The arrangement usually included corner rooms or buildings set at an angle, presumably so that the doorway would be aligned with the center of the court. The structures have a single entrance on the court side and a series of narrow chambers, created by making double walls around the entire structure and around a single large room.

At Chiripa there were 16 buildings around the sunken court, and the narrow chambers probably functioned as large storage bins judging by the basketry impressions and food remains found in them. At Ch'isi the sunken court was surrounded by burials. Whatever the specific function of the rooms, it seems likely that the separate chambers belonged to relatively independent social groups who gathered at the temple centers, with the autonomy-within-unity of the social organization expressed by the relatively autonomous, although similar, rooms situated next to one another around a commonly shared space.[62] Thus, while Altiplano ceremonial architecture and the rituals that took place within it were radically different from the Kotosh Religious Tradition, early socio-political organization in both regions was based on egalitarian principles in which different groups maintained separate ritual spaces at shared ceremonial centers.

Tall pillars carved with distinctive symbolic elements are a hallmark of Formative Period Titicaca Basin religious complexes, as well as ceramics and the sunken-court civic-ceremonial design. Together these are known as the Yaya-Mama Religious Tradition (see Figure 6.5).[63] The term is derived from the Quechua words for father (*yaya*) and mother (*mama*) because a dominant motif of the sculptures is a pair of stylized male and female figures, commonly portrayed with hands on chest and stomach. Additional elements include single-headed and bicephalic serpents, tadpoles, zig-zags, and distinctive crosses. Many of these symbols continued to be employed, with modifications, into later times.

Very few Yaya-Mama stone sculptures have been recovered in archaeological contexts. Many were retrieved from temple sites by local peoples and moved to other places where they often

S. & K. Chávez

Figure 6.5   Map of the Titicaca Basin showing variations of the Yaya-Mama style carvings, especially on stone monoliths.

remain objects of veneration today.[64] Consequently we do not know where these monoliths were originally located. An early southern phase (*circa* 800 to 200 BC) is characterised by designs pecked in low relief on long stone slabs, as well as four-sided pillars. Later phase Yaya-Mama stone monoliths (*circa* 200 BC to AD 200–300) are associated with the Pucara site on the north end of the lake, and the style also expanded into the Cusco region to the north and the Tiwanaku region to the south. In this later phase stelae were incised and carved with animal and geometric figures in low relief, and anthropomorphic figures were rendered in the round as three-dimensional statues. The Arapa Thunderbolt Stela weighs more than 2,268 kg (2.5 tons), is almost 6 m (20 ft) in length and is the largest stela of its kind in the Andes. After its use in Pucara times part of it was installed at Tiwanaku, 212 km (132 mi) distant.

It is interesting to note that large stone monoliths, known as *huanca* in Quechua today, were a fairly common feature at many ceremonial centers in Peru during the Late Preceramic and Initial Periods. Examples can be found at Aspero and Caral in the Supe Valley, and at Chavín de Huántar. However, the U-shaped centers of the Peruvian central coast seem not to have included such monoliths as cult items, and the tradition seems to stop in various parts of Peru at the beginning of the Initial Period. The relationship between the Titicaca stelae tradition and the earlier Peruvian practice is poorly understood. It may be significant, however, that many of the Titicaca monoliths have a distinct notch at the top, a feature shared with the Lanzón and the Tello Obelisk.[65]

Although the use of huancas may have been a continuation or revival of practices that had ceased elsewhere, they remained in use throughout prehistory in southern Peru and the greater Titicaca culture region. Titicaca ceremonial center buildings also employed entryways that appeared to contain a smaller doorway within a larger one and door jambs were stepped in two-tiers, emphasizing the door-within-a-door appearance. These were used only for buildings of the highest status and the practice continued into Tiwanaku times and through to the Incas.

People lived at Chiripa for at least four centuries before the first large scale ceremonial architecture was constructed. David Browman excavated in these earlier layers, occupied between 1450 and 850 BC, and recovered great quantities of fish, waterfowl, and lacustrine plant remains, including totora reeds that could have been used for making rafts.[66] This evidence strongly suggests that Early Formative people in the region depended to a great degree on resources gathered from Lake Titicaca. Some recovered seeds and tubers may be from cultivated varieties of potatoes and quinoa as well. In later times there were close relations between high altitude camelid pastoralists and lower altitude agriculturalists. It is likely that at least some domesticated camelids were already in use at Chiripa, although whether villagers practiced both agriculture and pastoralism is uncertain.

Recent research has suggested that the Titicaca Basin underwent several environmental changes in the half-millennium that constitutes the Middle Formative. At its beginning the lake level rose, creating more marshland, but later the level dropped again, providing more grazing land for camelids but fewer opportunities for fishing and resources from the marsh.[67] The environment was always harsh, however, and the densest areas of human habitation were always in places that were warm and protected from winds.

The sunken court complexes are assumed to have been political centers, but the nature of those politics is not fully known. The region is huge and it is quite likely that there were different language groups within it, as is the case for the historic and current eras. Albarracin-Jordan has suggested that the centers were foci for kin groups spread across the landscape, perhaps similar to the *ayllu* organizations of later times.[68] The centers may have been pilgrimage sites, places to gather for significant ceremonies during the year such as the solstices and equinoxes. Part of the incentive for movement across the landscape to and from these centers was likely the extraction, production, and circulation of precious goods such as sodalite beads, copper, bronze, and salt, and more distant goods such as shells from the coast or tropical plants for medicine and healing.

Some scholars emphasize the growth of political centralization at the centers as being mostly due to extra-basin trade, while others see environmental changes and the growth of pan-regional religious practices, albeit with local variations, as producing a peaceful era that raised the authority of the ceremonial centers into political powers. These two views are not necessarily mutually exclusive, however, and we should assume considerable dynamism and change in how societies interacted over the half-millennium of the Middle Formative.[69]

Starting around 500 BC, the iconography of Titicaca Basin art changed to include trophy heads, body parts, and other warrior imagery.[70] By this time the basin was filled with large multiple-sunken-court centers dispersed more or less equidistantly from one another, between 20 and 25 km (12 to 16 mi) apart. Between these were many smaller centers with only one or two courts, as well as villages and hamlets. In short, a multi-tiered settlement hierarchy appears to have developed with small centers and other settlements ranked lower but tied to the large centers.

On the northern side of the lake, Qaluyu reached 15 hectares (37 acres) in extent, but it was eclipsed by Pucara. Pucara grew to 1.5 square km (371 acres) in area, had three large sunken courts, more than a dozen smaller ones, and appears to have sustained a large resident population. As Qaluyu and Pucara are only 4 km (2.5 mi) from each other they may have formed a dual "capital," although this is not certain.

On the southern end of the lake, Taraco on the Rámis River appears to have become the dominant Late Formative site, reaching 1 square km (247 acres) in area. As the site now lies under a modern town the details of plazas and other structures have been difficult to identify, but the site is famous for many beautiful stone stelae. Excavations at Taraco uncovered extensive, intense burning in what appears to have been the highest status area of architecture. Although Taraco was occupied after the burning, more agricultural tools and less obsidian in this later phase suggest a marked reduction in the status of its occupants; they appear to have engaged in subsistence farming and they had less access to the valuable imported obsidian than in previous times. Furthermore, the material remains in the post-burn occupation appear to be in Pucara styles.

Taraco thus appears to have been conquered by Pucara, and radiocarbon dates suggest that this took place sometime between 200 BC and AD 200. In short, consolidation of power from numerous regional centers into concentrated loci appears to have been underway during this time: Pucara's rise to prominence took place through military might. Whether through militarism, trade, the creation of religious centers, or some combination of these, these general patterns of growth and expansion continued in the following centuries, leading to the eventual rise of the Tiahuanaco site complex at the southern end of the lake as the pre-eminent power that spread its influence throughout the Circum-Titicaca Basin Cultural Area and beyond.

THE END OF THE BEGINNING

In the Titicaca Basin a gradual growth and consolidation of political power expressed through ceremonial complexes led to increasingly large and more powerful centers. Through time, increasingly extensive regional centers arose until Pucara came to dominate the region by conquest over its rival Taraco. This view of ceremonial centers acting as aggressive military powers is a very different perspective from that which is assumed to characterise the spread of Chavín influence in Peru. Further north, however, the opposite process occurred when Chavín's hegemony over great areas of Peru disintegrated.

For reasons that are still somewhat unclear, Chavín's hold over the peoples of a vast region in what is now Peru eventually crumbled, ushering in a period of considerable instability. The great ceremonial center of Chavín de Huántar was eventually abandoned and squatters lived in the literal and figurative former glories of the complex. In many ways the sense of the barbarians camping in the Roman Forum is a direct parallel. Elsewhere, people who had lived by the side of their agricultural fields retreated to the hilltops, such as at the site of Castillo el Palmo, in the Chillón Valley on Peru's Central Coast.[71] The fact that fear was in the air is attested to by the great amounts of shellfish found high on the hilltop. For people to haul shellfish to those heights, they must have been fearful of spending too long on the beach.

In many ways, there is a logical progression in cultural ideas and practices in Peru from the Preceramic Period through the Initial Period and into the Early Horizon. Chavín's religion may indeed have been a revitalization movement that reworked older ideas as Richard Burger has suggested.[72] Chavín had a height from which to fall, however.

There is no evidence that Chavín had a political system that came close to resembling one which would have been familiar to the citizens of modern nation-states, or even those of European societies in the Middle Ages. Chavín's prestige and power came primarily through the power of its religious message and rituals. At the same time, however, there seems to have been a clear increase in hierarchy among different ceremonial centers, with Chavín at the top and exercising control over a considerable area of Peru. The chief priests at Chavín de Huántar used their status to control vital resources such as cinnabar mines, obsidian sources, perhaps exotic shells, and maybe the trade routes themselves. As distinctions between ceremonial centers sharpened there was also an increase in social ranking within the communities that lived in and around them, evident in the differential access to resources within the town of Chavín de Huántar itself, and probably at other centers as well. This increased social ranking within the Chavín sphere stands in marked contrast to the Altiplano, where systems with greater resemblance to earlier patterns in Peru were only manifest in the Middle to Late Formative. Elsewhere, either radically different patterns were followed, such as the rejection of hierarchy in Ecuador, or the situation is still unclear due to a lack of research, such as on the South Coast of Peru.

Were there any causal links between Chavín's collapse and the growth of ceremonial centers in the Titicaca Basin? Currently the two regions appear to have been on different trajectories with no known relations between them. Our knowledge of some of the regions between central highland Peru and Bolivia in the Early Horizon/Formative is still relatively poor, and so future research may clarify this issue. What is clear, however, is that in the area of Chavín's dominion a dark age began, which was only brought to an end when new systems emerged in the Early Intermediate Period.

NOTES

1 Cieza de León 1986 [1553].
2 Burger 1992, Lumbreras 1993, Rowe 1962b, Rick and Kembel 2004, Tello 1960.
3 Burger 1992 currently provides the most complete coverage of Chavín and its times, and much of the following is based on his work and publications.
4 Lumbreras 1970: 83.
5 Burger (1992: 177) refers to these as "reverse balconies."
6 See Cummins 2008 on the Lanzón.
7 Burger 2008: 689–690.
8 Burger 2011; Torres 2006.
9 For information on this bimetallic spoon and other Chavín and Andean art, see appropriate sections in Boone 1996.
10 Quilter 2012.
11 Lathrap 1973 and Urton 2008 on the Tello Obelisk.
12 There is an extensive bibliography on Chavín iconography. See Burger 2011 and Conklin and Quilter 2008 for references.
13 Burger 2012.
14 Burger et al. 1984.
15 Burger and Matos Mendieta 2012.
16 Clasby and Meneses B. 2013.
17 *Charqui* is a freeze-drying technique still used in the Andes today for meat, usually llama. It is also used for potatoes, with the product known as *chuño*. The English term "jerky" (as in beef jerky) derives from the Inca/Quechua *charqui*.
18 Miller and Burger 1995.
19 Elera 1994.
20 Discussions of the pros and cons of "shamanism" may be found in Francfort and Hamayon 2001.
21 Burger 2008: 699.
22 Burger 1992.
23 Richardson 1994; Sandweiss et al. 2001; Roscoe 2008.
24 Burger 1992: 284.
25 Roscoe 2008: 88–95.
26 Rick 2004; Rick & Kemebel 2004.
27 Yuichi Matsumoto personal communication, 2012.
28 See Vaughn 2009: 34–36.
29 Engel 1976: 140–142.
30 Isla Cuadrado 2009; Reindel 2009.
31 See Proulx 2008.
32 Menzel et al. 1964.
33 Paracas Cavernas was equated with Ocucaje Phases 8 and 9 and Paracas Necropolis with Ocucaje Phase 10. While Menzel and colleagues thought that the style originated in Ica, recent research by Reindel and Isla (Reindel 2009: 446) suggests that its origins lie in the Palpa and Rio Grande de Nazca drainages. The distinctive, plain but beautifully executed Topará ceramics may have first been made in the Cañete and Chincha valleys, whose people appear to have had a strong influence on their southern neighbors in Paracas near the end of the Early Horizon (Peters 1997; Proulx 2008).
34 The use of splayed or stretched imagery is seen without geometricization in the small ceramic vessel found at Pampa Gramalote in the Moche Valley.
35 Kaulicke et al. 2009.

36 The use of conical adobes is also found on the North Coast and in the tomb constructions at site BRiG 3117. Both Parsons (1980) and Toshihara (2002) suggest direct connections between Jequetepeque and the South Coast.

37 On Paracas culture in general see Paul 2008. On Carhua textiles see Wallace 1991 and Conklin 2008.

38 Wallace 1991: 106.

39 "Mummy bundles" is an incorrect term because the dead were not prepared as mummies, but as it is a popular one I will continue to use it.

40 Peters 2010.

41 Proulx 2010.

42 Canziani 2009.

43 This site was investigated by Max Uhle who thought it dated to Inca times, but Canziani 2009 makes a convincing case that it might be Formative in age.

44 On diets see Silverman 1996: 101. On sites near the shore see Garcia and Pinilla 1995.

45 Robinson 1994; Riddel and Valdez 1987–1988.

46 Silverman 1996: 112.

47 Engel 1966; 1976: 189–229 and Silverman 1996: 113 on Puerto Nuevo de Paracas. Santos Ramírez 1980 on La Ramada.

48 Kaulicke et al. 2009.

49 Wallace 1962.

50 Tomasto Cagigao 2009.

51 K. Chávez 1982; Bauer 2004: 39.

52 Burger et al. 2000: 289.

53 Dwyer 1971.

54 Bauer 2004: 42.

55 Bauer 2004: 45.

56 On Chokepukio: McEwan 1987. On Chusichaca area: Hey 1984. On Cuyo Basin: Covey 2003a.

57 Stanish and Cohen 2005: 3.

58 Hastorf 2008.

59 Bennett 1936. The site was also later investigated by Alfred Vincent Kidder and Michael Coe. See Kidder 1943, 1956.

60 Moseley 1992: 147.

61 S. Chávez 2004: 82.

62 Basketry impressions: K. Chávez 1988. Ch'isi: S. Chávez 2004: 74.

63 K. Chávez and S. Chávez 1997; S. Chávez 2004.

64 Rowe 1958; S. Chávez 2004: 75.

65 The predilection for pillars or stelae with notched tops is also found far to the north in Costa Rica, though at a later time period.

66 Browman 1986.

67 Hastorf 2008: 549.

68 Albarracin-Jordan 1996.

69 Trade: Browman 1986 and Stanish 2002. Religion: Bandy 2004.

70 Stanish and Levine 2011.

71 Quilter 1986.

72 Burger 1992.

7

THE EARLY INTERMEDIATE PERIOD

CONTINUITIES AND NEW BEGINNINGS

Chavín influence never extended far into Ecuador, except perhaps via long-distance trade. Chorrera ceramics have often been suggested as expressing Chavín influence, although they may simply be an expression of general widespread stylistic and ideological systems. In the northern highlands populations remained low in the wake of the Pululahua volcanic eruption, although the archaeological record is quite unclear because numerous smaller eruptions followed the massive one of *circa* 500 BC.[1] On the central Ecuadorian coast the Regional Developmental Period spans a thousand years from 500 BC to AD 500. Many archaeological cultures, such as La Bahía, appear to have continued from the Formative into the Regional Developmental, or else to have developed directly from earlier traditions such as Jama-Coaque. Unfortunately, little archaeological research has been carried out on many cultures that are chiefly known through their ceramics. The La Tolita culture of northern Ecuador and southern Colombia and the Guangala culture of Manabí Province are two of the better known of these traditions.

In the highlands, Cotocollao and Chaulluabamba are two sites that were established at an early stage, but they apparently grew thanks to their roles as key nodes in long-distance exchange systems. Similarly, the sites of Pirincay and Cerro Narrio are both located at control points in transmontane routes from coast to highlands, and they both yielded considerable quantities of Late Formative trade goods.

Trade in ceramics was clearly important and finely made wares were probably exchanged for their value in and of themselves, as well as for the symbolism that they carried. Marine shells were particularly popular trade goods, including the red-rimmed *Spondylus* and also large and small conches (*Strombus galeatus, Conus spp.*), mangrove oysters (*Anadara tuberculosa*), scallops (*Lyropecten sp.*) and mother of pearl (*Pinctada sp.*). Green-blue stones resembling turquoise and other semiprecious stones such as rock crystal were also favored. Shells and stones were mostly used for jewelry, while cotton and other specialized crops were traded between regions where they could be grown and places where they could not.[2]

One of the most valued trade items of all was obsidian. The major sources in Ecuador are near modern Quito, the source of all the obsidian found at highland Formative sites.[3] Less obsidian is found at sites further away from the source, suggesting "down-the-line" trade, although this was nevertheless considerable. Trade networks extended out beyond the Central Andes into Colombia.

CHRONOLOGY AND CULTURE CHANGE

The Early Intermediate Period is dated to between AD 0 and 650. The ceremonial center of Chavín de Huántar appears to have been abandoned before 200 BC, so it seems that its influence on ceramics on the South Coast lasted much longer than the center itself. The reasons for this are unclear, since the two or three centuries after the demise of the highland ceremonial center are quite murky in terms of our understanding of what was taking place, especially in Peru.

Whether environmental factors affected the collapse of Chavín or not, there appear to have been major upheavals in life and politics in Peru and a long period like a kind of dark age in many regions. The Pax Chavinensis seems to have broken down. This is shown in settlement patterns. In many areas people had lived for centuries on valley bottoms, close to rivers. However, in the early Early Intermediate Period these sites were abandoned in favor of settlements on high hills, such Castillo El Palmo noted at the end of the previous chapter.[4] This was a domestic occupation with a good view of the ocean, the coastline, and areas of the valley below. It was also defensible because of its steep slopes, and the remains of shellfish on the hilltop, which could have been eaten with much less effort at the beach instead, suggest that the occupants were concerned about their safety. The site of Media Luna, a "cheaply"-built series of platforms constructed into the slope of a hill below Castillo El Palmo, is indicative of the low-energy investments made in ceremonial architecture at the time, again probably due to concerns about safety.

In much of the region that was formerly under Chavín influence there appears to have been a hiatus in the construction of large temple complexes for a considerable period of time, with a concentration on hilltop sites and fort construction instead. There was also a sharp drop in long-distance trade, another sign that these were troubled times. This dark age, which may have lasted several centuries in some areas, seems to have been most hazardous on the North and Central Coasts of Peru and in the adjacent highlands, and less so in southern Peru and neighboring regions of Bolivia and Chile. Eventually, however, new regional systems emerged (see Figure 7.1).

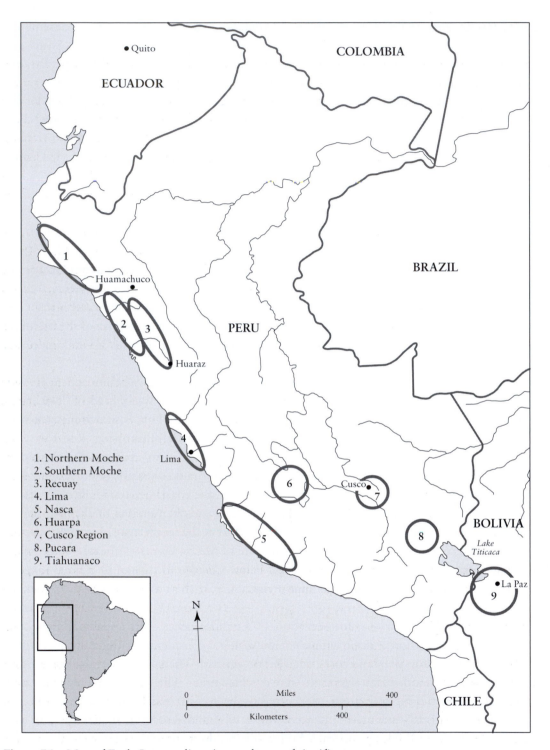

Figure 7.1 Map of Early Intermediate Area cultures of significance.

HIGHLAND CHIEFS

Sometime after 200 BC Chavín de Huántar became a ruin, and was occupied by squatters who had no respect for the ancient gods of the place or the rites they had demanded. The ceramics of these people were simple, decorated with geometric motifs of thin white paint on a red background. A general use of white-on-red decoration in ceramics is common throughout a great part of Peru in the post-Chavín era, but stylistic details in the Central Highlands distinguish the decoration there as the Huarás style. Simple motifs suggest a relatively low symbolic load in the designs suggesting that the Huarás society was relatively egalitarian, probably consisting of dispersed farmsteads or small communities that nevertheless represent the first phase of the Recuay tradition (see Figure 7.2).[5]

The Recuay archaeological culture is known for its distinct fine-ware ceramic style, stone sculpture, and architecture found in two major Peruvian central highland regions—the Callejón de Conchucos where Chavín is located, east of the Cordillera Blanca, and the Callejón de Huaylas formed by the Santa, the longest river in central Peru. Recuay sites are found over a great area of the north-central highlands covering about 15,000 square km (5,800 square mi), much of it high sierra and mostly in the modern Department of Ancash. Recuay is present in the archaeological record *circa* AD 250, reaching its apogee *circa* AD 400 to 600 with late Recuay dating to AD 600 to 700.

Recuay fancy ceramics are distinctive in the use of white kaolin clay, local to the region (see Figure 7.2). The overall ceramic style was completely new, with no known precedents. Decorative techniques were numerous, but most notable are three-dimensional modeling combined with red, white, and black painting, and the use of negative painting in the most elaborate vessels. Such complicatedly decorated vessels required multiple firings. Unique shapes included architectural models and representations of humans and animals. Indeed, Recuay is the first archaeological culture in Peru that clearly and consistently chose to depict humans involved in human affairs. These representations included images of high-ranking men, and sometimes women, posed in various groups in council or banqueting, as well as occasional representations of ritual sex, men leading llamas, groups peering out from fortified architectural complexes, and congregations attending mummy bundles or ancestor figures. Painted decoration included a wide range of geometric motifs and iconic figures that appear repeatedly, such as a crested animal (sometimes called a crested feline), a bodiless head with appendages (often snakes), and feline-serpent creatures (often bicephalic). The latter may be related to the Quechua and Aymara concept of the *amaru*, the "under-world" supernatural serpent associated with irrigation, water and fertility.

While ceramics were complex productions, stone sculpture was simple but impressive. Large boulders of granite and other hard stones were carved to resemble stout warriors or ancestor figures. These are mostly found near the modern city of Huaraz. Elsewhere, horizontal or vertical rectangular stone slabs were carved in low relief and inserted into architecture, forming lintels for doorways or flanking entries. Tenoned heads of humans and felines were also used in some buildings, a retention or emulation of a Chavín tradition.

Figure 7.2 Recuay culture. Top: Main wall at Yayno. Center: Bowl and carved lintel. Bottom: House model in kaolin clay, stone sculpture, and ceramic of lord with camelid.

There are small Recuay hamlets and farmsteads, corrals, shrines, and other architectural and landscape features. However, Recuay architecture is best known for its large, stone-built, multi-purpose complexes on ridges, hilltops, and other defensible positions. These included residential quarters, storage rooms, reservoirs, defensive bastions, and plazas and patios like those at Chinchawas, Pashash, Honco Pampa, Huacarpón, and Yayno, among many other sites. Many of these were protected not only by their locations and construction methods, but also by defensive ditches in areas that would otherwise have provided easy access to the complex.[6]

Although Recuay architecture was not as refined as the temples of Chavín, nonetheless it was impressive. Block-and-spall (*huanca-pachilla*) was the standard technique, in which small filler stones (*pachilla*) were inserted between large uprights (*huanca*). Although the stones were locally available, it took prodigious effort to build them into massive walls, such as the 15 m (49 ft) high Caserón at Pashash and the 12 m (39 ft) walls at Yayno that stand to this day (see Figure 7.2).[7] Many of the large stones seem to have been selected for their colors, but at the same time, ceramic architectural models indicate that the walls of some complexes were plastered and elaborately painted. Selecting fine stones and carefully building them into architecture only to cover them up with painted decoration may be another tradition inherited from Chavín: beauty had to be present, even if it was never to be seen by mortals.

Funerary chambers are the most ubiquitous Recuay form of architecture found within large architectural complexes, on ridge-tops and at various places in the countryside. For most of the Recuay era tombs were relatively hidden, consisting of subterranean facilities ranging from two rooms to large multi-chambered tombs with elaborate vestibules and decorations. Towards the later phases of Recuay, however, highly visible above-ground stone tombs known as *chullpas* became popular, suggesting that a different set of interests and concerns about relations between the living and the dead had developed.

There is a high degree of variability in Recuay material culture in different parts of the central sierra, all existing within a shared or overlapping set of forms, practices and beliefs. However, George Lau has noted the highly martial nature of Recuay imagery.[8] A "warrior aesthetic" is manifest in ceramics and stone sculpture with the depiction of high-ranking men as warriors with maces, shields, and battle regalia, and Recuay architectural complexes were built as fortifications. The standard Recuay weapon was a single-handed mace with a stone or bronze head. Although it is uncertain whether the metal mace heads were cast using a lost-wax process, elaborate metal pins for high status women were certainly made using that technique, making Recuay the earliest known Peruvian archaeological culture to use the lost-wax process extensively.[9]

Recuay consisted of a number of chiefdoms, among which the most powerful leaders were in charge of a central fortified town and the people and resources around it existed in a two- or three-tier political hierarchy. Leadership was maintained through kin relations, warrior skills, and rituals that propitiated and sought aid from ancestors in tombs as well as powerful cosmic forces in the landscape. Alliances may have been forged between chiefs, but they also probably fought one another. Variation existed even in this, however, because in the Huaráz area sites are not in defensible locations, perhaps due to the prestige or sanctity of the religious shrines in the region. In general, though, the Recuay world was a violent one.[10]

A critical aspect of understanding the emergence of Recuay is the location of many settlements at high altitudes between the *suni* and *puna* life zones, at about 4,000 m (13,000 ft) above sea level. These regions had been exploited previously in the Late Preceramic Period and more so in the Initial Period and the Early Horizon. Recuay people seem to have especially concentrated on exploiting this zone, and they were highly successful at it, working the landscape with previously unmatched success. Presuming that environmental regimes and zones were not radically different than they are today, in these locales Recuay people would have farmed potatoes and root crops in the *suni* and herded camelids in the *puna*. It is therefore no accident that camelids figure prominently in Recuay art. However, there also are various Recuay sites at lower altitudes and therefore a wide range of subsistence practices existed overall, but in general Recuay appears to have been largely a result of the exploitation and settlement of higher altitude resource zones. There is no evidence that the Recuay people practiced an organized system of "vertical" resource use; rather, they relied on a "compressed" ecological complementarity of tuber farming, pastoralism, and trade at the highest altitudes, and maize farming/trade and *yunga* farming/trade at lower elevations.[11]

The Recuay tradition, starting with the Huarás white-on-red pottery style, represents a clear break with Chavín and its legacy, and Recuay militarism is likely an outgrowth of the instability produced by Chavín's fall.[12] Subsequent Recuay people were unable or unwilling to reconstitute the Chavín religious and socio-political system. It is interesting to consider that in many ways continuities with Chavín were more strongly maintained on its former periphery, just as Byzantium rose on the geographical and political margins of the Roman Empire. Like Byzantium, what emerged in that peripheral zone was quite different from its predecessor, while carrying forward some aspects of the former power. In Peru, this new archaeological culture is known as Moche.

MOCHE PREDECESSORS

Some time in that long dark period after the collapse of Chavín, the peoples of the North Coast achieved a level of social stability and began to build huacas and produce various crafts and art associated with local religious systems. Some of these local religions achieved enough popularity that they began to spread across wider areas. Perhaps some of the processes associated with these developments were partly due to attracting pilgrims, as Chavín had done. In other places and areas, however, the growth of regional religious systems with distinctive gods, rituals, and artifacts may have been more tightly bound up with political events, including defense and war.

How and when the Moche culture emerged is rather unclear at present. Part of the uncertainty lies with the lack of a clear definition of what exactly Moche was, and how to recognize it. The Salinar and Gallinazo archaeological cultures are thought to have been Moche antecedents.

Salinar, like many Andean archaeological cultures, is best known through its ceramics. The finest examples have traits that could be considered to be transitional between Cupisnique and Moche, and available dates suggest that Salinar ceramics were made in the late Early Horizon or the early Early Intermediate Period. A number of distinctive stone mace heads, often elaborately carved but often showing chips and other signs of use, are commonly assigned to Salinar, suggesting that the culture was active at a time when the Pax Chavinensis had broken down and the warrior ethos of Recuay and the Moche were emerging.

The Gallinazo or Virú culture has long been seen as the predecessor of the Moche. Its region lies in the same general area: its largest site, the Gallinazo Group, is in the lower Virú Valley, and many practices are thought to be antecedent to the Moche culture. Chief among these is the construction of large temples made of adobe bricks in the shape of truncated pyramids with large plazas at their fronts. The Gallinazo Group is huge, consisting of over 30 architectural complexes spread over 600 hectares (2.3 square mi). However, some of these are not artificial mounds but island-like hills densely packed with architecture. It is not clear which of these are residential and which were temple structures built up from the flatlands. Furthermore, there is no evidence of occupation between the mounds, so that the total area of occupation and ceremonial architecture was about 40 hectares (99 acres), large but not huge by Andean standards.

While some recent field research has been carried out on the Gallinazo Group, the Gallinazo culture is mostly known through its fineware ceramics, which are seemingly less complex than Moche although they share some similar forms.[13] Unlike Moche, however, Gallinazo potters shared the Recuay penchant for the use of negative painting. The fanciest ceramics are distinct, but serving wares with simple decorations, particularly the Castillo Series, have been found in early and middle era Moche sites. Castillo Series ceramics appear to have been widely used by many different groups that also produced distinct finewares.

Even though Gallinazo is supposed to have preceded Moche, recent research at Huaca Santa Clara, a mid-sized Gallinazo site in the Virú Valley, indicates that it was occupied between the second century BC and the eighth century AD, thus spanning the entire time period commonly assigned to Moche. This is an area that needs further research, but it is possible that the Gallinazo style began earlier than the most recognizable Moche style ceramics, that it continued to be made at some huaca centers as the Moche style evolved, and then perhaps it ceased to be made before the final phases of Moche. Vicús, in a relatively isolated northern valley, is another example of a cultural style similar to Gallinazo in its preference for negative painting, but it appears to have been a local tradition that adopted Moche traits.

MOCHE IN TIME AND SPACE

The Moche culture is famous for finely made ceramics employing a "representational" ("veristic") art style (see Figure 7.3). While stirrup-spout bottles had long been in use, the

Figure 7.3 Moche culture. Top: Roll-out drawing of the Sacrifice Ceremony. Middle: Temple model from tomb at San José de Moro, stirrup-spout portrait bottle, and nose ornament from the Señora de Cao, Huaca Cao Viejo. Lower: Artist's conception of the Huaca de la Luna and woman dressed as the Señora de Cao.

Moche were particularly fond of the form, using it extensively for finewares as well as inventing new shapes such as the *florero* (flowerpot-shaped) bowl. They commonly used a bichrome color scheme of red-to-brown paired with cream-to-white slips and paints. Impressive vessels were made from many separate molds to create three-dimensional scenes which were often similar to painted versions made with fineline brushes. Gods, people, animals, and plants were portrayed in both media. Modeling was used to produce imagery not replicated in fineline painting. In turn, fineline painting by some schools of Moche ceramists produced highly complicated rendered scenes not feasible in modeled vessels.

Moche themes often show figures interacting.[14] The figures seem to be either the gods themselves, or else priests dressed as gods. Some themes are related to others, depicting episodes in long mythic narratives. Some are enigmatic, such as the Revolt of the Objects, while others show a mythic event but offer clues to the Moche culture, such as the Burial Theme depicting mortuary rites. Another series of scenes shows a wrinkle-faced god, usually with his iguana companion, in adventures that may be scenes from a "Hero Tale."

Moche ceramics are particularly noted for "portrait head vessels," some of which seem detailed enough to suggest that they are depictions of specific Moche individuals. These are mostly mature adult men of high status, although some show the same individuals in different life stages.[15] It is quite possible that some portrait vessels are of specific Moche lords or notable men, while others may portray gods or quasi- or fully mythic heroes, just as Alexander the Great was a real person who became mythologized over time.

Other Moche ceramics that draw special attention are "erotic vessels." Some show animals, including mice, copulating, while others show humans engaged in sex or exhibiting larger than normal sexual organs. Many of the human sex scenes show non-reproductive acts such as anal sex and fellatio. Like the portrait head vessels, it is probable that these different images have different symbolic meanings. Some, such as the copulating animals, may be associated with general concepts of fertility. Steve Bourget has argued that these are related to a supernatural realm in which the dead are transformed into ancestors, engaging in acts that are the opposite of those practiced in the land of the living.[16]

Differences in scenes and themes and their meanings are likely due to different ideas and practices throughout the great area and over the many years during which Moche ceramics were made. However, one of the most widespread and enduring themes is known as the Sacrifice Ceremony. It shows a set of deities presenting a chalice-like goblet to what appears to be a superior god (see Figure 7.3). The presenting deities sometimes vary in terms of who is portrayed, but the group almost always includes a priestess. The ritual goblet is generally interpreted to have been filled with the blood of sacrificed prisoners who were captured in war.[17]

Moche ceramics sometimes seem to stand apart from the pottery traditions from other parts of the Andes, particularly Peru.[18] In fact, however, Moche ceramics have much in common with earlier and contemporary styles in Ecuador, where bichrome painting and other methods and styles seen in Moche, such as the stirrup spout, occur quite early. The distinctions in regional styles during the Early Intermediate Period seem to be associated with realignments of long-distance relations in the Central Andes, or perhaps an increase in communication between regions.

Moche is famed for its ceramics, but few textiles are known. The many high status graves that have now been opened tend to show fairly poor preservation of organic materials. The comparatively moist conditions of the North Coast, combined with more frequent El Niño events than in regions to the south, may have contributed to the deterioration of textiles.[19]

Many Moche dead were buried with a small piece of copper placed in their mouths or hands, perhaps to act as "payment" so they could enter the underworld. The Moche continued earlier metallurgical traditions of making sheet metal ornaments for costumes and jewelry, favoring gold alloys. If they used bronze mace heads like their Recuay neighbors, they were not common or they were subsequently melted down for reuse. However, there are indications that some Moche warriors may have sported metal spikes at the butt ends of two-handed war clubs.[20]

MOCHE POLITICS

The numerous adobe-brick temple structures in the nine or so river valleys where Moche ceramics have been found have long attracted scholars. Some of these are of immense size. The Huaca del Sol, in the Moche Valley where the old colonial city of Trujillo was founded, was one of the largest human-made structures in the ancient New World: its ruin is currently 260 m long, 145 m high, and 41 m in height (837 × 477 × 135 ft). Across a broad plain next to the Huaca del Sol lies another large structure, the Huaca de la Luna, and together the two huacas and associated remains are known as the Huacas de Moche. There, in the last weeks of 1899 and the first weeks of 1900, the German archaeologist Max Uhle conducted one of the earliest professional archaeological excavations in Peru.[21]

The study of Moche ruins and ceramics continued at a relatively slow pace, but by the 1930s Rafael Larco Hoyle, the owner of a sugar cane hacienda in the Chicama Valley, had developed a passion for archaeology and he single-handedly defined Moche studies. Larco viewed the Moche as a state system based at the Huacas de Moche, which conquered valleys to the north and south and imposed its distinctive government and state religion. This interpretation was based on a view of a uniform Moche style of ceramics and huaca architecture. Larco developed a five-phase sequence of ceramic styles that he thought were present in all the valleys. The key to his view was that the earliest styles were found in the Moche and Chicama "heartland," while only late styles occurred in distant valleys and they were thus assumed to have been incorporated into the Moche state later in time.[22]

This view of Moche, as a conquest state with an evolved form of government which was usually thought of as being separate from the state religion, was the dominant interpretation for more than a half-century.[23] Beginning in the 1990s through to the 2000s, however, a number of studies gradually eroded confidence in this model. While some Moche specialists still adhere to this concept and a few believe that there was a single Southern Moche state system with valley-based polities in a Northern Moche region, even this view is now seriously in doubt.[24] The change in view was partly due to discoveries of élite Moche burials.

The discoveries made by Peruvian archaeologist Walter Alva in the late 1980s at the site of Sipán in the Lambayeque Valley, were remarkable not only in the richness of the tomb contents but also because individuals were found dressed in the costumes of some of the deities recognizable in the Sacrifice Ceremony. A similar discovery was made at the Huaca Úcupe in the Zaña Valley, while women buried in the costume of the Priestess were found at San José de Moro in the Jequetepeque Valley.[25]

This evidence strongly suggests that an important aspect of Moche religion was the enactment of important mythic events by priests and priestesses dressed as deities. Distinctive sets of ritual clothing and paraphernalia associated with the Sacrifice Ceremony have been found at a number of Moche huacas over a wide region. Many of the ceremonial centers have dense settlements close to the huacas, such as at the El Brujo complex and the Huacas de Moche. The most extensive study has been carried out at the latter site complex, where deep layers suggest an urban-like occupation lasting many centuries. A grid arrangement of streets ran along the sides of large residential compounds occupied by prestigious, large and extended families. Each compound appears to have been a relatively self-sufficient unit, and the issue of how the urban center functioned is still not entirely clear although the potential for a large population living between the huacas is clear.[26]

Not only were priests dressed as gods, their rites also included the taking of blood from prisoners as depicted in Moche art, very likely in the same manner as depicted in the Sacrifice Ceremony although other forms of torture and sacrifice are also shown in Moche art. Sacrificed young men of warrior age were found in ritual contexts at the Huacas de Moche and El Brujo.[27] Some scholars have interpreted these individuals, often with defensive wounds that were not fully healed when then died, as evidence that warfare occurred between huaca centers. Another possibility is that the huaca centers were not the instigators of warfare; rather, they may have been neutral places to which victorious armies based elsewhere brought their prisoners to be sacrificed. Still another interpretation is that the battles to take prisoners for sacrifice at the huacas were not "real" military campaigns but elaborately staged ritual events in which the outcome was predetermined. It is extremely difficult to prove or disprove any of these theories based solely on the archaeological data.[28]

However, there is considerable evidence that real warfare did occur between Moche communities away from the major huaca centers. In many North Coast valleys the remains of dense settlements composed of stone structures are present on hills rising above the valley floor and on the valley margins. Until very recently many of these sites were thought to be earlier than Moche, but changing views of the chronologies and the collapse of ceramic dating systems suggest that these settlements were contemporary with large Moche centers.

The buildings at these hillside residential sites consist of small rooms and patios that share common walls, with narrow alleys and streets between room clusters (agglutinated architecture), as seen from detailed studies at sites in the Jequetepeque, Moche, and Chao valleys.[29] In the Jequetepeque Valley many such sites were fortified, built in inaccessible locations with defensive walls and observation platforms placed at their highest points. Within these complexes there are often small platforms with ramps and the remains of postholes indicating that roofs or *ramadas* once covered sections of these small-scale temples.

A high status woman was buried in the Huaca Cao Viejo, at the El Brujo archaeological complex in the Chicama Valley. Known as the Señora de Cao, she was interred with a great amount of wealth including a sacrificed young woman (see Figure 7.3). Entombed with the Señora were 44 exquisitely crafted nose ornaments and 23 ceremonial spear throwers. Although other interpretations are possible, a reasonable conjecture is that the spear throwers, and possibly the nose ornaments as well, were tributary offerings given to the Señora in life or at her funeral. Although the Señora's role as a healer is suggested by a ceramic showing a woman healer founding her tomb, the nose rings are a distinctively male status symbol while the spear throwers also reference the male activities of hunting and warfare.[30]

Many tombs of both high and low status individuals have been uncovered at San José de Moro in the Jequetepeque Valley, excavated for over two decades by Luis Jaime Castillo. During one phase of its use the site was presided over by a series of priestesses who were buried near a major huaca in the costumes and paraphernalia of the Priestess-Woman character from the Sacrifice Ceremony. This suggests that the office of priestess, at least at this site, was taken by a succession of women, whether related or selected some other way.

In the plaza in front of the huaca, chamber tombs were constructed with a central space containing a high ranking individual, often buried in a cane or wooden coffin, accompanied by rich grave offerings that included metal objects, many ceramics, and sometimes sacrificed llamas or people. In one such tomb niches were made in the side walls of the chamber and small clay models of simple temples, like those seen at the hillside settlements, were placed in them (see Figure 7.3). Such a temple at Cerro Chepén, 4 km (2.5 mi) distant, is oriented directly towards San José de Moro. This and the models in the chamber tomb suggest that there were ties between the hillside communities and the San José de Moro ceremonial center. While the priestesses may have been the main religious practitioners at the site, the occupants of the chamber tombs may have been leaders at the outlying sites who were allied with the San José de Moro center and who were accorded the privilege of being buried there.[31]

The Señora de Cao's nose rings and spear throwers imply that political power in the Chicama Valley may have been tied to warfare and community allegiances. The dating of the Señora de Cao in relation to the tombs at San José de Moro is not clear, but the Señora de Cao burial has strong Salinar features. There is thus a suggestion that the earlier Salinar centers may have consolidated political relationships through military alliances, while the later Moche may have built links via religious rituals. Alternatively, these differences may be related less to changes through time and more to contemporary variations in different valleys.

INTRA-MOCHE RELATIONS AND CHANGE

Until recently the Moche style was thought to have begun in the Moche and Chicama Valleys and then spread uniformly through time and space by means of military conquest, as conceived by Larco. However, a much more complex process is now apparent, with some ceramic styles contemporary with one another while others succeeded older styles in particular valleys and not in others. So too, huaca centers rose and fell as a result of complex processes that are still only vaguely understood.

The relations between the Huaca de la Luna and the Huaca Cao Viejo is one of the clearest examples of these new views. In early construction phases the terraces of Huaca Cao Viejo were painted in solid colors, but in the final phase the terraces were decorated with the same designs as those at the Huaca de la Luna. The decorative scheme is much earlier at Huaca de la Luna (and it likely originated there), but it was adopted later at Huaca Cao Viejo indicating that Huaca de la Luna influenced Huaca Cao Viejo and not the other way around. Whether this process indicates conquest, alliance, or something else, is not clear.

These events took place sometime before about AD 650 when there were dramatic changes throughout the Moche region. Construction soon ceased at both the Huaca de la Luna and the Huaca Cao Viejo, and a new temple was built near the former site. The same pattern—the cessation of building at an old temple and the construction of a new form of temple nearby—also occurred at Licapa II, a mid-sized ceremonial center in the mid-Chicama Valley. There appears to have been a fairly dramatic reorganization of what "Moche" was in the late seventh century. Later huacas appear to have features that suggest feasting halls and places to bury dead ancestors. These changes may parallel the differences between the Señora de Cao and San José de Moro burials—that is, a shift from huaca sites as centers for military alliances and sacrifices to new roles as arbitrators in local disputes.

The Moche developed as irrigation systems and population levels reached their greatest levels to that point. While surveys in most of the north coast valleys have shown these changes, we know very little about non-huaca sites and everyday life at them; research at hillside sites such as those described for the Jequetepeque Valley is a quite recent phenomenon. Previously, some residential sites were considered to be Gallinazo because serving wares found across a wide area were interpreted as belonging to that culture. Now, however, it appears that some of these sites may have been inhabited by Moche populations who went to the temple complexes.

Wherever feasible, the full range of Andean domesticates was raised by the Moche and other Early Intermediate Area populations, including maize.[32] While the huacas may have been religious centers, the fact that many of them were located on or near major irrigation canals suggests that at least some of the temple centers, at some point in time, may have been involved in controlling the distribution of water, always an issue that could lead to strife. The idea of huaca centers as arbitrators of local disputes thus makes sense, although it is easy to wonder whether they could have been pulled into conflicts rather than always taking a mediating role.

Moche also was thought to have lasted for six or seven centuries, so it is logical to suggest that Moche at any one time or place may have meant something rather different than Moche elsewhere or at other times. It might be described as a distinctly religious system, intimately tied to politics, which underwent significant changes through time.

Finally, while it is hard to clarify the origins of Moche, there is a considerable amount of information about its end. A series of El Niño events, the arrival of new ideas from the Wari culture of the central highlands and from the central coast, and direct or indirect influence from Cajamarca and other northern highland regions all appear to have played a part in the great transformations that ended Moche. Indeed, if any general statement can be made about the north coast in the early Middle Horizon, it is that it was increasingly drawn into events and processes that were taking place on a much wider geographical scale.

THE CENTRAL COAST AND THE LIMA CULTURE

The Lima Culture is associated with the city of the same name, the capital of modern Peru, and it located in the Chancay through the Lurín Valleys (see Figure 7.4). It was more or less contemporary with Nasca to the south and Moche to the north. Research on the Lima Culture has a long pedigree because sites were close at hand for urban Peruvian intellectuals as well as visiting scholars who invariably began their Peruvian travels in the capital.[33] However, despite the great number of archaeologists who have worked on the Lima Culture, a robust understanding of it remains elusive. This is partly due to the urban growth of metropolitan Lima which has obliterated many small archaeological sites, with only the largest huacas sometimes remaining in what were once extensive architectural complexes. For some archaeologists research on Lima was often done while waiting to go elsewhere, while in other cases large sites have been excavated by many different archaeologists but syntheses are lacking.

The Lima Culture is perhaps best known by its distinctive ceramic style, which was carefully studied by American archaeologist Thomas Patterson who developed a nine-phase sequence of style changes.[34] Recently, however, Peruvian archaeologists have shifted to an Early-Middle-Late system with the exact time spans still being developed.

The most distinctive Lima ceramics have become known as the Interlocking or Playa Grande styles. These wares have an orange base or slip, with white, black, and red paints predominating in designs that commonly consist of long diagonal bands that parallel one another and then interlink so that the ends—often stylized serpent heads—are next to one another in patterns that appear to be reflections of the same element. Less rigid patterning occurs later in the style sequence, especially when Wari influence is apparent.

It is a sign of the lack of understanding and appreciation of Lima ceramics that they are commonly not included in surveys of ancient Peruvian pottery, but the finest examples of Lima ceramic artisanship equal those of Moche or Nasca.[35] Especially in the case of the interlocking motifs, the symbolic loads of the designs seem relatively low because of their high

Figure 7.4 Lima culture. Top: Huaca Pucllana from the north. Second row: Plaza with three-step altars and offering pits on Huaca Pucllana upper terrace. Third row (left to right, not to scale): Nieveria vessel of lucky fisherman, large feasting jar from Catalina Huanca, brown-on-yellow bottle from Huaca Pucllana. Bottom: Artist's conception of feasting at Huaca Pucllana with priests dressed as fish.

abstraction. Fish and bird imagery are common, as well as serpents, waves, and other maritime motifs. The style was employed on murals as well as ceramics, as shown in a painting estimated to have covered 65 m along a wall at Cerro Culebras in the Chillón Valley.[36] The interlocking style was not unique to Lima, of course, since it was used in textiles as early as Huaca Prieta, and contemporary murals at Moche sites, such as the Huaca Cao Viejo, also employed the technique. However, Lima took it to extremes.

White-on-red decorated ceramics were found over a very wide region of Peru in the aftermath of Chavín, and Lima developed from such earlier styles. In general, vessel forms such as the double-spout-and-bridge or slip-cast panpipes are much closer to Nasca styles than to Moche or Recuay ones, and there are no stirrup-spout Lima vessels. Detection of interchanges between Lima folk and highland peoples is difficult for the early and middle parts of the sequence, mostly because the Early Intermediate Period archaeology of the sierra adjacent to the Central Coast is one of the most poorly known areas of Peruvian prehistory. Nevertheless, the Lima style appears to be a distinctly coastal phenomenon. It may have developed first in the Chillón Valley and then spread to the others over time, based on the fact that Early Lima is found there while only Middle and Late Lima ceramics are present in some of the other valleys.[37]

Although many sites have suffered greatly due to looting and urban growth, those that remain are still impressive. They include Cerro Trinidad in the Chancay Valley, Cerro Culebra in the Chillón, Maranga, Cajamarquilla, Huaca Pucllana, and Catalina Huanca in the Rimac, and Pachacamac in the Lurín.

Huaca Pucllana lies in the fashionable Miraflores district of Lima and has been the subject of long-term investigations by Isabel Flores (see Figure 7.4). The main mound was built with adobes in successive layers, generally similar to Moche huacas. Lima builders preferred adobes that were squarer than the rectangular Moche ones, and they stacked them like books on library shelves rather than laying them flat. Yellow was the favored color to paint sacred spaces, such as a large plaza near the summit of the structure. Three-step stair altars—harking back to Cardal—were placed against a wall, while the plaza floor itself was covered with small holes into which worshipers placed offerings of fishes and mollusks. At lower levels there were various patios and rooms that were probably residences, shrines, and administrative offices. As is common in the Interlocking style, the site is filled with references to the sea and its resources, conforming to Lima interests in general and acknowledging the fact that the ocean is little more than a kilometer away.

Maranga is the largest known Lima site, more than a kilometer in width and covering between 150 and 200 hectares (370 to 494 acres). Much of what remains of Maranga now lies on the campuses of the University of San Marcos and the Catholic University of Peru. There are over 20 mounds known for the site, the largest of which, Amburú or San Marcos, is more than 300 m (984 ft) in length and between 180 and 250 m (591 to 820 ft) in width. No clear patterning of the arrangement of mounds is in evidence from old maps and aerial photos, except that the largest huacas are in a line and those that still retain some form are oriented 25° NE.[38] Recently the Catholic University of Peru conducted extensive and long-term excavations at

Huaca 20, one of the smaller mounds at the complex, likely a Late Intermediate Period structure underneath which was part of a Lima culture settlement with residences and burials next to a canal.

A curious fact regarding the Lima Culture is that there are no known high status burials. Even though élite Moche tombs were only found relatively recently, archaeologists had known for years that such interments existed based on looted luxury items such as gold ornaments sold on the international art market. The same is currently true for Nasca, but no similar materials are known for Lima.[39] It may be that lack of élite Lima burials is simply a question of luck, or perhaps it is an indication that Lima society was organized in a different way than other societies of its time.

Human skeletons buried in the walls at Huaca Pucllana bore evidence of violent deaths, particularly puncture wounds in the pelvis and lower spine and lesions on the head, and it is assumed that these were human sacrifices.[40] Ribs in the process of healing from wounds incurred at about two weeks prior to death fit the pattern of Moche sacrifices, suggesting that some of the individuals in these burials may have been captured warriors. Analysis of a group of burials from Huaca 20 indicates a population that generally conforms to preindustrial morbidity and mortality.[41] There was high mortality among children under three years of age, while adults lived into their late 20s and 30s. Almost all (98%) of the adults exhibited linear hypoplasia in their teeth, indicating periods of poor nutrition sometime in their lives. Interpersonal violence seems to have been high with about a fourth of adults showing traumatic lesions probably incurred from intentional causes, but not necessarily through the kinds of violence associated with war or raiding.

At all the large sites that have been investigated large patios with many posts in them are found, indicating that they were covered with roofs. These spaces suggest communal activities such as feasting and drinking, and so far there is a significant lack of highly structured spaces for rituals carried out by priests of various ranks. Similarly, the small offering pits at Huaca Pucllana suggest rituals carried out on an individual basis rather than by a priestly élite, so it is possible that the Lima Culture was not highly stratified, although inferring social organization from such data is very difficult.

In its final phases Lima experienced strong influences from the highland Wari culture. The massive complex of Pachacamac saw its first major constructions during Lima, but it was substantially expanded by Wari and later occupations. Catalina Huanca (aka Vista Alegre), in the Rimac Valley, was a massive huaca some 400 m (1,312 ft) long, 38 m (125 ft) high and with seven platforms, like Huaca Pucllana. However, the site appears to have been abandoned in the early Middle Horizon and later reutilized as a Wari burial ground. The Catalina Huanca population may have relocated to the large urban center of Cajamarquilla, and a nearby cemetery yielded both late Lima style ceramics as well as a distinctive style, named Nieveria after the cemetery, that had strong Wari as well as some Moche influence. While initial contact with Wari may have been relatively light or slow, dramatic changes eventually occurred on the Central Coast and in many other areas.

NASCA

As noted previously, the South Coast is rather isolated in relation to other littoral cultures and it generally maintained its strongest ties with the Southern Sierra in what might be called a South Central Andes Interaction Sphere. Nevertheless, in the Early Intermediate Period the remarkable and distinct Nasca archaeological culture emerged in the Ica and Nazca drainages (see Figure 7.5).

The Nasca have been compared and contrasted with their Moche contemporaries. They were quite different cultures, however, separated not only by great distances but also speaking different languages and following different fundamental practices, such as the Moche preference for extended, recumbent burial and the Nasca continuation of the Paracas tradition of flexed, seated burials. Perhaps the most striking difference is that whereas the Moche are generally known for bichrome ceramics, Nasca polychromes display one of the most colorfully diverse palettes in the New World, using 15 mineral-based pigments across the range with up to 13 colors known on a single vessel.[42] Until very recently it was through these ceramics that the basic chronology and cultural interpretations of the Nasca were formulated.

In many ways there appears to have been a relatively smooth transition from the Early Horizon to the early Intermediate Period in the Nasca region. Apparently the collapse of distant Chavín did not have social consequences that caused drastic changes of life and society, as happened closer to the Chavín heartland. Indeed, for many years separating aspects of Paracas and Nasca material culture, especially textiles, was difficult because of continuities between the Early Horizon and the Early Intermediate Period.[43]

For a while at least, there appear to have been two different social formations on the South Coast. The Paracas tradition continued, with its distinctive ceramics and elaborately embroidered textiles and a continuity in iconography. The Paracas Peninsula appears to have retained its role as a sacred burial ground to which high status dead were brought for burial as mummy bundles, often in groups, in abandoned habitation sites, although there is the possibility that the dead were locals.[44] Early Nasca textiles are not as impressive as their ancestors' handiworks, and burial patterns also differed. Nasca burials tend to be singular interments in shallow pits, cists, and large purpose-made jars, which were then covered over with cane or log roofs. Clearly a different social order was emerging.

In the Southern Nasca Region, Early Nasca society (Phases 2 to 4) consisted of small villages in the upper valleys, with subsistence systems based on floodwater agriculture combined with marine resources and camelid pastoralism.[45] There is little evidence of sharp social differences or hierarchy, and the polychrome ceramics were locally made and accessible to a wide range of people. Cultural and social unity was strengthened through pilgrimages to the large ceremonial center of Cahuachi.[46] It was at this time that Nasca culture existed in its most elaborated form.

Figure 7.5 Nasca culture. Nasca ceramics. Double-spout-and-bridge is early. Tall jar is late with more dense imagery. Hummingbird Nazca line. Geometrics at edge of pampa. Map of the central section of Cahuachi.

NASCA CERAMICS

Whereas the stirrup-spout vessel became popular in the late Initial Period in the central and northern highlands and on the north coast of Peru, it was not in favor among the Nasca. The analogy to the stirrup spout that expressed Nasca dualism was the double-spout-and-bridge vessel, in which, as the name states, two spouts were connected by a "bridge" of clay that could also serve as a handle to the pot. Bowls, jars, and other basically utilitarian vessel forms were also made in fineware forms, and Nasca figurines, especially of women, are well known. The Nasca also occasionally used modeling for vessels, although the technique is much less common than in Moche ceramics. Clay *antara* (panpipes) were particularly popular among the Nasca, being made in a wide range of sizes, and they were often elaborately decorated, as were ceramic drums.

There is a nine-phase ceramic sequence that has been developed in great detail. In general, it follows a progression from a few large painted images to increasingly more figures within the decorative field.[47] Favored images in early Nasca ceramic art seem to depict the natural world of the South Coast, and are thought to relate to general concepts of fertility. Various birds and fishes, foxes, and even insects such as spiders are shown. Natural and cultivated plants, especially beans, are also frequently depicted.

The "natural" plants and creatures on Nasca ceramics may all have had symbolic meanings, a point which may also be made for Moche ceramics as suggested by Christopher Donnan many years ago.[48] Clearly supernatural beings are difficult to identify. Orcas (killer whales) were seen as special and significant and felines are common, as are feline features on other beings. Anthropomorphic figures are often shown with cat-like whiskers and a tail stretching out behind an otherwise normal-looking, though elaborately dressed, humanoid figure. Various elements are often shown extending from tails, such as small animals, beans or other plants, and human heads. Some of the same features are depicted on quadrupeds, particularly a striped cat.

Whether the two-legged individuals are humans or gods who transform themselves from or into cats cannot be decided with certainty. To complicate matters, there are actual examples of gold "cat masks" as shown on painted images. It is likely that Nasca religious specialists costumed themselves as the beings shown in their art. Once again, there is a parallel with Moche art, in which it is sometimes hard to determine whether what is being portrayed are the gods themselves, or priests, priestesses, or shamans acting the parts of deities in rituals.

As time passed the themes on Nasca vessels became more ominous, and designs were more crowded within the available space. Warriors are more frequently shown, often holding a spear thrower in one hand and multiple darts in the other. Trophy heads, and heads in general, also become more abundant. A frequent motif shows the heads of deities with long tongues that reach out to connect with others in series. What are clearly trophy heads are shown on other ceramics, either by themselves, in multiples, or being grasped by warriors. Large caches of trophy heads have been found at Nasca sites, and combined with the culture's art, the impression is that warfare was constant and deadly in late Nasca society.

CAHUACHI AND THE LINES

Cahuachi is the largest Nasca site by far; indeed, at 1.5 square km (0.6 square mi) in area, it is large for ancient societies by any standard. Because of its size it has attracted the attention of archaeologists for many years, although much of the site remains to be investigated.[49] However, only about 25 hectares (62 acres) or 15% of the site is covered with architecture, with buildings widely spaced apart. There are at least 40 major mounds of wind-blown soil covering temples, plazas, and other architecture. Some structures, mostly temples, were built on hills to increase their apparent heights. The largest of these is the Great Temple, a stepped platform 20 m (66 ft) high with courts and rooms at its base and a large plaza some 47 by 75 m (154 × 246 ft) in size.

The South Coast is so dry that much of the water flows underground most of the time, but at Cahuachi water rises to the surface, and this is likely why the archaeological site is located where it is. As a pilgrimage center it probably did not support many residents, being manned by a group of priests and attendants. The nature of Nasca religion is the source of some debate, with some thinking that it was locally based and primarily shamanistic while others suggest that there may have been an organization of religious specialists based at Cahuachi.[50] Few small villages have been excavated, but Kevin Vaughn notes that his research at Marcaya and the small amount of other evidence available suggests that pottery making was not carried out at such settlements. In contrast, there is evidence that Nasca polychromes were manufactured at Cahuachi.[51] This suggests that the ceremonial center was the place where Nasca religious ideology was developed and elaborated, and from which it was disseminated.

Perhaps the best known aspect of Nasca culture are the Nazca Lines, the hundreds of markings made by removing the upper crust of desert rocks and pebbles "varnished" by the wind to reveal the lighter soil beneath (see Figure 7.5).[52] However, the Nazca Lines are not alone. "Geoglyphs," as they are sometimes called, are found throughout Peru and Chile dating from many different time periods, such as Initial Period Canto Grande, as discussed in Chapter 5. What makes the Nazca Lines special are the great number and diversity of geoglyphs concentrated in a single area covering between 400 and 500 square km (200 square mi). Despite their ubiquity on the Pampas de Nazca and Jumana, the geoglyphs were not known outside of the South Coast area until relatively recently.[53]

Although the lines have attracted the attention of sensationalist authors claiming that they were made by extra-terrestrial voyagers, research by many different scholars has demonstrated that they are the constructions of local people, who not only made many of the markings in styles also seen in their ceramics and textiles, but also left pottery vessels at places on the lines as offerings. There are different lines, made by different people for different purposes. Among the most famous and the earliest are about 70 images of animals (monkey, lizard, killer whale), birds (guanay, hummingbird, pelican), insects (spider), plants (trees, flowers), objects (loom, *tupu* [shawl pins]), and more enigmatic designs such as two human-like arms and hands.

Then there are actual "lines" in the desert, some as long as 10 km (6 mi) in length. These cut straight across the landscape, some parallel and others crossing. Ignoring hills and dales, many of them converge (or start out from) star-like "ray centers." There are at least 500 lines, of which approximately 100 link to 62 ray centers, accounting for about 80% of the total places of convergence.[54]

A third class of geoglyphs consists of trapezoids, rectangles, and triangles, many of which are also of immense sizes. Like the lines, they can often be found on the sides of hills as well as in flat areas. They were made by removing all surface cobbles and gravel in the interior of the geometric shape, making the whole image light in color. The removed stones are usually piled up along the edges of the design to further demarcate it. Heaps of stone, often with broken pottery scatters on top of them, are also frequently found at one or both ends of a clearing. Some lines appear to lead to or arrive at such accumulations.

The geoglyphs were not made for any single purpose, and they were made at different times. The figures appear to be the earliest. While some may date to the late Early Horizon, their similarities to some of the designs on Nasca pottery suggest that most were made in the Early Intermediate Period. The Nasca may also have made the other forms, but some appear to have been created in the Middle Horizon and Late Intermediate Period.[55]

A striking aspect of the figures is that they were made in one continuous line. This has led some scholars to believe that they were ceremonial pathways to be walked by people in a meditative state, similar to labyrinths in some Christian churches. Indeed, a Nasca labyrinth is known. Some figures may be associated with lines or geometrics, but whether they were made at the same time or whether the geometrics were later placed near figures is not clear. Many lines do appear to converge on Cahuachi, and so the idea that they may have been ceremonial pathways seems reasonable. A series of imaginary lines was thought to radiate from Cusco, the Inca capital, and therefore it is possible that a similar idea was expressed in the South Coast geoglyph lines.

Some lines appear to be aligned to celestial events. Gary Urton has studied the astronomical systems of contemporary Quechua people of the highlands, as well as Nasca farmers.[56] In modern Nazca the sun rises around the summer (December) solstice above Cerro Blanco, a giant sand dune referred to as a "Volcano of Water" because at this time of year subterranean waters start flowing in the region. In the highlands, Quechua people note that the sun rises into the central course of the Milky Way only during the December and June solstices. If ancient Nasca people followed similar practices, then these celestial phenomena and events may also have been important to them. However, Andean constellations were and are not the same as Eurasian ones. For example, the southern night sky is so bright with stars that it is the "dark clouds" lacking stars that are the most significant constellations, not imaginary lines connecting stars.

While some lines are oriented to celestial events, others appear to relate to water. Mejía Xesspe first suggested that the lines were ritual pathways and implied that they may have been associated with water tapping channels, and other archaeologists have developed this theory. Recent research suggests that some of the geoglyphs mark the paths of aquifers that carry water through geological faults.[57] The flow of water in the riverbeds of the region is relatively low, although we cannot be sure of conditions in the past. We do know, however, that in Nasca times water was accessed through digging wells (*pukios*) down to a relatively shallow water table where there was a steady flow of water. Indeed, the water was so abundant that filtration galleries and underground canals were created with pukio access points along their routes.[58]

WATER IN THE DESERT

In one of the driest parts of one of the driest deserts in the world water was critical, and so it is no wonder that some of the geoglyphs may have been associated with ensuring its abundance, whether via lines pointing to celestial events that marked the onset of flows or through trapezoids that followed the direction of those flows. This link between events above ground and beneath it is also typical of Andean thought, in which everything is connected.

The intensification of food production through the building of pukios increased the Nasca people's ability to grow maize. Studies indicate that both Nasca men and women of all social ranks show evidence of increased maize consumption. The difference between high and low status people was in the amount of meat they consumed and the generally more diverse diet enjoyed by higher ranking people. Higher-status people probably had more involvement in long-distance exchange systems that gave them access to camelids as well as to local coastal herds.[59] The general improvement provided by more maize in diets was short-lived, however.

Troubles manifested themselves in the Middle Nasca Period (phases 5 to 8), with Nasca society under increasing stress and with great changes occurring in the Late Nasca (Phases 6 and 7; *circa* AD 450 to 600). Construction ceased at Cahuachi and the site was eventually abandoned, while decorative schemes on polychrome ceramics became more abstract and less carefully executed. General health declined, as evidenced by increased dental caries and enamel hypoplasia.[60] Late Nasca was a time of increased conflict among Nasca communities. While warfare appears to have been endemic throughout the Nasca era, with different Nasca communities raiding one another regularly, in late Nasca warrior themes increased dramatically as represented in art. Trophy heads were more numerous, and populations gathered in a few large villages in each valley, very likely for defense. Presumably, Cahuachi had been a kind of neutral ground for regional worship. Whether Cahuachi ever assumed a dominant role is hard to assess, but our current view is that it never did, and that feuds and fighting intensified between individual Nasca communities. By the succeeding Middle Horizon significant sections of the region, especially the lower Ica Valley, were no longer occupied by settlements because the area was no longer fit for human habitation; instead it served mostly for cemeteries.

The increasing troubles in the Nasca region appear to have been at least partly due to human–environmental relations. David Beresford-Jones has conducted a study on the lost woodlands of ancient Nasca and how their disappearance may have undermined Nasca society.[61] Geomorphological, paleobotanical, and archaeological studies in the southern Nasca region revealed that the environment there was very different at the end of the Early Horizon and the beginning of the Early Intermediate Period, but deforestation caused a cascade of environmental changes that led to extreme desertification.

Drought resistant trees of the Acacia and Prosopis genera are dominant in coastal Peru, as they are across many of the earth's sub-tropical regions. To the Spanish, the latter tree resembled the *algarrobo*, which they already knew, and so they referred to the Prosopis as *algarrobo de las Indias*. Even though this, the carob tree, is a completely different plant, it is widely known as algarrobo throughout South America today.

Today, in much of Peru Prosopis trees rarely reach more than four or five meters in height, although larger examples are known from archaeological sites. On the South Coast, however, where it is known as the *huarango*, huge trees are known, some reaching 30 m (98 ft) in height with trunks 7 m (23 ft) in circumference, more than 2 m (6 to 5 ft) in diameter, and some have been dated at over 1,000 years old.[62] At the beginning of the Early Intermediate Period huarango forests covered the riverbanks and spread into the plains. With broad and deep roots, the trees stabilized the riverbanks and underpinned the floodplain. Prosopis trees fixed nitrogen from the air in the soil and further enriched it through leaf and litter fall. The soil was also kept moist via "hydraulic lift," a nocturnal process in which trees move water via taproots from deep layers to upper, drier soil layers where root mats would otherwise be dry.

Beresford-Jones suggests that Prosopis trees were part of a larger, complex woodland ecosystem in the southern Ica drainage in early prehistory, and that they played a "keystone" role in maintaining the system. The woodland not only stabilized the river channel and enriched the soil, but also served as a buffer against inundations when El Niño rains occurred. However, over time the cutting of trees and the conversion of woodland to farm fields changed this system dramatically. The more trees were cut down, the more desertification occurred. The ecology was further damaged by El Niño rains that washed away fertile soils, with further scrubbing by coastal winds to produce a desolate landscape. Various lines of evidence suggest that the region gradually declined in productivity, reaching a critical point sometime in the Middle Horizon.

It thus appears that the drastic changes in Nasca culture were in large part the result of changes in the South Coast ecosystem brought about by land-use practices. Once a threshold of change had been reached, these processes were virtually irreversible. As with the deforestation of the Central Coast lomas in the Middle Preceramic Period, it is quite likely that similar human–environmental relations also occurred elsewhere in the Andes, but the South Coast is, for the moment, simply the most detailed example that we have.

THE SOUTHERN HIGHLANDS AND ALTIPLANO

Relatively little archaeological research has been done on the Early Intermediate Period in the central sierra region, so that there is an impression of two distinct regions in the northern and southern Central Andes. However, while the trending patterns of mountain ranges and river valleys do create sub-regions of greater or lesser integrity, it is a fact that at various times geographical boundaries did not prevent cultural connections.

Huarpa was the dominant Early Intermediate Period archaeological culture in the southern highland valleys, with territory near the modern city of Ayacucho. In the Late Huarpa period sites tended to be located on hilltops, and the most elaborate of these were walled compounds made of fieldstones that served both civic and ceremonial functions. With their emphasis on defense, these sites show similarities with Recuay to the north.

Archaeological investigations like those at Nawimpukyo, as well as ceramic models, indicate that the most important sites consisted of a rectanguloid walled compound with a central plaza with a round building at each end, thought to be ceremonial structures, and two rectangular buildings facing each other across the plaza on its long axis. Once again dualism appears to have been an organizing principle at these sites and for the people who occupied them.[63]

Villages were small but great effort was put into terracing hillsides, a practice that began earlier but became a significant highland feature at this and in succeeding times. Some hillsides had more than a hundred terraces climbing their slopes, and spring-fed canals were well built, sometimes with clay linings and occasionally several kilometers in length.

Late Huarpa prestige pottery was influenced by Nasca designs, including a pinwheel-like motif and the use of more colors than in previous times. However, the direction of influence from coast to highlands was soon to reverse.

In the Cusco region populations that had begun to form chiefdoms in the Late Formative continued to grow in size. In earlier times the site of Wimpillay had apparently dominated the Cusco Valley. However, in the Qotakalli Period (AD 200 to 600) a cluster of sites were established in the western Cusco Basin. Power and wealth in the valley may have become divided between groups of élite households arranged in a series of separate but closely spaced kin-based settlements, perhaps similar to or the same as the later Inca *ayllu* organization.[64]

Qotakalli ceramics define the period and the archaeological culture. There are several variations of Qotakalli ceramics, the most common of which are bichromes (mostly black on cream) and polychromes (black and red on cream).[65] Designs consist of geometrical motifs painted within parallel lines. The symbolic loads of Qotakalli ceramics thus appear to have been quite low compared to those of Moche, Nasca, or Recuay. However, examples of ceramics from Pucara, 200 km to the east, are also found in the region, including fragments of incense burners (*incensarios*) with distinctive scalloped rims and puma-head adornments. These were used to burn incense in rituals, a practice generally uncommon outside of the Titicaca Region. Therefore, the area between Cusco and Pucara, where *incensarios* are found, appears to have been under Pucara influence in the Qotakalli Period.

The major Qotakalli site may have been at Cusco itself.[66] Settlements were more numerous near the best agricultural land, and a site hierarchy suggests that social organization may have been complex with secondary centers beyond the immediate vicinity of Cusco. The Qotakalli chiefdom may have covered an area roughly 50 km (31 mi) in diameter, although taking account the fact that much of this region would have been rugged mountainous terrain.[67] It is likely that much of the rest of the southern sierra of Peru consisted of chiefdom societies that occupied roughly similar areas, controlling sections of river valleys and varying in size depending on the amount of land available for agriculture and camelid pastoralism. Elsewhere, however, larger systems combining religion and politics were asserting themselves.

From early times many centers with sunken courts had been built in the greater Titicaca region, and there was a widespread sharing of architectural formats, iconography, and religious concepts. Over time certain centers gained greater power and expanded in size, such as Pucara (see Figure 7.6). There, the local chronology (Late Formative, 250 BC to AD 300) spans the late Early Horizon to the early Early Intermediate Period of Peru.[68] The site, one of the earliest and most studied in the basin, is 80 km (50 mi) from Lake Titicaca, on a river and in front of an impressive cliff. The complex eventually covered more than a square kilometer and consisted of a high terrace platform with three large sunken courts built on the same general plan as found in Chiripa architecture. A hemispherical enclosure received special attention with the use of carefully carved rectangular blocks and pilasters. Some of the interior chambers surrounding the sunken courts held human remains, probably the mummy bundles of local kin groups who came to worship at the site.

The Yaya-Mama religious imagery of early times morphed into and was augmented by iconography featuring hallucinogenic plants, human heads, men with knives, front-faced deities, and kneeling feline-masked humans (*chachapumas*). Many of these themes, such as the trophy heads, are also common in Nasca, as previously noted, but it is not completely clear whether there was direct influence from one region to another or simply a general increase in symbolism related to war and power due to changing socio-political conditions.

As Pucara power waned in the Late Formative, Tiahuanaco on the southern shore of Titicaca grew, and the two centers appear to have competed for the allegiance of the many medium-sized ceremonial centers that had grown up around the lake. Basic architectural formats, including details such as the placing of tenon-head sculptures in the walls of sunken courts, were practiced at both major sites, suggesting that the large centers competed for the allegiance of smaller centers.[69] However, while a general religious system may have been shared throughout the trans-Titicaca region, Pucara's economic and political ties extended westwards to Cusco and southwards to Nasca, whereas Tiahuanaco was oriented to the east, south, and southwest. The latter region included northern coastal Chile where the site of San Pedro de Atacama has produced remarkably well-preserved Tiahuanaco-style burials and other remains.[70]

The pathways to the dominance of Pucara and then Tiahuanaco may have been more complex than we currently understand. Recent research at Khonkho Wankane suggests that Tiahuanaco had local rivals as well as distant ones.[71] Khonkho Wankane lies only 28 km south of Tiahuanaco, on the Desaguadero River within the lake's primary drainage, and the site may have been larger and more important than Tiahuanaco. It grew to support a large and elaborate complex of ceremonial, residential, and mortuary areas centered around the largest plaza known in the region for the time (measuring 50 × 54 m [31 × 34 ft]), with an attached trapezoidal sunken court. The arrangement of platforms and mounds in relation to these courts suggests that there were two residential-ritual compounds at the site.

Figure 7.6 Top: Aerial photo of Pucara site. Bottom: Pucara ceramics (not to scale).

There are four impressive anthropomorphic sandstone monoliths at Khonkho Wankane, at least two of which may have been made as a pair, and several more fragments. Most of the complete sculptures stood over five meters in height, and although they are now eroded some still bear traces of carving. The iconography is an elaborated version of the Yaya-Mama style, showing young anthropomorphized catfish, paired felines, winged llamas, and other creatures combining the traits of different animals and of humans. These stelae were likely placed in the centers of courts and plazas to be the focus of ritual activities that included feasting, judging by recovered food remains.

For a while, Khonkho Wankane may have been tied to Tiahuanaco as part of a paired ceremonial system. By the end of the Formative Period (*circa* AD 500), however, Tiahuanaco had become the controlling power not only at the southern end of the lake or even in the entire Titicaca region, but over a large area of the Andean world, a dominance shared or rivaled only by Wari in Peru. That story is key to understanding the Middle Horizon.

NOTES

1 Lippi 2004.
2 Bruhns 2003.
3 Burger et al. 1994.
4 Quilter 1986.
5 Lau 2011.
6 Chinchawas: Lau 2011. Pashash: Grieder 1978. Honco Pampa: Tschauner 2003.
7 Lau 2011: 71.
8 Lau 2011.
9 Verlarde and Castro de la Mata 2007.
10 Lau 2011: 41.
11 Lau 2011: 61.
12 Lau 2011; Burger 1992: 228–229.
13 Millaire 2010.
14 Donnan 1978.
15 Donnan 2003: Chapter 8.
16 Erotic vessels: Bergh 1993; Weismantel 2004. Moche art in relation to death and sex: Bourget 2006.
17 The Sacrifice Ceremony, formerly known as the Presentation Theme, has an extensive bibliography. See Alva and Donnan 1993, Donnan 1978, and Quilter 1990 for discussions and further references.
18 Pasztory 1998.
19 Textiles on the North Coast are more common from late Middle Horizon times onwards than for earlier eras, and perhaps this is related to El Niño frequencies.
20 Quilter 2008.
21 Uhle 1913.
22 A discussion of the Larco sequence and new perspectives may be found in Castillo and Quilter 2010 and Quilter 2011.
23 Castillo and Quilter 2010.
24 Quilter and Koons 2012.
25 Information on these sites may be found in Pillsbury 2001. See also Benson 2012.

26 Uceda 2001.

27 Verano 2001 on warrior sacrifices at Huacas de Moche.

28 There are many articles on Moche warfare. See Quilter 2009 for one opinion and references to others.

29 Cerro Chepén is a good example of a fortified site in the Jequetepeque Valley. See Rosas Rintel 2007.

30 See Mujica Barreda 2007: 209–243. It is interesting that the number of nose ornaments (44) is close to but not exactly equal to double the number of spear throwers (23). If these items were presented by others and nose ornaments were made and presented in pairs, then speculatively, one funeral attendant may not have brought nose ornaments, only a spear thrower, or else one spear thrower was the Señora's own.

31 Castillo 2001 and http://sanjosedemoro.pucp.edu.pe/02english/index.html on San José de Moro.

32 Lambert et al. 2012.

33 Lima: Almost every adventurer-scholar who spent time in the Lima region conducted some fieldwork. However, Max Uhle, who excavated at Pachacamac (1991 [1903]) and elsewhere on the Central Coast, was the first to recognize the culture. He was followed by a number of researchers, among them Alfred Kroeber (1954) and Gordon Willey (1943), as well as the Peruvian Jiménez Borja (1985). In recent years most studies of the Lima Culture have been carried out by Peruvians with publications forthcoming.

34 Patterson 1966.

35 Donnan 1992 and Stone-Miller 2002 cover Peruvian ceramics, though there is little on Lima in either of these sources.

36 Fuentes S. and Carhuanina 2012.

37 Makowski and Vallenas 2012.

38 Canziani 2009: 282.

39 Burger 2012b.

40 Barreto 2012.

41 Vega 2012.

42 Vaughn 2008: 39.

43 Silverman 2002 on separating Paracas from Nasca textiles.

44 Cf. Dwyer and Dwyer 1975.

45 Schreiber and Lancho Rojas 2003; Vaughn 2005, 2009.

46 Silverman 1993.

47 Lawrence Dawson of the archaeology laboratory of the Kroeber (now the Phoebe Hearst) Museum at the University of California, Berkeley, was the key researcher in establishing the Nasca ceramic sequence into nine phases. This has since been modified because phase 1 is associated with the previous Paracas tradition (Van Gijseghem 2004, 2006), while phases 8 and 9 are associated with the following Middle Horizon (Schreiber 1998).

48 Donnan 1978 on religious symbolism in Moche art.

49 Strong 1957; Orefici 1992; Orefici and Drusini 2003; Silverman 1993; Vaughn 2009.

50 Silverman and Proulx 2002.

51 Vaughn 2009: 168–170.

52 They were "discovered" by Toribio Mejía Xesspe (1950), a student and colleague of Tello, in 1927. Study of them only began in earnest after World War II, however. That study was, to a great measure, inspired and promulgated by Paul Kosok (1965), a professor at Long Island University, and Maria Reiche, a charismatic German immigrant who devoted her life to recording, studying, and defending the lines from damage and destruction.

53 Publications on the Nasca Lines are extensive. Aveni 1990 and 2000 are good sources that can lead to others.

54 Aveni 2000.

55 Clarkson 1990.
56 Urton 1988.
57 Johnson et al. 2002.
58 Mejía Xesspe 1950. See Hadingham 1987: 254.
59 Kellner and Schoeninger 2012.
60 Kellner 2002 cited in Vaughn 2008.
61 Beresford-Jones 2011.
62 Beresford-Jones 2011: 129–133 discusses the complex and uncertain taxonomy of huarango trees.
63 Isbell 2008.
64 Bauer 2004: 52.
65 Glowacki 2002.
66 Covey 2003a; Bauer 2004: 52.
67 Bauer 2004: 54; Map 6.3.
68 Hastorf 2008.
69 Hastorf 2003; Couture 2004.
70 Rodman 1992.
71 Janusek et al. 2003.

8

THE MIDDLE HORIZON

TIAHUANACO AND HUARI

The conquistador Cieza de León not only described the ruins of Chavín de Huántar but also the remains of Tiahuanaco, the vast complex 15 km (9 mi) south of Lake Titicaca, now 72 km (45 mi) west of the modern city of La Paz in Bolivia. Like Chavín, Tiahuanaco was never hidden from view but remained a great abandoned mass of decaying structures on the altiplano, known to locals but familiar to few in the outside world. Like so many ancient Andean places, we do not know what the site's inhabitants called it or themselves. "Tiahuanaco" is the Inca name for the site, and its exact meeting is uncertain. It may derive from *taypiqala*, "stone in the center," the Aymara term dating from before the Inca came and built in the ruins.[1] As the highest and most southerly ancient city of any great size on the globe, and given its dramatic setting, it is easy to comprehend how it may have seemed to be a cosmic pivot point.

Because it was so large and so visible, Tiahuanaco drew archaeological attention from an early date. George Squier visited Tiahuanaco in the 1860s and published an account of it in his popular Andean travel book, and Adolph Bandelier, pioneer of southwestern US archaeology, visited and wrote about it as well. German geologist Alphons Stübel made a detailed map in 1876, and Max Uhle was familiar with Tiahuanaco through photographs of the ruins published by B. von Grumbkow. When Uhle excavated at Pachacamac in 1896 he saw imagery on ceramics and textiles at the Lurín Valley site that were almost identical to Tiahuanaco artifacts, and thus theorized that there had been relations between the two sites.

It can be argued that Uhle's greatest contribution to Andean archaeology was not his discoveries of sacrificial victims or elaborate artifacts, but his work on chronology. He concluded that the Tiahuanaco-like artifacts that Reiss and Stübel found in mummy bundles at Ancon Bay, near Lima, and similar remains that he had excavated on the coast of Peru demonstrated that the past could be divided into several different phases, rather than simply Inca and pre-Inca. He was able to build a chronology that had several different periods, even though he could not date them exactly and had to depend purely on stylistic analysis. He realized that the Tiahuanaco-influenced era had occurred in the remote past, and he called the coastal Tiahuanaco style "Epigonal" from a German word that refers to an imitator that is of lower quality than what it emulates.

Alfred Kroeber's support of Uhle's proposal was critical to the acceptance of the theory. However, as time passed suspicions grew that the Epigonal style may not have come solely from Tiahuanaco. A second major source was found at Huari, also a vast ruin, in the Huamanga Basin, some 11 km (6.8 mi) from the city of Ayacucho in the southern highlands of Peru. Once again Cieza de León had visited Huari, but it did not come to the attention of archaeologists until Julio C. Tello rediscovered it in another pioneering project in 1931 and identified it as the capital of Wari civilization.[2] Since that time, archaeologists have struggled to understand the relations between the two largest sites in the Andes in the Middle Horizon, and their influences throughout great regions of western South America. Although views have changed and are still in dispute, it is clear that the sites' roles were great and long-lasting.

The modern understanding of the Middle Horizon is based on the work of Dorothy Menzel, a research associate of John Rowe and a key contributor to the development of the Ica Valley sequence. She also accomplished a *tour de force* of ceramic analysis that divided the Middle Horizon into four epochs which are still in use today.[3]

Investigations of Tiahuanaco and Huari sites and their cultures (distinguished from the sites by the use of the terms "Tiwanaku" and "Wari") have followed very different paths, resulting in different kinds of information about each. Tiahuanaco has been the jewel in the crown of Bolivian archaeology. It has received extensive and intensive attention by Bolivian and foreign archaeologists, and its location near La Paz has made it easily accessible for study. Enthusiasm for Tiahuanaco has been so strong that various architectural complexes have been reconstructed, albeit not always accurately, for the benefit of the huge numbers of tourists who visit the site. Also, Tiahuanaco has inspired romance and fantasy such as in the publications of Arthur Posnansky in the early 1900s, who claimed the site was the "Cradle of American Man." Such transcendental appreciations continue today as Tiahuanaco serves as a cult center for New Age enthusiasts and others.[4]

Significant archaeological work at Tiahuanaco began in the 1940s with research by Wendell C. Bennett of Yale University, and continued in the late 1950s through to 1970 with the work of the Bolivian Carlos Ponce Sanginés. During the late 1970s through to the 1990s Alan J. Kolata and his Bolivian colleague Oswaldo Rivera conducted the largest project at the site to date. Further research projects on many different topics have since been carried out in various locales around the Titicaca Basin.

Neither extensive nor intensive investigations have been carried out at Huari. This is partly due to the fact that its importance was only noted relatively recently compared to Tiahuanaco, and partly because it is in a more remote region compared with the proximity of the Bolivian site to the national capital. In addition, beginning in the 1970s, the Shining Path (*Sendero Luminoso*) insurrection was based in the Ayacucho region, making research at Huari difficult for almost two decades. Consequently, Wari studies were mostly carried out at other sites. Since the mid-1990s this impediment has diminished, but the massive size of Huari still makes it difficult to work at or understand it easily. Research at other locales has nevertheless advanced knowledge considerably, particularly at Conchopata, a major Wari settlement near Huari.[5]

Middle Horizon iconography is rich and complicated, presenting challenges in separating out what styles pertain to each culture, their origins, their significances, and how they related to one another. Various researches in the last few decades have resulted in new views of Wari and Tiwanaku, at the same time confirming earlier scholarship that these cultures had profound influences on much of western South American between AD 600 and 1000.

TIAHUANACO

Tiahuanaco was a grand ceremonial center (see Figures 8.1 and 8.2).[6] For some scholars it was the seat of an expansive state or empire, while for others it was a holy pilgrimage site with far-reaching influence and trade connections. However it is conceived, all agree that at its height Tiahuanaco was very large, highly complex, and extremely influential.

The ruins of Tiahuanaco cover an area of 6 square km (2.31 square mi) or 600 hectares. A large rectangular ditch encloses between 65 and 70 hectares (161 to 173 acres) that contain architectural complexes at the center of the site, although important structures also lie outside the enclosure. It is uncertain how much of this area was occupied, however. This is important for a number of reasons, because the density of occupied space serves as an indication of the number of inhabitants and the nature of the city. Some of this area may have been uninhabited, but given its overall size it is possible that the area housed many hundreds of people, perhaps even thousands. Whether Tiahuanaco was a true city with a dense and diverse population or more of a huge ceremonial center with residents mostly devoted to religious activities and the support of pilgrims is another critical question that is not fully resolved.

Tiahuanaco's most famous feature is the "Gateway of the Sun," illustrated in Squier's travelogue and celebrated ever since.[7] The "gate" is a single block of andesite (similar to granite) 3 m (10 ft) high, 4 m (13 ft) wide and weighing 10 tons. Above a finely made doorway and two niches are carvings of a front-facing deity commonly called the "Staff God," flanked by Rayed Heads and Attendants, the most important deities in Tiwanaku religion, in this case possibly comprising a solar calendar.[8] While the monolith is impressive and the images are important icons of Tiwanaku religion, nevertheless it is only one of many masterworks of stone carving at the site. Indeed, Tiahuanaco stonework in buildings, patios, stelae, and freestanding sculpture was the finest in the Andes since Chavín, not to be matched again until the Inca.

A semi-subterranean temple and probably other structures had already been built before Tiahuanaco was radically transformed sometime in the seventh century. As noted in the previous

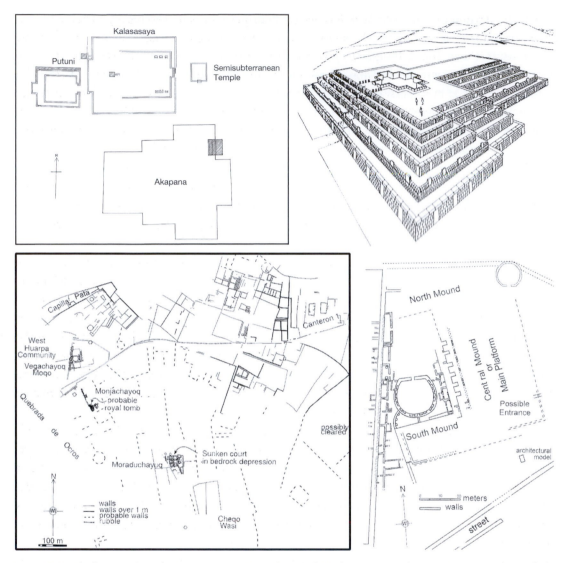

Figure 8.1 Tiahuanaco and Huari maps. Top: Core of Tiahuanaco with artist's conception of the Akapana at its height. Bottom: Core of Huari with detail of Morduchayuq.

chapter, this early ceremonial center followed the format of the many Formative temple complexes on the altiplano. Tiwanaku's apparent victory over Pucara was followed by a massive reorganization of the site that included extensive new building projects.

One of the new structures was the Akapana. Made with an earthen core covered in fine masonry, measuring 200 m (696 ft) on each side and 17 m (56 ft) high, for many years its ruins were thought to be a natural hill. The footprint of the structure and its six terraces appear to have been in the shape of a thick, stepped "T," a key symbol for the culture and ubiquitous in

Tiwanaku carvings and art.[9] Wide stairways led to a square sunken courtyard, 50 m (164 ft) on a side, which may have been in the shape of a stepped "Andean Cross" (*chakana*), the same form as in the Preceramic temple at Ventarrón in the Lambayeque Valley some 660 km (400 mi) distant. Complex construction techniques such as caissons ("boxes") built to contain stone fill also included "over-built" systems such as elaborate drainage canals, which served functional uses but were also symbolically powerful in making the Akapana a veritable life-giving water-mountain. Layers of green gravel brought from distant hills covered surfaces and expressed concepts of mountains, water, and fertility.[10]

Kolata and Rivera's excavations on the Akapana's summit found seated burials including the remains of a man, perhaps a shaman-priest, with a ceramic vessel in the form of a puma. Rich offerings were not placed with these dead, so they do not appear to have been élites. Perhaps they were religious specialists who lived modest lives, like monks, or perhaps they were sacrifices.

The top of the Akapana was severely looted in the past; if very rich burials of rulers were present there, all traces of them have vanished. However, in a nearby compound at Akapana East, human bodies had been carefully defleshed, grouped into bundles, and buried in a small mound sealed by meticulously prepared clay floors. These may have been the ancestors of Tiahuanaco leaders interred in a place of honor.[11] Furthermore, surrounding the patio on the Akapana summit were what appear to have been high status residences, which yielded llama and ceramic offerings and artifacts of obsidian, silver, and copper, suggesting that there had been people living there or buried close by who had access to prestige goods, in contrast to other, simpler burials nearby (see Figures 8.1 and 8.2).

There are other large architectural complexes near the Akapana. The Kalasasaya was built before the stepped pyramid, but was remodeled around the time that the Akapana was built. It is an immense (120 × 130 m; 394 × 427 ft) low platform with a sunken court, at the center of which was the large stone monolith known as the Ponce Stela (Figure 8.2). Next to it is the Semisubterranean Temple, more than two meters deep and remodeled on the same plan as one at Kalasasaya but with tenon heads facing inwards towards another large stone monument, the Bennett Stela.

Next to the Kalasasaya is the Putuni, built during a major remodeling effort at the height of Tiwanaku's power. It has features that suggest it may have been the palace of one or more élite individuals or families, since it had an elaborate system of canals, oven and storage areas, and polychrome murals on some of its walls. Elaborately dressed and ornamented burials were found underneath the corners of this apparent palace, one of which may have been of a priest or other high-ranking religious specialist.

The Pumapunku complex may have been the entry to the ceremonial center on its southeastern edge. It is a terraced, low mound in the emblematic T-shape. Covering 2 hectares (5 acres), the complex appears to have been left unfinished, as is also true for some other buildings, but it still contains some of the finest stonework at the ceremonial center, including splendid ashlar blocks held together by bronze clamps, a feature of the most prestigious stonework.[12]

Figure 8.2 Tiahuanaco architecture. Top: The Kalasasaya from the Semisubterranean court. Left: Tenon heads in the wall of the Semisubterranean court. Bottom: Gate of the Sun. Right: The Ponce Stela.

As at other ceremonial sites in the Andes, Tiahuanaco's architecture was integrated into a sacred landscape that included alignment with geographical features and celestial events. Three large snow-capped mountains rise up above the flat Altiplano, while the stars at this high altitude are remarkably dense and bright. The Semisubterranean Temple was aligned to view the Milky Way over one of the distant mountains and to observe the extremes of the movement of the moon. When the Akapana was built, however, it blocked the view of the southeastern horizon from the Kalasasaya, while a new wall tracked solar movement against the western horizon. These changes may indicate a shift in emphasis from a lunar to a solar religion as also represented on the Gateway of the Sun, a relatively late monument at the site.[13]

At the height of the center's power, as pilgrims walked from Lake Titicaca the lake would have vanished from sight as the snow-capped peak of Mount Illimani rose into view in the east. Once at Tiahuanaco, neither the lake nor the mountain would have been visible until the pilgrims climbed the Pumapunku and the snowy peak reemerged beyond the city skyline. The last rays of the sun setting over a sacred mountain passed through the megalithic entrance of the Kalasasaya, and where they touched beside the Sunken Court a number of caches of special artifacts were buried as offerings.[14] The alignment of architecture to landscape features that were seen as sacred and powerful probably began in the distant Andean past, as we have seen, just as the use of sightlines, light, and sound also had early origins and continued to be used throughout prehistory.

Tiahuanaco was thus not just a city, but also a sacred *axis mundi*. It is almost a certainty that the entire region around Lake Titicaca was considered to be invested with aspects of what Westerners would now call the "sacred." In the lake the Islands of the Sun and Moon had been sacred sites since the Late Archaic, by Tiwanaku times they were a pilgrimage center, and by Inca times one of the most important shrines in the land.[15] It is no accident that today one of the best-known Roman Catholic shrines in South America is the shrine of Our Lady of Copacabana on the shore by the islands.

HUARI

Like Tiahuanaco, Huari was huge, but an exact assessment of its size and nature has been hampered by a number of factors (see Figure 8.1).[16] In addition to being off-limits for scientific study for many years, the ground cover consists of cacti and other vegetation that make examining architecture and other features difficult. Also, the immensity of the site is challenging: the core of Huari is about 2 square km in area (0.8 square mi), but there are traces of walls and refuse in broken terrain over another three or four square kilometers.[17] As in the case of Tiahuanaco, we will not easily be able to gain an understanding of the size of Huari until much more work has been done.

Huari has no free-standing stelae or large pyramids, and to date there is no strong sense of an organization such as a grid of streets and avenues. Instead, the city grew through the construction of large walled compounds. Much of the architecture is made of rough fieldstones that were coated with smooth white plaster. However, there are known examples of very finely cut stones in some areas, and the site was looted for masonry slabs in colonial times.

The compounds are usually rectangular, divided into square units each containing a central open patio surrounded by long, narrow rooms which are often referred to as "Niched Halls" due to the features found inside them. These compounds, sometimes with sections two or three stories in height, may have been the residences of Huari élites, or else they may have been administrative centers. Similar compounds are found at Wari provincial sites, notably at Pikillacta near Cuzco.[18] The compounds were carefully built with secure foundations and drains at their bases supporting courtyards surrounded by long rooms or halls in a standard pattern known as a "patio group."

A distinctive form of Wari architecture is the D-shaped structure, the main form of Wari temples. As the name implies, they are built in the form of a "D" with the flat side containing the entry. D-shaped structures are relatively small, usually 10 m (33 ft) in diameter. Sixteen niches organized in four groups of four have been found in every known D-shaped structure, and excavations in these buildings have revealed small offerings around the exterior wall or at the structure's center in many cases.[19] At Conchopata, near Huari, there were large smashed chicha vessels on the floor of a D-shaped structure and human trophy heads placed as offerings, suggesting a feast related to success in war.[20]

Huari's architecture was constantly being torn down and built anew, and like cities everywhere, neighborhoods went through changes in status over time, from exclusivity to lower status, or else through changes in use. The Vegachayoq Moqo sector started as a palace, became an élite mortuary-temple complex, and then was later used as a cemetery for low- to mid-status folk.[21] There was a great amount of attention paid to cemeteries and mausoleums. In the Monqachayoc sector, four levels of subterranean chambers included galleries of tombs and ritual spaces.

While it has been difficult to work at Huari, research at Conchopata has been highly successful. Conchopata is on the edge of the modern city of Ayacucho, and it was discovered when a building project began at the site. It appears to have been a separate settlement, but one that was politically, economically, and in all other ways bound up closely with Huari's fortunes. The town covered between 20 and 40 hectares (49 to 99 acres) at its height, although research has been limited to an area of 3 hectares (7 acres). Conchopata also had a long history of occupation beginning in the late Early Horizon, although it was abandoned at the end of Wari.[22]

Excavations at Conchopata uncovered a large wall, perhaps for fortification, two patio compounds, two plazas, several temples, and more than 200 burials. The burials ranged from wealthy folk to servants, and stable isotope analysis suggests that diets were based on maize and camelid meat. Numerous recovered sets of pottery manufacturing tools suggest that some part of the town was devoted to the specialized production of ceramics, and recovered ceramics have themselves offered new appreciations of Wari culture.

While it had been known for some time that Wari feasts included the consumption of great amounts of chicha from very large jars that were smashed and ritually disposed of at the end of the festivities, details and variations of these practices were revealed at Conchopata.[23] Motifs on ceramics clarified aspects of Wari religion, showing connections with distant lands and peoples, such as the Moche, and offering new insights into the Wari themselves. For example, warrior imagery suggests that Huari's power may not have rested solely on proselytizing religion.

MIDDLE HORIZON RELIGION AND ART

For decades the relations between Tiwanaku and Wari have been the subject of much scholarly debate among Andeanists. Discussions began first by seeing the two art styles as different, despite superficial similarities, and then moved to interpreting them as having a single origin in one culture and then spreading to the other, where they diverged. In the last decade, however, enough research has been carried out at both Wari and Tiwanaku sites to support the idea that the two cultures shared a religion and its iconography, expressed in both large-scale public art (especially for Tiwanaku) and personal items and clothing (see Figures 8.2 and 8.3). William Isbell has suggested that the neutral acronym SAIS (Southern Andean Iconographic Series) be used to refer to the art style shared by both cultures. He proposes that the three main deities of the SAIS are those that appear on the Gateway of the Sun. The Staff God was the high god, although the objects held by representations of him are not always staves but may be a variety of things, such as spear throwers and darts or plants of various kinds. Similarly, there are variations of the Staff God that may express him in different incarnations or as a male-female couple, a conceptualization that would fit perfectly well with Andean dualism.[24] According to Isbell, the Rayed Head is second in importance, while Attendants rank third.[25] Attendants are always portrayed in profile, with one staff, and in a kneeling or running position.

There are other images as well, such as a "griffin" that has been seen as particularly associated with the Middle Horizon phase of the great site of Pachacamac on the Central Coast. Some of these other SAIS or related images are still to be fully understood. Indeed, it is only in the last few years that many of these iconographic details, as well as commonalities between Wari and Tiwanaku, have been confirmed. There are clear differences in how the main deities are portrayed through time and space. Some of the differences may be due to Wari embracing local religious ideas, while others may be local adaptations of Wari styles to local religion. There are also many depictions of humans, or perhaps mythological characters with completely human features. Patricia Knobloch has identified a number of these, including a figure known as the "Paramount Warrior" dressed in high status garments.[26]

There is no known direct link between the SAIS Staff God and the Staff God of the Raimondi Stone from Chavín de Huántar.[27] The image of a front-facing deity with arms to the side holding long objects seems to be a very ancient Andean motif. The rays around the deity's head might indicate that this is a solar god, but the "radiance" could also be associated with other qualities than sunshine. The rays often have the heads of animals or plants at their ends.

While there are precedents for the art style and imagery in the Yaya-Mama tradition and Pucara art, the SAIS appears to have been created mostly *de novo*. Isbell believes that the religion expressed in the SAIS appeared simultaneously, or nearly so, at both Huari and Tiahuanaco. Its simultaneous appearance at both cities, coupled with its originality, raise interesting questions about how and why the religion came about and what it signifies in terms of relations between the two cities and cultures. SAIS art partakes of long-standing Andean traditions, but it was also revolutionary in the way it reinterpreted old ideas and created new ones. The Staff God is presented as a deity in apotheosis, iconic in transcendent glory as s/he stands fully frontal, fearing nothing, arms outstretched and holding instruments of power. However, SAIS gods are not the monster deities of Chavín; they have more anthropomorphic features than animal ones. Even more revealingly, the stelae of Tiahuanaco appear to represent humans, as do various representations in Wari ceramics.

If Chavín priests became gods, Tiwanaku and Wari gods had become human, at least to a degree. There are images of monster deities, such as a large basalt *chachapuma*—an anthropomorphic puma—found at the base of the Akapana's western staircase, as well as other examples in both large and small artworks. However, there are many depictions of mortals, probably of high rank. This mixture of mortals and deities is a pattern that can be traced back at least as far as Chavín, and the Middle Horizon Staff God and Attendants appear to have their roots in that culture, but there is much greater emphasis on mortals in Middle Horizon art than ever before. The Staff God's assistants sometimes have avian or other animal heads but their bodies are quite human. So too, while human sacrifice was still common and there may have been mysteries that took place on the tops of pyramids or within the inner plazas, the new ritual programs instituted by the Middle Horizon societies were based around the festive aspects that had been part of Andean ceremonies for millennia but which were now being configured in new ways.

One distinctive feature, at least in Wari practice, was the use of huge urns made in the form of high ranking men, probably bureaucrats or other kinds of authorities, one of the emblems of authority for whom were four-cornered hats (see Figure 8.3). These huge jars-as-élites brought chicha to feasts, and this was an unmistakable, undeniable, three-dimensional metaphor for the "leader as great provider." However, the jars were ritually smashed at the end of festivals, perhaps an institutionalized acting-out of the rejection of authority, an opposition co-opted by the ruling class through its promotion of this act. Alternatively, it may simply have been a potlatch-like ritual smashing of prestige goods to proclaim the power and wealth of the givers of the feast. Either way, during the Middle Horizon, as always in the Andes, there was no clear separation between religion, politics, and economics.

The provision of great amounts of chicha and food to local leaders in a feasting venue appears to have been a key component of Wari political strategy.[28] The Wari even appear to have had their own chicha recipe, which involved the addition of Peruvian pepper (*Schinus molle*) tree fruits to the boiling corn mash, a brew that is still favored in the Moquegua Valley today.[29] At Cerro Baúl, high on a mesa in the same valley, a chicha brewery consisted of separate rooms for the various stages in brewing, and it was capable of producing 1,800 liters (475 gallons) of chicha.[30]

It was not only the large jars of chicha that persuaded people to adopt Wari or Tiwanaku practices, but also a suite of new goods made in distinctive, revolutionary styles that were highly appealing, such as the large jars themselves and other feasting and drinking gear (see Figure 8.3). One of the most noteworthy was a large flared tumbler that became so popular that variations of it—known to the Inca as a *kero*—continued to be used well into the Colonial Period. Indeed, they persist today in the form of the large chicha glasses common in the highlands.[31] There are a host of small objects as well, and while many are found as offerings they were probably also part of personal or group collections of goods. Individual items in metal or intricately inlaid wooden figurines were probably prized possessions, but sets of objects, large and small, also are prominent. These include small objects such as figurines in semiprecious stones or metal, as well as larger assemblages such as the groups of urns already mentioned.[32] One of the most spectacular finds of a set of objects was an apparent offering of 96 blue-and-yellow feather textile panels, rolled and placed in eight jars containing 12 panels each and found at the site of Robles Mojo in the Churunga Valley, near Arequipa.[33] The number of tropical birds required to make these textiles, probably wall hangings, and the amount of time to acquire the materials and fabricate the panels represent a huge investment of time and labor, and therefore a great deal of wealth.

The styles of Middle Horizon material culture varied from place to place and through time, but several features were shared in common. First, there was a delight in bright, multi-colored objects such as the polychrome ceramics that were popular throughout southern Peru and western Bolivia. Second, there was a tendency toward hieratic presentation of figures: the stiff, square-shouldered, front facing, arms-at-sides, soldier-like postures. Third, geometricization and abstraction become increasingly popular over time.

Among the most remarkable Andean art objects are Middle Horizon men's interlocking tapestry tunics, woven on looms staked out on the ground.[34] The tapestry work produced long decorative bands containing design squares of "abstract" motifs that ran horizontally when on the loom but hung vertically when worn, with the number of design bands probably indicating the status of the wearer.[35] A favored Wari technique was to create decorative bands of diminishing size moving outwards from the centerline of the garment. Each band contained the same geometric motifs as the others, but because the width of the band narrowed going outwards, the elements of the design were rendered in increasingly pared down, abstract and compressed forms. This "lateral distortion" technique is quite sophisticated and speaks of highly refined aesthetic senses among élites, as well as specialized motifs that served to mark status differences (see Figure 8.3).

Wari and Tiwanaku textiles appear similar to the untrained eye. Both cultures favored tapestry tunics and four-pointed hats, as well as unusual textile techniques such as discontinuous

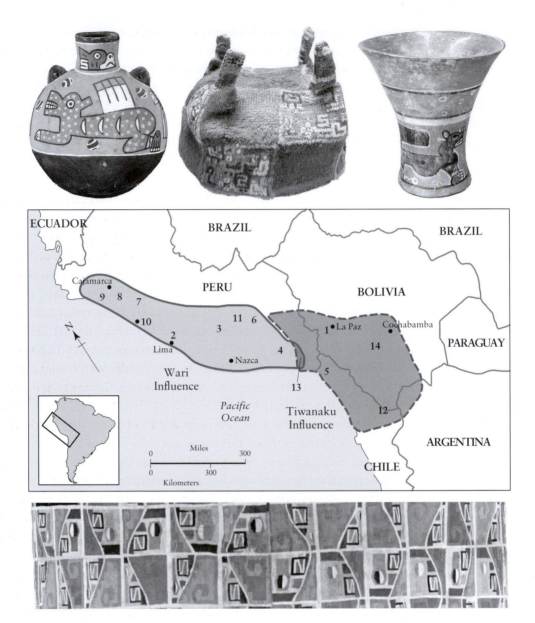

Figure 8.3 Middle Horizon South Andean iconography and artifacts. Top left: Wari "canteen" ceramic vessel. Top center: Wari Four-Corner Hat. Top right: Tiwanaku Kero. Center: Map of sites mentioned in the text. The boundaries of regions are tentative and were not necessarily all inclusive. 1. Tiahuanaco and Islands of the Sun and Moon. 2. Pachacamac, Rimac and Lurín Valley sites. 3. Huari, Conchopata, and modern Ayacucho. 4. Robles Mojo and modern Arequipa. 5. Alto Ramírez Culture. 6. Pikillacta and other Cusco sites. 7. Honco Pampa. 8. Marchuamachuco and Viracochapampa. 9. Pacatnamú, San José de Moro, and Cerro Chepén. 10. El Castillo de Huarmey. 11. Vilcabamba. 12. San Pedro de Atacama. 13. Cerro Baúl and Moquegua Valley sites. 14. Qeremita and Lake Poopó. Bottom: Detail of the width of a Wari tunic showing design compression towards the outer edges.

warps and wefts and tie-dye patchwork tunics.[36] On close examination, however, there are distinctions. Tiwanaku designs adhere more closely to the icons seen on Tiahuanaco sculpture, while Wari textiles appear to be more varied and less oriented to standards from a central place. There are also technical differences, such as the Wari preference for constructing tunics from two pieces of cloth while Tiwanaku tunics were woven whole.[37] While Wari favored lateral distortion increasing from the centerline outwards, late Tiwanaku men's tunics used lateral distortion going inwards, towards the centerline.[38] Both cultures surely knew the other's practices, and each was probably influenced by and played off new styles originating in the other, much like Paris fashions being reinterpreted in New York.

The degree to which such technical differences were meaningful when these textiles were in use is hard to assess, but concerns with details, invisible or hard to see structures or the essences of objects and materials have a deep history in Andean approaches to material culture.[39] These garments were not simply favored by aesthetes but were the apparel of choice, or perhaps the uniforms, of high-ranking administrators, warriors, or nobles, worn along with four-cornered hats as a privilege of rank within elaborate sumptuary laws.[40]

The role of garments in Wari and Tiwanaku is highly significant because both societies appear to have reinterpreted the importance of textiles as an art form and a social medium. Cloth was always important in the Andes, such as the exquisite Paracas mantles, and it has been earlier noted as the most important material good of the Inca.[41] Prior to the Middle Horizon the most elaborate textiles for which we have evidence were made by South Coast societies, so it appears that Wari and Tiwanaku either borrowed the tradition or shared it with South Coast peoples, increasing its role in tandem with greater social and political complexity and producing some of the finest weaving in the prehistoric New World.[42]

In some parts of the Tiwanaku realm, especially northern Chile and northwestern Argentina, feasts, rituals, and parties included not only the display of fancy clothing and the consumption of copious amounts of chicha but also the inhalation of snuff made from the seeds of various plants in the Genus *Anadenathera*. Its use had begun at least by the Initial Period, but its hallucinogenic properties were clearly elaborated and formalized into rituals by or in the Middle Horizon. It was known as *Vilca* to the Incas, and was popular with them as well. Elaborately carved wooden trays and elegant tubes were used to inhale the snuff: the Tiwanaku colony of San Pedro de Atacama in Chile contains the highest amount of snuffing paraphernalia from ancient South America, and the practice of taking snuff seems to have been particularly popular in this region.[43] The Alto Ramírez culture, also in northern Chile (*circa* 1000 BC to AD 600), built small villages where year-round water was available, and practiced a mixed economy in the otherwise barren environment. They were consistently influenced by altiplano cultures, including Tiwanaku.[44]

There is a bellicose aspect to Middle Horizon art. Warfare and sacrifice are not generally blatantly portrayed as they are in Moche art, and the static, hieratic style of Wari and Tiwanaku art tends to present rather formalized themes that make it easy to miss aggression. Whereas the Moche showed combat, Middle Horizon warriors stand or sit in repose and weapons are often only noticed at second glance. Nevertheless, martial and sacrificial themes are present, expressed by depictions of trophy heads, warriors, and weapons. Although the relation between art and life is not straightforward, enough warriors and weapons are depicted to suggest that warfare was an important part of Middle Horizon life, and likely one of the means by which the great cities extended their influence and élites maintained their power.

Feasting and drinking commonly occurred in the context of funerary rituals in the Middle Horizon, and Wari and Tiwanaku shared many funerary practices. The basic practice was interment of a tightly flexed, seated corpse in a pit or stone chamber with a few offerings. Following highland traditions as seen in the earlier Recuay culture, tombs were placed near the living such as under house floors, in patios, or on the edge of settlements. Although some specific practices, such as the use of stone-lined cists, were shared by both cultures, there are noteworthy differences, the most significant of which is that Wari emphasized social differences for some deceased, whereas Tiwanaku burial rites seem to have been the same regardless of age, gender, or other considerations.[45] There were at least eight different forms of Wari burial related to as many as six social ranks or classes, while Tiwanaku burials seem to only be distinguished between general classes of commoner and élite. Some Wari subterranean tombs had small orifices (*ttoco*) that were likely used to provide offerings to the dead, such as chicha, or to communicate with them. Wari tombs were also sometimes opened, with new burial bundles being added and sometimes bones removed from the deceased, a practice also known for Moche.[46] These different Wari mortuary practices were not followed by Tiwanaku, or only rarely. While mortuary rites do not necessarily directly reflect social organization, the differences in Middle Horizon burials tend to suggest rather distinct differences within their respective societies.

ECONOMICS AND POLITICS

What were the economic and political bases on which the vast sites of Tiahuanaco and Huari were built and by which they influenced other peoples in the Central Andes? Improved and expanded methods of food production appear to have played a role for both societies. Agro-pastoralism and agricultural production methods may have increased in intensity or in the ways in which they were employed (see Figure 8.4).

While there had been earlier art and religious traditions that featured llamas and other camelids, Tiwanaku continued that emphasis with vigor. Camelids provided not only meat and fine wool; they were also critical to the success of long-distance exchange systems. This appears to have been a key to Tiwanaku success: long-distance exchanges brought not only goods but also ideas to and from the Titicaca center. Llamas can carry between 25 and 40 kg (55 to 88 lbs) of goods and travel 15 to 20 km (9 to 12 mi) per day. A traditional journey was studied in 2007 in which 28 llamas traveled 90 km (56 mi) to trade salt for maize, tubers, and other goods.[47] If each animal carried an average of 32 kg (70.5 lbs) of goods, then 896 kg (1,975 lbs) were moved in each direction. It can easily be imagined that caravans many times larger than these 28 animals could have moved even more goods in the past.

The other component of Tiwanaku's economic success was the great investment of human labor in the creation of raised fields. This involved digging up the compacted soils of the Altiplano to create a raised bed of aerated soil resting on layers of gravel and with cobblestone bases for drainage. Each raised field was bounded by one or more ditches created by the borrow pit from which soil was excavated for the raised area. The ditches collected the water drained from the raised field, decayed plant matter in them provided rich fertilizer to be used on the ridges, and the water in ditches and canals absorbed heat from the sun that mitigated the effects of the severe frosts that would otherwise kill crops.

While raised field systems were used in many regions of the ancient New World, the Titicaca fields are among the largest and most elaborate. However, the technique ceased due to cultural collapse and depopulation through the centuries. Experimental archaeologists working in the Titicaca region tried to replicate ancient systems and had such success that raised fields were reintroduced into the region. On 12 experimental raised fields an average of 21 metric tons of potatoes were produced per hectare. This is twice the yield of traditional fields treated with chemicals, and over seven times the yield of unimproved traditional cultivation (see Figure 8.4).[48]

The raised fields were crucial in supporting Tiwanaku and Lukurmata, one of the most important secondary centers at the south end of Lake Titicaca.[49] In addition, Tiwanaku sites exploited lake fish resources. With fish and potatoes in abundance, camelid meat for special occasions, and llama caravans to trade for resources from lower altitudes, the Tiwanaku were well supplied with food and other goods.

Wari probably also exploited the use of llama caravans, but its art style does not emphasize camelids as much as Tiwanaku art. The appearance of Wari cultural influence in areas outside its homeland is commonly associated either with the introduction of or an increase in irrigated and terraced hillsides. Indeed, current evidence suggests that it was due to Wari that many regions of the Central Andes underwent massive landscape alterations including terracing and irrigation. Like raised fields, the creation of terraces is labor intensive. It is not simply the rearrangement of a hillside from a slope to a series of step-like platforms; in its most elaborate form, it is a recreation of the soil and landscape to retain and aerate the soil, bring water to it, and provide good drainage. The most impressive constructions in the Andes are not the massive temples but rather the dramatic transformations of entire landscapes through terracing and other engineering feats.

The importance of dualism in Andean culture in earlier times and how this has been interpreted to reflect socio-political organization has already been noted. Pierre Duviols has argued that a dual division in the central Peruvian Andes (the old Recuay region) came about when highland herding groups (the *llacuaz*) expanded into the lower areas occupied by sedentary agriculturalists (the *huari*).[50] Conflicts between the groups were contained by the creation of a dualistic society in which each group retained rights to their zones and resources of production, but assured the other of rights of access to its resources and enjoyed other reciprocal relations

Figure 8.4 Camelids and agriculture. Top: Llamas. Bottom: Revival of raised fields in the Titicaca Basin, Bolivia.

as well. Such a dual division of society may have been in operation for Tiwanaku or Wari, but whether this was a new system or a reworked one is hard to determine.[51] As noted in Chapter 6, a mixed economy of agriculture and pastoralism was practiced relatively early at Chavín de Huántar. The advantages of using high altitude land to raise llamas, which could be used for wool, meat, and transporting goods, and using land at lower altitudes for agriculture thus had been known in the Andes for at least a thousand years before the rise of the Middle Horizon cultures. Similarly, most of the basic engineering methods for agricultural intensification were already known, possibly from as early as the Late Preceramic.

It is apparent Tiwanaku and Wari both exploited resources from different environmental zones. It is highly likely that concepts of dualism were in operation in both societies and were present in religion, élite politics, and the lives of commoners. What is unclear, however, is why Tiwanaku and Wari rose to such great heights of power and influence. These two cultures might have developed new ways to increase food production, or they may have improved or intensified old systems to produce more food in addition to creating new religious and political systems to both draw people to them and colonize new regions.

GREATER TIWANAKU

Both Wari and Tiwanaku spread their influences over vast areas of the Central Andes (see Figures 8.4 and 8.5). How and why they spread, whether through religious cults, as military states, or via some other means, are topics of debate. We are only just beginning to understand the nature of occupations outside the heartlands in any detail for either of these great archaeological cultures.

As previously noted, Tiahuanaco was the product of many centuries of development and conflict, but it was one site among many in the Titicaca Basin, starting as a small village *circa* 300 BC. As the basin filled with people and small ceremonial centers, however, Tiahuanaco grew large, eventually eclipsing its rival Pucara, possibly through warfare and conquest. Local chronology traces the rise of Tiahuanaco in phases I and II (400 BC to AD 100) through various periods until its demise *circa* AD 1000. The similar dates for Conchopata, from 240 BC to AD 1000, suggest that Wari and Tiwanaku followed generally contemporary patterns of growth and eventual collapse. This stands in contrast to the Middle Horizon phases developed by Dorothy Menzel, which followed a relatively short sequence.[52] However, the Menzel sequence refers to the appearance of the Middle Horizon style traits in the Ica Valley, not to the origins of the highland Middle Horizon cultures themselves.

In the southern Peruvian highlands, as Huari grew in influence late hilltop Huarpa settlements in the Ayacucho region were abandoned and people moved down to new settlements on flat plains, often next to gorges. This trend in settlement relocation appears to have been due in large part to the increasing importance of irrigation agriculture, especially on terraced hillsides. The same process took place in the Cotahuasi Valley in the southern highlands where ten small villages from earlier times doubled in size and 15 new villages were established.

Tracing the growth and emergence of Tiwanaku and Wari from small communities to the large cities of the Middle Horizon is relatively easy compared with the thorny question of the nature of the mature societies and their influences beyond their homelands (see Figure 8.5). Were Tiwanaku and Wari states that spread their influence throughout the surrounding regions, were they even grander empires that incorporated ethnic and political groups different than those in their home territories, or were they something else altogether that does not fit into either of these categories? It is clear that both cultures were highly influential over broad regions, but how was that influence achieved? As always, it is difficult to move from archaeological data to issues of socio-political organization, but this is an important issue in archaeology so it is worth considering the issues that are involved, the data that is available, and how they may be linked.

Tiahuanaco has been subject to much more fieldwork than Huari. Although there are various lines of evidence pointing to signs of the presence of élites at the site, there is nevertheless no clear indication of the nature of the site's governance. The evidence strongly suggests that Tiahuanaco welcomed pilgrims, but on the Akapana the disarticulated remains of young men of warrior age had been left exposed to the elements before they were buried. These were probably enemies who were brought to the site and sacrificed, so it is quite likely that the site and Tiwanaku in general included violence as well as pilgrimage in its hegemonic strategy.[53]

The Titicaca Basin appears to have been under the control of Tiahuanaco, including second-order and smaller sites that were either under the direct control of authorities from Tiahuanaco or were in an asymmetrical power relationship with it. The larger sites within 75 km (47 mi) of Tiahuanaco have monumental architecture suggesting a direct association with the center. Beyond that distance, however, most sites with Tiwanaku affiliations have artifacts, often in burials that suggest the presence of Tiwanaku people, but they rarely show architectural features that would suggest subservience to or even alliances with the city on the Altiplano.

Tiwanaku had a strong role in the Cochabamba Valley, some 225 km (140 mi) from Tiahuanaco at a much lower altitude. Today the modern city of Cochabamba, at 2,800 m (9,200 ft) above sea level, is known as the "City of Eternal Spring." It was rich in tropical fruits, coca, maize, and other products that could not be produced or obtained on the Altiplano. However, the degree to which the highland center dominated or controlled the region is hard to assess.

An outcrop of a dense basalt that Tiwanaku people favored for heavy-duty tools and weapons was located at Qeremita, 300 km (186 mi) southeast of Tiahuanaco. Intensive exploitation at Qeremita occurred over a long period of time, but the Tiwanaku presence is clearly marked by small settlements on the shores of nearby Lake Poopó. Today the ground is littered with the detritus of mining and processing activities, to the point that Alan Kolata states that the scale of work was "the closest one comes to organized production in the ancient Andean world." However, whether that production was organized through a state bureaucracy or via a more independent entity—similar, say, to Aztec *pochtecas*—is hard to infer from the data.[54]

San Pedro de Atacama is an oasis in the desert in northern Chile, 500 linear km (310 mi) from Tiahuanaco, where, as noted previously, inhaling snuff was quite popular. There, the Coyo cemetery was organized into two separate clusters, one consisting of Tiwanaku dead with their distinct costumes, grave goods, and funeral rites, and the other of local people.[55] This suggests that the Tiwanaku were colonists whose relationships with locals were close enough for them to be interred in the same burial ground, but distinctive enough that they kept to themselves, probably in life as well as death. The Tiwanaku colonists were probably exploiting local minerals and metals to send back home.[56]

Yet another distant Tiwanaku colony was at Pasto Grande, in the Quebrada de Humahuaca in northwestern Argentina.[57] Just as in Cochabamba or northern Chile, however, while Tiwanaku was present, extracting local resources and interacting with local populations, specific political relations are difficult to identify. This is also true for the best example of Tiwanaku at a distance that we have, located in far southern Peru where not only Tiwanaku's dealings with locals may be examined but its relations with Wari as well.

Research in the Moquegua Valley, on the far South Coast of Peru, has been valuable in examining Tiwanaku and Wari relations between each other and with peoples outside their homelands because it is a region in which both cultures had influence. The local Huacarane Tradition consisted of small villages with no primary center, mixed floodplain agriculture, and plain ceramics. Tiwanaku colonists arrived *circa* AD 600 and brought their culture with them. They settled in formerly barren areas and built irrigation canals to water them.

Two distinct ceramic styles, Omo and Chen Chen, may represent two social or ethnic groups from different Tiwanaku lands. Both groups established towns with internal plazas that probably represented separate corporate or kin groups (ayllus, perhaps) and household patio group clusters that included storage units. Each town also had cemeteries around it with Tiwanaku-style burials of seated individuals facing east in cylindrical pits or stone-lined cists, dressed and accompanied by Tiwanaku clothing and artifacts although with few high status Tiwanaku objects.[58]

The lack of élite goods, the two different ceramic styles, and the location of settlements in previously uninhabited areas suggest that the Tiwanaku colonization of Moquegua was relatively peaceful. It is not easy to discern if colonization was ordered by a centralized Tiahuanaco authority or by some other Tiwanaku center. The general impression is that the movement into the valley was not part of a strategy authored by a political center, but rather resulted from a lower order, perhaps community-based, impulse.

The Tiwanaku colonists built a temple complex in the valley. Excavations by Paul Goldstein uncovered a centrally-located room with a U-shaped small altar- shrine, and six independently-accessed structures were arranged around a sunken court or chamber. The dry environment preserved masses of intricately-made thatch roofing material as well as bright paint on the walls of the structures. These various buildings suggest that ceremonial complexes had individual shrines for different social groups or deities and that they were bright, colorful places, features that have been lost on the Altiplano where preservation is poor.[59]

However, the Tiwanaku colonists were not alone, because Wari people also settled in Moquegua. Their most impressive settlement was atop the bulk of the steep-sided mesa of Cerro Baúl and at the nearby sites of Cerro Mejía and Cerro Petroglifo, which were occupied at about the same time as the Tiwanaku arrival in the region around AD 600.[60] Like the Tiwanaku colonists, Wari folk filled a previously unused ecological niche, establishing irrigated agricultural terraces on the flanks of Cerro Baúl.

Cerro Baúl may have begun as a deliberate colonization implemented by a Wari empire in the early Middle Horizon. The location of the site and the walls on the summit strongly suggest that the Wari established a fortified settlement. Another site, Cerro Tarpiche, in the mid-valley, had two defensible habitation sectors that show joint residential used by both Wari and local Huacarane folk, judging by the ceramics found in them. On the fortified peak, however, only Huacarane finewares are found and buildings in the local style are absent. The hilltop fortifications may thus have been an exclusive residential or refuge area for Wari élites in this part of the valley, who occasionally invited local Huacarane élites to the hilltop for rituals and celebrations.[61]

By the late Middle Horizon (AD 600 to 800) the nature of the Wari presence may have changed. Feasting and drinking parties were thrown for the locals to legitimate Wari authority, as shown by an extensive facility for the production of chicha in large quantities on the summit of Baúl, as well as the presence of both Huacarane and Wari ceramics. The impression from these lines of evidence is that Wari had successfully co-opted or converted locals to their culture.

The Moquegua Valley data offer tantalizing suggestions as to how the two most influential cultures of the Middle Horizon may have interacted with each other and with local populations. Nevertheless, pinpointing the nature of either Tiwanaku or Wari political organization is difficult, because even with archaeological data as robust as this case study, interpretations can vary. The dramatic and imposing hilltop site of Cerro Baúl suggests an imperial intrusion into local affairs, but do we interpret the use of previously unexploited environmental zones by both Tiwanaku and Wari as strategies to avoid disrupting the local populations, or as ways of showing them the proper way to live?

Despite the detailed information available on Tiwanaku and Wari in the Moquegua Valley, and the years of research that have been carried out in the area, it is still not entirely clear if Tiwanaku and Wari colonists interacted there. Moseley and colleagues see relationships, while Goldstein, Nash, and Williams believe that they did not interact.[62] Again, much work remains to be done. So far the Moquegua Valley is the only known region where the two great Middle Horizon cultures overlapped. While Tiwanaku's influence spread east and south to the fringes of the Central Andean region, Wari was extending its influence throughout much of present day Peru.

Figure 8.5 Beyond the Wari heartland. Top: Section of Pikillacta. Center left: Street in Pikillacta. Center right: Cerro Chepén. Bottom: Marcahuamachuco.

GREATER WARI

Excavations at Huari by Wendell Bennett, visits to the site by scholars including John Rowe, and research on artifact collections by Dorothy Menzel, all built a strong case that Wari was an expansive state.[63] Indeed, many scholars believe that Wari was a direct contributor to statecraft and other aspects of the Inca Empire. Subsequent research has affirmed that Wari's influence was great, but the issue of how it influenced regions beyond its homeland is debated, with arguments ranging between the extremes of an empire to a religious movement.[64]

In general, Wari appears to have acted more imperially in the highlands, especially the southern highlands, than on the coast and in the north.[65] In many highland regions there is ample testimony for the Wari presence. The site hierarchy of the Early Intermediate Period continued in the greater Cusco area. However, the newly built Pikillacta (see Figure 8.5) is one of the largest and best known Wari installations, only 35 km (22 mi) from Cusco. Terraces, canals, and reservoirs were built over 47 hectares (116 acres), as well as a huge central complex built on an orthogonal, cellular plan with many small rooms. What these rooms were used for is debated, with opinion divided between storage for the local crops or to house ancestral mummies.[66] Although Ak'awillay, 15 km (9 mi) from Cusco, is another Wari installation, elsewhere in the Cusco region Wari influence appears to have been light. There was no other Wari architecture, and scant Wari ceramics have been found at only a few sites. To complicate matters, Tajra Chullo is a distinctly Wari site at 4,100 m above sea level in the Virginiyoc Valley in the Department of Cusco, suggesting that Wari was in control of pastoral zones at high altitudes.[67] Perhaps Tajra Chullo and Pikillacta were sufficient to secure Wari hegemony over a local population that was mostly left to its own traditional practices, except for particular aspect that the empire demanded.

In the Callejón de Huaylas, the old Chavín and Recuay region, Honco Pampa has 18 patio groups, two D-shaped temples, and ceramics with strong Wari influences.[68] It is located along a major route into and out of the valley, and thus it likely played an important role in exchange systems. Indeed, Honco Pampa is one site among many that have been used to claim that Wari built roads, and this in turn has been raised as evidence to support claims for Wari's status as an empire.

Katharina Schreiber explains the variability in the nature of Wari's presence in different parts of Peru as a strategy employing a "mosaic of control."[69] In brief, the concept suggests that Wari set up administrative frameworks for direct control in some areas, while in other areas different strategies were employed, replacing a local ruler here, supporting a local puppet ruler there. Schreiber points to different strategies of control at different times during the Wari occupation at Pacheco, seen as an enforced Wari colony in the Nasca heartland, and even interprets smashed urns there as possible Nasca resistance rather than a Wari feast. In the high Sondondo Valley, south of Ayacucho, different strategies of control were employed.[70]

Other scholars interpret the data differently, however. Azángaro, in the Ayacucho Basin, is relatively small, a 7.8 hectare (19 acre) rectangular enclosure divided into three sections. Martha

Anders interpreted this site as being ruled by an élite who performed rituals for a local population, who gave their labor based on a calendrical system built into the complex's architecture.[71] Thus, in Anders' view, Wari was more of a religious system than a political one.

Religion and politics mixed at the grand site of Pachacamac, which was about 500 hectares (2 square mi) in size at the mouth of the Lurín Valley, near modern Lima. At the time of the Spanish arrival its temples and famous oracle were second to none in the Inca Empire, and it was so important that Pizarro delegated his brother to take control of it in the first few weeks of the Spanish invasion. Given its historical importance and its proximity to Lima, the site complex has played host to a long list of archaeologists. Until recently the general opinion was that while Pachacamac was of great antiquity, it experienced its most significant growth to date in the Middle Horizon when it fell under Wari rule. However, this view is under revision due to recent excavations at the site. The same is true in other parts of the Central Coast.

Most of the large sites from the late Early Intermediate Period in the area of what is now metropolitan Lima that have been studied in any detail show Wari influence, but the degree of control from Ayacucho is unclear. It appears that much of the Rimac Valley population was reorganized and resettled at Cajamarquilla, a large (160 hectares [395 acres]) urban complex in the mid-Rimac Valley. Recent excavations in two compounds show no extensive or intensive Wari occupations there, however.[72] As noted previously, Catalina Huanca was a 400 m (1,314 ft) long, 38 m (125 ft) high temple complex with seven platforms that appears to have ceased operation in the late Early Intermediate Period, a desertion that was perhaps associated with population shifts to Cajamarquilla. Nevertheless, in the Middle Horizon a large structure was built at the site to serve as a cemetery for Wari-style burials.[73]

One reason why Wari was once thought to have imposed itself directly on the Central Coast was the Nievería ceramic style. Nievería used local iconography with Wari influences, and the Pachacamac ceramic style, also local and also influenced by Wari, was thought to succeed it. However, based on recent stratigraphic excavations the styles now appear to have overlapped in time and date at least around the beginning of the Middle Horizon.[74]

The overall impression to be drawn from the current information is that major changes occurred on the Central Coast during the early Middle Horizon, and that such changes are correlated with the appearance of Wari-style ceramics and burials there. Economic differentiation increased, élites dominated ritual practices based on local symbols, and the same élite also emulated the activities and stylistic preferences of élites in Ayacucho. In short, the Lima Culture persisted although it was transformed by new ideas from Wari. The degree to which Wari may have involved itself in local affairs is still uncertain, but current evidence suggests much less direct involvement than previously thought.

Further up the coast from the Lima Culture region, research by a team of Polish and Peruvian archaeologists uncovered an extremely rich tomb complex at El Castillo de Huarmey in the valley of the same name.[75] The most important burials were of three high-ranking women who were accompanied by more than 60 seated individuals, perhaps sacrifices, buried in rows. There were thousands of artifacts in these tombs including weaving implements made of gold for the élite women. Ceramics showed local and Wari-influenced designs. Whether these remains express a Wari conquest or Huarmey adoption of élite Wari culture remains to be determined.

Similar issues of discerning the nature of Wari at a distance from Ayacucho are present in the northern highlands of Peru. In the Huamachuco region of the north highlands there are two large sites, Marcahuamachuco and Viracochapampa.[76] Marcahuamachuco is a site of monumental proportions on a 5 km (3 mi) long mesa overlooking the Condebamba Valley (see Figure 8.5). Massive masonry walls formed two kinds of structures. Galleries, sometimes more than 100 m (328 ft) long, appear to have been residences and occur in straight, circular, and curvilinear versions. Niched Halls were constructed in the form of quadrangular buildings with rows of niches in long walls. These Niched Halls were probably feasting places since high proportions of serving vessels and cups were found in them. The site was built and used from the fifth century to the tenth with its heyday in the 600s and 700s AD, and yet there are scant traces of contact with Recuay to the south, Moche to the west, or with Wari. Marcahuamachuco was a center for the maintenance of ancestor cults for a local population probably organized by a series of related lineages, and external contacts were mostly with people of the Cajamarca region to the north. The Niched Halls were a feature shared with Wari, or possibly even a source of influence on the empire, rather than a sign of the empire's presence.

Viracochapampa is less than three kilometers from Marcahuamachuco. Niched Halls and galleries also comprise the main features at this 34 hectare (84 acre) site, but its rectangular, cellular plan resembles Wari architecture. Although some have inferred that the site must be a Wari administrative center, John and Teresa Topic, who worked extensively at sites in the region, argue that it is not. They note that there are precedents for orthogonal layouts at other sites in the Huamachuco region, and that niches and galleries are not very common at Wari sites. They interpret Viracochapampa as a local attempt to reorganize society into dual divisions, based on patterning seen in architecture that was never finished and never occupied.

No account of Wari would be complete without a discussion of the question of its role in the demise of Moche. Earlier models suggested that there was a collapse of southern Moche sites and a new Moche order established in the north, such as the huge, square-kilometer site of Pacatnamú, located on a peninsula jutting into the Pacific at the far end of the Jequetepeque Valley, and Pampa Grande in the Lambayeque Valley. The degree to which Wari may have directly or indirectly contributed to these changes was a question with few responses until fairly recently. It now seems that Moche did not collapse in the Virú, Moche, and Chicama Valleys, but rather that it took on new forms everywhere, with ceremonial complexes built to host more participatory activities such as feasting rather than spectacles of sacrifice, as noted in the last chapter in relation to Licapa II, Huacas de Moche, and probably also at El Brujo.

The change in Moche site organization and function was accompanied by new ceramics, recognizably Moche in general style but taking different shapes. Notable among these are necked jars sometimes known as "King of Assyria" vessels due to the presence of the face of a man with long hair and a small moustache impressed on the neck of the vessel.[77] Perhaps the shift from sacrifices to feasting was due to Wari influences; the King of Assyria jars seem like a regional version of the large face-neck jars of Wari and Tiwanaku, although whether the Moche version depicts a god or human is not known.

For many years Wari centers north of Huamachuco or on the coast were unknown, but impressive sites with substantial Wari style architecture and artifacts have now been identified near the city of Cajamarca, particularly Yamobamba and El Palacio (aka El Castillo).[78] At these and other, smaller, sites local Cajamarca-style ceramics were found in association with Wari styles, although the political implications of such coexistence of pottery preferences is not easy to discern. Meanwhile, Wari presence has come into somewhat clearer focus on the North Coast, as well as in the adjacent highlands.

Towards the end of the period of use of San José de Moro, in the Transitional Period (*circa* AD 850 to 1000), some of the chamber tombs at the site were entered, the bones of the deceased were moved about, carelessly or even aggressively, and new burials were placed in the graves. Some of the ceramics associated with the new tomb occupants were in Cajamarca styles. Ceramics in the Nievería style of the Central Coast and Wari pottery from the southern sierra also appear in tombs, indicating that Wari ideas and tastes were being integrated into Moche life.[79]

The late Moche hilltop site at Cerro Chepén was expanded to the highest summit and a huge perimeter wall built around it (see Figure 8.5). Cajamarca-style ceramics found there indicate a highland influence, but other ceramics in different styles, including local wares, are also present. Whether it was conquered by folk from the highlands, whether sierra folk migrated there, or whether local people adopted Cajamarca styles or even intermarried with Cajamarqueños, is uncertain. Whatever the specifics, the massive walls high on the hilltop suggest that times were troubled. Further south, in the Moche Valley highland ceramic styles include utilitarian serving wares.[80] These and other indications suggest that there was a direct influx of highland people, either intermarrying with locals or migrating into the area in groups. There are forts in some locales that suggest that the local Moche folk resisted highland intrusions, but over several generations it is possible that some of the new arrivals came in peace while others came in war. The highlanders in Moche do not appear to have been strongly associated with Wari, but these large-scale movements of peoples from the highlands to the coastal valleys appear be part of larger processes that involved Wari in one way or another.

THE NATURE AND RISE AND FALL OF TIWANAKU AND WARI

The issue of whether Tiwanaku or Wari were states, empires, or something else, such as religious movements, is far from settled. New evidence collected in the last two decades has clarified many issues about the two major archaeological cultures of the Middle Horizon, but it has complicated other matters by the richness of the information now available. Where some scholars see local traditions, such as at Viracochapampa, others see Wari influence, and the different perspectives will not be resolved any time soon.

Years ago the anthropologist Robert Carneiro noted that the three Peruvian horizons all involved the expansion of highland systems into lowland regions.[81] He thought that the restricted resources of highland valleys led to more frequent population pressure crises in the sierra than on the coast, and thus the push to expand beyond highland valleys was strong. While this argument makes sense, estimating population levels and demographic pressure on resources are difficult tasks, and research on the Middle Horizon, as for so many other Central Andean periods and cultures, is not yet at the point at which these estimates can be made with confidence, although we are beginning to see some general patterns of how change occurred. Nevertheless, it is interesting to consider that the late Early Intermediate Period and Middle Horizon are times when irrigation agriculture seems to have reached maximum levels on the coast while grand irrigation and terracing programs occurred in the sierra, and recognize that these are indicative of population growth which, in turn, was related to culture change.

The two dominant cultures of the Middle Horizon not only expanded their subsistence systems but also formulated new ways to view the world and the relations between what we refer to as humans, nature, and the supernatural. They partook of a common "civilization" in the old-fashioned, somewhat discredited, but still useful sense of the term. As is common in archaeology and many other exploratory sciences, the current view of a single religion shared by Wari and Tiwanaku may change with further research. Were the differences in religion and "high" culture similar to the situation in Medieval Europe, where there was a common religion but local, subtle variations, such as different styles of cathedral architecture? Or were the differences more like those in nineteenth century Europe, when most nation states were Christian but some were Protestant and others Catholic?

While there are great similarities between Tiahuanaco and Huari, especially in terms of their common religious practices, the differences in the organization of the major sites are striking, as previously noted. If the architectural format of Tiahuanaco is open and inviting, Huari appears the opposite. If governance of an empire was seated at Huari it might have been arranged on very different principles than a single, centralized royal house or the equivalent, if the architecture reflects political organization in any direct way.

Today, Tiwanaku's realm lies in the heartland of speakers of Aymara, while Wari lies in the land of Quechua speakers. This was probably not the case in the past, when different languages were spoken in many places in the Central Andes. It is possible, however, that Wari and Tiwanaku were cultural expressions of different linguistic and/or ethnic groups that shared the same religion; this is one among many alternative interpretations. It is even possible that Huari and Tiahuanaco saw themselves as complementary members of a dualistic system, although how this might be inferred with confidence from the extant archaeology is difficult to imagine.

Human actions and intentions are always more than the material remains left behind. We may therefore consider that the influences of Tiwanaku and especially Wari on the Central Andes were greater than the archaeological record suggests. Recently a spectacular tomb belonging to a Wari "lord," containing high status Wari grave goods, has been discovered at Vilcabamba, in the *ceja de selva* east of Cusco.[82] The find was remarkable not only for the rich ornaments of silver and gold found with the badly decomposed human remains, but more importantly for the presence of a Wari nobleman in a semi-tropical region, suggesting that the Wari presence extended much further and ranged more widely than had previously been thought.

Tiwanaku and Wari may have been states and even empires for some decades or even centuries of their existence. They apparently brought new or improved ways of producing food and transporting staple and luxury goods from distant regions. However, their most profound impacts on peoples of the Andes were their religious, ceremonial, and feasting practices that were expressed in a new, distinctive and highly attractive art style. Again, analogies might be found in the Roman and British empires whose cultural influences and legacies were as profound and long-lasting as any political ones. Furthermore, like Rome and Britain, the Middle Horizon powers surely had complex histories that cannot easily be summarized.

Wari's and Tiwanaku's dealings with peoples beyond their home cities were likely sometimes peaceful and sometimes not. One of the most intriguing scenes on Conchopata ceramics depicts warriors armed with bows and arrows riding on reed boats. In general, bows and arrows are not considered Andean weapons, and Conchopata is far from bodies of water large enough for boats. The analysis of the trophy heads at Conchopata suggests that some of the skulls probably came from outside the Ayacucho heartland, and crania at Wari-affiliated sites in the Majes and Nazca Valleys showed high levels of violent trauma.[83] Wari, and probably Tiwanaku too, extended their influences violently in some times and places and peacefully at others. Elsewhere these two Middle Horizon cultures may have had little direct influence on local affairs, but their affairs likely had profound indirect consequences for people far from Huari and Tiahuanaco.

Both societies took old ideas and respected old ways—the bedrock feature at the Initial Period center of Huaca de la Cruz received its sacrificial victim in the Middle Horzion—but they repackaged them and added new and exciting ways of conceiving of the world and acting in it. Given that both Tiwanaku and Wari met their ends more than a millennium ago, the wealth of materials left behind in the ground and in terms of their marks on the landscape strongly suggests that these were powerful entities.

Perhaps they were something like empires, but we may need to be careful in how we conceive of their actions in their worlds in which religion, politics, society, and economics appear to have been virtually inseparable. Did they expand from their centers with specific governmental agencies and bureaucracies, or were their means more religiously based and less sharply defined as political actions? Some actions look distinctly political, while others seem more wrapped in religion—at least to our eyes. It is interesting to consider that while Wari and Tiwanaku had very different architectural formats, and therefore, we may presume, very different ways in which they mobilized groups of people in politico-ritual activities, both of them incorporated feasting groups of people and plying them with chicha and drugs as part of their strategies in order to gain support. However, throwing parties to win support is a practice found throughout the Andes and beyond, both in time and in space, even stretching as far as political rallies in modern nation states.

In global terms, Tiahuanaco and Huari were impressive. In the eighth century Saxon London was 60 hectares (0.23 square mi) in size. If Tiahuanaco covered an area of 6 square km (2.31 sq. mi), or 600 hectares, then it was ten times the size of the London of its day, and Huari seems to have been at least as large as Tiahuanaco. Thus, when these civilizations fell they fell very hard indeed, and there must have been a tidal wave of consequences in the wake of their collapse, albeit stronger in some regions than in others. Their influences had been great. They had created new styles of architecture, new kinds of bronze metallurgy, outstanding textiles, and many other cultural forms that were intimately connected with new ways of conceiving of the world and acting in it, although they nevertheless drew on a wide spectrum of old ideas. Just as Rome was maintained as a memory of a glorious past in Europe for centuries, so did the legacies of Tiwanaku and Wari persist.

What caused the ends of Tiwanaku and Wari? By AD 1000 both of the great centers were abandoned, their powers gone. As with other major changes in the past, one school of thought believes that severe environmental changes may have been a key to their collapse. Ortloff and Kolata have pointed to a long drought that significantly lowered the water level in Lake Titicaca.[84] The prolonged drought was a disaster for an agricultural economy in what was a precarious environment to begin with, and it undermined the authority of the priests and rulers of Tiahuanaco.

Bruce Owen suggests that social unrest may have been more important than environmental factors in the end of Tiwanaku.[85] He notes that in the Moquegua Valley the Chen Chen-style villages and temple were destroyed while the Omo-style communities were untouched, suggesting some kind of internal conflict. Owen also argues that the dates for the drought in the Titicaca Basin are after the abandonment of Tiahuanaco. Tiahuanaco may have been deliberately attacked and sacked. The Akapana might have been ritually desanctified, and there are signs of burning in the Putuni, the possible palace of Tiwanaku élites. Many Tiwanaku monoliths were smashed in the areas of their faces, while at Lukurmata fine stones were taken from the public architecture to be used in the tombs of poor folk.

We know much less about the end of Wari than of Tiwanaku. The movement of highlanders to the coastal valleys might be a sign of drought in the mountains, but other reasons might easily be conceived to explain the migration. It is interesting to consider that in the decades following the collapse of Tiwanaku the entire socio-political system on the Altiplano devolved into small polities, while on the North Coast of Peru large socio-politico-religious systems emerged out of the turmoil of the end of the Middle Horizon cultures in the Late Intermediate Period. Nevertheless, Tiwanaku and Wari left strong legacies that continued until the arrival of the Spanish, and as civilizations as rich and fascinating as any produced in the ancient world, their accomplishments should rightly elicit wonder and admiration today.[86]

While the imprints of Tiwanaku and Wari on Andean landscapes and cultures were strong and long-lasting, some peoples and areas avoided or were outside their direct influences. One of the most intriguing and poorly-known of such regions is in Chachapoyas, in the cloud forests of the eastern slopes of the Andes. Between 2,000 and 3,500 m in altitude (6,600 to 11,482 ft) the tropical forest was rich in resources and sustained extensive populations from very early times.

The region has been difficult for archaeologists to investigate due to its remoteness and the lack of easy visibility in the vegetation. Large sites display prodigious construction efforts consisting of high stone walls and hundreds of interior structures, probably dwellings. Caves in the limestone cliffs of the region often contain tombs, with tubular clay constructions that held the dead and were topped by eerie mask-like heads. Although the Chachapoyas continued to thrive in later prehistoric periods, large centers such as Kuélap and Gran Pajáten may have been built as defensive measures against Wari or perhaps other peoples outside of the Wari world, since they date to *circa* AD 750 to 800. When Tiwanaku and Wari collapsed, however, there was a reordering of societies and cultures throughout the Andes.

NOTES

1 See Kolata 1993 and Cummins 2008. The report of the older name was made to the Spaniard Bernabé Cobo in 1653 (1956).
2 Tello 1942.
3 Quoting Richardson 1994: 131.
4 Posnansky 1945.
5 Isbell and Cook 2002.
6 General coverage and synthetic treatment of Tiahuanaco and Tiwanaku may be found in Kolata 1993, Young-Sánchez 2004, and Janusek 2008.
7 Squier 1973 [1877].
8 Isbell (2008: 734) notes that the single Staff God added to the 11 Rayed Heads gives a total of 12, which might account for months, while the 30 Attendants create a 360 degree solar calendar.
9 Jorge Arellano L. (1991: 264) analyzed the structure and decided that it had five terraces and a flat top. If the ground is included, there would be a total of seven levels.
10 Kolata 1993: 107–134.
11 Blom and Janusek 2004; see also Verano 2008: 1048–1049.
12 In the Andes and around the world it is quite common to encounter large architectural complexes or cities that were "never finished." There is nothing necessarily mysterious about this, although the particular circumstances surrounding their incomplete state may be revelatory. For example, an architectural complex that was never finished and also never used is very different than a city that had a vibrant occupation which eventually ended, leaving some buildings unfinished.
13 Isbell 2008: 748.
14 Vranich 2001; Isbell and Vranich 2004.
15 Bauer and Stanish 2002; Stanish and Bauer 2004.
16 As in so many cases, we do not know what the people of the archaeological culture known as Wari or Huari called themselves. The term derives from a recent word for sedentary farmers, as discussed later in this chapter.
17 Schreiber 2005: 244.
18 G. McEwan 2006. See also Jennings and Craig 2001.
19 McEwan and Williams 2012: 72.
20 Cook 2001; Tung 2007, 2012.
21 Isbell 2008: 751.
22 Isbell 1984–85.

23 On smashing jars see Glowacki 2012 and Nash 2012. On the Conchopata smashed vessels see Cook 1984–85.
24 See Isbell and Knobloch 2006 and also Quilter 2012. The difference between a belted Staff God and an unbelted one may be symbolic of a male and female deity respectively.
25 Isbell 2008.
26 Knobloch 2012.
27 See Quilter 2012.
28 Nash 2012.
29 Nash 2012: 95.
30 Moseley et al. 2005.
31 Knobloch 2012.
32 Cook 1992.
33 King 2012.
34 Bergh 2012b, c, d, e.
35 Conklin 1996.
36 Rodman 2000 and A. Rowe 2012 on tie-dye.
37 Rodman and Fernández 2000.
38 Differences in lateral distortion in Wari and Tiwanaku derived from text about an exhibit at the Metropolitan Museum of Art, *The Andean Tunic*, March 7–October 16, 2011. Most Middle Horizon textiles have been found on the coast where preservation is good. Some information on highland textile styles can be found on ceramics and sculpture.
39 Lechtmann 1996.
40 It is possible, of course, that the tunics and hats were actual uniforms—specific clothing for specific offices held. However, this assumes a degree of bureaucratic organization for Wari or Tiwanaku that is neither clear nor proven as yet.
41 Murra 1962.
42 Relatively few Cupisnique, Recuay, or Moche textiles are known. This is probably partly due to factors of preservation that are less favorable on the North Coast than they are further south, and more frequent El Niños in the north may also have helped to destroy early textiles there. Textiles that have been found with high status burials, the most notable example of which is the burial of the Señora de Cao, exhibit fine craftsmanship such as elaborately made borders, but the main textiles are relatively simple. This suggests that textile arts were somewhat less valued in northern Peru than in the south.
43 Torres 1998.
44 Rivera 2008.
45 Isbell and Korpisaari ND on burial differences.
46 Verano 2008.
47 Tripcevich 2008.
48 Erickson 1984, 1985, 1999. See also Kolata 1991. Kolata and Ortloff 1989. Kolata 1993: 194 on raised field experiment yields.
49 Bermann 1994.
50 Duviols 1973.
51 Kolata 1993: 102.
52 Menzel 1964, 1968.
53 Blom and Janusek 2004; Blom et al. 2003.
54 Kolata 1993: 275.
55 Rodman, 1992. Also see Stovel 2008.
56 Lechtman and Macfarlane 2005; Rodman 1992.

57 Albeck 1994; Estévez Castillo 1992.

58 Goldstein 2005.

59 Goldstein: personal communication March 6, 2013.

60 Nash and Williams 2005.

61 Green and Goldstein 2010.

62 Moseley et al. 2005; Goldstein 2005; Nash and Williams 2005, 2009.

63 Bennett 1953; Rowe et al. 1950; Menzel 1968, 1977.

64 A review of Wari and its regional influences may be found in Jennings 2010a and interpretations of them in Jennings 2010b. Bergh 2012a also offers a great amount of information on Wari, including state-of-the-art assessments as well as new interpretations.

65 Isbell and McEwan 1991.

66 Local crops: Valencia Zegarra 2005. Ancestral mummies: G. McEwan 2005.

67 Wari in the Cusco region: Bélisle and Covey 2010. Tajra Chullo: Meddens 1989.

68 Isbell 2008, 1991.

69 Schreiber 1992.

70 Schreiber 1992, 2005.

71 Anders 1991.

72 Segura Llanos and Shimada 2010.

73 Maquera 2012.

74 Gayton 1927. A conference was held on the Lima Culture in Lima in August, 2012. Publications are pending.

75 Pringle 2013.

76 T. Topic and J.R. Topic 2010.

77 Ubbelohde-Doering 1967: 24.

78 Watanabe 2001.

79 Castillo Butters 2012.

80 Ringberg 2012.

81 Carneiro 1970.

82 Salcedo 2011.

83 Conchopata: Tung and Knudson 2008. Majes: Tung 2012. Nazca: Kellner 2002.

84 Kolata and Ortloff 1989.

85 Owen: personal communication 2012.

86 Isbell and Young-Sánchez 2012.

9

THE LATE INTERMEDIATE PERIOD

A QUICKENING PACE

There was probably a time of social turmoil when Tiwanaku and Wari collapsed, but the archaeological record once again is murky on what exactly occurred. The "recovery" time in the vacuum left by the highland powers seems to have been much shorter than in earlier transitions, however. The following era, the Late Intermediate Period, is another time of "regionalization," much like the Early Intermediate Period. In many places there is a strong sense of cultural vibrancy, while in others people retreated to defensive sites on hilltops. Some prosperous regions continued to flourish while others became backwaters. The overall impression of life in the Central Andes is one of generalized growth, of increased interconnectivity between different peoples, and of denser populations with more resources than ever in many regions while balkanization occurred in others (see Figure 9.1).

Real, living, Andean peoples and not just archaeological cultures come into sharper focus in the Late Intermediate Period as we enter into protohistory. In part, this is because the Inca can be seen as a highly successful Late Intermediate Period society, one that grew directly out of social, cultural, and political conditions that were shared over a wide swath of the Andes.[1] In addition, the Inca conquest of many regions took place only very shortly before the arrival of the Spanish in 1532. In areas where the Inca had not consolidated power or dramatically rearranged local social conditions, the nature and identity of local peoples often remained largely intact through the transconquest period. This was especially the case in the highlands where European diseases were less severe than on the coast. Although many peoples throughout the Central Andes certainly experienced wrenching changes due to the Inca and then the Spanish, nevertheless there were many continuities that help contemporary scholars to understand what prehistoric life was like in many regions.

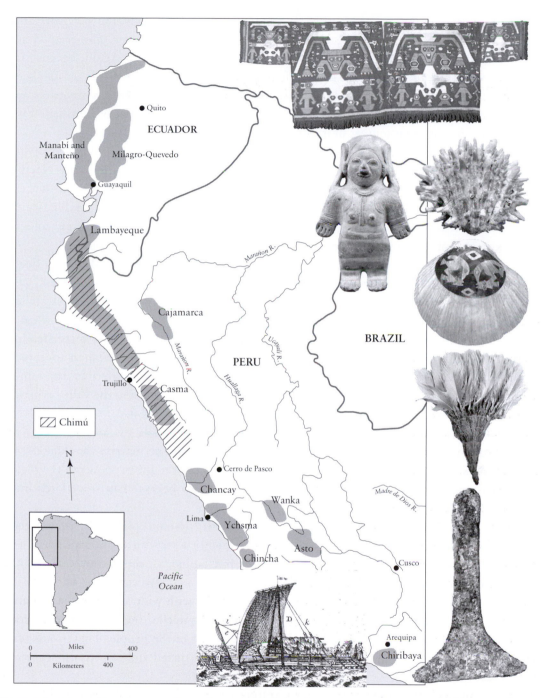

Figure 9.1 Map of Late Intermediate cultures and sites and trade items. From upper right: shirt (Chimú), Manteño ceramic figurine, *Spondylus princeps* shell, inlaid *Spondylus* shell (Chimú), parrot feather fan, copper axe-money, balsa raft with European style sail as depicted in the eighteenth century by Jorge Juan y Antonio de Ulloa.

In addition to continuities of identities and practices in some regions, the survivors of the traumas of the sixteenth century also told stories about olden days. Some tales seemed quite historical and factual while others have the flavor of myth and legend. Again, because Inca hegemony was quite recent in some places, there were old people who remembered life before the conquerors from Cusco or Spain arrived. Elsewhere, it may have been parents' or even earlier generations' tales that were recounted. Although such stories must be considered with caution, they do offer rich sources of information.

Two similar stories are known for the North Coast of Peru, one from the Lambayeque Valley region and the other from the Moche Valley. The protagonist of the former is known as Ñaymlap or Naylamp, while Taycanamo is the hero of the latter. The legends are similar in that each cultural hero was said to have come from elsewhere, arriving by sea to establish a dynasty that ruled for many years over large territories, the northern region associated with the archaeological culture known as Lambayeque or Sicán and the southern one as Chimú or Chimor.[2]

Ñaymlap, a man of great "valor and quality," came to the Lambayeque Valley on a fleet of balsa raft vessels.[3] He brought many concubines and his principal wife Ceterni, and other people as well. Many high officials accompanied Ñaymlap, and he is said to have established his court in a palace at a place called Chot. He also brought an important idol but when his work was done he grew wings and flew away. After a number of descendants succeeded him, Fempellec wanted to move the idol from its shrine at Chot. To tempt him a woman appeared in a vision and seduced him, causing rain for 30 days followed by a year of sterility and famine. Due to his sin the priests tied up Fempellec and threw him into the sea, and the valley remained without a ruler until the Kingdom of Chimor, to the south, conquered it.

Taycanamo also arrives on a balsa raft but spends a year learning the local language. He brings special yellow powders to be used in his ceremonies, and he marries the daughters of local leaders and takes the name of Chimor Capac. Eventually the Inca conquered the region, followed by the Spanish, and the descendants of Taycanamo became Christian lords under colonial rule.

Various archaeologists and ethnohistorians differ in their opinions of how far these legends can be taken as fact or not.[4] Since all myths must to greater or lesser degrees be grounded in the worlds of the people who heard them in order to be intelligible, aspects of the stories can be informative whether or not the historical reality of kings and dynasties are accepted. For example, there is a suggestion that huacas were associated with particular lords and named after them in late prehistory, while the priests' execution of Fempellec suggests that rulers could be deposed by religious specialists perhaps acting on behalf of the people. The discussion of rains and subsequent famine indicates that El Niño events occurred and sometimes devastated agricultural systems.

The Ñaymlap story is also valuable in suggesting what an Andean royal court might have been like in late prehistory. His retinue was said to have consisted of 40 officials including Pita Zofi, the Blower of the Shell Trumpet; Ninacola, Master of the Litter and Throne; Ninagintue, Royal Cellarer in charge of the king's chicha; and Fonga Sigde, Preparer of the Way, who scattered seashell dust in front of his lord's path. There was also Occhocalo, the Royal Cook; Muchec, Steward of the Face Paint; Ollopcopoc, Master of the Bath; and Llapchillulli, Purveyor of Feathercloth Garments.[5]

We cannot assume that the court of a high lord would have had 40 officials or even what their titles were, but the list provides an indication of what was considered important and appropriate for a king's court in late prehistory. There were shell trumpets, litters, feathercloth garments, and face paints, and it is reasonable to assume that these, along with fine food and luxuriant bathing, would have been highly valued and probably given special attention through high-status roles in the king's court, much like the titles of the courtiers who attended European royalty.[6] The statement that seashell dust was scattered in the lord's path is especially interesting, because for millennia the most highly-valued shell in the Andes had been *Spondylus*, and there is substantial evidence that trade in this luxury item increased dramatically in the Late Intermediate Period, one of the most telltale signs of the quickening pace of cultural interactions in the Andes.

SHELLS, METAL, AND LONG DISTANCE TRADE

Spondylus mollusks comprise their own genus (*Spondylidae*) (see Figure 9.1). They have a general shell shape similar to a scallop, but they can move and they have other features that resemble oysters. There are a great many varieties of the bivalve the world over. They were prized in antiquity at many times and places, but nowhere else did they achieve the importance of *Spondylus princeps* in the Central Andes. This shell has a pink-to-red colored exterior with large spine-like projections, leading some to refer to it as the spiny scallop or thorny or spiny oyster.

Red diatomite stone may have preceded *Spondylus* in terms of value in the Late Preceramic Period, as mentioned previously, and the earliest archaeologically retrieved examples of *Spondylus* are from the Middle Preceramic sites on the Central Coast.[7] Today it still is a crucial element in traditional Quechua rituals. In the past the thorny oyster was sometimes used for offerings in various forms—as whole shells or valves, carved into small images, and ground into powder. Often it was cut and polished as beads (Quechua: *chaquira*), or used as inlays to adorn objects, sometimes in conjunction with the less valuable purple-colored *Spondylus calcifer*. It is likely, then, that the dust scattered by Fonga Sigde was *Spondylus*.

The source of *Spondylus*, the coast from Ecuador northwards, was not only far from many of the regions where it was valued, but the shell also exists deep on ocean beds. Some recent research suggests that the shell can sometimes be found in shallower waters, but it seems that by late prehistory only deep-water specimens were available. The shell had been highly valued from very remote times.

The exact pace of *Spondylus* export from Ecuador and its importation into Peru through the prehistoric eras is difficult to judge. The shell is prominent in carvings at Chavín de Huántar, shown in contexts that indicate its highly sacral value in the religious system practiced there. It seems that there was a gradual increase in the importation of *Spondylus* over time, with an apparently dramatic surge in demand in the early Middle Horizon, especially on the North Coast. Many of the largest Moche huaca complexes were close to the shore, and part of the reason for their location may have been control of long-distance trade.[8]

Spondylus princeps was more precious than gold by the time the Spanish arrived in western South America, and the desire for it seems to have been a critical factor in the active and extensive long-distance commerce that was taking place there.[9] While various studies have suggested that the mollusk can sometimes be found further south, the densest and most extensive sources are in warm waters from Ecuador northwards to Mexico, as was also the case for the conch shell *Strombus galeatus*. However, *Spondylus* shells are found at archaeological sites as far distant as northern Chile, where they accompanied children to high mountain peaks for sacrifice.[10]

Interactions in the region from the North Coast of Peru to Ecuador were particularly intense, or perhaps they are simply the best documented by current research. The Ñyamlap story implies that large balsa raft vessels were plying the Pacific at least by the Late Intermediate Period, but the fact that Andean peoples were developing a maritime tradition as early as the Preceramic Period suggests that advanced seafaring was underway well before the Lambayeque Culture.

Our best view of late prehistoric balsa rafts and their trading ventures comes from the time of the Inca, when one of Pizarro's preliminary explorations along the coast encountered such a craft in full sail with a crew of twenty. Bartolomé de Ruiz, the captain of Pizarro's vessel, provided a fairly detailed description, perhaps because as a sailor he appreciated what he saw. His description of the craft with its large balsa logs, cotton sails, and stone anchors is one of the most important accounts we have of pre-Columbian marine technology, while the account of its cargo, housed in a cane superstructure that also served as crew quarters, gives us one of the best accounts of the goods that were traded. They included:

> many objects of silver and gold for personal ornament to barter with those with whom they were going to trade, among which were crowns and diadems and belts and bracelets and armor for the legs and breastplates and tweezers and bells and strings and masses of beads and mirrors adorned with the said silver and cups and other drinking vessels; they (also) brought many textiles of wool and cloth and shirts and tunics and capes and many other garments all of them finely woven with rich detail, and of colors such as red and crimson and blue and yellow and with all the other colors and varied craftwork and figures of birds and animals and fish and trees.[11]

Another important account was provided by a local chief in Panama when he was asked by Vasco Nuñez de Balboa (the "discoverer" of the Pacific Ocean) about gold. The chief supposedly replied that there was much more gold in lands far to the south, and made a small clay model of the strange animals that they had in those lands. From the available description, the animal appears to have been a llama. The man said that any travel to those distant lands should be delayed until the winds were right. Indeed, one of the controversies regarding ancient navigation along the Pacific coast is whether balsa rafts could tack against the wind. The evidence suggests that they could, and that part of their maneuverability depended on the use of centerboards rather than relying on a fixed keel.

While seafaring technology and other issues remain under-researched for western South America, there are nevertheless many other indications that trade was highly active in the Late Intermediate Period, proceeding by land as well as sea.[12] One of the most important of these is the growth in metallurgy and the widespread appearance of standardized copper alloy metal objects that likely served as units for trade. In short, forms of "proto-money" appear to have developed. One form, known as *naipes* (the Spanish word for a playing card), was made in standardized rectangular or bow-tie shaped forms, while another resembled small axes and so is often termed "axe-money."[13] These latter forms are found in northern Peru and Ecuador, but then they do not appear in the intervening area until West Mexico is reached. Materials scientist Dorothy Hosler has conducted scientific studies and concluded that there was a clear connection between the two geographically distant regions. Metallurgical techniques were introduced into Mexico in two waves, the first between AD 800 and 1250 and the second between 1250 and the arrival of the Spanish.[14]

For many years archaeologists have pointed out strong similarities between the cultures of West Mexico, especially the Tarascan area, and northern Peru and coastal Ecuador.[15] For example, in both regions boot-shaped shaft tombs were popular. Now, with new analytical tools, additional ways to identify connections have become available. Genetic studies are demonstrating that influences traveled in both directions, and this research has led to some surprising conclusions. For example, the chili pepper's original home was Peru. It traveled to Mexico in ancient times and is now found around the globe. On the other hand, hairless dogs were likely brought from Mexico and became popular in Peru in late prehistory.[16] Continuing research will certainly demonstrate many more kinds of contact.

There appears to have been a decline in the use of axe-monies and naipes a few generations before the arrival of the Spanish. Whether this reflects a decrease in trading activity, perhaps because of the interference of the Inca Empire in the affairs of formally independent traders, or whether it is due to some other factor is not known. While the quantity of axe-money may have decreased, overall there appears to have been an increasing trend for bronze tools employed for a variety of uses ranging from utilitarian to military.

The fact that axe-monies and similar systems became widespread and popular is evidence that metallurgy in general had greatly increased in importance. While Moche warriors may have added bronze spikes to the ends of their two-handed clubs and Recuay élites sported fancy bronze pins in their garments, utilitarian metal objects were relatively rare during Moche times and earlier. In the Late Intermediate Period, however, a great variety of metal weapons and tools appear in the archaeological record and the production of copper-arsenic bronze greatly increased.[17] Most of the metal artifacts that have been preserved consist of varieties of knives, various kinds of points such as for spears, and star-shaped and other forms of mace heads for weapons. Other objects include spuds, gouges, chisels, hoes, and crowbar-like devices. Some scholars believe that there is an unbroken tradition of these forms of tools from late prehistory to today.[18]

The various proto-monies used in trade may have had value in themselves, but they could also be reworked into tools, weapons, or other objects. The difficulty of ascertaining how widespread metal implements were in late prehistory in the Andes may lie in the fact that many of them were melted down to be made into new tools in later times, thus reducing the number of artifacts left for archaeologists to recover and study. The impression is that metal tools were fairly widespread but not universal, but again this is very hard to judge for societies from the Late Intermediate Period onwards. The one exception is the Lambayeque (aka Sicán) culture in which even the simple tombs of low-status people commonly held copper or bronze objects.[19]

What we can say is that in the Late Intermediate Period there appears to have been a substantial increase in the production of various goods and materials, and in the exchange of them across vast regions of the Andes and beyond. If this is so, rather than being simply a product of an archaeological record that is more dense for later periods than for earlier ones, there may have been a general increase in long-distance exchange systems. Perhaps increased population sizes made possible by improved agricultural technology could have been an important factor both increasing trade and fostering the production of goods for exchange, such as metal objects. Climate is often thought to play a role in the greater culture changes, and it is interesting to consider that the Medieval Warm Period took place between AD 950 and 1250. The initial date, give or take a century, is coeval with the end of many societies of the Middle Horizon, while the end date is close to shifts in regional politics in some places within the Late Intermediate Period. While the Medieval Warm Period was apparently a global phenomenon that produced milder temperatures in some places, its role in western South America is rather uncertain.[20] Whatever the reasons, however, the pace had quickened.

ECUADOR

While Ecuador had been "precocious" early in prehistory, its peoples took different paths during the subsequent centuries than those of people to the south. As noted earlier, while Real Alto had concentrated people in a central place, the site was eventually abandoned with populations spreading out to small farmsteads and hamlets. This pattern appears to have been constant over millennia. No large ceremonial centers, irrigation networks, or other collective construction works comparable to the large complexes of Peru and Bolivia were built—or at least, they were not undertaken with sufficient frequency that their remains are clearly visible to us today.

Again, as in so many other cases, the reasons for this trend are the subject of debate. Did ancient peoples in the lands now comprising Ecuador (and beyond into Central America) choose not to build great monuments, like some ancient hippies rejecting "civilization" in favour of the bucolic life on a small-scale? Or were they sidelined from achieving "high" levels of socio-political complexity?[21] A large-scale view of the matter points to the fact that the tropical forest and even highland regions of Ecuador are less harsh than similar ecological zones in Peru, Bolivia, or Chile, with the consequence that there was no overriding pressure to band together and work cooperatively.

By late prehispanic times, however, during what is referred to as the "Integration Period" (*circa* AD 500 to 1530), there were social hierarchies and large public works in both highland and coastal Ecuador.[22] Large earthen mounds—*tolas*—were erected in many places. Different regional traditions emerge in late prehistory that seem to be more or less linked to earlier traditions, often depending on the amount of research that has been carried out in one area or another.

In northern coastal Manabí, the Jama-Coaque tradition began in deep prehistory with an interruption due to a devastating, massive ash (tephra) fall *circa* AD 400.[23] The later Jama-Coaque culture produced one of the most innovative ceramic traditions in the New World, with many depictions of elaborately costumed warriors and fantastic deities. In the Guayas Basin, where the Valdivia culture once flourished, there were extensive raised field complexes and a three-tier site hierarchy. The Peñón del Río site had a long occupation and in late prehistory, in the local Milagro-Quevedo period, the site consisted of tolas arranged around open public spaces. Peñón del Río was probably a regulator of the flow of goods to and from the Gulf of Guayaquil and highland regions to the east. Axe-money and other metal objects were found at the site, and a variety of other remains also suggested highland–lowland interchanges.[24]

Manabí Province, on the central Ecuadorian coast, has one of the best-known records of late prehistoric occupations in the country. There, the Manteño archaeological culture flourished in the Late Intermediate Period and the Late Horizon. Relatively early in the Colonial Period the Italian traveler Girolamo Benzoni stated that the Spanish town of Manta had been a principal town of the region, and in the early twentieth century Marshall H. Saville reported that the remains of hundreds of house sites and mounds covered several square miles outside the town.[25] Based on archaeology and colonial reports, three principal sites and their associated polities (*señorios*) have been identified: Jocay (modern Manta), Picuaza (Picoazá), and Salangome (Agua Blanca).[26] At these sites and what appear to be secondary centers, sculpted U-shaped stone seats are present. They were likely used by the highest-ranking members of society, as indicated by large polished black Manteño vessels depicting a seated man with tattoos or body painting, large ear spools, and an elaborate hat or headdress.

The Manteño site that has received the most archaeological attention is Agua Blanca, eight kilometers up the Buenavista River Valley. Several hundred structures cover about four square kilometers over hilly terrain. A core area about 2 square km (0.7 square mi) in area consists of a modified hilltop with buildings on it. The largest of these is 50 m (164 ft) in length by 12 m (39 ft) in width, containing the greatest number of stone seats known for such sites, possibly as many as 20 arranged along the walls facing inward. Two pairs of smaller structures are nearby, outside the main building. The arrangements and sizes of the buildings suggest that the Andean concept of opposed, dual categories of slightly unequal partners was in operation at the site, while the many seats suggest that political organization consisted of a council of leading men, perhaps the heads of lineages or similar corporate groups.

Agua Blanca was probably the Manteño town of Salangome which was mentioned by name before Benzoni's visit in the account of the balsa raft trading vessel. The density of settlement and the wealth of the local lords at Salangome and other Manteño sites was likely due to the production of and trade in luxury goods. A shell workshop where mother-of-pearl was worked has been excavated at the site of Los Frailes, and on Isla de la Plata, at Puerto Lopez, hundreds of *Spondylus* shells were found at an apparent long-distance trade staging point, since Chimú and Inca ceramics were also present.[27] All major Manteño sites yield copper objects that were traded along with perishable items such as cotton, coca leaves, other tropical forest products and obsidian from the highlands.

Late prehispanic highland Ecuador, like the coast, was organized into a multitude of political units that the Spanish referred to as *cacicazgos,* from *cacique* (chief), a Taino word from the Caribbean that was frequently used by the Spanish to refer to *curacas* and other leaders.[28] Distinct socio-political regional groups are known for the highlands from Spanish sources reporting on who they met as well as what the Inca and locals told them about earlier times. Western Pichincha Province, in the sierra and slopes of the Andes just west of Quito, had been repopulated, probably from the coast, in the aftermath of the huge volcanic eruption in the Formative Period. By late prehistory, several different groups known collectively as the Niguas occupied the western Andean flanks, traded in tropical and highland products to the east and west, and specialized in the production of obsidian tools. At higher altitudes four powerful chiefdoms—the Caranqui, Cayambe, Otavalo, and Cochasquí—spoke the same language and struggled amongst themselves and with lesser chiefdoms in the region, but they united in a confederacy when they were finally faced with the threat of the Inca.[29]

The highest ranking caciques appear to have been linked to lower order leaders in principal villages, although the degree to which local groups considered themselves to be members of a single, larger community is uncertain.[30] Communities, known as *llactakuna,* shared rights over lands, labor, and other resources and recognized a leader who was probably linked to them through kinship. In addition to kin ties, caciques played key roles in ritual and economic systems, and long-distance exchange in prestige goods was highly important as shown by the existence of a special class of long-distance traders known as *mindaláes.*[31]

Large tolas are characteristic of late prehispanic highland Ecuador. Hemispherical mounds first appeared *circa* AD 700, ranging in size from 3 to 6 m (10 to 20 ft) in diameter and 1 to 2 m (3 to 6 ft) in height; they mostly seem to have served as mortuary facilities. Quadrilateral mounds may have ramps or not, and they can be quite large, up to 90 m (295 ft) on a side and 10 m (32 ft) or more in height. Their flat platform summits sometimes held structures or contained burials, and it seems reasonable to suspect that the structures could have served for rituals or as the residences of *caciques*, who probably combined both political and religious roles in their communities.[32]

In general, our view of ancient societies in Ecuador in late prehistory is one of dense populations of agriculturalists raising maize and other crops for their subsistence while engaged in craft production and long-distance trade. Many communities may have specialized as traders or as producers of raw materials, such as metals, or of particular goods such as metal jewelry or tools. Large tola sites indicate that surplus labor was marshaled to build impressive structures, but the evidence also suggests that political organization was locally based with relatively weak higher levels of integration. There are many fortresses known in highland Ecuador in particular, so it is likely that the political landscape was a complex one in which alliances and other political arrangements were common, especially in regards to trade networks and warfare. Generally, the late prehispanic peoples of Ecuador are commonly portrayed as more simply organized than their contemporaries in Peru. It is quite likely, however, that the kinds of socio-political and economic systems described above were the norm for most of the Central Andes in prehistory, and that the more complicated organization of political systems was the exception rather than the rule, in Peru and everywhere else.

THE LANDS OF ÑYAMLAP

The river valleys north of the Pampa de Paiján are generally considered to have been the territory of the Lambayeque archaeological culture, named after the largest valley in the region where the culture left its mark most strongly. The Lambayeque culture is also known as Sicán, a term said to mean "temple of the moon."[33] When the Spanish arrived a language known as Muchik was spoken north of the Pampa de Paiján in the region formerly occupied by the Lambayeque culture, while Quingnam was spoken south of Paiján in Chimú territory.[34] Lambayeque dates earlier than Chimú, and so the view that latter conquered the former seems to be supported by the archaeological evidence. Relations between the two are not entirely clear, however.

Lambayeque (*circa* AD 900 to 1350) seems to have arisen directly out of Moche, although there were turbulent times during its emergence. It continued many basic Moche patterns in its temple architecture, prestige goods, and religious practices, although there were some sharp distinctions (see Figure 9.2). Truncated pyramids continued as the primary ceremonial structure, but Lambayeque versions had a central ramp instead of a lateral one. Moche ceramics in red and white had been replaced by polychromes influenced by Middle Horizon styles in the Transition Period, but these styles were eventually abandoned in favor of dark-colored wares, and double-spout-and-bridge styles replaced stirrup spouts. Some other changes in technology also took place, such as the increased popularity of paddle-stamping (Spanish: *palateado*) to decorate everyday pottery and the use of the chamber-and-fill technique in construction.

Significant changes are also apparent in the great increase in popularity of head deformation, especially the "fronto-occiptal" form in which the front and back of the skull are molded to produce a wide, bun-like shape. Interment form also changed from the extended, supine Moche body position to seated, flexed positions among the Lambayeque. This practice occurred throughout society, from the humblest farmer to the mightiest lord. This suggests that there was a profound change in religious ideas and practices, and these were probably also closely tied to new social and political arrangements because flexed burials are the form that "mummy

Figure 9.2   Lambayeque culture. Top: Batán Grande. Center: Burial "mask," Sicán Lord bottle, detail of engraved gourd. Bottom: Túcume site.

bundles" take. Many of the changes are cultural preferences that originated in south coastal Peru.

Lambayeque iconography has not received a great amount of study compared to Moche, but a very popular image was of a figure known as the *Huaca Rey* (Huaca King) or Sicán Lord or Deity (see Figure 9.2). This is a depiction of a lord or deity wearing an elaborate mask and ear ornaments, which is often placed on the center of ceramics so that the vessel spout can also be read as a tall conical headdress. Like the earlier King of Assyria vessels, the body of the figure is often the body of the vessel, so that the idea of the lord or god as the source of bounty, as represented by the contents of the vessel, is emphasized.

The Huaca Rey is sometimes shown supported by two small aides, one on each side, as if the main individual is incapacitated or dead. Elaborate metal "masks" (no eye holes) with distinctive comma-shaped eyes as seen on the Huaca Rey are found in actual burials of high-ranking Lambayeque lords, and these are some of the most striking and emblematic prehispanic artworks (see Figure 9.2). Whether or not this imagery refers to a mythological ancestor, such as Ñyamlap, or a deity, or simply to a Lambayeque lord cannot be determined at present, but the image is very common in the art style. Several other images also appear frequently, including an "anthropomorphic wave" and other designs that are difficult to interpret. The range of images portrayed seems to be reduced from Moche times, and the hieratic nature of many of the presentations does not allow for ease of interpretation.

The dark ceramics depicting the Huaca Rey are ubiquitous, emblematic expressions of Lambayeque culture, as are the distinctive funeral masks found on high status burials as mentioned above. Small, simple versions made of alloys with low gold and high copper contents are known, as well as huge, elaborate versions made of high quality gold. Other emblematic objects are elaborate crescentic metal knives (*tumis*), often with long handles surmounted with highly decorated figures of the Huaca Rey.[35] Large keros—a continuance of Middle Horizon influences—made of precious metal are also common expressions of the great increase in the quantity of metal objects and their values in Lambayeque culture.

Lambayeque seems to have taken metal production to near industrial levels, with workshops under the control of élites producing utilitarian items as well as master artisans who worked in precious metals to craft the regalia of the highest lords. The metal worked included copper, gold-copper alloys, and pure gold, and there appears to have been a rank system in which the purer metal was more highly valued than alloys, even though great technical skills were employed in making alloys appear more golden in appearance than would be expected from their true composition.[36]

Two Lambayeque sites have received extensive study. These are Sicán (part of Batan Grande) and Túcume, both in the La Leche Valley, a small valley to the north of the larger Lambayeque Valley. Sicán consists of seven major huacas along the La Leche River, which have all been looted and studied to greater or lesser degrees.[37] One of the most impressive excavations occurred at Huaca Loro, a Middle Sicán (AD 900 to 1100) roughly square huaca with a western zig-zag ramp ascending its terraces and a massive 35 m (115 ft) wide, 200 m (656 ft) long platform extending from its northern flank. Two élite burials were found on either side of the intersection of the platform with the huaca. Each tomb by itself would rank as one of the wealthiest burials ever found in the New World. The East Tomb was smaller (3 × 3 × 11 m [10 × 10 × 36 ft]) than the West Tomb, but it contained more metal objects. The main burial was of a robust male between 40 and 50 years old at time of death, accompanied by four human sacrifices. The general suite of grave offerings followed old traditions of including ceramics, *Spondylus* and other shells, and items of personal adornment including crowns, ear spools, and staffs. Litter poles and arsenical copper implements were also found in the grave.

The West Tomb was grander than its neighbor and consisted of an upper antechamber (6 × 10 × 12 m [20 × 33 × 39 ft]) with a central chamber sunk in its center. The antechamber contained six square pits on each side of the central chamber, with one or two young women holding everyday objects in each pit to a total of nine per side. The main burial was a 30 to 35 year old adult male with a severe puncture wound in his pelvis. He was dressed in a Sicán mask, crown, pectorals, and other regalia including two large gold "gloves." Wealth was also expressed in eight camelid heads and the articulated feet of at least 25 camelids. There were niches in two opposing walls of the chamber in which the remains of young women were seated. One of these was beneath a rectangular basket filled with ornaments and paraphernalia including five cylindrical gold crowns, tumi-shaped crown ornaments, and other objects.

The immense wealth in these tombs is indicative of the power of the Lambayeque lords. In particular, the inclusion of so many sacrificed women expressed the ability of these powerful personages to gather resources unto themselves. Also, the general pattern of interment and mortuary ritual suggests strong continuities with earlier Moche practices, particularly in terms of symbolic references related to god personification. However, whereas Moche god impersonators were active, the lack of eye holes in Lambayeque masks suggests highly passive roles for Sicán lords, or else the assumption of deity roles only in death.

Túcume, also known as El Purgatorio, is another large impressive site, almost a square mile in area (220 hectares, 544 acres) accentuated by a natural hill jutting out of the plain which has been modified into a huge huaca, with 25 other huacas in the complex (see Figure 9.2).[38] The Huaca Larga measures 700 m (2,300 ft) in length, 280 m (910 ft) wide, and averages 20 m (65 ft) in height. The top was accessed by a long ramp and the entire structure abuts the large hill-huaca that dominates the site. The site is so massive that the extensive investigations under the direction of the famed explorer Thor Hyerdahl have still left many issues uncertain. Work on the small (7.5 × 8 m, 25 × 26 ft) Temple of the Sacred Stone found a *huanca* in the structure that had received offerings of potsherds, miniature metal objects including figurines, *Spondylus*, textiles, llamas, and humans. The roof of the temple was built with two triangular projections that reference a distinctive feature on the head of the Huaca Rey.

At the Huaca Chornancap a suite of rooms interpreted as a palace has recently been excavated, although it includes unusual features that suggest ritual spaces, such as a complex labyrinthine passageway. An impressive Lambayeque tomb was inserted into this space.[39] The principle burial was of a high ranking woman equipped with a face mask and accompanied by an elaborate scepter and gold, silver, and shell jewelry and ornaments, as well as many *Spondylus* shells. Notably, a group of very finely made "coastal" Cajamarca-style vessels were in the tomb, indicating the great influence of the highland style as first seen during the previous Transitional Period. The inclusion of seven humans buried with the élite woman are further indications of her high rank, although whether she was solely a priestess or if she had a direct political role is difficult to ascertain.

Discerning the nature of Lambayeque political organization is as difficult as for any other archaeological culture. The great amount of wealth invested in the tombs of élites such as those at Sicán and the great size of this and other architectural complexes clearly indicate that great amounts of time, trouble, and energy were invested in them. As always, however, the degree to which the élites who lived at and were buried in these centers controlled the people who went to such efforts is hard to evaluate. The ceremonial centers were places where craft and religious specialists resided or spent great amounts of time, but it is not clear who was making decisions about the production and distribution of essential goods and services.

As in all cases previously discussed, there is no indication of "government" for Lambayeque in the sense of a bureaucratic system operating independently of other forms of social relations. Still, Lambayeque lords could have exercised considerable political power by their control of long-distance exchange systems dealing in metals, emeralds, sodalite, cinnabar, amber, *Spondylus* and the production and distribution of prestige goods made with them, as well as through their claims of religious authority. So, too, the control of irrigation systems and the water that they distributed would also have been a critical aspect of political power. The line between roles as negotiators or arbitrators in disputes over water rights is a very fine one, and can be crossed, back and forth, with changing circumstances. Acting to settle disputes among contesting parties is very different than commanding that work be done by subjects. However, while these are very different forms of politics, viewing them archaeologically is very difficult indeed.

THE KINGDOM OF CHIMOR

It is generally believed that the Kingdom of Chimor conquered the Lambayeque. When the Spanish arrived the Chimú had been conquered by the Inca relatively recently, which means that there is a considerable amount of information derived from the chronicles that has been used to underpin archaeological research (see Figure 9.3).[40] Chimú is commonly assumed to have been a state, the Taycanamo legend has been used to interpret Chimú strategies, and the dates have been interpreted to fit with assumed patterns of growth and expansion both of the kingdom and of its greatest city, Chan Chan (see Figure 9.3).[41]

The Chimú heartland lay in the Moche and Chicama valleys, the same territory that had held important Moche sites, and Virú. In the early fourteenth century the Chimú conquered the Lambayeque center of Farfán in the lower Jequetepeque Valley. It became a major Chimú center with six large walled compounds stretched along four kilometers of road; the site controlled both the north-south coastal road and the route to Cajamarca in the highlands. Northward, Chimú expansion later extended at least as far as the Lambayeque Valley, where they also took control of Túcume. To the south Chimú established another center, Manchán, along the coastal road in the Casma Valley, with five free standing compounds and a very large set of agglutinated structures that included compound-like spaces.[42]

This view of the Chimor state was established 20 years ago, when Chimú was interpreted to have three or more levels in its settlement hierarchy and an imperial presence in the North Coast valleys and perhaps beyond, down to the Central Coast and possibly up to the region of the modern Peru–Ecuador frontier. However, subsequent research to confirm what was often speculation has tended not to support the level of complexity that was previously assumed to exist. For example, Chimú does not appear to have built any substantial centers in Tumbes, to the north, while the fortress of Paramonga on the Fortaleza River is still commonly referred to as the bastion of the southern reach of the empire, but it has been revealed not to be definitively Chimú judging from architecture and artifacts. Chimú sites in the valleys between the major occupations at Manchán, Chan Chan, Farfán, and Túcume vary in their number and character, with few that appear to be major centers of governance.

It does appear that road systems were consolidated and organized in Chimú times, while Chimú pottery is ubiquitous throughout the north coast. The problem is that something akin to state control can occur with very little need for a governmental bureaucracy, and direct evidence for military conquest can be highly elusive. In many places the Chimú presence appears to have been achieved without conflict, such as in the Casma Valley, and almost everywhere local religious practices appear to have been respected. At Túcume the Temple of the Sacred Stone was kept as a shrine, an act that makes sense as a political gesture that might not have occurred if Chimú was solely a religious system—unless, again, it was an open system that embraced local traditions. In short, the nature of Chimú as an expansionist state is not resolved.[43] Nevertheless, what is known about Chimú is highly impressive, and suggests that the culture marshaled resources and had great influence no matter what its specific political configuration.

At an approximate 20 square km (8 square mi) in area, Chan Chan was the largest city in South America in its day, and probably the largest urban center in the New World. An exact estimate of its full extent is difficult to determine, and much of it now appears to lie underneath the northern and western sectors of modern Trujillo. Chan Chan was a complex place, as expressed in the more than 20 different kinds of buildings identified in what remains of the city.[44] Fortunately, what was probably the most important sector to the city's residents has been preserved at this UNESCO World Heritage Site (see Figure 9.3). This area consists of ten large, rectangular walled enclosures with massive perimeter walls, some of which are more than half a kilometer (0.55 km or 0.34 mi) in length, known as *ciudadelas* (citadels). There also were smaller élite residential compounds, four mound-shaped huacas, and lower class housing.[45] Chan Chan also has the distinction of having been the focus of one of the largest research projects ever to have been carried out in South America, the Chan Chan–Moche Valley Project, throughout most of the 1970s.

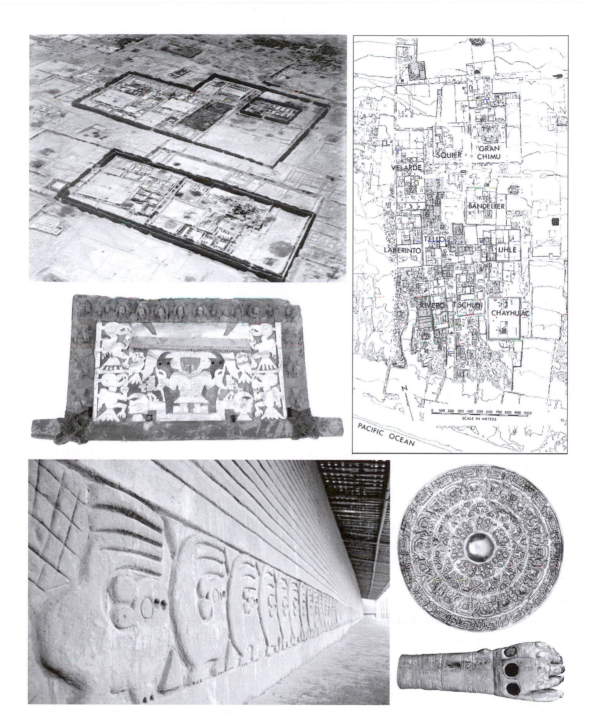

Figure 9.3 Chan Chan and Chimú. Upper left: Aerial view of Ciudadela Rivero (bottom) and Tschudi (top) at Chan Chan. Right: Map of Chan Chan core. Mid-left: The back of a Chimú litter. Lower left: Detail of restored adobe frieze in Chan Chan compound. Right: Chimú silver disk and gold "glove."

The ciudadelas have been the focus of much research and speculation. There is a general consensus about groups of early, middle, and late compounds, but the exact temporal relations of the structures and the significances of variations in their architectural plans leave open many questions about their uses and their relations to one another, and to Chimú culture in general. It has been suggested that they were built in succession by the ten successive kings of the Taycanamo legend.[46] Although there is considerable variation in their size, from 67,000 square m (17 acres) to 212,000 square m (52 acres), and in their organization, six are divided into three major sections: a large plaza near the entrance, small sets of rooms with patios in the center, a large space near the rear, and, commonly, a large walk-in well (*huachaque*).[47] Concentrations of domestic debris near the rear of compounds and kitchen areas are also known. This and other evidence strongly suggests that the ciudadelas were indeed the palaces of Chimú kings. Other features in the compounds include a single entryway and labyrinthine passageways that would have controlled and impressed visitors, especially when they were flanked by large, painted wooden guardian statues. The smooth adobe walls, made by pouring mud into molds known as *tapia,* similar to the way modern concrete is poured, were ideal surfaces to create impressive ornamental patterns of geometric or figurative designs or to display large painted cloths.

A distinctive Chimú architectural form is known as the *audiencia,* also referred to as U-shaped rooms, found in ciudadelas and smaller compounds. These are usually square or rectangular with one open side, they may have a central raised bench-like feature, and they always have banquettes of low bins, all made of adobe. Conceiving of Chimú as a governmental system has led some scholars to interpret audiencias as the offices or audience rooms of state officials, who received and distributed tribute stored in the bins and in larger storerooms nearby. However, it is also possible that these were ritual chambers rather than administrative ones.[48]

The fact that seven of the ten great compounds contain burial platforms implies that they were the palaces of Chimú kings in their lifetimes, but they also became their mausoleums at their deaths. Although it is not completely clear, it seems quite likely that the dead ruler's large extended family maintained his ciudadela after his death and continued to access the various resources that he had controlled. This practice was certainly followed by the Inca and it may have been adopted from the Chimú.

The burial platforms are the largest architectural features in the compounds, as well as the most heavily looted. The largest, in Gran Chimú, is 150 m (492 ft) long, 80 m (262 ft) wide and 12 m (39 ft) high. Excavations in the Laberinto ciudadela's platform and testing in others indicated that a basic plan for all consisted of a forecourt and ramp, with the platform itself consisting of a large, central principal chamber in the shape of a "T" with small chambers surrounding it. Found in the Laberinto were the remains of between 200 and 300 young women, likely sacrificial victims, and a great number of llama burials also were uncovered in a forecourt nearby.[49]

A remarkable wooden miniature of a simplified compound plaza was found as an offering at the Huaca de la Luna, which, although it was abandoned, was still considered sacred in Chimú times (see Figure 9.4). The model's courtyard is filled with miniature musicians and people in charge of large ceramic vessels that likely held chicha. Sentries or officials stand on side benches, while a mummy bundle sits on a raised bench at the far end of the compound. Behind the mummy a narrow chamber contains other mummies, perhaps ready to be brought to center stage for veneration. Other activities may have occurred in ciudadela plazas, but this model directs our attention to the importance of new forms of worship and, perhaps, governance in Chimú times.

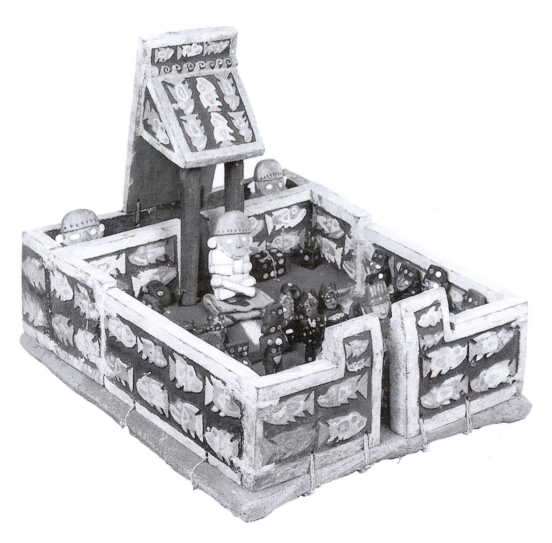

Figure 9.4 Chimú compound model found as an offering in the abandoned Huaca de la Luna, Moche Valley.

Chimú deities seem benign compared to Moche and earlier gods. A Staff God, a Goddess, and the Moon Animal, the latter a carry-over from Moche times, are often depicted. All lack fangs and have human-like features.[50] A number of lines of evidence suggest that Chimú politics and religion had shifted away from abstract gods to beliefs and practices that emphasized ancestor worship, a focus first seen in Recuay in the Early Intermediate Period which increasingly gained in importance in later times. Indeed, this shift is one of the great changes that can be seen in Andean religious practices through time, and it is very likely associated with the increased role of corporate kin groups, known as *ayllus*, by the time of the Inca.[51]

Resources under the control of Chimú rulers were considerable. Artisans made a wide variety of precious objects that demonstrated high skills in textiles, metal, and other materials. Chimú shared the Lambayeque preference for blackware ceramics, but although very fine vessels were made other materials tend to have received the most attention from modern scholars. Chimú silverwork is especially notable, for example, although work in gold was probably as extensive as for Lambayeque (see Figure 9.4).[52] *Spondylus* remained extremely important and there is substantial evidence that part of Chimú's power was due to its control of the *Spondylus* trade. Scenes depicting rafts and divers harvesting the shells were rendered in wall friezes in the ciudadelas as well as on large silver plates celebrating and emphasizing the city's wealth and power.[53]

The irrigation canals and agricultural fields appear to have been more extensive than ever before, and would have required a great number of people to build, maintain, and manage them. The most famous of these is the La Cumbre, or Intervalley, Canal, stretching 54 km (34 mi) in length. More remarkable still is the fact that La Cumbre was designed to transfer waters from the Chicama Valley to the Moche for the benefit of the Chan Chan population. Research has suggested that the canal was never completed and that there may have been mistakes in its engineering, but the size and effort alone is impressive whether it worked or not.[54] There are many other impressive Chimú engineering projects, including a huge wall at the northern limits of Chan Chan and the coastal road system that the Chimú consolidated from and built upon earlier systems.

There are also clear signs of organized, communal violence during the Late Intermediate Period. The Chimú reoccupied the city of Pacatnamú, which had been abandoned at the end of Moche. There, the bodies of 14 young men were placed in a defensive ditch next to the ramp leading into a compound. Their positions and wounds—multiple stabbings, decapitation, disarticulation and heart removal—suggest that they were sacrificed prisoners of war. All were males of warrior age (15 to 35 years) and date to Chimú times, *circa* AD 1270. The 14 individuals were buried in groups of 4, 8, and 2, suggesting three separate events, perhaps sacrificial rites in the aftermaths of three separate conflicts.[55]

In the Huarmey Valley, Punta Lobos is a small, isolated hill overlooking the Pacific Ocean. Sometime between AD 1250 and 1300 two hundred men and boys were assembled in this place, blindfolded and their wrists and ankles bound with ropes or cloths. Forced face down, their throats were slit multiple times and their bodies left to rot. Except for a few *Spondylus* shell fragments, no offerings were left with them. The age range, from boys of seven years to old men, does not fit the profile of a mass sacrifice of captured warriors so this event appears to be a reprisal killing, perhaps in response to resistance to the Chimú conquest by a community.[56] It is possible, of course, that some other inter-community conflict could have resulted in this massacre. Presumably the surviving women and girls were incorporated into another group, whether as slaves or concubines; this was common practice in many ancient societies. Who was responsible for the Punta Lobos massacre is uncertain, but unambiguously Chimú sacrifices have also been found close to Chan Chan.

At Huanchaquito, close to the Initial Period Gramalote site, 43 children and adolescents and 74 young llamas were sacrificed and left in mud, suggesting that they had been sacrificed during an El Niño event dated to between 1430 and 1450.[57] How the Chimú and other Andean peoples responded to the rains and droughts brought to the coast and the highlands, and what roles these reoccurring but sporadic events may have played in cultural change, are subjects still to be clarified.

OTHER KINGDOMS, OTHER PEOPLES

There were many other distinct regional cultures in the Late Intermediate Period, some of which have been known for many decades, mostly through their ceramic styles, and others which have only recently been identified. Melissa Vogel has suggested that there was a distinct polity with its capital city at El Purgatorio in the Casma Valley and a frontier outpost at Cerro la Cruz in the Chao Valley, a site that was 40 hectares (99 acres) in area.[58] The polity may have been a relatively loose confederation of affiliated communities that was dominated by El Purgatorio, a 5 square km (2 square mi) urban complex consisting of three distinct sectors of large compounds, habitational terraces, and cemeteries. Many of the architectural features found at El Purgatorio were repeated at Cerro la Cruz and distinctive Casma Incised and Casma Molded ceramics were also found at both sites, as well as variants in the valleys between the two. The Casma polity appears to have developed during the interregnum between the collapse of Wari and the rise of Chimú and the latter may have taken over the Chao Valley, forcing those loyal to Casma to flee.

The Chancay culture of the Central Coast is better known than many contemporary archaeological cultures, although details remain obscure (see Figure 9.5). It is most recognizable by its distinctive black-on-white ceramics and elaborate textiles. Although many finely-made Chancay ceramics are known, there are also huge quantities of poorer quality vessels. It appears that demand for ceramics was so great as to induce a near-industrial level of production, with sloppily painted and even fire-damaged vessels still sought after for inclusion in tombs as well as more refined pieces.

Ceramic and textile figurines were placed in burials and have become emblematic of the Chancay culture. Ceramic figurines, known as *cuchimilcos*, vary in style and size but a common version shows a pudgy male or female human figure standing erect with raised arms and hands.

Black paint was frequently employed on faces, hands, and arms and to depict headwear. They were also further elaborated by the addition of clothing.[59]

Chancay textile figurines, sometimes referred to as "Chancay Dolls," also commonly depict standing humans, and great attention was paid to adding details that provide rich suggestions for how their makers may have dressed. Carefully woven faces depict face paint, while arms and legs made of sticks wrapped with string add further color. Elaborate coiffures, headdresses, and tunics, as well as bead necklaces, decorate many examples. Figures sometimes carry objects such as staffs, or are depicted in daily activities such as weaving. In addition to humans, trees full of birds, elaborately-made llamas, and other creatures also are known.

The Chancay homeland lay in the Huara and Chancay valleys, and some kind of political or religious cohesion seems to have been in operation among the peoples of the sites found there. Pisquillo Chico and Lauri, in Chancay, are the two largest, over 20 hectares (49 acres) in size, with public buildings, élite and commoner residences, and cemeteries. Structures devoted to ritual or administration commonly consist of a rectangular adobe compound with a small, truncated pyramid inside, less than 8 m (26 ft) in height.[60] The pyramids have a side ramp and are surrounded by rooms and a large patio. Pisquillo Chico has a minimum of nine of these compounds and Lauri has at least six, while some small settlements have a single enclosure.

Whatever the degree of direct political control of rural valley populations exerted by the compounds such as Pisquillo Chico, the great quantity of Chancay-style ceramics and textiles in graves is an indication that funeral practices and the acquisition of the proper goods to include in graves was a driving force in how economics, politics, society, and religion interacted in the region. This is a pattern that seems common throughout many regions of the Central Andes in the Late Intermediate Period.

Although Chancay ceramics sometimes appear outside the key homeland valleys, the Chillón Valley to the south has no Chancay-style enclosures, and neither does it share the architectural formats known for the Rímac and Lurín Valleys. This suggests that the Chillón was a buffer or neutral territory between two distinct cultural traditions or polities. The Rímac-Lurín system had experienced strong Wari influences. At many of the large sites throughout the region, Pyramids With Ramps (*Pirámides con Rampa*) complexes are present. This term is somewhat misleading, however, because it is not simply the pyramid but the larger architectural complex as a whole that is significant. This consists of a rectangular adobe enclosure with limited access and a multilevel, terraced truncated pyramid with a short central ramp at its far end, as well as many other rooms in the entire complex.[61]

In the Lurín Valley the large site of Pachacamac contained 17 pyramid with ramp complexes which have been interpreted in a variety of ways, including the suggestion that they represented the shrines of distant polities or else embassy-like establishments at the pilgrimage center. With its origins at least in the Early Intermediate Period, Pachacamac was one of the most prominent religious centers in the Andean world, attracting pilgrims from great distances.[62] Ethnohistoric accounts state that before the Inca conquered it the site and valley were controlled by an ethnic group or polity called Ychsma.[63]

Figure 9.5 The Central Coast in the Late Intermediate Period. Top: Chancay Cuchimilco, black-and-white vessel in form of stacked pots; "Chancay Doll." Center: Panorama of the center court of a "Pyramid with Ramp" at Pachacamac. Lower left: Pachacamac walls. Lower right: Excavations by Izumi Shimada in the Plaza of the Pilgrims at Pachacamac, with Inca Sun temple in far rear.

More than 40 pyramids with ramps can be found at numerous sites in the Rímac and Lurín Valleys.[64] Nevertheless some of the largest sites in the region did not have them, such as Maranga in the Rímac Valley which had continued to grow since the Early Intermediate Period and was likely a major power in the Rímac-Lurín region, probably equaling or exceeding Pachacamac in importance.[65] However, while numerous studies have been carried out at Maranga, its urban setting combined with its massive size has limited a full understanding of its growth and importance.

While limited research may affect our view, the valleys south of Lurín appear to have continued to lack large-scale architectural complexes, as in previous times. A variant of Ychsma-style ceramics is found in the Asia and Cañete Valleys, indicating that people in them were oriented to the north.

THE SOUTH COAST

The South Coast is a region that seems to have shifted its external relations dramatically over time. While there appear to have been connections between it and the North Coast in the Initial Period, in the Early Intermediate Period and Middle Horizon it seems to have reduced its northward reach to become more involved with the south-central and southern highlands, especially in its ties to Wari. After the collapse of Wari, however, the South Coast regrouped into several different local cultures, the best known of which are Chincha and Ica.

The Inca claimed that the Chincha merchants were so well renowned that they received a special dispensation to continue their trade after their culture was incorporated into the Inca Empire.[66] The largest Late Intermediate architectural complex in the valley is La Centinela, overlooking the ocean, and it is assumed that this was the focus of the major political force in the region in its time. Between 30 and 40 other late sites are known in the valley, connected to La Centinela by straight roads suggesting both ritual and economic uses and including a connection to the Pisco Valley to the south.[67]

Not too far from La Centinela, in the Cañete Valley to the north, the relatively small site of Cerro Azul may have been a specialized fishing community that participated in interchanges with a larger center.[68] It was probably a fairly important community in the small Huarco polity in the Late Intermediate Period. The dozen mounds overlooking the Pacific appear to cover mostly multi-room residences for families, some of whom were more prosperous than others.

In the Ica Valley only Ica La Vieja has large-scale architecture, consisting of several large mounds in no discernable organization. The site was probably a center for religion and the production of the most desirable pottery on the South Coast, which is found throughout the region and beyond. Further south the Nazca, Acarí, and Yauca valleys also lack monumental architecture, although villages of agglutinated structures are common and appear to have increased in number in late prehistory. However, whether there was an organized, integrated polity is, at best, open to question. Fineware Chincha culture (*circa* AD 1000 to 1400) ceramics tended to emphasize utilitarian forms, such as globular jars, flat-bottomed, incurving-sided bowls, and large, steep-sided bowls that merge with kero forms. Decoration tended to favor bright colors, especially red and black, and repeated geometric patterns often separated by horizontal bands.

With the end of Wari and Tiwanaku colonization in the Moquegua Valley, the region shifted to a local ceramic style known as Chiribaya. Given the great amount of work carried out in the valley by numerous researchers, we know considerably more about this culture than many others of its time period. The ceramics are highly distinctive with multi-colored, geometric designs on a red background and with the unique feature of white dots on a black band on the rim of round-sided bowls and ovoid and globular jars, all with flat bottoms. Three phases of change in ceramic styles took place, and communities grew large with many sites in the valley, some up to 14 hectares (35 acres) in size.[69] Canals were built and a degree of economic specialization took place, with coastal communities focused on fishing and higher altitude ones on camelids. There was a clear hierarchy of status differences, with élites buried in larger tombs with more goods than commoners. Nevertheless, status differences in Chiribaya were much less marked than for the Chimú or even Chancay, and no large ceremonial complexes are known for the culture either.

The overall impression of Chiribaya in its heyday is of a prosperous society that filled the valley with its own traditions and practices. However, Chiribaya ended as a distinct culture in a massive flash flood that brought a liquid avalanche of mud and rocks to cover major settlements at some time close to AD 1350. While not every site was destroyed or every person killed, the disaster appears to have been severe enough that the society collapsed. Chiribaya ceramics end abruptly in the archaeological record, to be replaced by the Estuquina style that may have been brought by highlanders who repopulated the valley. The Chiribaya style also seems to have ended suddenly in northern Chile, where similar localized cultures had developed. In the first half of the Late Intermediate Period northern Chilean sites containing San Miguel ceramics also include some Chiribaya wares, but in Gentilar, in the second half of the period, Chiribaya ceramics are completely absent in northern Chile.

THE HIGHLANDS

This chapter has mostly discussed coastal cultures, largely because research on Late Intermediate societies in the sierra generally lags far behind research elsewhere—with the exception of the southern highlands, where the Inca and their neighbors are known both through archaeology and ethnohistory. The reasons for the paucity of our knowledge about late highland cultures are varied. Late Intermediate Period sierra sites are often very large, but they do not contain key features such as large huacas that draw the attention of archaeologists. Excavating them requires huge resources without clear gain in terms of spectacular finds such as royal tombs. Research is made all the more difficult because it appears that many of the largest or most interesting sites are located at high altitudes by the standards of modern researchers, making investigations arduous. However, this is indicative of one way in which Andean civilization was special, in its successful exploitation of unique resource zones. Nevertheless, few such sites are excavated, and as in other cases the transitions between archaeological cultures are poorly known.[70] Consequently, many of them are mostly known through their ceramics and other materials and through settlement surveys.

Many highland sites have been identified during surveys, often consisting of many hectares of agglutinated domestic architecture, agricultural terraces, and camelid pens. The lack of large huacas suggests that the de-emphasis on large huaca construction and a shift towards more secular societies that focused on ancestor worship rather than temple gods was even stronger in the highlands than on the coast. Despite a relatively low amount of information regarding the sierra overall, some regions are better known than others, notably those around Cajamarca, Huamachuco, the upper Mantaro River, Junín, and Chachapoyas.

With the collapse of Wari influence in the Cajamarca region the number of settlements first dropped, but then gradually increased by the Final Cajamarca phase (AD 1250 to 1532). Cajamarca apparently maintained its prestige for some time, as shown by the influence its ceramics still had on the coast. In Final Cajamarca site-wide hierarchies also emerged, with élite residential areas common in larger communities, while differences in ceramic and architectural styles at major sites suggest that there was no strong regional political integration.

In the Huamachuco region, Marcahuamachuco was abandoned followed by Cajamarca influence. By the early Late Intermediate Period the Yuraccama tradition is present in the region and possibly represents an intrusion of Quechua-speaking people who migrated from the south.[71] Yuraccama is associated with intensive terrace agriculture and the fading of Cajamarca influence. Hilltop fortified settlements also appear at this time, a phenomenon that occurred in many regions in the Late Intermediate.

Three different late regional traditions have been identified for the upper Mantaro River Valley, north of the modern city of Huancayo. Furthest upstream, populations represented by the Chinchaycocha and Tarama traditions expanded from Early Intermediate Period and Middle Horizon times to reach a maximum size of two or three times larger during the Late Intermediate and Late Horizon periods. The growth seems to have been due to the successful integration of herding at high elevations and agriculture at lower altitudes, with special function settlements located at the contact zone between them.[72]

Wanka is the third tradition in the Upper Mantaro, near the modern town of Huancayo. The region had been under Wari influence to some degree, but local ceramic styles did not change drastically over long periods of time making the identification of sites of different ages difficult. Nevertheless, three Wanka phases are known (I: AD 1000 to 1350; II: 1350 to 1460; III: 1460 to 1533), the final stage representing the culture's incorporation into the Inca Empire.[73]

As in the other regions there was significant population growth between Wanka I and II, accompanied by an increase in settlement sizes. Political centralization and social differentiation also took place. Social differentiation may have been demonstrated by some families having better houses and more access to prized foods (camelid meat, maize, coca, hot peppers) and exotic goods (obsidian, metals) than others. Also, while some sense of community bound people together within settlements, each household produced its own goods and evidence of textile production is only found where other signs of higher status are also present.

Two sites, Hatunmarca and Tunanmarca, are larger than any others in the region. Nevertheless, many sites are in defensive locations, such as on hilltops, indicating a considerable degree of inter-community conflict. Growing populations and increased conflict were also found in many other regions of Peru, especially the highlands, and in Bolivia and elsewhere in the southern Central Andes. It was out of this turmoil that the Inca arose.

South of modern Huancayo, in the region where the provinces of Lima, Junín, and Huancavelica meet, documentary evidence from the Colonial Period indicates that there were three small ethnic groups or polities in the Late Intermediate Period, the Asto, the Chunku, and the Laraw, with the former two occupying small valleys east of the high mountains and the Laraw on the Pacific side. The Asto have received particular attention from the studies of Danièle Lavallée and Michèle Julien, French archaeologists who are part of a long national tradition of interest in and research on Andean subjects.[74]

The Asto communities were probably organized as *ayllus* or some similar system, practicing a mixed subsistence economy that emphasized pastoralism and high altitude crops, augmented by the importation of lower elevation resources, such as maize, as well as opportunistic hunting. Population was dense with many settlements located at 4,000 m (13,000 ft) above sea level. Five villages were studied in detail. Round stone houses were arranged according to a few basic patterns in these communities, ranging in number from a high of 832 to 864 at Astomarka to a low of 78 to 81 at Chuntamarka. Because the walls of houses were well preserved at these settlements rough population estimates could be derived, indicating a maximum of 5,000 individuals at Astomarka and 500 at Chuntamarka.

The archaeological assemblage for the Asto is plain and simple, consisting of bone pins and tools, chipped stone knives and scrapers, roughly-hewn stone grinding surfaces, mortars and clod-breakers, and simple pottery. A few stone mace heads indicate that warfare was not unknown. These traits, along with the general ways of life and settlement patterns of the Asto, were common throughout the highlands, but the apparent simplicity of the remains of their material culture under-represent textiles and other crafts that have vanished due to preservation factors. However, the density of settlement and the inferred population estimates indicate that such communities were fairly prosperous in their humble ways. Nevertheless, such communities were about to experience the impact of the successful, expansive highland society known as the Inca.

SUMMARY

Summing up, it is worth noting that while the Late Intermediate Period was a time of increasing interactions across wide areas of the Andes, there were distinct local and regional practices that took place, as well as a general cultural shift of considerable import. Value systems were shared more widely than ever before, both horizontally across the landscape and apparently vertically within societies, as more people were allowed or demanded access to precious goods such as metals and *Spondylus*. These changes happened at the same time that the symbolic loads of ceramic, textile, and metal objects decreased precipitously. Simultaneously there was a pronounced growth in metallurgy for tools, most clearly observable on the North Coast.

While some gods and myths were portrayed, decorative motifs increasingly consisted of benign or abstract designs in many craft traditions throughout the Andes. Some scholars may warn that fish designs or even geometric motifs may have high symbolic import, but it appears that the design motifs in the kinds of goods available to common people became less associated with local or even regional religious systems. They used more broadly shared, relatively benign, and apparently secular motifs, such as birds and fish, than the kinds of symbols that had been used in earlier art, and also employed simple geometric motifs such as triangles, hatched bands and the like.

Although it is hard to quantify, there is a distinct sense that more people had more material goods than ever before in many places during the Late Intermediate Period. This could partly be due to the simple fact that more materials were preserved from later time periods. Nevertheless, people seem to have had more goods, and more goods seem to have been made by and for them. New religious systems that focused on cults of the ancestors followed by individual families would have created demands for more products to satisfy the needs of people engaged in such rituals. The simpler forms and plainer decoration of the ceramics of Chimú, Chancay, and Chincha are but three examples. The proper burial of relatives and their continued veneration through offerings would have required more material goods than attending a ritual at a ceremonial center. The added wealth and the shift in religious emphasis created by the ancestor cults probably also loosened sumptuary rules and generated more "service-oriented" wealth, as signaled by the increase in head deformation that we see from Moche to Lambayeque times.

Although tall huacas were still built in some places, in general there is a distinct leveling out of ceremonial precincts and corporate architecture from the vertical to the horizontal, whether it is expressed in the *ciudadelas* at Chan Chan or the dense agglutinated communities of the sierra. These changes in architecture and ceremonialism expressed new social relations as well as relations with deities. In particular, large, walled adobe compounds found distinct expressions on the North Coast (Chimú), Chancay, and Rímac-Lurín (Ychsma) areas, but all shared the basic idea of enclosing large spaces with platforms or huacas inside them. Perhaps Wari introduced compounds to the coastal region, and with them new forms of social relations, but the nature of how they were adopted is unclear.[75]

Another distinct change was the near-disappearance of large stone monuments and finely crafted stone masonry. On the coast the fine stone carvings of the Initial Period and Early Horizon had not been continued in the Early Intermediate Period, but the stonemason's craft had been followed in the highlands to a considerable degree, in Recuay and Middle Horizon Bolivia in particular. By the Late Intermediate Period, however, the emphasis everywhere was on construction techniques that could build large, impressive structures, but not on fine stone carving. This situation was soon to change with the Inca.[76]

What can be said with more certainty is that the regional systems that first become clear in the Late Preceramic Period appear to have been maintained through prehistory. These included continuing and seemingly intensified interactions along the coast and continuous relations with neighboring highland regions, although waves of influence pulsed, mostly emanating from the highlands towards the coast, throughout prehistory. While there were long-standing traditions, even down to the shape of three-step altars on the coast, there were also great changes in how people organized themselves in relation to one another and to the wider world.

It is interesting to consider that in Moche times a few retainers were sacrificed to accompany their lords and ladies into the afterlife. However, in the West Tomb at Huaca Loro of the Lambayeque culture, 20 young women were sacrificed with two dozen camelids. Later, at Chan Chan, more than ten times that number of sacrifices were included in a royal burial. It is likely that the amount of wealth in gold, silver, *Spondylus*, and other materials also was proportionately greater. The important point in this is not that there was simply an increase in sacrifices, but that lords increasingly came to control more resources and that such wealth was primarily focused on the reproductive capacities and symbolism of women and camelids.

These changes—the emphasis on compounds and the shift away from verticality, great numbers of sacrifices of women and camelids, new burial rites, especially flexed burials and mummy bundles, a decrease in highly charged symbolism—were all tied together in a wider culture change. Many of these trends began, or at least they first appear in the archaeological record, during the Early Intermediate Period (especially Recuay) and the Middle Horizon. However, the impression from the archaeological record is that by the time the Late Intermediate Period cultures were at their heights, there had been a fundamental transformation of social relations in major ways, even though many things remained constant. Religious systems that emphasized the veneration of ancestors ranked in order of importance probably reflected social systems that did the same thing. Therefore, the growth of *ayllu*-like social systems appears to have occurred in conjunction with a growth in ancestor worship. As with the ancestors, placement within the hierarchy of kin relations denoted greater rank, and this system produced both highland chiefs and Grand Chimús. Thus, the Andean version of the universal struggle of the weak to defend themselves from the predations of the strong and of the strong to exploit the weak had not changed, but the ways in which those struggles took place had altered. The Inca Empire that grew in the Late Intermediate Period world is an expression of these concepts with its own unique interpretation.

NOTES

1 Partly because of this, most of the present chapter focuses on the coast while highland Late Intermediate Period cultures are discussed in the next chapter.

2 The archaeological culture is known as "Chimú" while the kingdom discussed in historical records is called "Chimor." They are closely related. Writers in English vary on the use of the accent to stress that last syllable, as in Spanish (Chimú). Here, I choose to not use it.

3 Rowe's (1948) article that discusses many issues, including the environment of the North Coast and the legends of Ñaymlap and Taycanamo, remains valuable reading for anyone interested in these topics more than 60 years after publication.

4 Cordy-Collins 1990 and Donnan 1990 attempt to relate aspects of the tales to prehistorical peoples and places. Zuidema 1990a argues that the legends are statements about Andean dynastic structures. These different views run throughout discussions of Andean issues, especially for late prehistory, between the "Roweista" and "Zuidemista" schools of thought, as discussed in Chapter 1.

5 Ramírez (1990: 516) suggests that other court officials may have included jesters or buffoons, an official in charge of time or astronomy, and a keeper of armaments, based on word lists of the Yunga language spoken on the coast.

6 Skeptics might suggests that even though 1586 is quite early for Colonial Period reporting, there had been enough time and contact that indigenous peoples could have learned of European courts and developed views of their own past that conformed to them. Others might argue that "royal" courts worldwide develop independently to include similar positions for high ranking officials.

7 Patterson (1973: 3) reports an example from a site in Lurín that is said to be Middle Preceramic (Patterson, personal communication), and an example was found at Paloma (Quilter 1989: 29) although its exact date within the Middle Preceramic is uncertain.

8 "Trade" here is used in a generalized sense, as equivalent to "exchange," and is not intended to refer to a specific form of economic interaction.

9 Paulsen 1974.

10 Reinhard and Ceruti 2010.

11 Translation from McEwan and Delgado-Espinoza (2008: 515) from an original text by Samano-Xerez dating to 1528.

12 The late Thor Heyerdahl (1990) was a proponent of long-distance contacts, suggesting that Polynesia was colonized from Peru partly through his attempt to reproduce such a voyage on the Kon-Tiki raft and by other similar efforts. While most scholars do not believe that South Americans colonized the Pacific, Heyerdahl's contributions to the study of ancient sailing were considerable.

13 Hosler et al. 1990.

14 Hosler 1994.

15 Scholars have addressed the question of long-distance contacts between Mexico/Central America and South America for many years. See, for example, Coe 1960 and Fonseca Z. 1978.

16 As no hairless dogs are known for Peru before the Late Intermediate Period but they are known from earlier times in Mexico, the introduction from the latter to the former seems highly likely. Several breeds of dogs may have come with the first immigrants to the New World. See Leonard et al. 2002.

17 Quilter 2008 on Moche military gear and strategies.

18 Mayer 1992 and 1998 on tools. Hocquenghem and Parodi 2005 on tools and continuities.

19 Shimada et al. 2004.

20 Timing is everything. Correlating climatic changes with cultural ones is difficult and it does not necessarily prove causation. Kellerhals et al. 2010 have studied ammonia records in ice cores from the Bolivan Andes which suggest that there were relatively warm conditions between AD 1050 and 1300, followed by cooler temperatures from the fifteenth to the eighteenth centuries.

21 Burger 2003.

22 Bray 2008 for highland and McEwan and Delgado-Espinoza 2008 for coastal Ecuador. Because the Inca conquered Ecuador quite late in their expansion, many of the peoples described in this chapter could as easily be discussed in the following Late Horizon chapter.

23 Zeidler and Issacson 2003. For a detailed discussion of the ethnobotany of the region see Pearsall 2004.

24 Delgado-Espinoza 2005.

25 Benzoni 1985 [1550]; Saville 1907, 1910. Significant researches in the region and elsewhere in Ecuador and Peru were later carried out by Jacinto Jijón y Camaño and by Betty Meggers, Clifford Evans, and Emilio Estrada. See McEwan and Delgado-Espinoza 2008 for more discussion on Manteño culture, especially the stone seats, and their sites as related in the following section.

26 Different sites have been claimed to be Salangome by different scholars. See McEwan and Delgado-Espinoza (2008: 515) for a review of contending theories.

27 Mester 1985 on Los Frailes. Currie 1995 on Puerto Lopez. We await a full report on La Plata Island since most information is currently available through word of mouth.

28 Bray 2008.

29 Lippi 2004 covers the prehistory of the region from remote times to the Spanish Conquest.

30 Salomon 1986 on *llactakuna*. Also see Lippi 2004 on the issues of linking archaeological data with ethnohistorical and historical information.

31 Salomon 1977.

32 Bray 2008 summarizes these mound sites succinctly and provides bibliographical references on details.

33 "Sicán" has been promoted by archaeologist Izumi Shimada (2000). "Sí" is "moon" in the Muchik language.

34 See Quilter et al. 2010. These two regions are also distinguished as "Northern" and "Southern" Moche for earlier times as well.

35 Some archaeologists suggest that the term "crescentic knife" should be used, with "tumi" reserved only for a specific form of the knife used by the Inca. However, as "tumi" tends to be in general use I use it here.

36 Scholarship on Andean metallurgy, like textiles, has a small but dedicated scholarly community that has produced extensive and important works. See Lechtmann 1996 and Hosler 1994 for introductions to the subject.

37 Izumi Shimada has carried out research at the Sicán site and about the Lambayeque culture for many decades. See the bibliography in Shimada 2000 for a sampling of his publications.

38 Heyerdahl et al. 1995.

39 Wester de La Torre 2012.

40 Rowe 1948; Moore and Mackey 2008.

41 Moseley and Cordy-Collins 1990; Moseley and Day 1982.

42 Mackey and Klymyshyn 1990.

43 See Moore and Mackey 2008: 787–797 for details on Chimú expansionism and sites.

44 Kolata 1982.

45 Conrad (1982: 117 [FN 1]) refers to ten compounds, distinguishing between *ciudadelas* which have tripartite internal divisions and *cuadros* without three divisions. For brevity's sake I refer to all ten as *ciudadelas* or compounds. The compounds are named mostly after famous researchers: Bandelier, Tschudi, Rivero, Velarde, Laberinto, Uhle, Tello, Squire, Chayhuac, and Gran Chimú. Recent attempts to rename them with more "indigenous" names, even though we do not have much information on what language the Chimú spoke, have not been greeted with great enthusiasm by either scholars or the general public.

46 See also Pillsbury and Leonard 2004. Ciudadela Squier appears never to have been completed.

47 Chan Chan is one of the most investigated and discussed archaeological sites in Peru, and it has an extensive literature. The greatest single research project carried out there was Harvard's Chan Chan–Moche Valley Project in the 1970s and early 1980s. In subsequent years Peruvian archaeologists have also carried out important research. Major publications include Moseley and Day 1982. See Moore and Mackey 2008 for further discussion and bibliographical sources.

48 Andrews 1974; Moore 1992; West 1970.
49 Conrad 1982: 99–100.
50 Moore and Mackey 2008: 798–800.
51 See Isbell 1997 on the issue of the development of ancestor worship and *allyus*.
52 Although there are many features that distinguish Lambayeque from Chimú crafts there is a lot of overlap that has yet to be untangled.
53 Pillsbury 1996.
54 For the debate on the canal see Ortloff et al. 1982, 1983; Farrington 1983.
55 Verano 1986. Heart extraction sacrifice is new in the Andes, beginning in the Late Intermediate Period. Given the increasing evidence of contacts between the Andes and Mesoamerica, it is likely that the practice was adopted from Mesoamerican sources.
56 Verano 2008: 1053–1055. The total count of individuals at Punta Lobos is 200 but only 100 burials were found undisturbed.
57 Prieto et al. (in press).
58 Vogel 2012.
59 Cuchimilcos are commonly displayed in museums and galleries without clothing where their smooth bodies and sexual organs are visible. The discovery of five clothed versions in the collections of Harvard's Peabody Museum in March, 2013, by the author, Richard Burger, and Lucy Salazar suggests that all such figurines were once dressed. It also is quite possible that these figurines were originally made in male-female pairs.
60 Krazanowski 1991, who has conducted the most recent research on Chancay, refers to these enclosures or compounds as *"montículos piramidales tronco-cónicos"* (pyramidal truncated-conical mounds).
61 Jimenez Borja 1985.
62 At the time of writing there is disagreement as to when Pachacamac rose to prominence, although the details of the arguments remain to be published in full.
63 Rostworowski de Diez Canseco 2004.
64 Dulanto 2008: 769. See also Eeckhout 2004 for detailed coverage of Rímac-Lurín.
65 Dulanto 2008.
66 Rostworowski de Diez Canseco *op. cit.*
67 Wallace 1962, 1991.
68 Marcus 1987.
69 On Chiribaya ceramics and general introduction: Jessup 1991.
70 Dulanto 2008. Much of the following is taken from this fine discussion.
71 Krzanowski 1980.
72 Parsons et al. 2000.
73 D'Altroy 1992.
74 Lavallée and Julien 1983.
75 Isbell (1997) sees a direct introduction of compounds from Wari to other societies. See McEwan 1990 for a comparison of architectural forms between Wari and Chimú.
76 I owe this insight to Richard Burger.

10

THE LATE HORIZON

INCA ORIGINS

The Southern Sierra and the Altiplano were fragmented into small competing communities after the collapse of Wari. Some old Middle Horizon sites, especially those that were close to the rich agricultural fields of the valley floors, continued to be occupied such as in Paruro Province south of Cusco, but in many places, especially to the north and east, lower lands were abandoned in favor of fortified settlements on hilltops.[1] Hilltop forts, *pucaras,* are particularly well documented for the plains surrounding the Titicaca Basin, where Tiwanaku's collapse left a power vacuum that was filled by a number of small groups, each often confined to a single valley, which engaged in complex, shifting alliances and conflicts.[2]

It was out of this fractured political landscape that the Inca rose to become the predominant power in the Andes, establishing the largest empire the New World had known to that point. However, interpreting how that process took place is both difficult and fascinating. If the Inca can be said to have stepped into the light of history, then it is the light of the high Andes: a chiaroscuro of blinding brightness and black shadows that enlightens and confuses at the same time. The blinding brightness comes from too much information on some matters—too many different historical accounts that contradict one another. The shadows are all the things that we do not know, that the chroniclers do not tell or clarify, or that the archaeological data fail to address.

The baseline for understanding the origins of the Inca is the Killke ceramic series, which, like other Late Intermediate Period wares, is characterized by geometric decoration. In use from the twelfth century to the beginning of the Imperial Inca style, it is found in the Cusco Basin and some surrounding regions where Killke variants are present. The Killke series was first identified by John Rowe in the 1940s, and further research combined with surveys around Cusco have since suggested that there were a number of ethnic groups or polities within a relatively small area of a 100 km (62 mi) or so radius from Cusco during the Killke Period. In some valleys bottomlands continued to be occupied in peacetime, while in others troubles spurred the construction of hilltop forts. Based on a careful reading of colonial documents and archaeology, it appears that the Inca employed marriage alliances and other peaceful links with some of their neighbors while conquering others as they came to dominate the region.[3]

The Lucre Basin, southeast of Cusco, was relatively wide and fertile where the Wari sites of Pikillacta and Waru had been abandoned in the eleventh century. Between the Lucre and Cusco valleys the smaller Oropesa Basin had sustained numerous dispersed settlements along the valley floor, but with the collapse of Wari these were all abandoned in favor of a single large settlement, Tipón, which was later to become a royal Inca estate (see Figure 10.2). However, in the Lucre a number of large Late Intermediate Period sites were built, the best known of which is Chokepukio. Both the Oropesa and Lucre regions resisted Inca incursions for a considerable period, although they too eventually fell to Inca power.[4]

The origins of the Inca vary in different accounts recorded after the conquest by the Spanish.[5] Versions differ with who was telling the story, who was recording it, and when the tale was told, among other factors. One origin myth stated that the founders of the Inca dynasty emerged at Tiahuanaco, originating at the Island of the Sun in Lake Titicaca that became one of the great Inca pilgrimage centers.[6] Another common version, although with variants, is that mythical ancestors emerged from three caves in a rock formation called Pacariqtambo, south of Cusco.[7] From this place of origin (*paqarina*) a group of brothers and sisters walked northwards, having various adventures along the way, including some in which some of the travelers turned into rock formations. Eventually they reach the Cusco Valley and colonize it, in one version because the leader of the group throws a golden staff that sinks into the soil of the valley, marking the Inca claim to the place and signaling its richness.[8]

The leader of the group becomes the first Sapa Inca, the Inca King. Different versions of Inca history recount varying numbers of successive Inca monarchs. Modern scholars differ in the degree to which they accept these lists as mythological or true, and whether the lists are taken to indicate a succession like European royalty or some kind of dual division of leadership that was then misinterpreted by Spanish chroniclers and subsequent scholars.[9] All accounts focus on a dramatic event that is often assumed to have actually happened.

Whatever the specific details, the Inca appear to have been one of several small kingdoms in the southern Andes that fought against local rivals, as indicated by the archaeological data in the Cusco Basin. The stories state that the Inca's main enemies were the Chanka. Surprisingly, perhaps, archaeological research on the Chanka has only very recently been carried out, and perhaps more surprisingly, the archaeological remains do not suggest a powerful kingdom.[10] Thus, either the Inca tales are exaggerated, or the archaeology fails to fully express power politics in the Late Intermediate Southern Highlands. Be that as it may, the traditional story of the Inca–Chanka war is a tale eminently suitable for Hollywood.

Sensing doom as the Chanka army advances on Cusco, the Inca king, his heir, and most of the court flee the city. However, a stalwart young prince, Inca Yupanqui, stays on to fight. He seeks aid from Cusco's allies but they fail in their duties, and things look grim for the future of the Inca. At that point Inca Yupanqui has a vision promising him victory and greatness, and so he rallies his troops to face the Chanka hordes. Despite overwhelming odds, the Inca rout the Chanka with supernatural aid: the very stones of the battlefield rise up to become soldiers to defend the Inca city. In the battle's aftermath the stones are gathered up and placed in Cusco shrines and the young prince assumes the *mascaipacha,* the headdress with the "royal fringe" on it, the traditional crown of Inca monarchs. In becoming the *Sapa Inca* (the Great or Only Inca), the prince also took on a new name, Pachacuti. Like an earthquake, he overturned the status quo and launched the Inca on their road to empire through further conquests, an expansion method followed by all subsequent monarchs.

At its height the empire stretched from a small area of southern Colombia, through Peru, to include substantial parts of Bolivia, northwest Argentina, and northern Chile. In most accounts these territories were conquered by three successive monarchs: Pachacuti, Topa Inca Yupanqui, and Huayna Capac. Attempts have been made to fix the date of the Inca–Chanka War, with many scholars estimating that it occurred in 1438. However, radiocarbon dates suggest that Inca expansion began earlier, with dates for Inca presence in some parts of the empire suggesting their influence as early as 1400.[11] Even adding extra years to the traditional chronology, the Inca seem to have expanded very rapidly, with their empire rising late in prehistory.[12] Thus, many provinces experienced very little Inca presence before the disruptions caused by the Spanish conquest. A date of 1470 is commonly attached to the Inca conquest of the North Coast, and many people who remembered life in the pre-Inca Chimú times would still have been alive in 1532 when the Spanish arrived. The chronicles state that the Inca commonly offered people the choice to join the empire willingly. If they accepted, the new subjects were treated leniently. If they resisted, however, Inca military might was fierce and relentless and the vanquished were harshly treated, as were any subject peoples who dared to attempt revolt.

The Inca claimed that the peoples of the Andes were barbarians who had lived in darkness and squalor before they brought true religion and good government to them. Of course, this is what most empires say about their subjects, as if the new rulers are doing the conquered people a favor by dominating them. While different regions may have felt the weight of the imperial yoke to greater or lesser degrees, all were on a journey of dramatic change under the dominion of Cusco, while the imperial heartland was enriched by the Inca imperial project.

CUSCO AND THE INCA HEARTLAND

If Caesar Augustus found Rome a city of bricks and left it a city of marble, Pachacuti and his heirs transformed Cusco from adobe to stone (see Figure 10.1).[13] The city was not simply the capital of the empire—it was a holy pivot point of space, time, and all within them. The Inca referred to their land as Tawantinsuyu: "the four parts taken together as one." The four parts were the divisions of the empire that radiated from the center at Cusco. Following long-held patterns, these were organized in concepts of asymmetrical dualism so that two of the four *suyus*, Chinchasuyu and Collasuyu, were large while Cuntisuyu and Antisuyu were small. The capital itself was also divided into lower (Hurin Cusco) and upper sectors (Hanan Cusco) that were not only spatial but also social, with the residents of each sector ranked accordingly. Thus there were multiple ways of organizing and conceptualizing Cusco and the people in it, divided into sets of two, three, four, and other units (see Figure 10.1).

One of the most discussed aspects of the Inca capital is the *ceque* system, imaginary lines that radiated from the Coricancha, the temple of the sun near Cusco's center, along which huacas were located. Bernabé Cobo is the most detailed of the colonial authors on the subject, stating that 42 lines were organized into groups within each suyu and that there were at least 328 huacas within the system. Within each suyu there were further groupings and rankings associated with subdivisions of Inca lineages that were responsible for maintaining huacas on each ceque. While recent research has demonstrated that the placement of shrines along each line is not straight, the system was conceived of as such.[14]

The ceque huacas included rock formations and springs, but also included places where travelers caught their first or last glimpses of Cusco on roads leading into and out of the city, important points on irrigation canals, legendary and historical places where famous events occurred, and fables such as a point where a large stone rested because it was "too tired" to move to its intended destination (see Figure 10.1). The huacas thus incorporated the experiences of living people interacting with the city and with official histories and myths to form a seamless, holy present.

The complexities of the ceque system go beyond an elegant and dramatic incorporation of space and time, history and the present into a single system. The lines also mapped the irrigation districts of Cusco, which were administrative subdivisions of wards or precincts of the social groups (*panacas* and ayllus) residing in the city. The connection of ceque points to socio-political groups, reservoirs, main canals, and branch canals was thus a map of political and economic power as well as a cosmological charter of those rights that evolved and grew over time, which is why the lines were not straight.[15]

Like all great cities Cusco had many epithets, among which was *Mama Aqha* (Mother Beer). However, multiple conceptual and experiential layers were also emphasized physically, for the streets, plazas, and buildings of Cusco were laid out in the form of a puma.[16] The fortress of Sacsayhuaman was its head, and the neighborhood where two rivers join, now covered by streets, is still called *Pumakchupan*, "the puma's tail." The Coricancha is located where the testicles of the puma would be, with appropriately shaped, rounded walls and symbolic power in terms of the link between the generative powers of gonads and the sun.[17]

The compacting of time and space was carried further in Cusco's central plaza. Sand from Pacific beaches filled the trapezoidal main plaza, which was bisected into upper and lower halves by a canal. Nearby, an *ushnu*, a combined throne-altar, was the focus of rituals in which huge amounts of chicha were consumed. Urine from ritual festive imbibing and blood from

Figure 10.1 Inca Cusco. Clockwise from upper left: Map of the city with major features; The Coricancha under colonial church; Interior rooms of Coricancha; Sacsayhuaman fortress; The shrine of Kenqo; The "tired stone" (foreground) with Sacsayhuaman fortress in distance.

sacrifices entered the canal, so that the center of Cusco was the source of the circulation of the vital fluids that kept the world in motion.

The Inca time system noted the passage of the sun past towers placed on a hill in the valley. Many celestial events were significant, such as the rising of the Pleiades, but the movement of the Sun, the principle deity of the Inca pantheon, was of special significance. The solstices were especially important, being celebrated at the Inti Raymi and the Capac Raymi, the winter and summer solstices. At the Capac Raimi the Sapa Inca and his entire royal court stood in the plaza before dawn, faced the eastern horizon, and chanted the rising of the sun throughout the entire day, reaching a sonic crescendo at noon and fading as the sun set.[18] Solemn ceremonies were counterpointed by dances and foot races, such as the rites of passage marking the point at which boys became men.

It is hard to judge whether Cusco was a city in the European sense of the term, with a large residential population divided into classes and neighborhoods and different sectors engaged in varied activities. It may have been more like the Vatican, with residents restricted to the Inca élite, religious specialists, servants, and pilgrims, as well as subjects who lived in the wider empire but who were called to present themselves at the center of the world.

The heart of modern-day Cusco still has streets that were trod by Inca feet, as well as substantial remains of the walls of ancient buildings. Inca buildings tended to be rectangular in plan and used two architectural forms, the *kallanka* and *cancha*, as modules to make groupings.[19] The former was a gabled hall with internal posts, multiple doorways, and interior niches. Most kallankas were quite large and served as meeting and feasting halls as well as temporary quarters when necessary. Canchas were compounds consisting of a perimeter wall and multiple one-storey buildings surrounding a patio within. This was a fundamental unit of Inca architecture; for example, the Coricancha should be literally translated as the "Golden Compound" because it contained multiple buildings within it. These forms were placed in groups in various settings; part of the impressiveness of Inca architecture lies not merely in the individual buildings or even groups of them, but in how they were placed within the landscape, such as at Machu Picchu.[20]

Inca architecture favored thatched gabled roofs, canted to shed the highland rains. Some thatching was elaborately executed to grace the most important buildings. Just as the Inca took great pains to make their roofs beautiful, they also made extraordinary efforts to create impressive stonework. Indeed, while Inca art excelled in a many areas, their stonework stands is one of their most outstanding achievements.

Inca stonework is so impressive that the technology used to create it is often presented as a "mystery" (especially by tour guides). In fact, however, most aspects of Inca stone working technology are fairly well understood. Stone quarries are known, and it is clear that the raw material was roughed out at them. The stones were then moved to construction sites where they were individually trimmed and fitted. Sometimes only the front faces of the stones were carefully shaped, but this still took a tremendous amount of effort and skill whereby each stone was carefully worked to join its neighbors.[21] A variety of different techniques are known, with some constructions favoring highly refined, rectilinear arrangements, others using irregular polygons, and others using rough field stones (*pirca*). Different symbolic, political, and economic factors were probably at work in determining which technique was used at a particular building site. In addition to the stonework itself, various distinctly Inca architectural details were also employed, such as trapezoidal doorways and niches. Such features may have been used to denote status, such as double- and sometimes triple-jambed portals.

It is likely that ancient peoples unfamiliar with Inca stone artistry were as astonished as modern visitors when visiting sites such as Machu Picchu. While precedents can be found for various aspects of Inca stone working, their overall approach was completely new. Their emphasis on blending natural formations with artificial constructions underwrote their claims to their own divine authority to conquer and rule others. Just as caves had produced the founding fathers and mothers of the Inca empire, so the earth brought forth temples and other concrete forms of Inca dominion. Irrigation canals and agricultural terraces had conformed to the landscape for centuries, and Inca-built engineering works continued to do so. However, Inca stonework insisted on demonstrating that its masters could make the crooked straight and the straight crooked, the smooth sharp and the sharp smooth. In this way, Inca architecture and engineering constantly surprise, instilling awe and respect.

The sites of various palaces and temples are still known in Cusco today, having been pointed out to the Spanish, and many of the walls of these places still stand, incorporated into later architecture just as many Inca plazas have been modified from their original trapezoidal shapes into square Spanish-style town squares. Whether Cusco was a city in the European sense or not, the Inca monarchs chose to build their own country estates, often at lower elevations than Cusco to take advantage of the milder climates (see Figure 10.2). Many of these are also known, and the most famous of them all is Machu Picchu which is said to have been one of many estates built by Pachacuti.[22] These estates were not simply pleasure palaces, but also religious centers.

Whether Cusco can be classed as a "true" city or not depends largely on how one defines the term. Present-day Cusco retains enough Inca architecture and we have enough Spanish accounts of what they witnessed or heard about it to assure us that it was a spectacular place in which the riches of an empire were employed for the pleasure of rulers and to impress visitors. For example, there is the famous description of the garden in the center of the Coricancha, in which life-sized figures of a man and a woman and a great variety of plants and animals all were rendered in precious metals. So too, there is a description of the impressive royal palace:

> The royal palace ... had two magnificent gateways, one at the entrance to the palace, and another farther inside where the finest and most impressive of these portals made its appearance ... In the entrance of the first doorway there were 2,000 indian guards ... [and this first gateway] opened into a plaza. Here all those who accompanied the Inca from the outside entered and remained there. The Inca and the four *orejones* of his cabinet entered the second gate, where there was another guard [composed of kinsmen] ... Beside the second gateway was the armory ... [and] another great plaza or patio for the officials of the palace,

and those who had regular jobs there were conducting tasks assigned them according to their responsibilities. Continuing on, one enters the quarters, apartments, and buildings where the Inca lived that were filled with pleasures and delights for there were trees, gardens with a thousand varieties of birds that went about singing: lions, tigers, and pumas; and every species of beast and animal found in this kingdom. These buildings were large and spacious and worked with great skill ... Within the house of the Inca was a treasure room ... where the jewels and gold and silver of the king were kept.[23]

RELIGION

The Spanish described the Inca pantheon. Viracocha was the source of creation. Inti was the Sun God, the Inca's patron deity, and he was worshiped in different forms such as a young boy at dawn or a more mature and abstract solar disk. Illapa controlled the weather and was associated with rains both good and bad; his sling hurled lightning bolts. Pachamama was the earth, Pachacamac the (old) creator god, Mamaquilla the moon, and Mamacocha the sea. These latter four were old gods, not specifically Inca in origin. The Inca insisted that subject peoples must build a temple to Inti and set aside and maintain fields and flocks to support the temple personnel, but they were not opposed to their subjects' continued worship of their existing local gods.

The degree to which these deities were thought of as personalities is difficult to assess, and it may be that the Spanish, greatly influenced by early Renaissance interests in Classical Antiquity, over-interpreted the Andean deities as similar to the Greco-Roman pantheon. Many of the gods and goddesses seem more like general concepts about sources of power and energy, and the processes by which these are channeled into action, than personages in their own right. Then again, it is likely that conceptions of deities were arranged according to rank, ethnicity, and understanding. In addition to the high gods belonging to the élites of conquered peoples, lesser local deities also continued to be worshipped under Inca rule. An early seventeenth century account of the beliefs of the people of Huarochiri, in the sierra directly east of Cusco, shows a remarkable and vibrant local religion.[24]

Camay, the life force, was everywhere, like a field spread throughout the universe. At some places the force was concentrated and powerful, while at other places it could erupt suddenly without warning as a *pachacuti*. Asymmetrical dualism meant that forces were always shifting, and change was constant, with more stable entities considered to be more powerful and reliable. Thus, soft, bubbly babies were full of potential and were valuable offerings due to their abundance of *camay*, but old people offered constancy and stability. The mummies of ancestors or Sapa Incas were not separated from the living by the gulf of death, but rather were more highly evolved beings who required the *camay* of offerings, in return for which they gave fertility to crops, herds, and people.[25] Even more stable and powerful than mummies were great mountains, worshiped as ancestors (*apu*).

268

Life and death were not sharply differentiated, so that sacrificed children, like mummified monarchs or boulders as transformed ancestors, were still thought to have agency to protect or punish the living. Human sacrifice had been part of Andean society since early times, and young children were highly regarded as appropriate and powerful offerings. *Capacocha* ceremonies brought young children from the provinces to the capital city, where ceremonies sanctified them and then sent them out again. Some were taken to high mountains, where they were quickly dispatched and buried in fine clothing and valued offerings.[26] However, human sacrifice among the Inca was not a daily occurrence, as best we can judge. Rather, it was carried out at critical times, such as the death of monarchs, or for the most sacred of ceremonies.

While *camay* flowed, junctures and confrontations were also important and were marked in the Andean cosmovision. Consequently, places where two things meet, *tinkuy*, were powerful and creative, whether they were two pieces of cloth, a man and a woman in love, or two rivers joining as one. Ritual battles fought in highland communities today are also known as tinkuy.[27] Both flow and juncture were thus considered in Inca thought, and this is also seen clearly in Inca stonework.

Many of the huacas in and around Cusco were carved rock formations in which the transitions from natural stone to artifice are manipulated to produce different effects (see Figure 10.2). Sculpted stone sometimes appears to arise out of bedrock in a flow. At other times sharp lines and angles delineate the break between natural and carved rock. Elsewhere natural formations, carved flowing rock, and rectangular masonry are combined, often sequentially. This was not simply the expression of an Inca aesthetic; it represents a much deeper and more sophisticated philosophical stance about the relationship between things, recognizing both continuity and disjunction.

What we might consider as rupture, punctuation, and distinctiveness were all associated in Inca thought, whether in time, space, or form. For this reason huacas included unusually shaped stones or llamas born with two heads, as well as mythological or historically grounded things and places. From small pebbles to the massive stone walls with their carefully fitted masonry, Inca religion was deeply wrapped up with visual experiences: rainbows were powerful and troubling signs, the most holy shrines cast no shadows at noon, while their fantastically carved walls shimmered like mirrors. A metaphysics of brilliance was widespread in the New World, and the Inca excelled in expressing it.[28] Indeed, much of what the Inca Empire was about was its ability to reformulate long-standing ideas in new ways, particularly in terms of the way in which politics and religion were conceived and acted out.

THE INCA EMPIRE

While considering the nature of politics and religion in prehispanic times necessitates a good deal of supposition and guesswork, we know a lot about these matters for the Inca. While interpretations of the Inca "state" are sometimes discussed as if the system approximated a

Figure 10.2 Inca places. Top: royal estate of Tipón. Center: Artist's interpretation of the Quispiguanca, the estate of the Sapa Inca Huayna Capac in the Urubamba Valley. Bottom left: Agricultural terraces at Pisac, Urubamba Valley, with ruins on distant hill. Bottom right: Inca administrative center of Tambo Colorado, Pisco Valley, South Coast of Peru.

nineteenth century European nation state, the evidence generally favors the view that in fact politics and religion were one, or at least they were greatly enmeshed together.

The nature of the Inca ruler is fairly clear because the Spanish, themselves living under a monarchy, were particularly interested in him. The Sapa Inca was treated as if he were a huaca, a sacred phenomenon that could only be approached with caution because of the intensity of the *camay* concentrated in him. Only the highest nobles were allowed to have an audience with the king, and even they had to carry a ritual burden on their back when they entered his presence. That presence was usually unseen because the Sapa Inca sat on his royal stool behind a finely woven gauze textile so that no one could look at his face. When the Sapa Inca traveled in his veil-covered litter anyone within sight of him, no matter how distant, stopped and worshipped with the *mochar*, the same special gesture made to other huacas: left arm outstretched with open fingers, as if blowing a kiss. Honorific forms of address were shouted out as he and his retinue passed by. Well-off people offered coca leaves, while the poor pulled out their eyelashes and blew them in his direction.[29]

The Sapa Inca did not simply live in Cusco. He *was* Cusco. Better yet, he was *the* Cusco, the center and source of all (see Figure 10.3). The title originally was applied to a person, not a place, and representatives of the four suyus carried the Sapa Inca's litter so that Tawantinsuyu was mobile. The concept of the sovereign as embodying or being the political unit was marked in many other ways as well, such as an *uncu* (tunic) decorated with the badges of the realm, known as *tocapu* (see Figure 10.4). These enigmatic emblems are mostly undeciphered, but one is known to refer to the uniform of an élite army corps.[30]

The Sapa Inca was the son of the Sun and the chief priest for its worship, while his wife, the *Coya*, was in charge of the worship of the Moon. Lieutenants may have supervised many of the great numbers of shrines, rituals, and priests involved with them, but nevertheless the highest Inca in the land was deeply involved with religion. That religion drew upon deep, long-lasting Andean ideas, but packaged them in new ways and added new ideas and practices. Furthermore, "religion" must be considered broadly here, to include both formal theology and rituals but also customary and traditional ways of acting.

Commensality was an extremely important aspect of the Inca worldview. Sharing food and usually drink is universally considered to be an act that signals an alliance and a positive bond, however temporary, between those participating. The Inca economy, like so many others, stored wealth in the form of food in towers and bins, and used it to feed and feast those who fought and built for it. Key to Inca diplomacy was drinking together. For the most important diplomacy, the Sapa Inca himself would offer the chief of his enemies the opportunity to drink a fine chicha from a beautiful *aquilla*, a metal tumbler.[31] The drinking vessels were near equal in size, but the Sapa Inca's was the larger of the two. If the ruler of the foreigners accepted the drink, a close but asymmetrical relationship was established between the two realms.

This view of Inca politics as rooted in ancient but reworked Andean religious and social concepts might seem to run counter to conceptions of the Inca state as a highly organized political machine. That view has tended to dominate Western European thinking about the Inca

Figure 10.3   The Inca as the Cusco, as illustrated by Guamán Poma.

for a long time. In fact, the Inca have been cited by European philosophers and political scientists as both the ultimate example of a fascist state at one end of the political spectrum, in which every movement of its subjects was under its watch and control, or as the ideal communist state at the other extreme, by which each gave according to his ability and received according to her needs.

The chroniclers reported a highly structured society in which the suyus were divided into smaller and smaller units on a decimal numbering system, down to the level of ten families in each community.[32] Men were in charge of each unit, so that a clear pyramidal hierarchy ascended to the four governors of the suyus who reported to the Sapa Inca. Government spies informed on locals, and punishment was harsh even for "minor" offenses. Travelers on the Inca road system could only move with permission, and they had to wear their traditional costume, especially their headgear, on pain of death.

A bureaucracy managed the empire. The road system was organized with small way-stations (*tambos*) and administrative centers at key nodes, such as at junctions between the long coastal and major highland routes and connecting roads. There had been earlier roads, but the Inca integrated and systematized them and built new ones. The two major north-south routes—the *Capac Ñan* or "Great Roads"—were given special treatment. In mountains these roads were narrow, sometimes only a meter (3.3 ft) or so in width, but they were often paved with stones to prevent erosion during the rainy season.[33] In other places, such as on the coast, they were 4 m (13 ft) across and flanked by tall walls that blocked wind-blown sand and concealed the movements of troops or government agents on their secret missions.

As with roads, there had been earlier recording systems that the Inca appear to have adopted and elaborated through their development of *quipu,* the knotted string recording device. The survival of hunters, fisher-folk, and herders depends on manipulating cordage such as snares, nets, and leads, and other devices, such as slings. These tendencies, combined with the Andean love of textiles, were the foundations of a recording system based on knots on strings.[34] *Quipucamayoc* (Quipu "Masters") recorded information in duplicate, so that one or more copies would be available for comparison, and censuses, tribute records, and other information were all recorded and kept on quipu. While they have sometimes been thought to be mnemonic devices, it seems much more likely that quipu pushed the limits of recording complex and sophisticated information, including narratives, in their knots and strings.

Without a monetary economy, taxes were paid through labor. Runners renowned for being fleet of foot were specially selected from tribute peoples, while communities near chasms were responsible for the construction and maintenance of rope bridges spanning them. Coastal communities specialized in fishing, while inland, often only a few kilometers away, farming communities tilled the land.[35] As in other matters, these specializations and systems of exchange between them may have been in operation prior to the Inca, who merely formalized them. Inca political and economic policies were tolerant and flexible, especially when subject peoples were cooperative. It was better to let existing systems continue to work well for the benefit of the empire than to disrupt them.

As noted in the beginning of this book, one of the great distinctions of Inca civilization has been a claim that it had few to no markets. Although the subject has previously been discussed at length, it bears briefly repeating here. Whereas a market brings different goods to a central place for redistribution, the Inca system moved people to the different resource zones in what has come to be known as the "Vertical Archipelago" model of Andean economics, a concept popularized by John V. Murra in the late twentieth century.[36] In some cases the colonists stayed, sending caravans of goods back to the mother community, while in others the colonists would work for a season or so and then return to the home community with the goods they had gathered or produced while away. However, a recent review of archaeological, historical, and ethnographical evidence from the Central Andes suggests that there was greater variability in economic systems in late prehispanic times than had previously been thought, and markets may have existed at various times and places.[37]

The vertical archipelago model recognizes that, in general, Andean resources are distributed like a chain of islands stretching through a sea. While marketplaces are usually located in central places roughly equidistant from the locations of all those participating in them, such locales are not easily found in a vertical landscape. A solution to the problem of efficiently gathering resources from different environmental zones is to send colonists from the parent community, wherever it is located, and then use a variety of systems to get the resources from each zone distributed to residents in the others.

The vertical archipelago model has been buttressed by colonial reports of the Inca practice of sending colonists to distant lands. These groups, known as *mitimae*, often consisted of peoples who had resisted incorporation into the empire, and so they were punished by being removed from their homelands and resettled in a distant part of the empire. Surrounded by local people who resented the intrusion of foreigners into their territories, the mitimae were made to work for the Inca and were effectively controlled by being strangers in a strange land. There are quite a number of communities in the contemporary Andes who claim to be the descendants of mitimae, such as the Salasaca of south highland Ecuador who say that their ancestors originated in the Titicaca Basin.[38] The mitimae system and the vertical archipelago model, however, are not necessarily linked; each could have operated without the other.

The mitimae were colonists who were deliberately mandated by the Inca to work far from their homelands. Their efforts were distinctly different than the labor taxes that local people gave in service to the Inca in a non-monetary economy. Furthermore, the labor tax was also different than the concept of *m'ita*, in which communities or segments of them provided labor or other services in the expectation that their efforts would be reciprocated by the group they served. However, the ideology promulgated by the Inca state was that all relations were reciprocal with the Inca providing for the people working for them. In light of the fact that many rose in rebellion against Inca rule, it would seem that not everyone was convinced that this was so. M'ita refers to the idea of a "turn" that expects reciprocity. When populations did their labor tax work on a road or bridge, they were taking their "turn" in expectation of Inca generosity in return for doing so. The provision that the Inca offered in return often took place at an Inca administrative center in the provinces, but which was linked to the imperial center through the road system.

Huanuco Pampa was a large Inca administrative center in the Peruvian sierra, and it is the only such site that has received extensive archaeological investigation. Different forms of Inca architectural complexes were all constructed around an expansive central plaza, while rows of storage towers overlooked the complex from a position high on a nearby hill. Excavations around the edge of the plaza revealed great quantities of smashed serving ware ceramics. Inca statecraft was clearly manifested in the extant archaeology: local people had been conscripted to work on Inca projects, and when the work was done their rulers had feasted them in the main plaza.

Each side had taken its reciprocal "turn." The locals had done work that benefited the Inca, and then the Inca had feasted the workers with food and drink in abundance. The work had been carried out over weeks or months, perhaps, and was an immediate contribution to some project, but the Inca took their turn in providing for the long term: when the Spanish later broke into storage towers they marveled at the quantity of materials in storage for future use. While the locals had offered their hands and their knowledge of the particulars of the surrounding environment and its resources, the Inca brought the excitement of a cross-cultural way of doing things. In particular, the styles of the ceramics used for eating and drinking at the feasts were highly appealing.

The Inca continued the Middle Horizon practice of producing large storage vessels with highly distinctive designs, sometimes known as *aryballos*,[39] as the equivalent of "beer kegs." These and other distinctive serving wares came in imperial Cusco styles, but many examples of "Provincial Inca" wares also have been found, indicating that locals copied the more desirable foreign wares.[40] The Inca Empire thus spread and controlled its subjects through a combination of setting style and fashion standards, finding new and exciting ways to do things that were attractive to non-Inca peoples, and also using force when necessary.

Although the chroniclers describe the bureaucracy of the Inca Empire in theory, in fact its day-to-day operation appears to have varied considerably from the ideal. There may have been differences in Inca administration in particular areas due to short intervals of time between the Inca conquest and the arrival of the Spanish, but similarly there may have been fully implemented different policies of control, and it is difficult to differentiate these two situations. For example, the relatively non-intrusive Inca presence on the North Coast seems to be due to the short time between their arrival and the Spaniards' appearance. On the South Coast, however, Inca influence is light on the coast but heavier in the warm middle regions of the valleys (the *chaupi yunga*), apparently as a deliberate strategy.[41] Like Wari policies before them, Inca statecraft varied in its form and intensity depending on a number of factors. However, we can come much closer to understanding how the overall system worked for the Inca, than we can for the Wari, because we have both archaeology and the Spanish chronicles from which to draw information.

ISSUES OF INCA STATECRAFT

At various points in this book I have noted the difficulty of using Western European concepts to describe or discuss Andean realities. This is particularly true for the Inca, because the great amount of information we have tempts us with the possibility of a deep understanding that is not possible for societies known only through archaeology. Searching for concepts and terms that help us to understand the past is natural, desirable, and a goal of anthropology. However, we must be cautious that we do not overly simplify qualitatively different ways of doing and thinking about things in the process of trying to understand them.

It might be helpful to consider how different the Western European experience was in comparison with the Inca. Starting in the Classical World, distinctions were made between customary practices and the laws that drew from the former but were codified, rationalized, and subject to amendments to adapt to new circumstances. After they were colonized by the Romans the peoples of Western Europe were subject to foreign laws, but in general they maintained them after the collapse of the Roman Empire because they had been integrated into the empire as citizens. In the Middle Ages another distinction was made between civil society and religion as two separate spheres of human behavior, and this trend continues in the present day with religion continuing to lose its (legal) powers to directly affect human behavior. Still another trend has seen government and economics also becoming distinct in human affairs. While politics and economics are inseparable, in most Western nation states and societies economic life involves individuals (including corporations legally conceived of as "individuals") while governmental affairs involve collective concerns, at least in principle.

In short, over the centuries the Mediterranean–Western European tradition has defined and then separated out human behaviors into different concepts and spheres of interaction, and has attempted to create societies based on these ideas. However, this runs counter to the way many peoples behaved in other parts of the world and at different times.

Some Western ideas are still relatively new, such as the concept of a political body comprised of citizens. Louis XIV of France could not conceive of a political system different from his personal ownership of lands and riches, famously stating that *L'état, c'est moi* (I am the state)—although the French revolutionaries clearly thought otherwise especially two reign later. A consequence of the throwing off of aristocratic rule in Europe has been that the bureaucracies that developed in the nineteenth century have increasingly come to be seen as the day-to-day manifestations of "the state" in operation. With their quipucamayocs and chasquis (couriers), the Inca have been interpreted by Europeans as something like a corporate, bureaucratized state, whether this is conceived of as communist, socialist, fascist, or some other variation.

However, there is little evidence to suggest that considering the Inca as a state resembling Western bureaucracies is useful beyond general heuristic purposes. How the Inca system was perpetuated is a good example of these important differences. There is fairly widespread acceptance of the suggestion that the rapid spread of the Inca Empire was due to unique inheritance laws. Every Sapa Inca came to power with a great many resources at his disposal, but with no inherited wealth from his predecessor. It is worth emphasizing again that there was no way to store wealth in currency or banks, so that it was the control over wealth and its production that was critical to maintaining a Sapa Inca and his court. Women and camelids had long been considered to be sources of wealth. By the time of the Inca, artisans may also have been considered as wealth (see Figure 10.4).

Each Sapa Inca became the head of a new social unit known as a *panaca*, generally interpreted as a royal ayllu.[42] This was the foundation of his power, but it also was his obligation to provide for his panaca for eternity. There was also a reciprocal obligation, according to which panaca members would serve the Inca during their lives and generations unborn would maintain his mummy while working for and profiting from the wealth and estates that he had provided. Some scholars believe that this or a similar system was first practiced at Chan Chan, explaining the series of ciudadelas there, and the system was possibly adopted from the Chimú by the Inca.[43] Whether this is true or not, the system impelled Inca sovereigns to conquer new lands as their quickest way to gain new wealth to support their panacas.

Conquering new territory to add to one's kingdom is an activity followed by contemporary Old and New World kings alike. In Europe, however, the problems of inheritance and potential feuds among claimants to the throne were addressed by restricting who could inherit, generally the first-born son of the king and his sole wife, the Queen. However, enough inconsistencies and serendipitous events occurred in Europe to incite numerous wars between rival claimants. For the Inca, their system was apparently new enough that problems inherent in it did not manifest themselves until shortly before the arrival of the Spanish.

One critical aspect of the Inca system that was not present in the Old World is the prominent role of women. There are many accounts to suggest that they played much more significant roles, had more freedoms, and were more equal to men than in contemporary European societies. For instance, this can be seen in the high status roles of Moche women, among other examples.[44] However, the Inca took a different route.

It was reported that the Sapa Inca's principal wife was his sister, justified by the claim that since he was divine, he could only marry another deity to produce a divine heir. However, this claim runs counter to substantial evidence that royal succession was not fixed by any rigid principles. Furthermore, while the Sapa Inca may have married his sister as his principal wife there is ample evidence that he had many other wives as well, with whom he produced numerous offspring. Indeed, the monopolization of a great number of fertile women was a key source of élite power.

The most well-known examples of Inca women are the *aclla*, sometimes known as the "chosen women." The Spanish found them remarkable and reminiscent of Roman Vestal Virgins and Catholic nuns. While there were some similarities, the differences were nevertheless important (see Figure 10.4). There were several categories of aclla, selected or offered as tribute ("taxes") and taken from their homes to serve in Cusco or a regional Inca center. The highest ranking acllas were known as *mamaconas*. They were chaste, holy, and nun-like in their consecrated service in temples. After them, however, there were the *huayrur aclla*, beautiful

Figure 10.4 Inca prosperity. Top: "All-Tocapu" tunic, which may be a royal garment. Guamán Poma depictions of acllas who wove, made chicha, and reproduced, and work made into a festival at planting time.

girls who were taken by the Sapa Inca as secondary wives. Then came a group which the Sapa Inca gave to high-ranking lords in return for their services, and there were other groups that included singers and dancers as well as servants. Acllas were said to be highly skilled in weaving the finest cloth in the realm, and in brewing high quality chicha. Control over aclla was maintained by capital punishment meted out to those who dared profane them, and by keeping them apart from normal society by housing them in special facilities known as *acllahuasi*.

In a society without money, the greatest gifts a servant of the Inca could receive included the finely woven cloth made by acllas, known as *cumbi*, as already noted (see Figure 10.4). We have already seen that feasting, especially accompanied by copious amounts of chicha, was another aspect of Inca statecraft. Thus, control of the aclla also constituted control of two of the main sources of wealth and power in the Andean world. Women were not only creative and lucrative in weaving cumbi and brewing beer, but in their reproductive capacities as well.

Ethnohistorian Susan Ramírez makes a strong case that the Inca Empire was not a territorial state in which land was the primary resource, but rather the number of people under one's command was the basis of power and wealth.[45] The importance of the reproductive capacities of women and llamas had been recognized and expressed for centuries through their roles as sacrificial victims. While the Inca continued these practices, they also "banked" women's reproductive potential by "storing" it in the institution of the aclla. Equally importantly, the Sapa Inca was able to exploit this resource by having a great number of wives who produced many children. He literally produced his own political group through his offspring, creating subsequent generations to serve in his panaca. Offering chosen women to loyal subjects was thus a way of providing them with opportunities to increase their following as well, although the Sapa Inca still maintained his monopoly on the resource overall.

The Inca did not have a concept of "property" that encompassed the idea of "real estate." Indeed, this idea only developed gradually in Western Europe as well. In the Andes, land that was not in use was wasteland, but it could not be legally or physically cordoned off simply because someone, including an abstract entity such as "the state," claimed ownership of it. Therefore, wealth was only accumulated through an agency, an act of creation, as embodied in the concept of *camay* that implies a sense of making something happen. It was the agency of quipu masters (quipucamayoc) that made the strings speak, and it was the agency of planted fields and camelids and women bearing offspring that produced wealth.

There is much that we do not know about Inca society. A class of people known as *yanaconas* is mentioned in the chronicles, serving as laborers and servants. These people were of low social rank, but whether their status could be raised, and if so, how, is unclear. Issues are compounded by the problem of biased reporting from the Spanish. The yanaconas may have been people who had somehow lost their kin affiliations, so that consequently their political connections would have been severely curtailed. The yanacona class was supposedly created specifically to work the lands of the panaca estates.[46]

Given all this information, the growth of the Inca Empire might be interpreted as something that happened as a consequence of ideas and actions that were not fully thought out when they were developed. What we might term Serendipitous States happened more than once in the past, but the Inca do seem to have been able to form a spectacularly successful one. However, this interpretation works best in conjunction with the view that the Inca state grew relatively quickly—within the lifespan of three or four kings at most.

One aspect of Inca politics that has drawn much recent attention is the role of oracles.[47] Oracles played important roles at least as early as the Early Horizon, when there is clear evidence of one in the sanctum sanctorum at Chavín de Huántar as discussed in Chapter 6. The Spanish chroniclers reported that Peru was a "land of oracles" in the sixteenth century, and it seems logical to assume that oracles had remained important in the great span of time between Chavín and the Late Horizon.[48] We have a considerable amount of specific information about oracles in late prehispanic Peru. Shortly after Pizarro captured the Sapa Inca Atahualpa in north highland Peru, he also sent his lieutenants to seize Pachacamac where the most important coastal oracle was located. Later the high priest of the Apurimac oracle committed suicide at the approach of the Spanish by jumping into the deep chasm next to the site.

Beyond these dramatic incidents, we also know that there were many oracles throughout Peru when the Spanish arrived. One view suggests that these oracles could only have existed because of the Inca bureaucratic government that organized and supported them, but the evidence actually suggests a very different scenario.[49] Rather than serving as part of the Inca bureaucracy, oracles were independent institutions that served as alternate, sometimes even opposing, forces to Inca hegemony. Oracles consisted of a primary center, with satellite or "daughter" oracles in distant parts of the Central Andes. While they may have served the concerns of local people in their personal affairs, they were also actively engaged in politics in ways similar to Old World counterparts.

The most famous example of an oracle's engagement in political affairs is the case of Catequil, with its main shrine in the highlands of La Libertad Province.[50] Shortly before the arrival of the Spanish there was a civil war between two rival claimants to the leadership of the empire. Catequil was approached by agents of one of them, Atahualpa, and asked which side would win. The oracle replied that Atahualpa's brother and rival, Huascar, would be the victor. However, Atahualpa won, and wreaked vengeance on Catequil by killing the oracle priests and obliterating the huaca and shrine complex.

We cannot know for certain if the political involvement of Catequil was a unique event sparked by the civil war, but it seems likely that it was the rule rather than the exception for oracles to be consulted. Because the voices of oracles are supposedly those of the gods, they can offer expressions of displeasure and disapproval of the powerful with impunity. This was not the case for Catequil, but it was probably seen as sacrilege to kill the oracle, and Atahualpa appeared to pay for his sin shortly thereafter when he forfeited his own life at the hands of the Spaniards.

The story of Catequil implies that the Inca Empire made claims of great authority in the Andes, but the oracles represented at least one system that challenged the empire's hegemony, although at some risk. The chronicles also suggest that many conquered peoples rose up in rebellion against the empire, often paying dearly for their attempts at reestablishing their independence. However the Inca Empire is conceived, whether as a complex of governmental agencies run by bureaucrats or as a much looser religious system and army that worked for the benefit of a monarch anxious to gain resources for his panaca, it was probably never in complete control of its subject peoples. Rather, like many empires, it was likely a constant work in progress in which new challenges demanded innovative solutions. Nevertheless, the Inca Empire was a new phenomenon on the Andean landscape. It took old ideas and reworked them, and added new concepts and new ways of doing things to the old ways. Then, however, it too faced a challenge of a form and scale that had never been encountered before.

A signal illustration of Inca statecraft, religion, the roles of women and men, huacas, and oracles is encapsulated in the story of Tanta Carhua, told to the Spaniard Hernández Príncipe in the Colonial Period.[51] The tale demonstrates the ways in which the Inca were like our conceptions of a state and how they were not, the reworking of old ideas into new ones, and how the promulgation and acceptance of a religious-political ideology allows the creation and maintenance of asymmetrical power relations.

Tanta Carhua was a ten-year-old girl, the only daughter of Cacique Poma of Urcon, near the town of Recuay in the Department of Ancash. She was of extraordinary beauty, and much admired by all who knew her. Her father offered to sacrifice his beloved child, dedicating her to be one of the four noble children sacrificed to the Sun in Cusco during the festival of Inti Raymi at the winter solstice. So, in great pomp and circumstance, she traveled with her father and retinue from her home in Urcon to Cusco, hailed and adored by local people on the roads on the way. On arriving at the capital city she marched in procession in the great square, participated in elaborate rituals that involved festival eating and drinking, and was consecrated by the Sapa Inca himself. Once the festivals ended she returned home as an *aclla-capacocha* with her father and retinue, where she was buried alive on a hilltop overlooking royal lands and those of the local *ayllu*. The elders of her *ayllu* who remembered this event said that her last words were, "Finish now with me, for the celebrations which were made in Cusco were more than enough!"

Cacique Poma was elevated in status by the sacrifice of his daughter, receiving a hereditary governorship. The Sapa Inca had decreed that Tanta Carhua was a huaca to be reverenced, and lands and herds were set aside to support her worship. Tanta Carhua remained a vital part of the community, not only ensuring the prosperity of the fields and flocks but also aiding her *ayllu* in sickness and in health. Old people told Hernández Príncipe that when people fell ill or were in trouble they would consult the oracle of Tanta Carhua, staffed by priests who spoke for her in high falsetto voices.

THE END OF AN EMPIRE

So we return to that fateful day in the Cajamarca plaza when two very different worlds confronted each other. Neither would ever be the same again. The standard story so often recounted is the view from the Spanish side. It focuses on the confrontation of Friar Valverde armed with his Bible and the Sapa Inca's ignorance that black scribbles in a book could speak, interpreting this as the pivot point on which the world tipped from prehistory into history. The story goes that the friar bravely left his hiding place, strode across the plaza and confronted the Sapa Inca. He presented the ruler with a Bible, and through a translator he explained that God spoke through it. The Inca took the book, held it to his ear, said that he heard no God and threw it to the ground. At this moment the friar called upon the Spaniards to attack. The rest, quite literally, is history.

We also have an indigenous account of the event, however, taken down in 1570.[52] In that version the crisis of confrontation occurred when the priest refused to drink with the Inca. The gesture of hospitality, the offer of a reciprocal relationship between near-equal partners, was as incomprehensible to the Spanish as the written word was to the Inca.

The subsequent slaughter that took place in Cajamarca that day was not the end of the Inca Empire, or of Andean civilization. The empire held on and fought on for many years. That civilization was as deep, as rich and as complex as the one it faced, and it was not about to be snuffed out like a church candle. While details of the Spanish invasion and battles lost and won may be found in many different accounts, some issues concerning the period immediately prior to the Spanish arrival are noteworthy because of what they suggest about the Inca Empire in its final years before it faced its mortal enemy.

The accounts written down by the Spanish, years later, state that the last independent Sapa Inca was Huayna Capac, who extended the empire into Ecuador and a little beyond, just across the border into modern Colombia. He followed common Inca practice in building temples and palaces, constructing another "Cusco" in the newly conquered lands. Huayna Capac supposedly liked Ecuador and spent much time there. However, he was suddenly struck with a severe illness and died. It is said that on his deathbed he named his heir, but he too was struck by a plague that was raging through the kingdom. When that heir expired the empire was thrown into confusion because there was no clear line of succession after him.[53]

Two rivals gathered armies to fight for the mascaipacha. Huascar was at the head of the Cusco faction and Atahualpa led a group based in Ecuador. Atahualpa won a decisive victory that created the possibility of seizing the entire empire rather than just a part of it. It was in the wake of that victory that he traveled to Cajamarca, where he planned to recuperate from the campaign by taking advantage of the hot springs which may still be enjoyed there today.

Like so many aspects of the past, we do not know how much of this story is true, how much was an invention of various Inca, especially Atahualpa and his supporters, who reworked the story to their advantage, and how much is due to accidental or deliberate misinterpretations by the Spanish. If the outlines of the narrative are close to what actually occurred, they are instructive on several issues.

There is the claim that the civil war began because of the lack of a clear policy of royal succession. If there was no policy and succession depended solely on the deathbed statements of the monarch, this would tend to support the idea that the Inca Empire was a relatively new phenomenon that had not yet created a governmental system that allowed for smooth transitions of power, a critical issue in any system where great advantages are to be gained in high political office. Again, this is not that different from Medieval monarchies in Europe, in which there often were rival claimants to the throne who went to war with each other in support of their claims. However, such conflicts and unsettled affairs of state could last for centuries, so that by itself the problems of inheritance do not indicate unambiguously that the Inca Empire was young in 1532.

Another issue that the account raises is whether the Inca Empire had extended beyond the capacity of a pre-industrial society. Stretching from the Colombia–Ecuador border to central Chile, it was one of the largest pre-modern states ever to have existed. While Inca roads and administrative centers, and the chasquis and army that utilized them, may have brought a level of integration rare for any ancient society, it could also be that the empire had gone beyond the limits of effective management. This would especially be the case if the mechanisms for integrating the royal estates of the panacas of deceased monarchs into a single managerial system were relatively weak. The tendencies for individual units to want to manage their own affairs without outside interference would have been exacerbated.

Whatever the specifics of the nature of the Inca Empire on the eve of conquest, when the Spanish arrived they were opposed every step of the way as they moved from Cajamarca towards Cusco. The Spanish spent almost a year in Cajamarca before they executed Atahualpa, and they were not idle during this time. While only a handful of Europeans had been in the plaza in November 1532, a steady stream of reinforcements had been arriving while they waited for Atahualpa's ransom. As in the case of Cortés and Mexico, the Spaniards could not have conquered Tahuantinsuyu without the aid of a multitude of former Inca subjects, who now rose up against their imperial masters. For example, the Chachapoyas in the high altitude cloud forests of the eastern *ceja de selva* had rebelled against the Inca many times.[54] So too had the Cañaris of Ecuador, bitter foes who had resisted the Inca valiantly and paid heavily for their tenacity when they were finally conquered. Now, heading towards Cusco, these native groups were in the vanguard of the attack on the Inca, and they fought so bravely that the Spaniards granted them a place of honor ever afterwards in the yearly Corpus Christi parades held in Cusco.[55]

The Inca fought for Cusco, and when they lost it they fought from ever more remote centers in the Urubamba Valley, at Ollantaytambo, and, eventually from their jungle capital in exile at Vilcabamba. They not only fought; they also adapted. They learned how to reduce the effectiveness of Spanish cavalry by attacking from steep hillsides in narrow gorges whenever possible, and they even learned to make Spanish weapons when they planned a massive uprising in the 1560s.

Andean people also had a change of consciousness. When the Spanish arrived, Andeans were embroiled in their own affairs and recognized much too late that Pizarro's forces comprised the thin tip of a huge spear of invaders that would drive deep into their world. This had happened in Mexico and in many other places, and the Andean people were no exception. Even today people tend to identify more with their town or region than they do with larger national identities, and the same was true in the past. Many people who had been happy to throw off the yoke of the Inca Empire (another reason to indicate that it really had existed) learned too late that the Spanish yoke was even more heavy and severe.

By the 1560s more than a generation of Andean people had passed through decades of incessant disease, starvation, and war, and it became clear that the Spanish were a fundamentally different kind of enemy than any they had ever faced before. Previous foes, whether from over the next hill or from afar, and no matter how fierce, had at least shared basic, common assumptions about the nature of reality and the proper relations between humans and the natural world. The Spanish were different in that they did not share any of those assumptions. They engaged in what has been aptly described as a "plunder economy," in which the land and people were ravaged solely for what they could provide the conquerors.[56] Indeed, the lust for wealth was so great that much of the period between the initial successes of Pizarro's expedition and the following two decades was characterized by wars between different Spaniards all vying for control of the Andes.

Word spread throughout the different native communities that the Inca gods had been thoroughly defeated by the Spanish god and saints, but there was hope. The huacas, the locally based, autochthonous spirits of the mountains, valleys, and rivers would rise up and aid in destroying the foreign invaders. Thus the concept of a common cause, a common Andean identity that underpinned or crosscut the local distinctions long held so dear, was born.[57]

This new sense of Andean identity was expressed in the *Taqui Onqoy* movement, a phrase meaning "Singing Sickness." It resembled many other revitalization movements that emerged in the face of colonialism, in which a mystical vision captured the imagination of the oppressed, with revitalized communities and gods driving out oppressors through a combination of communal rituals and, often, armed insurrection. Lasting from about 1564 to 1572, *Taqui Onqoy* was eventually defeated when the Spanish heard of the impending uprising and crushed it mercilessly.

A new Viceroy Francisco de Toledo, arrived in Peru. He was the first truly effective Spanish administrator of the vast region under his command, and for better and worse he brought it under control. This included more systematic means of exploitation, with the slight saving grace that the resource extraction was regulated rather than uncontrolled as it had been previously. However, it was Toledo who managed to capture Tupac Amaru, the last Sapa Inca directly descended from the royal line, bring him to Cusco, and execute him in the Plaza de Armas, the main city square, to the consternation of Andeans as well as many Spaniards.

Even the execution of Tupac Amaru was not the end of the conquest. There were very few Spanish in the New World for a very long period of time, and while Andean peoples suffered greatly at the hands of the invaders, they were resilient. Andean societies rebounded and persisted. True, the arrival of the Spanish was a profound event because it pulled the Central Andes into participating in a much larger world than it had known of before. Andean ways of doing and thinking about things were greatly influenced by these changes—but then again, changes had always been taking place. Andean peoples did not simply yield to European ways of life and belief. Like many people subjected to colonial rule they accepted some things, such as technologies and plants and animals, that made life easier or richer. However, they resisted other attempts at imposing European ways using the various methods that all in such circumstances will apply, sometimes subtly and sometimes overtly. In other matters Andean people absorbed or appropriated European practices and beliefs, often reworking them to their own liking or conforming to their own tastes and standards.

Today, Andean peoples continue to draw upon their rich heritages while facing the challenges and opportunities provided by new ways of doing and thinking about things, just as they have always done. The worlds of the Colonial (AD 1532 to 1821) and Republican Periods (AD 1821 to the present) were and are as rich and complex as any of the periods that preceded them. Indeed, the purpose of this book has been to demonstrate to those who think that "history" began when Europeans started to write about the Andes that the Andean prehistory was as rich and complex as any of the eras that have succeeded it.[58]

NOTES

1 Dulanto 2008: 775.
2 Arkush 2011.
3 Rowe, 1944. Bauer and Covey 2004 offer a review of the history of studies and current understandings of pre-Inca Cusco.
4 McEwan 2006: 63–66 and McEwan et al. 2002 argue that Chokepukio was *the* major center southeast of Cusco in the Late Intermediate Period. Bauer and Covey (2004: 84–87) discuss the Oropesa and Lucre basins in detail, however, and note that Chokepukio is one of many large Late Intermediate Period sites in the region and that, at the time, Cusco was at least as extensive.
5 Publications on the Inca are the most numerous of any subject within the wider area of the ancient Andes. Patterson (1991) is the most succinct and focuses on politics. Rowe's (1946) article is still a valuable introduction and is especially useful on rituals and everyday life. D'Altroy (2003), Morris and von Hagen (2012), and McEwan (2006) are the most recent book-length treatments in English. Maria Rostworowski de Diez Canseco wrote an authoritative book in Spanish (1988) that has also been translated into English (1999). Many Spanish chronicles on the Inca are also available in edited or full versions, some in English and more in Spanish. Interested readers should consult the recent books for further listings.
6 Bauer and Stanish 2002.
7 Urton 1990.
8 Both the archaeological and mytho-historical versions of the origins of the Inca place importance on migrations or invasions by people from elsewhere into Cusco or nearby. See Clastres (1987) on invasions as class justifications; Gose 2008 on invaders as ancestors.
9 Rowe 1946 presents the kings as succeeding one another. Zuidema 1990b provides a structuralist interpretation. Julien 2000 offers a commentary on the problem of interpreting Inca history.
10 Bauer et al. 2010.
11 Morris and von Hagen 2012: 30–31.
12 Covey 2003b suggests a much earlier date for state formation, between AD 1000 and 1400, than most scholars believe.

13 Works on Cusco include Bauer 2004 and Zuidema 1990b.

14 Jeanette Sherbondy (1979, 1982, 1987) was the first to recognize that the reason the ceque lines were not straight is because they were mapping irrigation/political districts. Her work has since been used to inform the thinking of many other scholars. See Bauer 1998 for a detailed discussion of the ceque system.

15 Sherbondy 1987.

16 Herring 2010: 80.

17 Caution must be exercised in assuming that modern or even colonial terms were used in ancient times, because "puma's tail" and other notions could have been created more recently. Susan Niles suggested to me that the Coricancha was the scrotum of the puma.

18 See MacCormack 1993.

19 See McEwan 2006: 175–177; Gasparini and Margolies 1980.

20 The best general introduction to Machu Picchu is Burger and Salazar 2004.

21 Protzen 1985, 1986, 1993.

22 Salazar 2004; Niles 1987, 2004.

23 Pillsbury and Leonard 2004: 253–254, translating and citing Murúa 1987 [1611–16], book 2, chapter 2, 345–348.

24 Salomon and Urioste 1991.

25 Salomon 1995.

26 Reinhard and Ceruti 2010. See description of rite in Silverblatt 1987.

27 Harrison 1989 on tinkuy in general.

28 Herring 2010 on stonework and architecture as light. Saunders 1998 and 2003 on the importance of shiny things in the New World.

29 Descriptions of Inca worship are taken from numerous sources as discussed by Julien 2000: 264–265.

30 Susan Ramírez (2007) makes the strongest argument for "Cusco" as the title of a person, not a place. See Cummins (2007: 288–290) on the suyu litter carriers and other matters, and the same author and Stone (2007) on the uncu. The precise meaning and role of tocapu are debated, but it seems that they were something like badges or identifiers of some kind.

31 Carved (wooden) tumblers were called *queros* while hammered metal ones were called *aquillas*. See Cummins 2002 and 2007 on these issues and much more.

32 Julien 1988.

33 Hyslop 1984.

34 There is an extensive literature regarding quipu (or *khipu*). See Quilter and Urton 2002 and Urton 2003 for introductions. On Middle Horizon quipu see Conklin 1982.

35 Sandweiss 1992.

36 On the Vertical Archipelago, see Murra 1972.

37 Van Buren 1996; Hirth and Pillsbury 2013.

38 Corr 2009.

39 The term derives from the shape of classical Greek vessels that the Inca versions resemble.

40 Bray 2004. Malpass 1993.

41 Covey 2000, 2009.

42 Sherbondy (1996) suggests that panacas were originally administrative units of the Inca state that were developed to collect and store tribute, including labor, from distant regions to the core of the Inca Empire and to carry out ritual obligations for sacred sites within the valley of Cusco. These were later reinterpreted as ayllu-like kinship groups to save them from being seized by the Spanish. If Sherbondy's claim is correct, one may ask whether the inheritance rules and the rest of the justification of the spread of the Inca Empire were also invented as a means to try and safeguard resources.

43 Conrad (1981) on split inheritance.

44 Silverblatt 1987.

45 Ramírez 2007.

46 Rostworowski de Diez Conseco 1962.

47 Curatola Petrocchi and Ziólkowski 2008.

48 I have suggested that oracles were key aspects of Moche huacas. See Quilter 2011.

49 Stanish and Bauer 2007.

50 Topic et al. 2002.

51 Tanta Carhua's story is told at greater length in Silverblatt 1987: 94–100.

52 Legnani 2006.

53 It is generally thought that the plague was a European disease, probably smallpox, which preceded the physical arrival of the Spanish, but we know very little about autochthonous diseases in ancient America. Kiracofe and Marr (2008) suggest that it was Bartonellosis, a fatal bacterial disease that is found exclusively in the New World.

54 Schjellerup 1997.

55 Dean 1999 for Cañaris and Corpus Christi in Cusco.

56 Spalding 1988.

57 Stern 1993.

58 Books and articles on the post-prehistoric Central Andes are numerous. Stern 1993 is a good book with which to begin.

AFTERWORD

Any attempt to offer a grand synthesis of Central Andean prehistory is fraught with difficulty. Each person who takes the time and trouble to study the rich and deep sources on the subject will certainly draw their own, distinct conclusions. Nevertheless, after having covered so many millennia, regions, and cultures of the past, I will offer some of my own thoughts on these matters for the reader to contemplate, and perhaps to use as a comparison for their own reflections. I do so in the form of an essay rather than a more studied presentation, as in the previous chapters.

In my view, there are three topics of interest. The first is the major trends and patterns to be found within the Central Andes as a region in its own right. The second involves a consideration of the prehistory of the Andes in light of the comparative study of civilizations and with regard to the fundamental mission of anthropology as a cross-cultural, comparative discipline. Finally, the third topic notes how the study of the ancient Central Andes bears upon matters beyond anthropology, reaching the social sciences, History, and even academics. All three of these topics, are interlinked beyond their generalities, although in some ways more than in others.

Fifty years ago a basic framework for understanding the Andean past was established in the chronological systems of Luis Lumbreras and of John Rowe and Dorothy Menzel. Despite some major theoretical implications in terminologies, these chronologies are more similar than they are different. Although the pace and intensity of investigations have greatly increased in the last half-century, the frameworks that Lumbreras, Rowe and Menzel created remain more or less intact, despite some significant reworking and clarifications of older concepts within the larger chronological frames.

Although qualifications abound, the horizon concept remains intact with three defined eras in which people participated in pan-regional systems across great areas of the Central Andes. Those times are encapsulated in the concepts of the Early Horizon with the strong influence of

Chavín de Huántar, the Middle Horizon dominated by Wari–Tiwanaku, and the Late Horizon characterized by the Inca. The Preceramic Period and the Early and Late Intermediate periods are becoming better known, but there is still much work to be done in understanding the times of transition between periods and horizons. As those times are clarified, the resulting understanding will, in turn, affect our interpretations of the major eras themselves. Furthermore, as noted at the beginning of this book, ultimately the chronological eras merely simplify a much messier and more interesting reality, in which cultural and other changes occurred at different paces and in different ways across different areas of the Central Andes.

One significant change from a half-century ago is the full recognition of the importance of the Preceramic Period as a crucible of Andean civilization. Within the last decade, research elsewhere in the world has had an effect in allowing us to appreciate the remote past of the Early and Middle Preceramic in more detail than ever. Archaeologists tend to be a conservative lot, and there is simply less evidence—fewer artifacts, fewer sites, more erasure of traces of the past—for remote antiquity than for later times. Consequently, archaeologists are reluctant to speculate on what happened and how events came about when evidence is lacking. However, research in other parts of the world is driving home the message that the earliest humans to enter the Americas, whether 14,000 years ago or twice that period, arrived with already well-developed cultures that were much more complex than has previously been imagined. Some of those early immigrants probably arrived in boats rather than on foot, and they brought with them a suite of technologies, social patterns, and religious beliefs that already had long histories. The similarities that are often noted in New World cultures, especially along the Pacific shores, may thus be partly explained by one or more cultural patterns that came to the New World in very early times and then developed on different pathways as time progressed.

In one way or another, early cultures in western South America shared many common ways of dealing with the world ranging from practical to spiritual matters, although most of them would not have made such a distinction. Populations were undoubtedly relatively small at first, although it is possible that we may be significantly underestimating the density of the human presence in early times. Shared patterns diverged, perhaps gradually at first, but by 1500 BC peoples in what we now call Ecuador, Peru, Bolivia, northwestern Argentina and Chile were doing very different things while still sharing some of those inherited practices and beliefs from earlier times.

Older conceptions of Environmental Determinism, in which people are at the mercy of natural forces, have given way to more nuanced understandings of human–environmental interactions in which "natural" landscapes are thought to have vanished at a very early stage due to human effects on the environment. Nevertheless, it is clear that the broad ecologies of the major regions of the Central Andes correspond with very different cultural trajectories in prehistory. In Ecuador social stratification remained relatively low throughout prehistory. The same holds true in the Altiplano, northwestern Argentina, and northern Chile, completely different environments than Ecuador, although there was a rapid increase in socio-political complexity in these regions beginning in the Late Formative, equivalent to the Early Horizon in Peru.

It can be debated whether the cultures of the region from the Central to the North coasts and the Highlands of Peru were more "advanced" or "complex" than those from other regions of the Central Andes in the Late Preceramic Period through the Early Horizon, but it is indisputable that some very different things were taking place there during these times. Again, the reasons for this are controversial, but the richness of the offshore fisheries, the great agricultural potential of the river valleys, especially under irrigation, and the compactness of the vertically stacked resource zones in the highlands seem to have been critical factors.

The case for the precocity of the Central-North Peruvian region is reinforced by an examination of the region south of Lima, with its different configuration of coastal valleys, long distances to the highlands, and severe aridity. It is perhaps a testament to how cultural patterns can overcome environmental restrictions that the South Central Andean interaction region became such a powerful center of political and economic power in later prehistory. The links between the South Coast of Peru and the southern highlands of Peru and the Bolivian Altiplano gave rise to both Wari and Tiwanaku, and eventually to the Inca. The relatively late rise of the southern region may be partly due to the collapse of the large interaction sphere to the north, when Chavín fell, followed by a resurgence and eventual demise in succeeding cultures. It may also be due in part to the use of agricultural techniques such as terracing, which had been known for centuries but were apparently only intensely deployed in the fifth or sixth centuries AD, and partly to the intensification of llama caravans.

In many ways there is a strong sense of continuity in the archaeological record from the Late Preceramic Period through the Initial Period. Chavín was both a culmination of those trends and at the same time a whole new reinterpretation of them. Certainly the differences between each of the three eras were dramatic enough to leave different archaeological remains by which we can make distinctions, but at the same time there are clear continuities in temple styles, symbol systems, and even subsistence economies from any one of these periods to the next. As in all cases when we examine complex events represented by evidence strained through the sieve of time, one's view of such changes is partly due to how much one cares to note the differences or the similarities.

We can now discuss Late Preceramic Period regional architectural styles that probably reflect larger cultural patterns, and in general the period still stands as an impressive example of how achievements in the building of large structures can be accomplished with what appear to be relatively simple subsistence and social systems. In recent years there has been a trend for suggesting that these societies were more "complex" than previously thought. To my way of thinking, the opposite is true. These societies were "simple" in the sense that political organizations were relatively egalitarian and subsistence systems were unelaborated, but through high levels of organization and coordination impressive collective works were nevertheless accomplished.

The same is true for the Initial Period. Whereas the Late Preceramic demonstrates that large-scale architecture, elaborate ceremonialism, and long-distance trade networks can develop without stratified societies or elaborated agricultural systems, the Initial Period points to the introduction of new technologies—pottery and weaving—not necessarily as causes of culture change, but as two agents among many that resulted in social transformations. The driving forces in these changes were not the pots and textiles themselves, but the rearrangements in social relations among people that called for new ways to interact with one another and the world around them. At the same time, however, new technologies and modes of expression can also have effects on how people interact. The relationships between people and the things that they use to survive, prosper, and express themselves are complex and reciprocal; people make things because of social and other needs, and in turn, the things that have been made to fulfill these needs have effects on the people and societies in which they are produced. In recent times the invention of different modes of transportation (railroads, airplanes, automobiles) and communications systems (telegraph, telephones, computers), food preservation, and even indoor lighting have had profound consequences on society and politics.

There is considerable evidence, which is being strengthened by further research, that while Chavín acquired power through its religious ideology, it was also a power in control of resources such as obsidian and cinnabar, and very likely other desirable goods. The differences between what Chavín did and what the Initial Period centers that preceded it did probably exist in the realm of human activities, which are hard to pinpoint because they are less archaeologically observable than architectural formats or iconography. However, tracing economic power is feasible for resources originating at distinct points, such as obsidian, cinnabar, and *Spondylus* shells. Continuing research is also beginning to demonstrate that Chavín's influence was not uniform throughout the central part of the Central Andes. As more detailed information becomes available about where it had influence and how this influence was expressed, we will be better able to determine how Chavín employed a mixture of religious proselytization and other forms of influence.

The causes of Chavín's demise are as obscure as the changes in cultural patterns in the preceding and subsequent eras. Many archaeologists today consider that environmental changes, such as periods of intense El Niño events, may have had something to do with one or more of these cultural shifts. While this may be the case, there are two serious problems in relying on such theories as explanations. The first is that the identification and dating of many of the significant environmental changes that have been proposed is often quite dubious, although there are some notable exceptions. There is also a larger issue at play, in that archaeologists of the Central Andes generally do not have refined chronologies for the times that they study. This is due in part to an over-reliance on relative chronologies which are often based on ceramic seriations that have recently been dismantled, thereby also disassembling the chronologies that they supported. The case of the Moche is perhaps the most salient example of this trend.

Even major environmental changes are often hard to identify in the archaeological record, and even when they can be dated they then have to be linked to culture changes that themselves are often hard to identify and date. These concerns lead to the second problem, which is the degree to which severe environmental changes may or may not affect culture change. Although

I noted above that from a very broad perspective the patterning of the different sub-regions of the Central Andes suggests causal links between environments and cultural practices, precisely how societies fared within those broad frameworks varied greatly due to a number of factors. Human resilience is impressive, and reaction to an environmental disaster such as an earthquake or El Niño in one society in one time and place may be very different than for a different society in slightly different circumstances. When dealing with the interpretation of past human behavior *and* past environmental change through studies of material culture, geological features, and the like, the task of reaching reliable conclusions is very difficult—although it is nevertheless worth the effort because of the significant insights that can be gained into what happened in the past.

Chavín had held sway mostly in central and northern Peru, especially in the highlands, with significant connections to some parts of the coast. It had some special kind of connection, perhaps indirectly through the Jequetepeque Valley, to the South Coast. When the Chavín system fell apart, whatever the reasons, the homeland reverted to relatively simple ways followed by the chiefdoms of Recuay. Moche also seems to have reworked Chavín beliefs and practices, to the point where they took on unique forms, perhaps due to Moche's north-south relations along the coast, including into Ecuador. Furthermore, it is at this time that the southern Central Andes came into its own through a reworking of ties between the Altiplano, the southern Peruvian highlands, the South Coast, and beyond into northern Chile.

The long sequence of North Coast cultures—Salinar, Gallinazo, Moche—has recently been compressed due to the collapse of the ceramic dating system. This leaves open the question of how long these systems endured before they were strongly affected by either peaceful, aggressive, or mixed intrusions by highland peoples from Cajamarca, Huamachuco, and other regions. A better understanding of these processes will be gained when a clearer picture emerges of the political systems that were extant in "Mochelandia." While the idea of a unitary, expansionist state or states still remains in favor in some quarters, the nature of Moche politics appears to have been extremely complex and may have included different systems emerging and collapsing in very rapid succession in a complex political world where the dividing lines between religion and politics may have been impossible to separate in operation, and even harder to discern today. While contemporary scholars struggle with understanding Moche in new ways, they have made tremendous progress in understanding this ancient culture. Once known mostly through its art, we now have a much richer and deeper appreciation of how that art was linked to religious and social practices, and we are challenged in how to account for these relationships. Again, the collapse of Moche has often been blamed on periods of frequent and intense El Niño events, but in fact there may have been a set of interlinked natural and human agents involved in Moche's eventual demise.

One of the great questions of 50 years ago was the nature of Wari and Tiwanaku, particularly the relations between them and the effects that one or both had on other peoples of the Central Andes. One of the signal advances in Andean scholarship over the past five decades has been a much clearer understanding of these issues, despite a research hiatus of more than a decade due to modern political upheavals in the Wari heartland. Ironically, that research has shown Wari and Tiwanaku to be both more similar and more different than was previously imagined. Differences in religion and in the general symbolic systems and paraphernalia and arts associated with them have lessened, while at the same time distinct practices such as mortuary customs have been found to be quite different. Despite closer links between their religions and perhaps their general ideologies, their spheres of influence have been more sharply delineated with their intriguing overlap and apparently relatively peaceful coexistence in the Moquegua Valley. However, clear differences are apparent in their capital cities with Tiahuanaco's pyramids, orderly plan, and extensive sculptural tradition contrasting with the apparently unorganized compounds of Huari and its lack of public monuments. As noted in the chapter on the Middle Horizon, some of these differences may be due to language or ethnic differences that are hard to detect in the archaeological record. However, the similarities may be explained in terms of religion and élite culture that were shared between the two major centers.

While both Wari and Tiwanaku clearly had great influences across extensive regions surrounding them, it was the former that appears to have dramatically transformed the other complex cultures of the Central Andes. While Wari influence was hinted at and occasionally pinpointed in some regions of Peru half a century ago, today its influence has been confirmed in many places where it was not recognized in the past. The consequence of this is an increased pressure to determine what Wari was, but the answers to this question are not easy to tease from the archaeological record. The degree to which Wari was a political force in the way Westerners commonly think of such things is hard to assess, although it does seem that that Wari's influences consisted of a combination of different strategies and practices at various times and places, perhaps somewhat akin to Chavín.

Whatever Wari was, it seems to have dramatically reshaped the social, political, religious, and cultural landscape of the Central Andes. Although trends can be seen in earlier times, such as the depiction of lords and ladies in Recuay ceramics, Wari seems a much more human-oriented society than many previous archaeological cultures. Religion was likely the main vehicle through which life was constructed and acted out, but the Wari–Tiwanaku (SAIS) *gestalt*, as far as it can be interpreted, seems much less fearsome than that of Chavín or Moche. There is ample room for urns made in the shape of fat officials, and if the front-facing SAIS Staff God was somehow a legacy or revival of Chavín ideology, he seems to have been taught some manners; the Wari version is less fierce and snarling, more transcendent.

Architecture went horizontal. Huacas were still built in various parts of the Central Andes and the Akapana is formidable in its size and organization, but the Wari preference for compounds appears to have been widely adopted throughout much of Peru and it stayed in fashion to the time of the Incas. However, even Wari and Tiwanaku had their limits: some societies were selective in the religious tenets and other highland practices that they accepted. Although Wari's influence now seems to have been even greater and more widely spread than was previously understood, nevertheless there were other currents that shifted some societies in different directions.

In northern Peru, one of those different trends was Lambayeque or Sicán. In many ways this was a reformulation of Moche culture. Large huacas were still built, massive sacrifices were still carried out, and trade up and down the coast appears to have accelerated from previous times. The increase in trade may partly have been due to greater social stratification, in which ruling élites were able to organize both the production of valued and luxury items, such as metal tools and ornaments, and the trading systems that brought them to and from different lands. It was with the Manteño Culture in the Late Intermediate Period on the North Coast and into Ecuador that signs of long-distance trade are in clear and abundant evidence. That trade not only brought hairless dogs to Peru and metal to Mesoamericans, but it may also have brought new ideas to Peru such as pyramids with central ramps, a practice perhaps long forgotten since they were employed at places like Caral in the Late Preceramic Period or, indeed, a practice both stimulated from afar and revived from the past.

It is also quite possible that improved sailing systems or more vigorous pursuit of maritime adventures brought people from different places along the shore to new lands. The Ñyamlap legend may have a basis in fact. Be that as it may, the issue of large-scale population movements is a topic that has waxed and waned in archaeology in general. But with new methods to study such patterns through DNA studies and the analysis of isotopes that tell us much about place of birth and early childhood, we should soon be able to say much more about population movements. The highland-coastal interactions of people moving from one major zone to another appear to have formed long-term patterns that had great effects on cultural history, with movement down from the highlands seemingly more common than the reverse.

The transition from Lambayeque to Chimú is relatively unclear at present, and tales told to conquistadors hundreds of years after the fact should be interpreted with caution. The fact that Chimú leaders were fond of large compounds suggests that ideas either shared with or, more likely, came directly from Wari were important in the rise of Chimor at the apparent expense of Lambayeque. Both Lambayeque and Chimor also appear to have been stratified societies, and it is likely that sharply ranked or stratified socio-political systems were extant throughout the Andes by the Late Intermediate Period or earlier.

While the Central and Northern Central Andean regions experienced a growth in hegemonic systems over fairly large regions after the collapse of Wari and Tiwanaku, the Southern Highlands and Altiplano were plunged into a world of intense rivalries between petty kingdoms. The South Coast Late Intermediate Period is not well known despite finely constructed chronologies, but it appears that some places, such as Chincha, maintained strong regional systems, perhaps due to coastal connections including trade. This situation also seems to pertain in Ecuador, where trading systems and complex chiefdoms are common for the period. Around this time the furthest reaches of Tiwanaku influence in northwestern Argentina and northern Chile seem to have reverted back to local practices and relative isolation with regard to their northern neighbors. They may have consolidated themselves around local and regional interests and concerns.

The Southern Highlands of Peru is where the Inca rose to prominence. The Cusco Basin is not that far from and is in a chain of valley connections to the Titicaca Basin; indeed, one Inca origin myth, among several different ones, is that their ancestors came from Tiahuanaco.

Although in some ways the Inca are the best-known ancient Andean culture, much about them remains elusive. However, the multiple information sources do show us how one Andean civilization both continued old traditions and invented entirely new ones, a pattern that almost certainly reflects the way in which previous great systems were able to expand beyond their homelands.

As noted throughout this book, it is highly dubious that the Inca or any other ancient Andean society ran its government in a manner resembling modern, bureaucratic, nation-states. As also noted, for years many scholars and others have attempted to understand Andean societies from their own points of view and with their own agendas, from utopianists who saw the Inca as the ideal communist state to those who saw a dark, fascist bureaucracy exploiting conquered peoples.

The trick in studying the peoples of the ancient Andes—or any other prehistoric culture, for that matter—is to be open to understanding very different ways of doing things than the ways we know, while at the same time appreciating that there are common patterns of surviving and prospering, making a living out of the land and its resources, organizing people into communities, and religion and ideology. This is the basic goal of anthropology in its broadest sense: to compare and contrast, to note difference and sameness, and to seek explanations for why things are the way that they are in the realms of human behavior and belief.

Studies comparing how people made the transition from hunter-gatherers or fisher-foragers to agriculturalists, how they changed from relatively egalitarian societies to ones in which there were social classes, are important as part of the larger enterprise of the comparative study of peoples through time and space. The challenge is to do this in such a way that the general categories necessary to make comparisons do not overwhelm the distinctions. Those scholars who favor evolutionary models are sometimes accused of being too generalizing, while they in turn scoff at those who see what they study as unique and incomparable with any other society or culture. Anthropology has always swung between these two poles, and will likely continue to do so. It is up to the individual to find a place where he or she is most comfortable, by finding the right framework or system within which to view such phenomena.

Anthropology was the child of imperialism and colonialism, but that does not necessarily mean that its goal to seek understanding of the differences and similarities between humans though time and space is unworthy. Nevertheless, the study of the past is not the sole province of anthropological archaeology. Today, the peoples of the nation states that exist in what was once Tawantinsuyu have various agendas to do with the past, its remains, and what should be done with them. As in Europe or the United States, some wish to wipe away all but the most impressive monuments in order to make way for "progress," while others are concerned that archaeological sites are even more fragile than animal species or plants, and once destroyed they cannot be reconstituted. Sites, especially the large and important ones, can bring tourists and their money and instill national pride. In this way, archaeological remains can easily become commoditized into yet another "resource" to be used for economic development—although sadly they are sometimes over-exploited.

The case for saving archaeological sites and studying them and their contents can be made in several different ways. From a scientific perspective, studying the past can tell us about ancient human–environmental interactions and how people coped in the face of stresses, for better and worse. Perhaps we do not need archaeology to tell us that we are currently damaging our environment, but understanding how people used and abused resources in societies with much simpler technologies than the ones available to us can sometimes offer "low-tech" solutions to today's challenges; the case of Titicaca's raised fields is perhaps the easiest one to cite, but there are many others.

Knowledge for its own sake is to be treasured, and this, above all, is a reason to study the ancient Central Andes or any other subject. Columbus was right on his last voyage when he began to refer to the lands he had come across as an "Other" World. It was not a New World; it had been there all along, as rich in its complexities and subtleties as any other.

Inti Raimi, 2013
Magdalena de Cao, La Libertad, Peru

REFERENCES CITED

Adorno, Rolena (2000) *Guaman Poma: Writing and Resistance in Colonial Peru*, 2nd edn. Austin: University of Texas Press.

Albarracín-Jordán, Juan (1996) *Tiwanaku: Arqueología Regional y Dinámica Segmentaria*. La Paz, Bolivia: Editores Plural.

Albeck, María E. (1994) La Quebrada de Humahuaca en el Intercambio Prehispánico, in M. Albeck (ed.) *De Costa a Selva, Producción e Intercambio entre los Pueblos Agroalfareros de los Andes Centro Sur*. Tilcara, Argentina: Instituto Interdisciplinario Tilcara.

Aldenderfer, Mark (1998) *Montane Foragers: Asana and the South-Central Andean Archaic*. Iowa City: University of Iowa Press.

Aldenderfer, Mark, Nathan M. Craig, Robert J. Speakman, & Rachel Popelka-Filcoff (2008) Four-thousand-year-old gold artifacts from the Lake Titicaca basin, southern Peru. *Proceedings of the National Academy of Sciences of the United States of America* 105 (13): 5002–5005.

Allen, Catherine (2002) *The Hold That Life Has: Coca and Cultural Identity in an Andean Community*. Washington, D.C.: Smithsonian Books.

Alva, Walter (1986) Investigaciones en el Complejo Formativo con Arquitectura Monumental de Purulén, Costa Norte del Perú. *Beiträge Zur Allgemeinen und Vergleichenden Archäologie* 8: 283–300.

Alva, Walter & Christopher B. Donnan (1993) *The Royal Tombs of Sipán*. Los Angeles: Fowler Museum of Cultural History, University of California.

Anders, Martha (1991) Structure and Function at the Planned Site of Azángaro: Cautionary Notes for the Model of Huari as a Centralized Secular State, in William H. Isbell & Gordon F. McEwan (eds) *Huari Administrative Structure: Prehistoric Monumental Architecture and State Government*. Washington, D.C.: Dumbarton Oaks Research Library and Collection.

Andrews, Anthony P. (1974) The U-Shaped Structures at Chan Chan, Peru. *Journal of Field Archaeology* 1: 241–264.

Andrus, C. Fred T., Daniel H. Sandweiss, & Elizabeth J. Reitz (2008) Climate Change and Archaeology: The Holocene History of El Niño on the Coast of Peru, in Elizabeth J. Reitz, C. Margaret Scarry, & Sylvia J. Scudder (eds) *Case Studies in Environmental Archaeology*, 2nd edn. New York: Springer.

Arellano L., Jorge (1991) The New Cultural Contexts of Tiahuanaco, in William H. Isbell & Gordon F. McEwan (eds) *Huari Administrative Structure: Prehistoric Monumental Architecture and State Government*. Washington, D.C.: Dumbarton Oaks Research Library and Collection.

Arkush, Elizabeth (2011) *Hillforts of the Ancient Andes: Colla Warfare, Society, and Landscape*. Gainesville: University Press of Florida.

Armitage, Simon J., Sabah A. Jasim, Anthony E. Marks, Adrian G. Parker, Vitaly I. Usik & Hans-Peter Uerpmann (2011) The Southern Route "Out of Africa": Evidence for an Early Expansion of Modern Humans into Arabia. *Science* (28 January) 331 (6016): 453–456.

Arriaza, Bernardo T. (1995) *Beyond Death: The Chinchorro Mummies of Ancient Chile*. Washington, D.C.: Smithsonian Institution Press.

Aveni, Anthony F. (1990) (ed.) *The Lines of Nazca*. Philadelphia: American Philosophical Society.

——(2000) *Between the Lines: The Mystery of the Giant Ground Drawings of Ancient Nasca, Peru*. Austin: University of Texas Press.

Bandy, Matthew S. (2004) Fissioning, scalar stress, and social evolution in early village societies. *American Anthropologist* 106 (2): 322–333.

Barreto, Inés (2012) *Sacrificios Humanos en Huaca Pucllana: El Espacio Consagrado y la Muerte*. Paper presented at Arqueología y Patrimonio de la Cultura Lima. 14–16 August at the Museo de Arte de Lima (MALI), Lima, Peru.

Bauer, Brian S. (1998) *The Sacred Landscape of the Incas: The Cuzco Ceque System*. Austin: University of Texas Press.

——(2004) (ed.) *Ancient Cuzco: Heartland of the Inca*. Austin: University of Texas Press.

——(2007) (ed.) *Kasapata and the Archaic Period of the Cuzco Valley*. Cotsen Institute of Archaeology Monograph 57. Los Angeles: Cotsen Institute of Archaeology Press, University of California.

Bauer, Brian S. & R. Alan Covey (2004) The Development of the Inca State (AD 1000–1400), in Brian S. Bauer (ed.) *Ancient Cuzco: Heartland of the Inca*. Austin: University of Texas Press.

Bauer, Brian S., Lucas S. Kellett & Miriam Aráoz Silva (2010) *The Chanka: Archaeological Research in Andahuaylas (Apurimac), Peru*. Cotsen Institute of Archaeology Monograph 68. Los Angeles: Cotsen Institute of Archaeology Press, University of California.

Bauer, Brian S. & Charles Stanish (2002) *Ritual and Pilgrimage in the Ancient Andes: The Islands of the Sun and Moon*. Austin: University of Texas Press.

Bélisle, Véronique & R. Alan Covey (2010) Local Settlement Continuity and Wari Impact in Middle Horizon Cusco, in Justin Jennings (ed.) *Beyond Wari Walls: Regional Perspectives on Middle Horizon Peru*. Albuquerque: University of New Mexico Press.

Bell, Catherine (2009) *Ritual: Perspectives and Dimensions*. New York: Oxford University Press.

Benfer, Robert A. (web) http://rcp.missouri.edu/bobbenfer/index.html

——(1986) Holocene Coastal Adaptations: Changing Demography and Health at the Fog Oasis of Paloma, Peru, in Ramiro Matos Mendieta, Solveig A. Turpin & Herbert H. Eling, Jr. (eds) *Andean Archaeology*. Institute of Archaeology Monograph 27. Los Angeles: Institute of Archaeology, University of California.

——(1990) The Preceramic Period Site of Paloma, Peru: Bioindications of Improving Adaptation to Sedentism. *Latin American Antiquity* 1 (4): 284–318.

——(1999) Proyecto de Excavaciones en Paloma, Valle de Chilca, Perú, in Peter Kaulicke (ed.) El Período Arcaico en el Perú: Hacia una Definición de los Orígenes. *Boletín de Arqueología PUCP* 3: 213–237. Lima: Fondo Editorial, Pontificia Universidad Católica del Perú.

Bennett, Wendell C. (1936) Excavations in Bolivia. *Anthropological Papers of the American Museum of Natural History* 35, part 4. New York: American Museum of Natural History.

——(1948) A Reappraisal of Peruvian Archaeology. *Memoirs of the Society for American Archaeology* no. 4. Menasha, WI: published jointly by the Society for American Archaeology and the Institute of Andean Studies.

——(1953) Excavations at Huari, Ayacucho, Peru. *Yale University Publications in Archaeology* 49. New Haven.

Benson, Elizabeth P. (2012) *The Worlds of the Moche on the North Coast of Peru*. Austin: University of Texas Press.

Benzoni, Girolamo (1985 [1550]) *La Historia del Nuevo Mundo (Relatos de Su Viaje por el Ecuador, 1547–1550)*. Guayaquil: Museo Antropológico y Pinacoteca, Banco Central del Ecuador.

Beresford-Jones, David (2011) *The Lost Woodlands of Ancient Nasca: A Case-Study in Ecological and Cultural Collapse*. Oxford: Published for the British Academy by Oxford University Press.

Bergh, Susan (1993) Death and Renewal in Moche Phallic-Spouted Vessels. *RES* 24: 78–94.

Bergh, Susan E. (ed.) (2012a) *Wari: Lords of the Ancient Andes*. New York and Cleveland: Thames and Hudson and the Cleveland Museum of Art.

——(2012b) Tapestry-woven Tunics, in Susan E. Bergh (ed.) *Wari: Lords of the Ancient Andes*. New York and Cleveland: Thames and Hudson and the Cleveland Museum of Art.

——(2012c) Inlaid and Metal Ornaments, in Susan E. Bergh (ed.) *Wari: Lords of the Ancient Andes*. New York and Cleveland: Thames and Hudson and the Cleveland Museum of Art.

——(2012d) Figurines, in Susan E. Bergh (ed.) *Wari: Lords of the Ancient Andes*. New York and Cleveland: Thames and Hudson and the Cleveland Museum of Art.

——(2012e) Wood Containers and Cups, in Susan E. Bergh (ed.) *Wari: Lords of the Ancient Andes*. New York and Cleveland: Thames and Hudson and the Cleveland Museum of Art.

Berman, Marc (1994) *Lukurmata: Household Archaeology in Prehispanic Bolivia*. Princeton, NJ: Princeton University Press.

Bird, Junius B. (*ca.* 1985) personal communication.

——(1988) *Travels and Archaeology in South Chile*. Iowa City: University of Iowa Press.

Bird, Junius B. & John Hyslop (1985) The Preceramic Excavations at The Huaca Prieta Chicama Valley, Peru. *Anthropological Papers of the American Museum of Natural History* 62, part 1. New York: American Museum of Natural History.

Bischof, Henning (1994) Toward the Definition of Pre- and Early Chavín Art Styles in Peru. *Andean Past* 4: 169–228.

——(2000) Los Mates Tallados de Huaca Prieta ¿Evidencias del Arte Valdivia en el Arcaico Centroandino? in El Périodo Arcaíco en el Perú: Hacia una Definición de los Orígenes. *Boletin de Arqueología PUCP* 3: 85–120.

——(2008) Context and Contents of Early Chavín Art, in William J. Conklin & Jeffrey Quilter (eds) *Chavín: Art, Architecture and Culture*. Cotsen Institute of Archaeology Monograph 61. Los Angeles: Cotsen Institute of Archaeology Press. University of California.

Blom, Deborah E. & John W. Janusek (2004) Making Place: Humans as Dedication in Tiwanaku. *World Archaeology* 36 (1): 123–141.

Blom, Deborah E., John W. Janusek & Jane Buikstra (2003) A Re-Evaluation of Human Remains from Tiwanaku, in Alan L. Kolata (ed.) *Tiwanaku and Its Hinterland: Archaeology and Paleoecology of an Andean Civilization, volume 2: Urban and Rural Archaeology*. Washington, D.C.: Smithsonian Institution Press.

Boaretto, Elisabetta, Xiaohong Wu, Jiarong Yuan, Ofer Bar-Yosef, Vikki Chu, Yan Pan, Kexin Liu, David Cohen, Tianlong Jiao, Shuicheng Li, Haibin Gu, Paul Goldberg & Steve Weiner (2009) Radiocarbon Dating of Charcoal and Bone Collagen Associated with Early Pottery at Yuchanyan Cave, Hunan Province, China. *Proceedings of the National Academy of Sciences of the United States of America* 106 (24): 9537–9538.

Bonavia, Duccio (2009) *The South American Camelids*. Cotsen Institute of Archaeology Monograph 64. Los Angeles: Cotsen Institute of Archaeology Press, University of California.

Bonavia, Duccio & Alexander Grobman (1999) Revisión de las Pruebas de la Existéncia de Maíz Preceramico de los Andes Centrales, in Peter Kaulicke (ed.) El Periodo Arcaico en el Perú: Hacia una

Definición de los Orígenes. *Boletín de Arqueología PUCP* 3: 239–261. Lima: Fondo Editorial, Pontificia Universidad Católica del Perú.

Bonnier, Elizabeth (1997) Preceramic Architecture in the Andes: The Mito Tradition, in Elizabeth Bonnier & Henning Bischof (eds) *Archaeologica Peruana 2, Prehispanic Architecture and Civilization in the Andes*. Manhein: SAPA–Reiss Museum.

Boone, Elizabeth Hill (1996) (ed.) *Andean Art at Dumbarton Oaks* (2 volumes). Washington, D.C.: Dumbarton Oaks Research Library and Collection.

Bourget, Steve (2006) *Sex, Death, and Sacrifice in Moche Religion and Visual Culture*. Austin: University of Texas Press.

Bradley, Bruce & Dennis Stanford (2004) The North Atlantic Ice-Edge Corridor: A Possible Paleolithic Route to the New World. *World Archaeology* 36 (4): 459–478.

Braun, Robert (1982) The Formative as Seen from the Southern Ecuadorian Highlands, in Jorge G. Marcos & Presley Norton (eds) *Primer Simposio de Correlaciones Antropológicas Andino-Mesoamericano*. Guayaquil, Ecuador: Escuela Superior Politécnica del Litoral.

Bray, Tamara (2004) La Alfarería Imperial Inka: Una Comparación Entre La Cerámica Estatal del Área de Cuzco y La Cerámica de Las Provincias. *Chungará (Revista de Antropología Chilena)* 36 (2): 365–374.

——(2008) Late Prehispanic Chiefdoms of Highland Ecuador, in Helaine Silverman & William H. Isbell (eds) *Handbook of South American Archaeology*. New York: Springer.

Briceño Rosario, Jesús G. (1999) Quebrada Santa María: Las Puntas en Cola de Pescado y La Antigüedad del Hombre en Sudamérica, in Peter Kaulicke (ed.) El Periodo Arcaico en el Perú: Hacia una Definición de los Orígenes.*Boletín de Arqueología PUCP* 3: 19–39. Lima: Fondo Editorial, Pontificia Universidad Católica del Perú.

Brinkbaümer, Klaus & Clemens Höges (2006) *The Voyage of the Vizcaína: The Mystery of Columbus's Last Ship* (transl. Annette Streck). New York: Harcourt Inc.

Browman, David L. (1986) Chenopod cultivation, lacustrine resources, and fuel use at Chiripa, Bolivia. *Missouri Archaeologist* 47: 137–172.

Bruhns, Karen O. (1989) Intercambio entre la Costa y Sierra en el Formativo Tardó: Nuevas Evidencias del Azuay, in Jean-François Bouchard & Mercedes Guinea Bueno (eds) *Relaciones Interculturales en el Area Ecuatorial del Pacífico Durante la Epoca Precolombina*. BAR International Series 50. Oxford: British Archaeological Reports.

——(2003) Social and Cultural Development in the Ecuadorian Highlands and Eastern Lowlands during the Formative, in J. Scott Raymond & Richard L. Burger (eds) *Archaeology of Formative Ecuador*. Washington, D.C.: Dumbarton Oaks Research Library and Collection.

Burger, Richard L. (1985) Concluding Remarks: Early Peruvian Civilization and its Relation to the Chavin Horizon, in Christopher B. Donnan (ed.) *Early Ceremonial Architecture in the Andes*. Washington, D.C.: Dumbarton Oaks Research Library and Collection.

——(1987) The U-shaped Pyramid Complex, Cardal, Peru. *National Geographic Research* 3 (3): 363–375.

——(1992) *Chavín and the Origins of Andean Civilization*. London and New York: Thames and Hudson.

——(2003) Conclusions: Cultures of the Ecuadorian Formative in Their Andean Context, in J. Scott Raymond & Richard L. Burger (eds) *Archaeology of Formative Ecuador*. Washington, D.C.: Dumbarton Oaks Research Library and Collection.

——(2008) Chavín de Huántar and Its Sphere of Influence, in Helaine Silverman & William H. Isbell (eds) *Handbook of South American Archaeology*. New York: Springer.

——(2011) What Kind of Hallucinogenic Snuff Was Used at Chavín de Huántar? An Iconographic Identification. *Ñawpa Pacha* 31 (2): 123–140.

——(2012a) Central Andean Language Expansion and the Chavín Sphere of Interaction, in Paul Heggarty & David Beresford-Jones (eds) *Archaeology and Language in the Andes*. Proceedings of the British Academy, 173. Oxford: Published for the British Academy by Oxford University Press.

——(2012b) Comments on papers presented at Arqueologiá y Patrimonio de la Cultura Lima. 14–16 August at the Museo de Arte de Lima (MALI), Lima, Peru.

Burger, Richard L., Frank Asaro & Helen Michel (1984) The Source of the Obsidian Artifacts at Chavín de Huántar, in Richard L. Burger (ed.) *The Prehistoric Occupation of Chavín de Huántar.* Berkeley: University of California Press.

Burger, Richard L., Frank Asaro, Ernesto Salazar, Helen V. Michel & Fred H. Stross (1994) Ecuadorian Obsidian Sources Used for Artifact Production and Methods for Provenience Assignments. *Latin American Antiquity* 5 (3): 257–277.

Burger, Richard L. & Ramiro Matos Mendieta (2012) Atalla: A Center on the Periphery of the Chavín Horizon. *Latin American Antiquity* 13 (2): 153–177.

Burger, Richard L., Karen L. Mohr Chávez & Sergio J. Chávez (2000) Through the glass darkly: Prehispanic obsidian procurement and exchange in Southern Peru and Northern Bolivia. *Journal of World Prehistory* 14 (3): 267–362.

Burger, Richard L. & Lucy C. Salazar (2004) (eds) *Machu Picchu: Unveiling the Mystery of the Incas.* New Haven: Yale University Press.

——(2008) The Manchay Culture and the Coastal Inspiration for Highland Chavín Civilization, in William J. Conklin & Jeffrey Quilter (eds) *Chavín: Art, Architecture, and Culture.* Cotsen Institute of Archaeology Monograph 61. Los Angeles: Cotsen Institute, University of California.

Burger, Richard L. & Lucy Salazar-Burger (1985) The Early Ceremonial Center of Huaricoto, in Christopher B. Donnan (ed.) *Early Ceremonial Architecture in the Andes.* Washington, D.C.: Dumbarton Oaks Research Library and Collection.

——(1986) Early Organizational Diversity in the Peruvian Highlands: Huaricoto and Kotosh, in Ramiro Matos Mendieta, Solveig A. Turpin & Herbert H. Eling Jr. (eds) *Andean Archaeology, Papers in Memory of Clifford Evans.* Institute of Archaeology Monograph 27. Los Angeles: University of California.

——(1991) The Second Season of Investigations at the Initial Period Center of Cardal, Peru. *Journal of Field Archaeology* 18 (3): 275–296.

——(1993) The Place of Dual Organization in Early Andean Ceremonialism: A Comparative Review, in Luis Millones & Yoshio Onuki (eds) *El Mundo Andino.* Senri Ethnological Studies, no. 37. Osaka: National Museum of Ethnology.

Burger, Richard L., Lucy C. Salazar & Victor Vasquez (2012) *Rethinking Agricultural Staples for the Initial Period Population of the Lurin Valley: Scraping the Bottom of the Olla.* Paper presented at the Between Pachacamac and Pariacaca Symposium, 77th Annual Meeting of the Society for American Archaeology, April 20th, Memphis, TN.

Campbell, K. E. (1982) Late Pleistocene Events Along the Coastal Plain of Northwestern Peru, in Ghillean T. Prance (ed.) *Biological Diversification in the Tropics.* New York: Columbia University Press.

Canziani Amico, José (2009) *Ciudad y Territorio en Los Andes: Contribuciones a la História del Urbanismo Prehispánico.* Lima: Fondo Editorial, Pontificia Universidad Católica del Perú.

Capriles Flores, José Mariano (2011) *The Economic Organization of Early Camelid Pastoralism in the Andean Highlands of Bolivia.* Ph.D. dissertation, Department of Anthropology, Washington University in St. Louis.

Cardich, Augusto (1958) *Los Yacimientos de Lauricocha, Nuevas Interpretaciones de la Prehistoria Peruana.* Studia Praehistórica I. Centro Argentino de Estudios Prehistóricos, Buenos Aires.

——(1964) *Lauricocha: Fundamentos para una Prehistoria de los Andes Centrales.* Studia Praehistórica III. Centro Argentino de Estudios Prehistóricos, Buenos Aires.

——(1980) Origen del hombre y de la Cultura Andina. In *Perú Antiguo: Historia del Perú,* volume 1: 29–156. Lima: Editorial Mejía Baca.

Carneiro, Robert L. (1970) A Theory of the Origin of the State. *Science* (New Series) 169(3947): 733–738 (August 21, 1970).

Castillo, Luis Jaime (2001) The Last of the Mochicas: A View from the Jequetepeque Valley, in Joanne Pillsbury (ed.) *Moche Art and Archaeology in Ancient Peru*. Washington: National Gallery of Art, New Haven: Distributed by Yale University Press.

Castillo Butters, Luis Jaime (2012) Looking at the Wari Empire from the Outside, in Susan E. Bergh (ed.) *Wari: Lords of the Ancient Andes*. New York and Cleveland: Thames and Hudson and the Cleveland Museum of Art.

Castillo Butters, Luis Jaime & Jeffrey Quilter (2010) Many Moche Models: An Overview of Past and Current Theories and Research on Moche Political Organization, in Jeffrey Quilter & Luis Jaime Castillo Butters (eds) *New Perspectives on Moche Political Organization*. Washington, D.C.: Dumbarton Oaks Research Library and Collection.

Chapdelaine, Claude & Victor Pimentel (2008) Personaje de Alto Rango en San Juanito Valle del Santa, in Krzysztof Makowski (ed.) *Señores de Los Reinos De La Luna*. Lima: Banco de Crédito.

Chauchat, Claude (1988) Early hunter-gatherers on the Peruvian coast, in Richard W. Keatinge (ed.) *Peruvian Prehistory: An Overview of pre-Inca and Inca Society*. Cambridge: Cambridge University Press.

Chauchat, Claude & Jean-Paul Lacombe (1984) El Hombre de Paiján: ¿el más antiguo peruano? *Gaceta Arqueológica Andina* 11: 4–6, 12.

Chauchat, Claude, E. S. Wing, J. P. Lacombe, P. Y. Demars, S. Uceda & C. Deza (1992) *Préhistoire de la Côte Nord du Pérou; Le Paijanien de Cupisnique*. Cahiers du Quaternaire, 18. Bordeaux: CNRS-Editions, Centre Régional de Publication de Bordeaux.

Chávez, Karen L. M. (1982) Resumen de los Trabajos en Marcavalle, in I. Obert R. (compiler) *Arqueología del Cuzco*. Cuzco: Instituto Nacional del Cultura del Perú.

——(1988) The Significance of Chiripa in Lake Titicaca Basin Developments. *Expedition* (Special Issue) 30: 17–26.

Chávez, Karen L. M. & Sergio Chávez (1997) The Yaya-Mama Archaeology Project, Bolivia. *Willay* 44: 5–7.

Chávez, Sergio J. (2004) The Yaya-Mama Religious Tradition as an Antecedent of Tiwanaku, in Margaret Young-Sánchez (ed.) *Tiwanaku: Ancestors of the Inca*. Lincoln, NE: University of Nebraska Press and Denver Art Museum.

Childe, V. Gordon (1956) *Piecing Together the Past: The Interpretation of Archaeological Data*. New York: Praeger.

Cieza de León, Pedro de (1986/1553) *Crónica del Perú, Primera Parte*. 2nd edition. Lima: Pontificia Universidad Católica del Perú; Fondo Editorial: Academia National de la Historia. (1986 is the 2nd edition.)

——(1998) *The Discovery and Conquest of Peru: Chronicles of the New World Encounter*. Alexandra Parma Cook & Noble David Cook (eds). Durham, NC: Duke University Press.

Cipolla, Lisa M. (2005) Preceramic Period Settlement Patterns in the Huancané-Putina River Valley, Northern Titicaca Basin, Peru, in Charles Stanish, Amanda B. Cohen & Mark S. Alderderfer (eds) *Advances in Titicaca Basin Archaeology – 1*. Cotsen Institute of Archaeology Monograph 54. Los Angeles: Cotsen Institute of Archaeology Press, University of California.

Clarkson, Persis B. (1990) The Archaeology of the Nazca Pampa, Peru: Environmental and Cultural Parameters, in Anthony F. Aveni (ed.) *The Lines of Nazca*. Memoirs of the American Philosophical Society, 183. Philadelphia: American Philosophical Society.

Clasby, Ryan & Jorge Meneses Barata (2013) Nuevas Investigaciones en Huayurco: Resultados Iniciales de la Excavaciones de un Sitio de la Ceja de Salva de los Andes. *Arqueología y Sociedad* (Lima) 25: 303–326.

Clastres, Pierre (1987) *Society Against the State: Essays in Political Anthropology*. New York: Zone Books; Cambridge, MA: distributed by the MIT Press.

Cobo, Bernabé (1956/1653) *Obras del P. Bernabé Cobo.... Historia del Nuevo Mundo.* Biblioteca de Autores Españoles 91–92. Madrid: Ediciones Atlas.

Coe, Michael D. (1960) Archaeological Linkages with North and South America at La Victoria, Guatemala. *American Anthropologist* 62: 363–393.

Collier, Donald and John V. Murra (1943) *Survey and Excavations in Southern Ecuador.* Field Museum of Natural History Publication 528. Chicago: Field Museum of Natural History.

Conklin, William J. (1982) The Information System of the Middle Horizon Quipus, in Anthony F. Aveni and Gary Urton (eds) *Ethnoastronomy and Archaeoastronomy in the American Tropics.* Annals of the New York Academy of Sciences, 385. New York: New York Academy of Sciences.

——(1996) Structure as Meaning in Ancient Andean Textiles, in Elizabeth H. Boone (ed.) *Andean Art at Dumbarton Oaks*, Volume 2. Washington, D.C.: Dumbarton Oaks Research Library and Collection.

——(2008) The Culture of Chavín Textiles, in William J. Conklin & Jeffrey Quilter (eds) *Chavín: Art, Architecture, and Culture.* Cotsen Institute of Archaeology Monograph 61. Los Angeles: Cotsen Institute of Archaeology Press, University of California.

Conklin, William J. & Jeffrey Quilter (2008) (eds) *Chavín: Art, Architecture and Culture.* Cotsen Institute of Archaeology Monograph 61. Los Angeles: Cotsen Institute of Archaeology, University of California.

Conrad, Geoffrey W. (1981) Cultural Materialism, Split Inheritance, and the Expansion of Ancient Peruvian Empires. *American Antiquity* 46 (1): 3–26.

——(1982) The Burial Platforms of Chan Chan: Some Social and Political Implications, in Michael E. Moseley & Kent C. Day (eds) *Chan Chan: Andean Desert City.* Albuquerque: School of American Research Advance Seminar Series, University of New Mexico Press.

Cook, Anita G. (1984–1985) The Middle Horizon Ceramic Offerings from Conchopata. *Ñawpa Pacha* 22–23: 49–90.

——(1992) Stone Ancestors: Idioms of Imperial Attire and Rank Among Huari Figurines. *Latin American Antiquity* 3 (4): 341–364.

——(2001) Huari D-Shaped Structures, Sacrificial Offerings and Divine Rulership, in Elizabeth P. Benson (ed.) *Ritual Sacrifice in Ancient Peru: New Discoveries and Interpretations.* Austin: University of Texas Press.

Cooper, John M. (1949) Stimulants and Narcotics, in Julian H. Steward (ed.) *Handbook of South American Indians, Volume 5: The Comparative Ethnology of South American Indians.* Washington, D.C.: United States Government Printing Office.

Cordy-Collins, Alana (1990) Fonga Sigde, Shell Purveyor to the Chimu Kings, in Michael E. Moseley and Alana Cordy-Collins (eds) *The Northern Dynasties: Kingship and Statecraft in Chimor.* Washington, D.C.: Dumbarton Oaks Research Library and Collection.

Corr, Rachel (2009) *Ritual and Remembrance in the Ecuadorian Andes.* Tucson: University of Arizona Press.

Couture, Nicole C. (2004) Monumental Space, Courtly Style, and Elite Life at Tiwanaku, in Margaret Young-Sánchez (ed.) *Tiwanaku: Ancestors of the Inca.* Lincoln, NE: University of Nebraska Press and the Denver Art Museum.

Covey, R. Alan (2000) Inca Administration on the Far South Coast of Peru. *Latin American Antiquity* 11 (2): 119–138.

——(2003a) A Processual Study of Inca State Formation. *Journal of Anthropological Archaeology* 22: 333–357.

——(2003b) *The Vilcanota Valley (Peru): Inka State Formation and The Evolution of Imperial Strategies.* Ph.D. dissertation, Department of Anthropology, University of Michigan. Ann Arbor: University Microfilms International.

——(2009) Inca Agricultural Intensification in the Imperial Heartland and the Provinces, in Joyce Marcus & Patrick Ryan Williams (eds.) *Andean Civilization: A Tribute to Michael E. Moseley.* Cotsen

Institute of Archaeology Monograph 63. Los Angeles: Cotsen Institute of Archaeology, University of California.

Cummins, Thomas B. F. (2002) *Toasts with the Inca: Andean Abstraction and Colonial Images on Quero Vessels*. Ann Arbor: University of Michigan Press.

——(2007) Queros, Aquillas, Uncus and Chulpas: The Composition of Inka Artistic Expression and Power, in Richard L. Burger, Craig Morris & Ramiro Matos Mendieta (eds.) *Variations in the Expression of Power*. Washington, D.C.: Dumbarton Oaks Research Library and Collection.

——(2008) The Felicitous Legacy of the Lanzón, in William J. Conklin & Jeffrey Quilter (eds.) *Chavín: Art, Architecture and Culture*. Cotsen Institute of Archaeology Monograph 61. Los Angeles: Cotsen Institute of Archaeology Press, University of California.

Curatola Petrocchi, Marco & Mariusz S. Ziólkowski (2008) (eds) *Adivinación y Oráculos en el Mundo Andio.* Lima: Instituto Francés de Estudios Andinos; Fondo Editorial: Pontificia Universidad Católica del Perú.

Currie, Elizabeth J. (1995) Archaeology, Ethnohistory, and Exchange along the Coast of Ecuador. *Antiquity* 69: 511–526.

D'Altroy, Terence N. (1992) *The Incas*. Hoboken, NJ: Wiley-Blackwell.

Damp, Jonathan E. (1982) Ceramic Art and Symbolism in the Early Valdivia Community. *Journal of Latin American Lore* 8 (2): 155–178.

——(1984) Environmental Variation, Agriculture, and Settlement Processes in Coastal Ecuador (3300–1500 BC). *Current Anthropology* 25 (1): 106–111.

Damp, Jonathan E. & Deborah M. Pearsall (1994) Early Cotton from Coastal Ecuador. *Economic Botany* 48 (2): 163–165.

Damp, Jonathan E., Deborah M. Pearsall & Lawrence T. Kaplan (1981) Beans for Valdivia. *Science* 212 (4496): 811–812.

Davidson, Iain (2013) Peopling the Last New Worlds: The First Colonization of Sahul and the Americas. *Quaternary International* 285: 1–29.

De la Vega, Garcilaso (2006) *The Royal Commentaries of the Incas and General History of Peru* (ed. Karen Spalding, trans. Harold V. Livermore). Cambridge, MA: Hackett Publishing.

De Rivero, Mariano & Juan Diego de Tschudi (1851) *Antigüedades Peruanas*. Vienna: Imperial Court and State Press.

Dean, Carolyn (1999) *Inka Bodies and the Body of Christ: Corpus Christi in Colonial Cuzco, Peru*. Durham, NC: Duke University Press.

DeBoer, Warren R. (2003) Ceramic Assemblage Variability in the Formative of Ecuador and Peru, in J. Scott Raymond & Richard L. Burger (eds) *Archaeology of Formative Ecuador*. Washington, D.C.: Dumbarton Oaks Research Library and Collection.

Delgado-Espinoza, Florencio (2005) Organización Politica en la Baja Cuenca del Río Guayas, Ecuador (*ca.* 500 D.C.–Contacto Español). *Cuadernos de Investigación* 6: 255–276.

Diamond, Jared M. (1997) *Guns, Germs, and Steel: The Fates of Human Societies*. New York: W.W. Norton.

Dillehay, Tom D. (1989) *Monte Verde*, Volume 1. Washington, D.C.: Smithsonian Institution Press.

——(2008) Early Population Flows in the Western Hemisphere, in Thomas H. Holloway (ed.) *A Companion to Latin American History*. Malden, MA; Oxford: Blackwell.

——(2012) personal communication.

Dillehay, Tom D., Duccio Bonavia, Steve L. Goodbred Jr., Mario Pino, Victor Vásquez & Teresa Rosales Tham (2012) A Late Pleistocene Human Presence at Huaca Prieta, Peru, and Early Pacific Coastal Adaptations. *Quaternary Research* 77 (3): 418–423.

Dillehay, Tom D., Herbert H. Eling Jr. & Jack Rossen (2005) Preceramic Irrigation Canals in the Peruvian Andes. *Proceedings of the National Academy of Sciences of the United States of America* 102 (47): 17241–17244.

Dillehay, Tom D., Jack Rossen & Patricia J. Netherly (1997) The Nanchoc Tradition: The Beginnings of Andean Civilization. *American Scientist* 85 (1): 46–55.

Donnan, Christopher B. (1964) An Early House from Chilca, Peru. *American Antiquity* 30 (1): 137–144.

——(1978) *Moche Art of Peru*. Los Angeles: Museum of Cultural History, University of California, Los Angeles.

——(1990) An Assessment of the Validity of the Naymlap Dynasty, in Michael E. Moseley & Alana Cordy-Collins (eds) *The Northern Dynasties: Kinship and Statecraft in Chimor*. Washington, D.C.: Dumbarton Oaks Research Library and Collection.

——(1992) *Ceramics of Ancient Peru*. Los Angeles: Fowler Museum of Cultural History, University of California.

——(2003) *Moche Portraits from Ancient Peru*. Austin: University of Texas Press.

——(2009) The Moche Use of Numbers and Number Sets, in Joyce Marcus & Patrick Ryan Williams (eds) *Andean Civilization: A Tribute to Michael E. Moseley*. Cotsen Institute of Archaeology Monograph 63. Los Angeles: Cotsen Institute of Archaeology Press, University of California.

Dulanto, Jalh (2008) Between Horizons: Diverse Configurations of Society and Power in the Late Pre-Hispanic Central Andes, in Helaine Silverman & William H. Isbell (eds) *Handbook of South American Archaeology*. New York: Springer.

Duncan, Neil A., Deborah M. Pearsall & Robert A. Benfer, Jr. (2009) Gourd and Squash Artifacts Yield Starch Grains of Feasting Foods from Preceramic Peru. *Proceedings of the National Academy of Sciences of the United States of America* 106 (32): 13202–13206.

Duviols, Pierre (1973) Huari y Llacuaz, Agricultores y Pastores: Un Dualismo Prehispánico de Oposición y Complementaridad. *Revista del Museo Naional* 39: 153–192.

Dwyer, Edward Bridgeman (1971) A Chanapata Figure from Cuzco, Peru. *Ñawpa Pacha* 9: 33–40.

Dwyer, Edward B. & Jane P. Dwyer (1975) The Paracas Cemeteries: Mortuary Patterns in a Peruvian South Coastal Tradition, in Elizabeth P. Benson (ed.) *Death and the Afterlife in Pre-Columbian America*. Washington, D.C.: Dumbarton Oaks Research Library and Collection.

Eeckhout, Peter (2004) *Arqueología de la Costa Central del Perú en los Periodos Tardios*. Lima: Instituto Francés de Estudios Andinos.

Elera, Carlos (1994) El Shaman del Morro Eten: Antecedentes Arqueológicos del Shamanismo en la Costa y Sierra Norte del Perú, in Luis Millonies & Moises Lemlig (eds) *En el Nombre del Señor: Shamanes, Demonios y Curanderos del Norte del Perú*. Lima: Biblioteca Peruana de Psicoanálisis.

Elera, Gustavo (1994) Anexo No. 4; Análisis Radiográfico, Comentarios, y Resultados de los Femurs Derecho e Izquierdo del Individuo Correspondiente al Entierro 4 de la Unidad 14-D del Morro de Eten. Appendix to article by C. Elera in Luis Millonies & Moises Lemlig (eds) *En el Nombre del Señor: Shamanes, Demonios y Curanderos del Norte del Perú*. Lima: Biblioteca Peruana de Psicoanálisis.

Engel, Frédéric André (1963) A Preceramic Settlement on the Central Coast of Peru: Asia, Unit 1. *Transactions of the American Philosophical Society*, New Series, volume 53, part 3. Philadelphia: The American Philosophical Society.

——(1966) *Paracas: Cien Siglos de Cultura Peruana*. Lima: Editorial Juan Mejía Baca.

——(1969) On Early Man in the Americas. *Current Anthropology* 10 (2–3): 255.

——(1970) Exploration of the Chilca Canyon, Peru. *Current Anthropology* 11: 55–58.

——(1976) *An Ancient World Preserved: Relics and Records of Prehistory in the Andes*. New York: Crown Publishers.

——(1988) *Ecología Andina: El Hombre, Su Establecimiento, y el Ambiente de los Andes, La Vida en Tierras Áridas y Semiáridas*. Universidad Nacional Agrária del Perú. Atlantic Highlands, NJ: Humanities Press (US Distributor).

Erickson, Clark L. (1984) Waru Waru: Una Tecnología Agrícola del Altiplano Prehistórico. *Boletín del Instituto de Estudios Aymaras* 18(serie 2): 4–37.

——(1985) Applications of Prehistoric Andean Technology: Experiments in Raised Field Agriculture, Huatta, Lake Titicaca, Peru, 1981, 1983, in Ian Farrington (ed.) *Prehistoric Intensive Agriculture in the Tropics*. British Archaeological Reports, International Series No. 232. Oxford, UK.

——(1999) Agricultura en Camellones Prehispánicos en las Tierra Bajas de Bolivia: Posibilidades de Desarollo en el Trópico Húmedo, in Juan José Jiménez-Orsornio & Véronique M. Rorive (eds) *Los Camellones y Chinampas Tropicales: Memorias del Simposio-Taller Internacional Sobre Camellones y Chinampas Tropicales*. Mérida, México: Ediciones de la Universidad Autónomo de Yucatán, Mérida.

Erickson, David L., Bruce D. Smith, Andrew C. Clarke, Daniel H. Sandweiss & Noreen Tuross (2005) An Asian Origin for a 10,000-year-old domesticated plant in the Americas. *PNAS* (Proceedings of the National Academy of Sciences, December 20) 102 (51): 18315–18320.

Erlandson, Jon M., Michael H. Graham, Bruce J. Bourque, Debra Corbett, James A. Estes & Robert S. Steneck (2007) The Kelp Highway Hypothesis: Marine Ecology, the Coastal Migration Theory, and the Peopling of the Americas. *The Journal of Island and Coastal Archaeology* 2(2): 161–174.

Estévez Castillo, José (1992) Pasto Grande: Centro Productivo Tiwanaku e Inka en las Sud Yungas Bolivanas. *Gaceta Arqueológica Andina VI*, No. 21: 109–137.

Farrington, Ian S. (1983) The Design and Function of the Intervalley Canal: Comments on a Paper by Ortloff, Moseley, and Feldman. *American Antiquity* 48: 360–375.

Feldman, Robert Alan N. (1980) *Aspero, Peru: Architecture, Subsistence Economy, and Other Artifacts of a Preceramic Maritime Chiefdom*. Ph.D. dissertation. Department of Anthropology, Harvard University.

Fonseca, Z. Oscar M. (1978) South American and Mayan Cultural Contacts at the Las Huacas Site, Costa Rica. *Annals of the Carnegie Museum*, 47, article 13, 299: 317. Pittsburgh: Carnegie Museum of Natural History.

Francfort, Henri-Paul & Roberte N. Hamayon (2001) (eds) *The Concept of Shamanism: Uses and Abuses*. Budapest: Akadémiai Kiadó.

Fried, Morton H. (1967) *The Evolution of Political Society: an Essay in Political Anthropology*. New York: McGraw-Hill.

Fuchs, Peter R., Renate Patzchke, Claudia Schmitz, Germán Yenque & Jesús Briceño (2006) Investigaciones Arqueológicas en el Sitio de Sechín Bajo, Casma. *Boletín de Arqueología PUCP* No. 10: 111–135.

Fuentes S., José Luis & Diana Cahuanina (2012) *Las Pinturas Murals de Cerro Culebras: Esbozos para una Contribución a la Iconografía de los Lima*. Paper presented at Arqueología y Patrimonio de la Cultura Lima Conference, Museo de Arte de Lima (MALI), August 15.

Gálvez Mora, Cesár A. (1999) Quebrada Santa Maria: Nuevos Datos Y Problemas Sobre El Paijanesnse en el Chicama: Aportes Para una Evaluación de la Occupación Temprana en el Norte del Perú, in Peter Kaulicke (ed.) *El Periodo Arcaico en el Perú: Hacia una Definición de los Orígenes. Boletín de Arqueología PUCP* 3: 41–54. Lima, Peru: Fondo Editorial, Pontificia Universidad Católica del Perú.

Garcia, Rubén S. & José Pinilla B. (1995) Aproximación a una Secuencia de Fases con Cerámica Temprana de le Región de Paracas. *Journal of the Steward Anthropological Society* 23: 43–81.

Gasparini, Graziano & Luise Margolies (1980) *Inca Architecture* (trans. Patricia J. Lyon). Bloomington: University of Indiana Press.

Gayton, A. H. (1927) The Uhle Pottery Collections from Nievería. *University of California Publications in American Archaeology and Ethnology* 21, no. 8. Berkeley: University of California Press.

Gilbert, M. Thomas P., Dennis L. Jenkins, Anders Götherstrom, Nuria Naveran, Juan J. Sanchez, Michael Hofreiter, Philip Francis Thomsen, Jonas Binladen, Thomas F. G. Higham, Robert M. Yohe II, Robert Parr, Linda Scott Cummings & Eske Willerslev (2008) DNA from Pre-Clovis Human Coprolites in Oregon, North America. *Sciencexpress*, www.sciencexpress.org/3 April 2008.

Glowacki, Mary (2002) The Huaro Archaeological Site Complex: Rethinking the Huari Occupation of Cuzco, in William H. Isbell & Helaine Silverman (eds) *Andean Archaeology 1: Variations in Sociopolitical Organization*. New York: Kluwer Academic/Plenum Publishers.

——(2012) Shattered Ceramics and Offerings, in Susan E. Bergh (ed.) *Wari: Lords of the Ancient Andes*. New York and Cleveland: Thames and Hudson and Cleveland Museum of Art.

Goldstein, Paul (2005) *Andean Diaspora: The Tiwanaku Colonies and the Origins of South American Empire*. Gainesville: University Press of Florida.

——(2013) (March) personal communication.

Gose, Peter (2008) *Invaders as Ancestors: On the Intercultural Making and Unmaking of Spanish Colonialism in the Andes*. Toronto: University of Toronto Press.

Green, Ulrike Matthies & Paul S. Goldstein (2010) The Nature of War Presence in the Mid-Moquegua Valley: Investigation Contact at Cerro Trapiche, in Justin Jennings (ed.) *Beyond Wari Walls: Regional Perspectives on Middle Horizon Peru*. Albuquerque: University of New Mexico Press.

Greenberg, Joseph H., Christy G. Turner II & Stephen L. Zegura (1986) The Settlement of the Americas: a Comparison of the Linguistic, Dental, and Genetic Evidence. *Current Anthropology* 27 (5): 477–497.

Grieder, Terence (1978) *The Art and Archaeology of Pashash*. Austin: University of Texas Press.

Grieder, Terence, Alberto Bueno Mendoza, C. Earle Smith Jr. & Robert M. Malina (1988) *La Galgada, Peru: A Preceramic Culture in Transition*. Austin: University of Texas Press.

Grobman, Alexander, Duccio Bonavia, Tom D. Dillehay, Dolores R. Piperno, José Iriarte & Irene Hoist (2011) Preceramic Maize from Paredones and Huaca Prieta, Peru. *Proceedings of the National Academy of Sciences (PNAS) Early Edition* www.pnas.org/cgi/doi/10.1073/pnas.1120270109.

Gruhn, Ruth & Alan L. Bryan (1977) Los Tapiales Paleo-indian Campsite in Guatemalan Highlands. *Proceedings of the American Philosophical Society* 121 (3): 235–273.

Guamán Poma de Ayala, Felipe (2006) *The First New Chronicle and Good Government* (abridged; trans. and ed. David Frye). Indianapolis: Hackett Publishing Company.

Guidon, Niède & G. Delibrias (1986) Carbon-14 Dates Point to Man in the Americas 32,000 years ago. *Nature* 321: 769–771.

Guillén, Sonia & Gerardo Carpio (1999) Violencia en el Desierto: Un Entierro Arcaico en el Sitio del MAR-IPSS, Ilo, in Peter Kaulicke (ed.) El Periodo Araico en el Perú: Hacia una Definición de los Orígenes. *Boletín de Arqueología PUCP* 3: 365–373. Lima, Peru: Fondo Editorial Pontificia Universidad Católica del Perú.

Haas, Jonathan, Winifred Creamer, Luis Huamán Mesia, David Goldstein, Karl Reinhard & Cindy Vergel Rodríguez (2013) Evidence for Maize (Zea mays) in the Late Archaic (3000–1800 BC) in the Norte Chico Region of Peru. *Proceedings of the National Academy of Sciences of the United States of America* 110(13): 4945–4949.

Hadingham, Evan (1987) *Lines to the Mountain Gods: Nazca and the Mysteries of Peru*. New York: Random House.

Halpern, Jake (2012) The Secret of the Temple. *The New Yorker* 88 (11): 48–57.

Harrison, Regina (1989) *Signs, Songs, and Memory in the Andes: Translating Quechua Language and Culture*. Austin: University of Texas Press.

Hastorf, Christine (1999) Early Settlement at Chiripa, Bolivia: Research of the Taraco Archaeological Project. *Contributions of the University of California Archaeological Research Facility*, 57. Berkeley: University of California.

——(2003) Community with the ancestors: Ceremonies and social memory in the Middle Formative at Chiripa, Bolivia. *Journal of Anthropological Archaeology* 22 (4): 305–322.

——(2008) The Formative Period in the Titicaca Basin, in Helaine Silverman & William H. Isbell (eds) *Handbook of South American Archaeology*. New York: Springer.

Herring, Adam (2010) Shimmering Foundation: The Twelve-Angled Stone of Inca Cusco. *Critical Inquiry* 37 (1): 60–105.

Hey, Gillian (1984) Early Occupation on the Huillca Raccay Promontory Site, Cusichaca: The Archaeological Evidence, in E. Ann Kendall (ed.) *Current Archaeological Projects in the Central Andes*. EBAR International Series, 210. Oxford: British Archaeological Reports.

Heyerdahl, Thor (1990) *Kon-Tiki: Across the Pacific on a Raft*. New York: Simon and Schuster.

Heyerdahl, Thor, Daniel H. Sandweiss & Alfredo Narváez (1995) *Pyramids of Túcume: The Quest for Peru's Forgotten City*. New York: Thames and Hudson.

Hirth, Kenneth & Joanne Pillsbury (2013) (eds) *Merchants, Markets, and Exchange in the Pre-Columbian World*. Washington, D.C.: Dumbarton Oaks Research Library and Collection.

Hocquenghem, Anne Marie & Luisa Vetter Parodi (2005) Las Puntas y Rejas Prehispánicas de Metal en los Andes y su Continuidad hasta el Presente. *Bulletin de l'Institut Français d'Études Andines* 34 (2): 141–159.

Hosler, Dorothy (1994) *The Sounds and Colors of Power: The Metallurgical Technology of Ancient West Mexico*. Cambridge, MA: MIT Press.

Hosler, Dorothy, Heather Lechtman & Olaf Holm (1990) *Axe-Monies and Their Relatives*. Studies in Archaeology No. 30. Washington, D. C.: Dumbarton Oaks Research Library and Collection.

Hyslop, John (1984) *The Inca Road System*. New York: Academic Press.

Isbell, William H. (1984–1985) Conchopata, Ideological Innovator in Middle Horizon 1A. *Ñawpa Pacha* 22–23: 91–126.

——(1991) Architecture and Spatial Organization at Huari, in William H. Isbell & Gordon F. McEwan (eds) *Huari Administrative Structure: Prehistoric Monumental Architecture and State Government*. Washington, D.C.: Dumbarton Oaks Research Library and Collection.

——(1997) *Mummies and Mortuary Monuments: A Postprocessual Prehistory of Andean Social Organization*. Austin: University of Texas Press.

——(2008) Wari and Tiwanaku: International Identities in the Central Andean Middle Horizon, in Helaine Silverman & William H. Isbell (eds) *Handbook of South American Archaeology*. New York: Springer.

Isbell, William H. & Anita G. Cook (2002) A New Perspective on Conchopata and the Andean Middle Horizon, in Helaine Silverman & William H. Isbell (eds) *Andean Archaeology II: Art, Landscape, and Society*. New York: Kluwer Academic/Plenum.

Isbell, William H. & Patricia J. Knobloch (2006) Missing Links, Imaginary Links: Staff God Imagery in the South Andean Past, in William H. Isbell & Helaine Silverman (eds) *Andean Archaeology III: North and South*. New York: Springer.

Isbell, William H. & Antti Korpisaari (ND) *Burial in the Wari and the Tiwanaku Heartlands: Similarities, Differences, and Meanings*. Manuscript in possession of the authors.

Isbell, William H. & Gordon F. McEwan (1991) (eds) *Huari Administrative Structure: Prehistoric Monumental Architecture and State Government*. Washington, D.C.: Dumbarton Oaks Research Library and Collection.

Isbell, William H. & Helaine Silverman (2006) Rethinking the Central Andean Co-Tradition, in William H. Isbell & Helaine Silverman (eds) *Andean Archaeology III: North and South*. New York: Springer.

Isbell, William H. & Alexi Vranich (2004) Experiencing the Cities of Wari and Tiwanaku, in Helaine Silverman (ed.) *Andean Archaeology*. New York: Blackwell.

Isbell, William H. & Margaret Young-Sánchez (2012) Wari's Andean Legacy, in Susan E. Bergh (ed.) *Wari: Lords of the Ancient Andes*. New York and Cleveland: Thames and Hudson and the Cleveland Museum of Art.

Isendahl, Christian (2011) The Domestication and Early Spread of Manioc (Manihot esculenta Crantz): A Brief Synthesis. *Latin American Antiquity* 22 (4): 452–468.

Isla Cuadrado, Johny (2009) From Hunters to Regional Lords: Funerary Practices in Palpa, Peru, in Markus Reindel & Günther A. Wagner (eds) *New Technologies for Archaeology*. Berlin and Heidelberg: Springer-Verlag.

Jackson, Donald, César Méndez, Roxana Seguel, Antonio Maldonado & Gabriel Vargas (2007) Initial Occupation of the Pacific Coast of Chile during Late Pleistocene Times. *Current Anthropology* 48 (5): 725–731.

Janusek, John W., Arik T. Ohnstad & Andrew P. Roddick (2003) Khonkho Wankane and the Rise of Tiwanaiku. *Antiquity* 77 (296): http://antiquity.ac.uk/ProjGall/janusek/janusek.html.

Janusek, John Wayne (2008) *Ancient Tiwanaku.* Cambridge, UK: Cambridge University Press.

Jennings, Justin (ed.) (2010a) *Beyond Wari Walls: Regional Perspectives on Middle Horizon Peru.* Albuquerque: University of New Mexico Press.

——(2010b) *Beyond Wari Walls,* in Justin Jennings (ed.) *Beyond Wari Walls: Regional Perspectives on Middle Horizon Peru.* Albuquerque: University of New Mexico Press.

Jennings, Justin & Nathan Craig (2001) Polity Wide Analysis and Imperial Political Economy: The Relationship between Valley Political Complexity and Administrative Centers in the Wari Empire of the Central Andes. *Journal of Anthropological Archaeology* 20 (4): 479–502.

Jessup, David A. (1991) *General Trends in the Development of the Chiribaya Culture, South-Coastal Peru.* Paper presented at the annual meeting of the Society for American Archaeology, New Orleans. Available at: http://bruceowen.com/research/jessup1991-200dpi.pdf

Jiménez Borja, Arturo (1985) Pachacamac. *Boletín de Lima* 38: 40–54.

Johnson, David W., Donald A. Proulx & Stephen B. Mabee (2002) The Correlation Between Geoglyphs and Subterranean Water Resources in the Río Grande de Nazca Drainage, in Helaine Silverman & William H. Isbell (eds) *Andean Archaeology II: Art, Landscape, and Society.* New York: Kluwer Academic/Plenum Publishers.

Julien, Catherine (1988) How Inca Decimal Administration Worked. *Ethnohistory* 35 (3): 257–279.

——(2000) *Reading Inca History.* Iowa City: University of Iowa Press.

Kaulicke, Peter (1998) (ed.) *Max Uhle y El Peru Antiguo.* Lima: Pontificia Universidad Católica del Perú.

——(1999) Contribuciones Hacia La Cronologia del Périodo Arcaico en Las Punas de Junín. *Boletín de Arqueología PUCP* No. 3: 307–324.

Kaulicke, Peter, Lars Fehren-Schmitz, María Kolp-Godoy, Patricia Landa, Óscar Loyola, Martha Palma, Elsa Tomasto, Cindy Vergel & Burkhard Vogt (2009) Implicancias de un area funeraria del Periodo Formativo Tardío en el departamento de Ica. *Boletín de Arqueología PUCP* 13: 289–322.

Keefer, David K., Susan D. DeFrance, Michael E. Moseley, James B. Richardson III, Dennis R. Satterlee & Amy Day-Lewis (1998) Early Maritime Economy and El Niño Events at Quebrada Tacahuay, Peru. *Science* (18 September) 281 (5384): 1833–1835.

Kellerhals, T., S. Brütsch, M. Sigl, S. Knüsel, H. W. Gäggeler & M. Schwikowski (2010) Ammonium Concentration in Ice Cores: A New Proxy for Regional Temperature Reconstruction? *Journal of Geophysical Research* Vol 15: D16123. http://onlinelibrary.wiley.com/doi/10.1029/2009JD012603/abstract

Kellner, Corina Marie (2002) *Coping with Environmental and Social Challenges in Prehistoric Peru: Bioarchaeological Analyses of Nasca Populations.* Doctoral dissertation, Department of Anthropology, University of California, Santa Barbara.

Kellner, Corina M. & Margaret J. Schoeninger (2012) Dietary Correlates to the Development of Nasca Social Complexity (AD 1–750). *Latin American Antiquity* 23 (4): 490–508.

Kidder, Alfred II (1943) *Some Early Sites in the Northern Lake Titicaca Basin.* Papers of the Peabody Museum, Harvard University. Volume 27, No. 1. Cambridge, MA.

——(1956) Digging in the Titicaca Basin. *University Museum Bulletin* (University of Pennsylvania) 20 (2): 16–29.

King, Heidi (2012) Featherwork, in Susan E. Bergh (ed.) *Wari: Lords of the Ancient Andes.* New York and Cleveland: Thames and Hudson and Cleveland Museum of Art.

Kiracofe, James B. & John S. Marr (2008) Marching to Disaster: The Catastrophic Convergence of Inca Imperial Policy, Sand Flies, and El Niño in the 1524 Andean Epidemic, in Daniel H. Sandweiss &

Jeffrey Quilter (eds) *El Niño, Catastrophism, and Culture Change in Ancient America*. Washington, D.C.: Dumbarton Oaks Research Library and Collection.

Klink, Cynthia J. & Mark Aldenderfer (2005) A Projectile Point Chronology for the South-Central Andean Highlands, in Charles Stanish, Amanda Cohen & Mark Aldenderfer (eds.) *Advances in Titicaca Basin Archaeology – 1*. Los Angeles: Cotsen Institute, University of California.

Knobloch, Patricia J. (2012) Archives in Clay: The Styles and Stories of Wari Ceramic Artists, in Susan E. Bergh (ed.) *Wari: Lords of the Ancient Andes*. New York and Cleveland: Thames and Hudson and Cleveland Museum of Art.

Kolata, Alan (1982) Chronology and Settlement Growth at Chan Chan, in Michael E. Moseley and Kent C. Day (eds) *Chan Chan: Andean Desert City*. Albuquerque: University of New Mexico Press.

——(1991) The Technology and Organization of Agricultural Production in the Tiwanaku State. *Latin American Antiquity* 2: 99–125.

——(1993) *The Tiwanaku: Portrait of an Andean Civilization*. Cambridge, MA: Basil Blackwell.

Kolata, Alan & Charles Ortloff (1989) Thermal Analysis of Tiwanaku Raised Field Systems in the Lake Titicaca Basin of Bolivia. *Journal of Archaeological Science* 16: 233–263.

——(1993) Climate and Collapse: Agro-Ecological Perspectives on the Decline of the Tiwanaku State. *Journal of Archaeological Science* 20: 195–221.

Kosok, Paul (1965) *Life, Land and Water in Ancient Peru*. New York: Long Island University Press.

Krazanowski, Andrzej (1980) *Przedkolumbijskie osadnictwo w dorzeczu Alto Chicama, Pólnocne Peru* (Pre-Columbian Settlement patterns in the Alto Chicama Basin, Northern Peru). Doctoral Dissertation, University of Warsaw, Poland.

——(1991) Observaciones Sobre la Arquitectura y Patrón de Asentamiento de la Cultura Chancay, in Andrzej Krazanowski (ed.) *Estudios Sobre La Cultura Chancay, Perú*. Warsaw: Uniwersytet Jagiellonski.

Kroeber, Alfred (1954) Proto-Lima: A Middle Period Culture of Peru. *Anthropology* 44. Chicago: Chicago Natural History Museum.

Lamb, Simon (2006) *Devil in the Mountain: A Search for the Origin of the Andes*. Princeton, NJ: Princeton University Press.

Lambert, Patricia M., Celeste Marie Gagnon, Brian R. Billman, M. Anne Katzenberg, José Carcelén & Robert H. Tykot (2012) Bone Chemistry at Cerro Oreja: A Stable Isotope Perspective on the Development of a Regional Economy in the Moche Valley, Peru, During the Early Intermediate Period. *Latin American Antiquity* 23 (2): 144–166.

Lanning, Edward P. (1967) *Peru Before the Incas*. Englewood Cliffs, NJ: Prentice Hall.

Lanning, Edward P. & Thomas C. Patterson (1964) Changing Settlement Practices on the Central Peruvian Coast. *Ñawpa Pacha* 2: 113–124.

Lathrap, Donald W. (1970) *The Upper Amazon*. New York: Praeger.

——(1973) Gifts of the Cayman: Some Thoughts on the Subsistence Basis of Chavín, in Donald W. Lathrap & Jody L. Douglas (eds) *Variations in Anthropology: Essays in Honor of John C. McGregor*. Urbana: Illinois Archaeological Survey.

——(1977) Our Father the Cayman, Our Mother the Gourd: Spinden Revisited, or a Unitary Model for the Emergence of Agriculture in the New World, in Charles A. Reed (ed.) *Origins of Agriculture*. The Hague: Mouton.

Lathrap, Donald W., Donald Collier & Helen Chandra (1975) (eds) *Ancient Ecuador: Culture, Clay, and Creativity, 3000–300 BC*. Chicago: Field Museum of Natural History.

Lathrap, Donald W., J. G. Marcos & J. A. Zeidler (1977) Real Alto: An Ancient Ceremonial Center. *Archaeology* 30 (1): 2–13.

Lau, George F. (2011) *Andean Expressions: Art and Archaeology of the Recuay Culture*. Iowa City: University of Iowa Press.

——(2012) The First Millennium AD in North-Central Peru: Cultural Perspectives on a Linguistic Prehistory. *Proceedings of the British Academy* 173: 163–195.

Lavallée, Danièle & Michèle Julien (1983) *Asto: Curacazgo Prehispánico de los Andes Centrales.* Lima: Instituto de Estudios Peruanos.

Lavallée, Danièle, Michèle Julien & Jane Wheeler (1982) Telamarchay, Niveles Precerámicos de Occupación. *Revista del Museo Nacional* 45: 55–133.

Lavallée, Danièle, Michèle Julien, Jane Wheeler & Claudine Karlin (1985) *Telamarchay, Chasseurs et Pasteurs Préhistoriques Des Andes, I & II.* Paris: Institut Français D'Études Andines.

Lechtman, Heather (1996) Cloth and Metal: The Culture of Technology, in Elizabeth H. Boone (ed.) *Andean Art at Dumbarton Oaks*, Volume I. Washington, D.C.: Dumbarton Oaks Research Library and Collection.

Lechtman, Heather & Andrew Macfarlane (2005) La Metalúrgia del Bronce en los Andes Sur Centrales: Tiwanaku y San Pedro de Atacama. *Estudios Atacameños* 30: 7–27.

Legnani, Nicole Delia (adaptor) (2006) *Titu Cusi: A 16th Century Account of the Conquest.* Series on Latin American Studies 15. Cambridge, MA: David Rockefeller Center for Latin American Studies, Harvard University.

Leonard, Jennifer A., Robert K. Wayne, Jane Wheeler, Raúl Valadez, Sonia Guillen & Carles Vilà (2002) Old World Origin of New World Dogs. *Science* 298: 1613–1616.

Lippi, Ronald D. (2004) *Tropical Forest Archaeology in Western Pichincha, Ecuador.* Case Studies in Archaeology. Belmont, CA: Wadsworth/Thompson Learning.

Llagostera, M. A., H. R. Weisner, G. G. Castillo, G. M. Cervellino & M. A. Costa-Junqueira (2000) El Complejo Huentelauquén Bajo Una Perspectiva Macroespacial y Multidisciplinaria. *Contrubución Arqueológica* 5 (1): 461–482.

Lumbreras, Luis G. (1970) *Los Templos de Chavín.* Lima: Corporación Peruana de Santa.

——(1974a) *La Arqueología Como Ciencia Social.* Lima: Ediciones Histar.

——(1974b) *The Peoples and Cultures of Ancient Peru* (transl. Betty J. Meggers). Washington, D.C.: Smithsonian Institution Press.

——(1993) *Chavín de Huántar: Excavaciones en la Galeria de la Ofrendas.* Materialien zur Allgemeinen und Verglesichenden Archäologie Band 51. Mainz am Rhein: Verlag Philipp von Zabern GmbH.

Lynch, Thomas F. (1980) *Guitarrero Cave: Early Man in the Andes.* New York: Academic Press.

Maasch, Kirk Allen (2008) El Niño and Interannual Variability of Climate in the Western Hemisphere, in Daniel H. Sandweiss & Jeffrey Quilter (eds) *El Niño, Catastrophism, and Culture Change in Ancient America.* Washington, D.C.: Dumbarton Oaks Research Library and Collection.

MacCormack, Sabine (1993) *Religion in the Andes: Vision and Imagination in Early Colonial Peru.* Princeton, NJ: Princeton University Press.

McEwan, Colin & Florencio Delgado-Espinoza (2008) Late Pre-Hispanic Polities of Coastal Ecuador, in Helaine Silverman & William H. Isbell (eds) *Handbook of South American Archaeology.* New York: Springer.

McEwan, Gordon F. (1987) *The Middle Horizon in the Valley of Cuzco, Peru: The Impact of Wari Occupation on the Lucre Basin.* Austin: University of Texas Press.

——(1990) Some Formal Correspondences Between the Imperial Architecture of the Wari and Chimu Cultures of Ancient Peru. *Latin American Antiquity* 1(2): 97–116.

——(ed.) (2005) *Pikillacta: The Wari Empire in Cuzco.* Iowa City: University of Iowa Press.

——(2006) *The Incas: New Perspectives.* New York: W. W. Norton.

McEwan, Gordon F., Melissa Chatfield & Arminda Gibaja (2002) The Archaeology of Inca Origins: Excavations at Chokepukio, Cuzco, Peru, in William H. Isbell & Helaine Silverman (eds) *Andean Archaeology I: Variations in Sociopolitical Organization.* New York: Kluwer Academic/Plenum.

McEwan, Gordon F. & Patrick Ryan Williams (2012) The Wari Built Environment: Landscape and Architecture of Empire, in Susan E. Bergh (ed.) *Wari: Lords of the Ancient Andes*. New York and Cleveland: Thames and Hudson and the Cleveland Museum of Art.

Mackey, Carol J. & Ulana Klymyshyn (1990) The Southern Frontier of the Chimu Empire, in Michael E. Moseley and Alana Cordy-Collins (eds) *The Northern Dynasties: Kinship and Statecraft in Chimor*. Washington, D.C.: Dumbarton Oaks Research Library and Collection.

MacNeish, Richard S., R. K. Vierra, A. Nelkin-Terner, R. Lurie & A. García Cook (1983) *Prehistory of the Ayacucho Basin, Peru, Volume IV: The Preceramic Way of Life*. Ann Arbor: The University of Michigan Press.

MacQuarrie, Kim (2008) *The Last Days of the Incas*. New York: Simon and Schuster.

Makowski, Krzystof & Alain Vallenas (2012) *El Inicio de la Occupación Lima en Pachacamac: Templo Viejo y Templo del Sol*. Paper presented at Arqueologia y Patrimonio de la Cultura Lima, 14–16 August at the Museo de Arte de Lima (MALI), Lima, Peru.

Malpass, Michael A. (ed.) (1993) *Provincial Inca: Archaeological and Ethnohistorical Assessment of the Impact of the Inca State*. Iowa City: University of Iowa Press.

Maquera, Erik (2012) *Complejo Arqueológico Catalina Huanca, Un Asentamiento de la Sociedad Lima de Horizonte Medio*. Conference paper presented at Arqueología y Patrimonio de la Cultura Lima, Museum of Art of Lima, July 16.

Marcos, Jorge G. (2003) A Reassessment of the Ecuadorian Formative, in J. Scott Raymond & Richard L. Burger (eds) *Archaeology of Formative Ecuador*. Washington, D.C.: Dumbarton Oaks Research Library and Collection.

Marcus, Joyce (1987) *Late Intermediate Occupation at Cerro Azul, Peru: A Preliminary Report*. Technical Report 20. Ann Arbor: University of Michigan Museum.

Martin, Paul (1984) Prehistoric Overkill: The Global Model, in Paul S. Martin & Richard G. Klein (eds) *Quaternary Extinctions*. Tucson: University of Arizona Press.

Matos M., Ramiro (1975) Prehistoria y Ecología en Las Punas de Junín. *Revista del Museo Nacional* 41: 37–74.

Matsumoto, Yuichi (2012) Personal communication.

Mayer, Eugen F. (1992) *Armas y Herramientas de Metal Prehispánicas en Ecuador*. Mainz am Rhein: Verlag Philipp von Zabern.

——(1998) *Armas y Herramientas de Metal Prehispánicas en Perú*. Mainz am Rhein: Verlag Philipp vo Zabern.

Meddens, Frank M. (1989) Implications of Camelid Management and Textile Production for Huari, in R. Michael Czwarno, Frank M. Meddens & Alexandra Morgan (eds) *The Nature of Wari: A Reappraisal of the Middle Horizon Period in Peru*. BAR International Series 525. Oxford: British Archaeological Reports.

Meggers, Betty J. (1981) La Reconstrucción de la Prehistoria Amazónica. *Amazonía Peruana* III, 7: 15–30.

Megoni Goñalons, Guillermo L. & Hugo D. Yacobaccio (2006) The Domestication of South American Camelids: A View from the South-Central Andes, in Melinda A. Zeder, D. G. Bradley, E. Emshwiller, & B. D. Smith (eds) *Documenting Domestication: New Genetic and Archaeological Paradigms*. Berkeley: University of California Press.

Meighan, Clement W. & D. L. True (eds) (1980) *Prehistoric Trails of Atacama: Archaeology of Northern Chile*. Los Angeles: Institute of Archaeology, University of California.

Mejía Xesspe, Toribio (1950) Historia del Descubrimiento de la Cultura Paracas. El Más Importante Hallazgo Arqueológico de los Últimos Años. *El Comercio* (Lima) 26 July.

Mellars, Paul, Katie Boyle, Ofer Bar-Yosef & Chris Stringer (eds) (2007) *Rethinking the Human Revolution: New Behavioural and Biological Perspectives on the Origins and Dispersal of Modern Humans*. Cambridge: McDonald Institute for Archaeological Research.

Meltzer, David J. (2009) *First Peoples in a New World: Colonizing Ice Age America*. Berkeley: University of California Press.

Menzel, Dorothy (1964) Style and Time in the Middle Horizon. *Ñawpa Pacha* 2: 1–106.

——(1968) New Data on the Huari Empire in Middle Horizon Epoch 2A. *Ñawpa Pacha* 6: 47–114.

——(1977) *The Archaeology of Ancient Peru and the Work of Max Uhle*. Robert H. Lowie. Berkeley: Robert H. Lowie Museum of Anthropology, University of California.

Menzel, Dorothy, John H. Rowe & Lawrence E. Dawson (1964) *The Paracas Pottery of Ica: A Study In Style and Time*. University of California Publications in American Archaeology and Ethnology, 50. Berkeley: University of California Press.

Mester, Ann M. (1985) Un Taller Manteño de Madre Perla del Sitio Las Frailes, Manabei, Ecuador. *Antropológica Ecuatoriana* 5: 101–111. Boletín del Museos del Banco Central del Ecuador, Quito.

Millaire, Jean-François (2010) Primary State Formation in the Virú Valley, North Coast of Peru. *Proceedings of the National Academy of Sciences of the United States of America* 107 (14): 6186–6191.

Miller, George R. & Richard L. Burger (1995) Our Father the Cayman, our Dinner the Llama: Animal Utilization at Chavín de Huántar, Peru. *American Antiquity* 60 (3): 421–458.

Miller, George R. & Anne L. Gill (1990) Zooarchaeology at Pirincay, a Formative Period Site in Highland Ecuador. *Journal of Field Archaeology* 17 (1): 49–68.

Miotti, Laura (1999) Pedra Museo (Santa Cruz): Nuevos Datos Para el Debate de la Ocupación Pleistocénica, in J. Gómez Otero (ed.) *Arqueología Sólo Patagonia*. Puerto Madryn: Centro Nacional Patagónico.

Miotti, Laura L. & Mónica C. Salemme (2004) Poblamiento, Movilidad y Territorios entre las Sociedades Cazadoras-recolectoras de Patagonia. *Complutum* 15: 177–206.

Moore, Jerry D. (1992) Pattern and Meaning in Prehistoric Peruvian Architecture: The Architecture of Social Control in the Chimu State. *Latin American Antiquity* 3 (2): 95–113.

Moore, Jerry D. & Carol J. Mackey (2008) The Chimú Empire, in Helaine Silverman and William H. Isbell, (eds) *Handbook of South American Archaeology*. New York: Springer.

Morales Chocano, Daniel (1998) Chambira: Una Cultura de Sabana Árida en la Amazonía Peruana. *Investigaciones Sociales* 2 (2): 61–75.

Morris, Craig & Adriana von Hagen (2012) *The Incas*. New York: Thames and Hudson.

Moseley, Michael E. (1975) *The Maritime Foundations of Andean Civilization*. Menlo Park, CA: Cummings Press.

——(1992) *The Incas and Their Ancestors: The Archaeology of Peru*. New York: Thames and Hudson.

Moseley, Michael E. & Alana Cordy-Collins (eds) (1990) *The Northern Dynasties: Kinship and Statecraft in Chimor*. Washington, D.C.: Dumbarton Oaks Research Library and Collection.

Moseley, Michael E. & Kent C. Day (1982) *Chan Chan: Andean Desert City*. SAR Advanced Seminar Series. Albuquerque: University of New Mexico Press.

Moseley, Michael E., Donna J. Nash, Patrick Ryan Williams, Susan D. DeFrance, Ana Miranda & Mario Ruales (2005) Burning Down the Brewery: Establishing and Evacuating and Ancient Imperial Colony at Cerro Baul, Peru. *Proceedings of the National Academy of Sciences* 102 (48): 17264–17271.

Moseley, Michael E. & Luis Watanabe (1974) The Adobe Sculpture of Huaca de los Reyes. *Archaeology* 27: 154–161.

Mujica Barreda, Elias (2007) *Huaca Cao, Centro Ceremonial Moche en el Valle de Chicama/Huaca Cao, A Moche Ceremonial Center in the Chicama Valley*. Lima: Fundación Wiese.

Murra, John V. (1962) Cloth and Its Functions in the Inca State. *American Anthropologist* 64: 717–722.

——(1972) El "Control Vertical" de un Máximo de Pisos Ecológicos en la Economia de las Sociedades Andinas, in John V. Murra (ed) *Visita de la Provincia de León de Huánuco 1562*. Huánuco: Universidad Hermillio Valdizán.

Murúa, Martín de (1987) Historia General del Perú in Manuel Ballesteros (ed.) *Crónicas de América*, 35. Madrid: Historia 16.

Nash, Donna (2012) The Art of Feasting: Building an Empire with Food and Drink, in Susan E. Bergh (ed.) *Wari: Lords of the Ancient Andes*. New York and Cleveland: Thames and Hudson and the Cleveland Museum of Art.

Nash, Donna & Patrick Ryan Williams (2005) *Architecture and Power on the Wari-Tiwanaku Frontier*. Archaeological Papers of the American Anthropological Association 14.

——(2009) Wari Political Organization on the Southern Periphery, in Joyce Marcus & Patrick Ryan Williams (eds) *Andean Civilization: A Tribute to Michael E. Moseley*. Cotsen Institute of Archaeology Monograph 63. Los Angeles: University of California.

Nesbitt, Jason S. (2012) *Excavations at Caballo Muerto: An Investigation into the Origins of the Cupisnique Culture*. Doctoral Dissertation, Department of Anthropology, Yale University.

Niles, Susan A. (1987) *Callachaca: Style and Status in an Inca Community*. Iowa City: University of Iowa Press.

——(1999) *The Shape of Inca History: Narrative and Architect in an Andean Empire*. Iowa City: University of Iowa Press.

——(2004) The Nature of Inca Royal Estates, in Richard L. Burger and Lucy C. Salazar (eds) *Machu Picchu: Unveiling the Mystery of the Incas*. New Haven: Yale University Press.

Núñez, Lautaro, Rodolfo Casamiquela, Carolina Villagrán & Juan Varela (1994) Reconstrucción Multidisciplinaria de la Ocupación Prehistórica de Quereo, Centro de Chile. *Latin American Antiquity* 5(2): 99–118.

O'Connell, James F. & Jim Allen (2004) Dating the Colonization of Sahul (Pleistocene Australia-New Guinea): A Review of Recent Research. *Journal of Archaeological Science* 31 (6): 835–853.

Orefici, Giuseppe (1992) *Nasca: Archeologia per una Ricostruzione Storica*. Milan, Italy: Jaca Book.

Orefici, Giuseppe & Andrea Drusini (2003) *Nasca: Hipótesis y Evidencias de su Desarrollo Cultural*. Brescia, Italy: Centro Italiano Studi E Ricerche Archeologiche Precolombiane.

Ortloff, Charles R., Michael E. Moseley & Robert A. Feldman (1982) Hydraulic Engineering Aspects of the Chimu Chicama-Moche Intervalley Canal. *American Antiquity* 47 (3): 572–595.

——(1983) The Chicama-Moche Intervalley Canal: Social Implications and Physical Paradigms. *American Antiquity* 48 (2): 375–389.

Ossa, Paul P. & Michael E. Moseley (1971) La Cumbre: A Preliminary Report on Research into the Early Lithic Occupation of the Moche Valley, Peru. *Ñawpa Pacha* 9: 1–16.

Owen, Bruce (2012) Personal communication.

Oyuela-Caycedo, Augusto & Renée M. Bonzani (2005) *San Jacinto 1: A Historical Ecological Approach to an Archaic Site in Colombia*. Tuscaloosa: University of Alabama Press.

Parsons, Jeffrey R., Charles Hastings & Ramiro Matos (2000) *Prehistoric Settlement Patterns in the Upper Mantaro and Tarma Drainages, Junín, Peru, Volume 1*. Memoir No. 34. Ann Arbor: The University of Michigan Museum of Anthropology.

Parsons, Lee A. (1980) *Pre-Columbian Art: The Morton D. May and the Saint Louis Art Museum Collections*. New York: Harper and Row.

Pasztory, Esther (1998) *Pre-Columbian Art*. New York: Cambridge University Press.

Patterson, Thomas C. (1966) Pattern and Process in the Early Intermediate Period Pottery of the Central Coast of Peru. *University of California Publications in Anthropology*, volume 3. Berkeley and Los Angeles: University of California.

——(1971) The Emergence of Food Production in Central Peru, in Stuart Struever (ed.) *Prehistoric Agriculture*. Garden City, NY: Natural History Press.

——(1973) *America's Past: A New World Archaeology*. Glenview, CA: Scott-Foresman and Co.

——(1985) The Huaca La Florida, Rimac Valley, Peru, in Christopher B. Donnan (ed.) *Early Ceremonial Architecture in the Andes*. Washington, D.C.: Dumbarton Oaks Research Library and Collection.

——(1991) *The Inca Empire: The Formation and Disintegration of a Pre-Capitalist State*. New York: Berg.

Paul, Anne (2008) *Paracas Art and Architecture: Object and Context in South Coastal Peru*. Iowa City: University of Iowa Press.

Paulsen, Allison C. (1974) The Thorny Oyster and the Voice of God: Spondylus and Strombus in Andean Prehistory. *American Antiquity* 39 (4): 597–607.

Paunero, Rafael S., Ariel D. Frank, Fabiana Skarbun, Gabriela Rosales, Manuel Cueto, Gonzalo Zapata, Matías Paunero, Natalia Lunazzi & Martín Del Giorgio (2007) Investigaciones Arqueológicas en Sitio Casa del Minero 1, Estancia La María, Meseta Central de Santa Cruz, in Flavia Morello, Mateo Martinic, Alfredo Prieto & Gabriel Bahamonde (eds) *Arqueología de Fuego-Patagonia. Levantando Piedras, desenterrando huesos... y develando arcanos*. Punta Arenas, Chile: Ediciones CEQUA.

Pearsall, Deborah M. (1992) The Origins of Plant Cultivation in South America, in Wesley Cowan & Patty Jo Watson (eds) *The Origins of Agriculture: An International Perspective*. Washington, D.C.: Smithsonian Institution Press.

——(2003) Plant food resources of the Ecuadorian Formative: an overview and comparison to the Central Andes, in J. Scott Raymond & Richard L. Burger (eds) *Archaeology of Formative Ecuador*. Washington, D.C.: Dumbarton Oaks Research Library and Collection.

——(2004) *Plants and People in Ancient Ecuador: The Ethnobotany of the Jama River Valley*. Case Studies in Archaeology. Belmont, CA: Wadsworth/Thompson Learning.

Pearsall, Deborah M. & Dolores R. Piperno (1990) Antiquity of Maize Cultivation in Ecuador: Summary and Revaluation of the Evidence. *American Antiquity* 55 (2): 324–337.

Peters, Ann H. (1997) *Paracas, Topará, and Early Nasca: Ethnicity and Society on the South Coast Central Andean Coast*. Ph.D. dissertation. Department of Anthropology, Cornell University.

——(2010) Paracas: Liderazgo Social, Memoria Histórica, y lo Sagrado en el Necrópolis de Wari Kayán, in Krzysztof Makowski (compiler) *Señores de los Imperios del Sol*. Lima: Banco de Crédito.

Pillsbury, Joanne (1996) The Thorny Oyster and the Origins of Empire: Implications of Recently Discovered Spondylus Imagery from Chan Chan, Peru. *Latin American Antiquity* 7 (4): 313–340.

——(ed.) (2001) *Moche Art and Archaeology in Ancient Peru*. Washington, D.C.: National Gallery of Art.

——(ed.) (2008) *Guide to Documentary Sources for Andean Studies, 1530–1900* (3 volumes). Norman, OK: University of Oklahoma Press.

Pillsbury, Joanne & Banks Leonard (2004) Identifying Chimú Palaces: Elite Residential Architecture in the Late Intermediate Period, in Susan Toby Evans & Joanne Pillsbury (eds) *Palaces of the Ancient New World*. Washington, D.C.: Dumbarton Oaks Research Library and Collection.

Piperno, Dolores R. & Karen E. Stothert (2003) Phytolith Evidence for Early Holocene Cucurbita Domestication in Southwest Ecuador. *Science* 299 (5609): 1054–1057.

Platt, Tristan (1986) Mirrors and Maize: The Concept of Yanantin Among the Macha of Boliva, in John V. Murra, Nathan Wachtel & Jacques Revel (eds) *Anthropological History of Andean Polities*. Cambridge, UK; New York: Cambridge University Press; Paris: Editions de la Maison des sciences de l'homme.

Poma de Ayala, Guaman (2006/1600–1616) *The First New Chronicle and Good Government (Abridged)*. Indianapolis, IN: Hackett Publishing Company.

Posnansky, Arthur (1945) *Tihuanacu: The Cradle of American Man: Tihuanacu: La Cuna del Hombre Americano*. 4 volumes in 2. New York: J.J. Augustín.

Pozorski, Shelia & Thomas G. Pozorski (1987) *Early Settlement and Subsistence in the Casma Valley, Peru*. Iowa City: University of Iowa Press.

——(2011) The Square-Room Unit as an Emblem of Power and Authority within the Initial Period Sechín Alto Polity, Casma Valley, Peru. *Latin American Antiquity* 22 (4): 427–451.

Pozorski, Thomas G. (1980) The Early Horizon Site of Huaca de los Reyes: Societal Implications. *American Antiquity* 45 (1): 100–110.

Pozorski, Thomas G. & Shelia Pozorski (1987) Chavin, the Early Horizon, and the Initial Period, in Jonathan Haas, Shelia Pozorski & Thomas Pozorski (eds) *The Origins and Development of the Andean State*. Cambridge, UK; New York: Cambridge University Press.

Prescott, William H. (1843) *History of the Conquest of Mexico, with a Preliminary View of the Ancient Mexican Civilization and the Life of the Conqueror, Hernando Cortés*. New York: Harper and Brothers.

——(1847) *History of the Conquest of Peru, with a Preliminary View of the Civilization of the Incas*. New York: Harper and Brothers.

Prieto, Gabriel (2012) (November) Personal communication.

Prieto, Gabriel, Nicolas Goepfert & Katya Valladares (in press) Sacrificios de Niños, Adolescentes y Camélidos Jóvenes durante el Intermedio Tardío en la periferia de Chan Chan, valle de Moche, costa norte del Perú. *Arqueologia y Sociedad*, 26. Lima.

Pringle, Heather (2013) *First Unlooted Royal Tomb of Its Kind Unearthed in Peru*. http://news.nationalgeographic.com/news/2013/06/130627-peru-archaeology-wari-south-america-human-sacrifice-royal-ancient-world/. Published on June 27, 2013.

Protzen, Jean Pierre (1985) Inca Quarrying and Stone Cutting. *Ñawpa Pacha* 21: 183–214.

——(1986) Inca Stonemasonry. *Scientific American* 254 (2): 94–105.

——(1993) *Inca Architecture and Construction at Ollantaytambo*. New York: Oxford University Press.

Proulx, Donald A. (2008) Paracas and Nasca: Regional Cultures on the South Coast of Peru, in Helaine Silverman and William H. Isbell (eds) *Handbook of South American Archaeology*. New York: Springer.

——(2010) Curacas y Guerreros en la Costa sur del Perú, in Krzysztof Makowski (compiler) *Señores de Los Imperios Del Sol*. Lima: Banco de Crédito. Proyecto Arqueológico Sechín Bajo Casma, Peru 2008 Web http://www.restaurierung-am-oberbaum.de/index.php?article_id=158

Pulgar Vidal, Javier (1987) *Geografía del Perú: Las Ocho Regiones Naturales, La Regionalización Transversal, La Microregionalización*. 9th edition. Lima: PEISA.

Quilter, Jeffrey (1985) Architecture and Chronology at El Paraíso, Peru. *Journal of Field Archaeology* 12 (3): 279–297.

——(1986) Cerro de Media Luna: an Early Intermediate Period Site in the Chillón Valley, Peru. *Ñawpa Pacha* 24: 73–98.

——(1989) *Life and Death At Paloma: Mortuary Practices and Social Organization in a Preceramic Peruvian Village*. University of Iowa Press, Iowa City.

——(1990) The Moche Revolt of the Objects. *Latin American Antiquity* 1 (1): 42–65.

——(1991) Late Preceramic Peru. *Journal of World Prehistory* 5 (4): 387–438.

——(1992) To Fish in the Afternoon: Beyond Subsistence Economies in the Study of Early Andean Civilization. *Andean Past* 3: 111–125.

——(2008) Art and Moche Martial Arts, in Steve Bourget & Kimberly L. Jones (eds) *The Art and Archaeology of the Moche: An Ancient Andean Society of the Peruvian North Coast*. Austin: University of Texas Press.

——(2009) Art and Moche Martial Arts, in Steve Bourget & Kimberly L. Jones (eds) *The Art and Archaeology of the Moche: An Ancient Andean Society of the Peruvian North Coast*. Austin: University of Texas Press.

——(2011) *The Moche of Ancient Peru: Media and Messages*. Cambridge, MA: Peabody Museum Press.

——(2012) The Staff God: Icon and Image in Andean Art, in Linea Sundstrom & Warren DeBoer (eds) *Enduring Motives: The Archaeology of Tradition and Religion in Native America*. Tuscaloosa: University of Alabama Press.

Quilter, Jeffrey & Michele L. Koons (2012) The Fall of the Moche: A Critique of Claims for South America's First State. *Latin American Antiquity* 23 (2): 127–143.

Quilter, Jeffrey, Bernadino Ojeda, Deborah M. Pearsall, Daniel H. Sandweiss, Elizabeth Wing & John Jones (1991) Subsistence Economy of El-Paraíso, An Early Peruvian Site. *Science* 251 (4991): 277–283.

Quilter, Jeffrey & Gary Urton (eds) (2002) *Narrative Threads: Accounting and Recounting in Andean Khipu*. Austin: University of Texas Press.

Quilter, Jeffrey, Mark Zender, Karen Spalding, Régulo Franco J., Cesar Gálvez M. & Juan Castañeda M. (2010) Traces of a Lost Language and Number System Discovered on the North Coast of Peru. *American Anthropologist* 112 (3): 357–369.

Rademaker, Kurt, Gordon R. M. Bromley & Daniel H. Sandweiss (in press) Peru Archaeological Radiocarbon Database, 13,000–7000 14C BP. *Quaternary International*. (www.elsevier.com/locate/quaint).

Rademaker, Kurt, David A. Reid & Gordon R. M. Bromley (2012) Connecting the Dots: Least Cost Analysis, Paleogeography, and the Search for Paleoindian Sites in Southern Highland Peru, in Devin A. White & Sarah L. Surface-Evans (eds) *Least Cost Analysis of Social Landscapes: Archaeological Case Studies*. Salt Lake City: University of Utah Press.

Ramírez, Susan E. (1990) The Inca Conquest of the North Coast: A Historian's View, in Michael E. Moseley & Alana Cordy-Collins (eds) *The Northern Dynasties: Kinship and Statecraft in Chimor*. Washington, D.C.: Dumbarton Oaks Research Library and Collection.

——(2007) *To Feed and Be Fed: The Cosmological Bases of Authority and Identity in the Andes*. Palo Alto, CA: Stanford University Press.

Ranere, Anthony J. & Richard G. Cooke (1991) Paleoindian Occupation in the Central American Tropics, in Robson Bonnichsen & Karen L. Turnmire (eds) *Clovis: Origins and Adaptations*. Corvallis, Oregon: Center for the Study of the First Americans.

Ravines, Rogger (1985) Early Monumental Architecture of the Jequetepeque Valley, in Christopher B. Donnan (ed.) *Early Ceremonial Architecture in the Andes*. Washington, D.C.: Dumbarton Oaks Research Library and Collection.

Raymond, J. Scott (2003) Social Formations in the Western Lowlands of Ecuador during the Early Formative, in J. Scott Raymond & Richard L. Burger (eds) *Archaeology of Formative Ecuador*. Washington, D.C.: Dumbarton Oaks Research Library and Collection.

Redfield, Robert (1956) *The Little Community and Peasant Society and Culture*. Chicago: University of Chicago Press.

Reich, David, N. Patterson, D. Campbell, A. Tandon, S. Mazieres, N. Ray, M. V. Parra, W. Rojas, C. Duque, N. Mesa, L. F. Garcia, O. Triana, S. Blair, A. Maestre, J. C. Dib, C. M. Bravi, G. Bailliet, D. Corach, T. Hunemeier, M. C. Bortolini, F. M. Salzano, M. L. Petzl-Erler, V. Acuna-Alonzo, C. Aguilar-Salinas, S. Canizales-Quinteros, T. Tusie-Luna, L. Riba, M. Rodriguez-Cruz, M. Lopez-Alarcon, R. Coral-Vazquez, T. Canto-Cetina, I. Silva-Zolezzi, J. C. Fernandez-Lopez, A. V. Contreras, G. Jimenez-Sanchez, M. J. Gomez-Vazquez, J. Molina, A. Carracedo, A. Salas, C. Gallo, G. Poletti, D. B. Witonsky, G. Alkorta-Aranburu, R. I. Sukernik, L. Osipova, S. A. Fedorova, R. Vasquez, M. Villena, C. Moreau, R. Barrantes, D. Pauls, L. Excoffier, G. Bedoya, F. Rothhammer, J.-M. Dugoujon, G. Larrouy, W. Klitz, D. Labuda, J. Kidd, K. Kidd, A. Di Rienzo, N. B. Freimer, A. L. Price & A. Ruiz-Linares (2012) Reconstructing Native American Population history. *Nature (Online)*: doi.10.1038/doi:10.1038/nature11258.

Reiche, Maria (1968) *Mystery in the Desert*. Stuttgart: Eigenerlag.

Reindel, Markus (2009) Life at the Edge of the Desert – Archaeological Reconstruction of the Settlement History in the Valleys of Palpa, Peru, in Markus Reindel & Günther A. Wagner (eds) *New Technologies for Archaeology: Multidisciplinary Investigations in Palpa and Nasca, Peru*. Natural Science in Archaeology. Berlin: Springer-Verlag.

Reinhard, Johan & María Constanza Ceruti (2010) *Inca Rituals and Sacred Mountains: A Study of the World's Highest Archaeological Sites*. Cotsen Institute of Archaeology Monograph 67. Los Angeles: Cotsen Institute of Archaeology Press, University of California.

Reinoso Hermida, Gustavo (1973) Punín and Chalán. *Revista de Antropología (Cuenca)* 4: 130–175.

Reiss, Wilhelm & Althons Stübel (1880–1887) *The Necropolis of Ancón in Peru*, 3 volumes. Berlin: A. Asher & Co.

Richardson, James B. (1978) Early Man on the Peruvian North Coast, Early Maritime Exploitation and the Pleistocene and Holocene Environment, in Alan L. Bryan (ed.) *Early Man in America from a Circum-Pacific Perspective*. Occasional Papers of the Department of Anthropology, University of Alberta, 1. Edmonton: Archaeological Researches International.

——(1981) Modeling the Development of Sedentary Maritime Economies on the Coast of Peru: A preliminary statement. *Annals of the Carnegie Museum* 50: 139–150.

Richardson III, James B. (1994) *People of the Andes*. Washington, D.C.: Smithsonian Books.

Richardson III, James B. & Daniel H. Sandweiss (2008) Climate Change, El Niño, and the Rise of Complex Society on the Peruvian Coast During the Middle Holocene, in Daniel H. Sandweiss & Jeffrey Quilter (eds) *El Niño, Catastrophism, and Culture Change in Ancient America*. Washington, D.C.: Dumbarton Oaks Research Library and Collection.

Rick, John W. (1980) *Prehistoric Hunters of the High Andes*. New York: Academic Press.

——(2004) The Evolution of Authority and Power at Chavín de Huántar, Peru, in Kevin J. Vaughn, Dennis Ogburn & Christina A. Conlee (eds) *Foundations of Power in the Prehispanic Andes*. Archaeological Papers of the American Anthropological Association 14. Arlington, VA: American Anthropological Association.

Rick, John & Silvian R. Kembel W. (2004) Building Authority at Chavín de Huántar: Models of Social Organization and Development in the Initial Period and Early Horizon, in Helaine Silverman (ed.) *Andean Archaeology*. Malden, MA: Blackwell Publishers.

Riddel, Frederick A. & L. M. Valdez (1987–1988) Hacha y la occupación temprana del valle de Acarí. *Gaceta Arqueológica Andina* 16: 6–10.

Ringberg, Jennifer Elise (2012) *Daily Life at Cerro León, an Early Intermediate Period Highland Settlement in the Moche Valley, Peru*. Doctoral dissertation, Department of Anthropology, University of North Carolina at Chapel Hill.

Rivera, Mario (2008) The Archaeology of Northern Chile, in Helaine Silverman & William H. Isbell (eds) *Handbook of South American Archaeology*. New York: Springer.

Rivero, Diego E. (2012) La Ocupación Humana Durante La Tansición Pleistoceno-Holoceno (11,000–9,000 a.P.) en las Sierras Centrales de Argentina. *Latin American Antiquity* 23 (4): 551–564.

Robinson, Roger W. (1994) Recent excavations at Hacha in the Acarí Valley, Peru. *Andean Past* 4: 9–37.

Rodman, Amy O. (1992) Textiles and Ethnicity: Tiwanaku in San Pedro de Atacama, North Chile. *Latin American Antiquity* 3 (4): 316–340.

——(2000) *Of Gods and Men, Ancestors and Tapestry in the Central Andes*. Textile Society of America Symposium Proceedings In Approaching Textiles, Varying Viewpoints: Proceedings of the Seventh Biennial Symposium of the Textile Society of America, Santa Fe, New Mexico.

Rodman, Amy O. & Arabel Fernández (2000) Tejidos de Huari y Tiwanaku: Comparaciones y Contextos. *Boletín de Arqueología PUCP* 4: 119–130.

Rollins, Harold B., James B. Richardson III & Daniel H. Sandweiss (1986) The Birth of El Niño: Geoarchaeological Evidence and Implications. *Geoarchaeology* 1: 3–15.

Roosevelt, Anna C., M. Lima da Costa, C. Lopes Machado, M. Michab, N. Mercier, H. Valladas, J. Feathers, W. Barnett, M. Imazio da Silveira, A. Henderson, J. Sliva, B. Chernoff, D. S. Reese, J. A. Holman, N. Toth & K. Schick (1996) Paleoindian Cave Dwellers in the Amazon: The Peopling of the Americas. *Science* 272 (5260): 373–384.

Roosevelt, Anna C., John Douglas & Linda Brown (2002) Migrations and Adaptations of the First Americans: Clovis and Pre-Clovis Viewed from South America, in Nina G. Jablonski (ed.) *The First Americans: The Pleistocene Colonization of the New World*. Berkeley: University of California Press.

Ros Fonseca, Paul (2008) Catastrophe and the Emergence of Political Complexity: A Social Anthropological Model, in Daniel H. Sandweiss & Jeffrey Quilter (eds) *El Niño, Catastrophism, and Culture Change in Ancient America*. Washington, D.C.: Dumbarton Oaks Research Library and Collection.

Rosas Rintel, Marco (2007) Nuevas Perspectivas Acerca del Colapso Moche en el Bajo Jequetepeque: Resultados Preliminares de la Segunda Campaña de Investigación de Proyecto Arqueológico Cerro Chepén. *Bulletin de L'Institut Français d'Études Andines* 36 (2): 221–240.

Roscoe, Paul (2008) Catastrophe and the Emergence of Political Complexity: A Social Anthropological Model, in Daniel H. Sandweiss & Jeffrey Quilter (eds) *El Niño, Catastrophism, and Culture Change in Ancient America*. Washington, D.C.: Dumbarton Oaks Research Library and Collection.

Rose, Courtney E. (2001) Organización Residencial en una Aldea del Periodo Formativo Temprano: El Sitio Warankani de La Brca, Oruro. *Textos Antropológicos* 13 (1–2): 147–166.

Rosselló Truel, Lorenzo (1997) *Canto Grande y su Relación con los Centros Ceremoniales de Planta en "U." Lima*: Published by the author.

Rostworowski de Diez Canseco, María (1962) Nuevos Datos Sobre Tenencia de Tierras Reales en el Incario. *Revista del Museo Nacional* 31: 130–164.

——(1988) *Historia de Tahuantinsuyu*. Lima: Instituto de Estudios Peruanos.

——(1999) *History of the Inca Realm* (trans. Harry B. Iceland). Cambridge, UK; New York: Cambridge University Press.

——(2004) *Costa Peruana Prehispánica: Prólogo a Conflicts over Coca Fields in XVIth Century Peru*. 3rd edition. Obras Completas, 3. Lima: Instituto de Estudios Peruanos.

Rowe, John H. (1944) An Introduction to the Archaeology of Cuzco. *Papers of the Peabody Museum of American Archaeology and Ethnology*, 27(2). Cambridge MA: The Museum.

——(1946) Inca Culture at the Time of the Spanish Conquest, in Julian H. Steward (ed.) *Handbook of South American Indians* Volume 2. Bureau of American Ethnology Bulletin 143. Washington, D.C.: Government Printing Office.

——(1948) The Kingdom of Chimor. *Acta Americana* 6 (1–2).

——(1958) The Adventures of Two Pucara Statues. *Archaeology* 11 (4): 255–261.

——(1962a) Stages and Periods in Archaeological Interpretation. *Southwestern Journal of Anthropology* 18 (1): 40–54.

——(1962b) *Chavín Art: An Inquiry into Its Form and Meaning*. New York: Museum of Primitive Art.

Rowe, John H., Donald Collier & Gordon R. Willey (1950) Reconnaissance Notes on the Site of Huari, near Ayacucho, Peru. *American Antiquity* 16 (2): 120–137.

Rowe, Ann (2012) Tie-Dyed Tunics, in Susan E. Bergh (ed.) *Wari: Lords of the Ancient Andes*. New York and Cleveland: Thames and Hudson and the Cleveland Museum of Art.

Rundel, Phillip W. & Michael O. Dillon (1998) Ecological Patterns in the Bromeliaceae of the Lomas Formations of Coastal Chile and Peru. *Plant Systematics and Evolution* 212 (3–4): 261–278.

Rundel, Phillip W., Michael O. Dillon, H. A. Mooney, S. L. Gulmon & J. R. Ehleringer (1991) The Phytogeography and Ecology of the Coastal Atacama and Peruvian Deserts. *Aliso* 13: 1–50.

Sakai, Masato & Juan José Martinez (2008) Excavations at the Templete de Limoncarro in the Lower Valley of Jequetepeque. *Boletin de Arqueología PUCP* 12: 171–202.

Salazar, Lucy C. (2004) Machu Picchu: Mysterious Royal Estate in the Cloud Forest, in Richard L. Burger & Lucy C. Salazar (eds) *Machu Picchu: Unveiling the Mystery of the Incas*. New Haven: Yale University Press.

Salcedo, José Victor (2011) Increíble Pero Cierto: Hallan Señor Wari en el Cusco. Article in *La Republica* newspaper, Lima, Peru, February 24th, 2011.

Salomon, Frank (1977) Pochteca and Mindalá: A Comparison of Long-Distance Traders in Ecuador and Mesoamerica. *Journal of the Steward Anthropological Society* 9 (2): 231–246.

——(1986) *Ethnic Lords of Quito in the Age of the Incas: The Political Economy of North-Andean Chiefdoms*. Ithaca, NY: Cornell University Press.

——(1995) The Beautiful Grandparents, in Tom Dillehay (ed.) *Tombs for the Living: Andean Mortuary Practices*. Washington, D.C.: Dumbarton Oaks Research Library and Collection.

Salomon, Frank & George L. Urioste (1991) *The Huarochirí Manuscript: A Testament of Ancient and Colonial Andean Religion*. Austin: University of Texas Press.

Samaniego, Lorenzo (2011) Punkurí y El Valle de Nepeña. Arqueología De La Costa De Ancash, Miłosz Giersz & Iván Ghezzi (eds). *Andes* 8: 59–96.

Samaniego, Lorenzo, Enrique Vergara & Henning Bischof (1985) New Evidence on Cerro Sechín, Casma Valley, Peru, in Christopher B. Donnan (ed.) *Early Ceremonial Architecture in the Andes*. Washington, D.C.: Dumbarton Oaks Research Library and Collection.

Sandweiss, Daniel H. (1992) Cronología de Lo Demás, Valle de Chincha e Implicancias Para la Prehistoría Tardía de Chincha. *Boletín de Lima* 79: 33–42.

——(2003) Terminal Pleistocene through Mid-Holocene Archaeological Sites as Paleoclimatic Archives for the Peruvian Coast. *Palaeography, Palaeoclimatology, Palaeoecology* 194: 23–40.

——(2008) Early Fishing Societies in Western South America, in Helaine Silverman & William H. Isbell (eds) *Handbook of South American Archaeology*. New York: Springer.

——(in press) Early Coastal South America, in Colin Renfrew & Paul Bahn (eds) *The Cambridge Prehistory*. Cambridge: University of Cambridge Press.

Sandweiss, Daniel H., Kirk A. Maasch, Richard L. Burger, James B. Richardson III, Harold B. Rollins & Amy Clement (2001) Variation in Holocene El Niño Frequencies: Climate Records and Cultural Consequences in Ancient Peru. *Geology* 29 (7): 603–606.

Sandweiss, Daniel H., Heather McInnis, Richard L. Burger, Asunción Cano, Bernardino Ojeda, Rolando Paredes, Maria del Carmén Sandweiss & Michael D. Glascock (1998) Quebrada Jaguay: Early Maritime Adaptations in South America. *Science* 281: 1830–1832.

Sandweiss, Daniel H. & Jeffrey Quilter (2009) *El Niño, Catastrophism, and Culture Change in Ancient America*. Washington, D.C.: Dumbarton Oaks Research Library and Collection.

Sandweiss, Daniel H., James B. Richardson III, E. J. Reitz, J. T. Hsu & R. A. Feldman (1989) Early Maritime Adaptations in the Andes: Preliminary Studies at the Ring Site, Peru, in Don S. Rice, Charles Stanish & Phillip R. Scarr (eds) *Ecology, Settlement, and History in the Osmore Drainage, Peru*. BAR International Series, 545(i). Oxford, UK: B.A.R.

Sandweiss, Daniel H., James B. Richardson III, E. J. Reitz, Harold B. Rollins & Kirk A. Maasch (1996) Geoarchaeological Evidence from Peru for a 5000 Years BP Onset of El Niño. *Science* 273 (5281): 1531–1533.

Sandweiss, Daniel H., Ruth Shady Solis, Michael E. Moseley, David Keefer & Charles R. Ortloff (2009) Environmental Change and Economic Development in Coastal Peru Between 5,800 and 3,600 Years Ago. *Proceedings of the National Academy of Sciences of the United States of America* 106 (5): 1359–1363.

Santos Ramírez, René (1980) Cerámica Temprana Estilo La Ramada. *Arqueos Perú* 1: 3–29.

Sauer, Carl O. (1952) *Agricultural Origins and Dispersals*. New York: American Geographical Society.

Saunders, Nicholas J. (1998) Stealers of Light, Traders in Brilliance: Amerindian Metaphysics in the Mirror of Conquest. *RES* (Spring) 33: 225–252.

——(2003) "Catching the Light": Technologies of Power and Enchantment in Pre-Columbian Goldworking, in Jeffrey Quilter & John W. Hoopes (eds) *Gold and Power in Ancient Costa Rica, Panama, and Colombia*. Washington, D.C.: Dumbarton Oaks Research Library and Collection.

Saville, Marshall H. (1907) *The Antiquities of Manabí, Ecuador: Preliminary Report. Contributions to South American Archaeology*. New York: The Heye Foundation.

——(1910) *The Antiquities of Manabí, Ecuador: Final Report. Contributions to South American Archaeology 2*. New York: The Heye Foundation.

Schjellerup, Inge R. (1997) *Incas and Spaniards in the Conquest of the Chachapoyas: Archaeological and Ethnohistorical Research in the North-Eastern Andes of Peru*. Copenhagen: National Museum of Denmark, Department of Ethnography.

Schreiber, Katharina J. (1992) *Wari Imperialism in Middle Horizon Peru*. Anthropological Papers of the Museum of Anthropology No 87. Ann Arbor: University of Michigan.

——(1998) Afterword, in Patrick H. Carmichael (ed.) *The Archaeology and Pottery of Nazca, Peru: Alfred L. Kroeber's 1926 Expedition*. Walnut Creek, CA: Alta Mira Press.

——(2005) Imperial Agendas and Local Agency: Wari Colonial Strategies, in Gil J. Stein (ed.) *The Archaeology of Colonial Encounters: Comparative Perspectives*. Santa Fe, NM: School of American Research.

Schreiber, Katharina J. & J. Lancho Rojas (2003) *Irrigation and Society in the Peruvian Desert: The Puquios of Nasca*. Lanham, MD: Lexington Books.

Segura Llanos, Rafael & Izumi Shimada (2010) What Role did Wari Play in the Lima Political Economy? in Justin Jennings (ed) *Beyond Wari Walls: Regional Perspectives on Middle Horizon Peru*. Albuquerque: University of New Mexico Press.

Seiichi, Izumi (1971) Development of the Formative Culture in the Ceja de Montaña of the Central Andes, in Elizabeth P. Benson (ed.) *Dumbarton Oaks Conference on Chavín*. Washington, D.C.: Dumbarton Oaks Research Library and Collection.

Seiichi, Izumi & Kazuo Terada (1972) *Andes 4: Excavations at Kotosh, Peru, 1963 and 1966*. Tokyo: University of Tokyo Press.

Service, Elman R. (1968) *Primitive Social Organization*. New York: Random House.

Shady, Ruth (1976) Investigaciones Arqueológicas en la Cuenca de Utcubamba. *Actos del Congreso Internacional de Americanistas* 3: 579–589.

Shady, Ruth & Christopher Kleihege (2010) *Caral: The First Civilization in the Americas/La Primera Civilización de America*. Singapore: CK Photo Publications.

Shady Solis, Ruth, Jonathan Haas & Winifred Creamer (2001) Dating Caral, a Pre-ceramic Site in the Supe Valley on the Central Coast of Peru. *Science* 292 (5517): 723–726.

Sherbondy, Jeannette E. (1979) Les Réseaux d'Irrigation dans la Géographie Politique de Cuzco. *Journal de la Société des Americanistes* 66 (1): 45–66.

——(1982) *The Canal Systems of Hanan Cuzco*. Doctoral dissertation, Department of Anthropology, University of Illinois, Champaign-Urbana.

——(1987) Incaic Organization of Terraced Irrigation in Cuzco Peru, in William M. Denevan, Kenty Mathewson & Gregory Knapp (eds) *Pre-Hispanic Agricultural Fields in the Andean Region*, Part II. Proceedings of the 45 International Congress of Americanists, Bogotá, Colombia, 1985. BAR International Series, 359(ii). Oxford, UK: B.A.R.

——(1996) Panaca Lands: Re-Invented Communities. *Journal of the Steward Anthropological Society* 24 (1&2): 173–201.

Shibata, Koichiro (2011) Cronología, Relaciones Interregionales y Organización Social en el Formativo: Esencia y Perspectiva del Valle Bajo de Nepeña. Arqueología de la Costa de Ancash, Miłosz Giersz and Iván Ghezzi (eds). *Andes* 8 (2011): 113–134.

Shimada, Izumi (2000) Late Prehispanic Coastal States, in Laura Laurencich Minelli (ed.) *The Inca World: The Development of Pre-Columbian Peru, AD 1000–1534*. Norman: University of Oklahoma Press.

Shimada, Izumi, Ken-ichi Shinoda, Julie Franum, Robert Corrunccini & Kirokatsu Watanabe (2004) An Integrated Analysis of Pre-Hispanic Mortuary Practices: A Middle Sicán Case Study. *Current Anthropology* 45 (3): 369–402.

Silgado Ferro, Enrique (1978) História de los Sismos Más Notables Ocurridos en el Perú (1513–1974). *Boletín, Serie C. Geodinámica e Ingenería Geológica*, no. 3. Lima: Instituto de Geología y Minería.

Silverblatt, Irene M. (1987) *Moon, Sun, and Witches: Gender Ideologies and Class in Inca and Colonial Peru*. Princeton, NJ: Princeton University Press.

Silverman, Helaine (1993) *Cahuachi in the Ancient Nasca World*. Iowa City: University of Iowa Press.

——(1996) The Formative Period on the South Coast of Peru: A Critical Review. *Journal of World Prehistory* 10(2): 95–146.

——(2002) Differentiating Paracas Necropolis and Early Nasca Textiles, in Helaine Silverman & William H. Isbell (eds) *Andean Archaeology II: Art, Landscape, and Society*. New York: Plenum/Kluwer.

Silverman, Helaine & Donald A. Proulx (2002) *The Nasca*. Malden, MA: Blackwell Publishers.

Spalding, Karen (1988) *Huarochiri: An Andean Society Under Inca and Spanish Rule*. Palo Alto, CA: Stanford University Press.

Spaulding, Albert C. (1960) The Dimensions of Archaeology, in Gertrude E. Dole & Robert L. Carneiro (eds) *Essays in the science of culture in honor of Leslie A. White*. Crowell, NY. [Reprinted in Deetz, James (1971) *Man's Imprint From the Past: Readings in the Methods of Archaeology*. Boston: Little, Brown.]

Squier, Epharim George (1877) *Peru: Incidents of Travel and Exploration in the Land of the Incas*. New York: Harper and Brothers.

——(1973[1877]) *Peru: Incidents of Travel and Exploration in the Land of the Incas*. New York: AMS Press.

Stahl, Peter W. (1985) The Hallucinogenic Basis of Early Valdivia Phase Ceramic Bowl Iconography. *Journal of Psychoactive Drugs* 17 (2): 105–123.

Staller, John E. (1991) *Valdivia Tardío en la provincia del Oro*. Revista de la Universidad de Guayaquil.

——(2001) The Jelí Phase Complex at La Emerenciana, a Late Valdivia Site in Southern El Oro Province, Ecuador. *Andean Past* 6: 117–174.

Staller, John E. & Robert G. Thompson (2002) A Multidisciplinary Approach to Understanding the Initial Introduction of Maize into Coastal Ecuador. *Journal of Archaeological Science* 29: 33–50.

Stanish, Charles(2002) Tiwanaku political economy, in William H. Isbell & Helaine Silverman (eds) *Andean Archaeology I: Variations in Socio-political Organization*. New York: Kluwer Academic.

——(2010) *Prehistoric State Formation in the Lake Titicaca Basin, Andean South America*. Lecture presented in the Department of Anthropology, Harvard University, May 5th.

Stanish, Charles & Brian S. Bauer (eds) (2004) *Archaeological Research on the Islands of the Sun and Moon, Lake Titicaca, Bolivia: Final Results from the Proyecto Tiksi Kjara*. Los Angeles: Cotsen Institute of Archaeology Press.

——(2007) Pilgrimage and the Geography of Power in the Inka Empire, in Richard L. Burger, Craig Morris & Ramiro Matos Mendieta (eds) *Variations in the Expression of Inka Power*. Washington, D.C.: Dumbarton Oaks Research Library and Collection.

Stanish, Charles & Amanda B. Cohen (2005) Introduction to Advances in Titicaca Basin Archaeology-1, in Charles Stanish, Amanda B. Cohen & Mark S. Alderderfer (eds) *Advances in Titicaca Basin Archaeology* volume 1. Los Angeles: Cotsen Institute of Archaeology Press, University of California.

Stanish, Charles & Abigail Levine (2011) War and early state formation in the northern Titicaca Basin, Peru. *Proceedings of the National Academy of Sciences of the United States of America* 108 (34): 13901–13906.

Stern, Steve J. (1982) *Peru's Indian Peoples and the Challenge of the Spanish Conquest: Huamanga to 1640*. Madison, WI: University of Wisconsin Press.

——(1993) *Peru's Indian Peoples and the Challenge of the Spanish Conquest: Huamanga to 1640*. 2nd ed. Madison, WI: University of Wisconsin Press.

Stirling, Stuart (2000) *The Last Conquistador: Mansio Serra de Leguizamón and the Conquest of the Incas*. Stroud, UK: Sutton Publishers.

Stone, Rebecca R. (2007) "And All Theirs Different from His": The Dumbarton Oaks Royal Inka Tunic in Context, in Richard L. Burger, Craig Morris & Ramiro Matos Mendieta (eds) *Variations in the Expression of Power*. Washington, D.C.: Dumbarton Oaks Research Library and Collection.

Stone-Miller, Rebecca (2002) *Art of the Andes from Chavín to Inca*. London and New York: Thames and Hudson.

Stothert, Karen E. (1985) The Preceramic Las Vegas Culture of Coastal Ecuador. *American Antiquity* 50: 613–637.

Stothert, Karen E. & Jeffrey Quilter (1991) Archaic Adaptations of the Andean Region, 9000 to 5000 BP. *Revista de Arqueología Americana*, 4: 25–53.

Stovel, Emily (2008) Interaction and Social Fields in San Pedro de Atacama, Northern Chile, in Helaine Silverman & William H. Isbell (eds) *Handbook of South American Archaeology*. New York: Springer.

Strong, William Duncan (1957) *Paracas, Nazca, and Tiahuanacoid Cultural Relationships in South Coastal Peru*. Memoirs of the Society for American Archaeology 13. Salt Lake City, UT: Society for American Archaeology.

Surovell, Todd A. & Brigid S. Grund (2012) The Associational Critique of Quaternary Overkill and Why It Is Largely Irrelevant to the Extinction Debate. *American Antiquity* 77 (4): 672–687.

Tello, Julio C. (1942) *Orígen y Desarollo de las Civilizaciones Prehistóricas Andinas*. Lima: Librería e Imprenta Gil.

——(1960) Chavín: *Cultura Matríz de la Civilización Andina, Primera Parte*. Publicación Antropológica del Archivo "Julio C. Tello" de la Universidad Nacional Major de San Marcos, Volumen II. Lima: Universidad de San Marcos.

Thompson, Robert G. (2006) Documenting the Presence of Maize in Central and South America through Phytolith Analysis of Food Residues, in Melinda A. Zeder, Daniel G. Bradley, Eve Emschwiller & Bruce D. Smith (eds) *Documenting Domestication: New Genetic and Archaeological Paradigms*. Berkeley: University of California Press.

Tomasto Cagigao, Elsa Lucila (2009) *Caries Dental y Dieta en Poblaciones Prehispánicas de los Valles de Palpa Costa Sur del Perú (3500 a.C. – 1000 d.C.)*. Graduate thesis, Ponifical Catholic University of Peru (PUCP), Lima.

Topic, John, Theresa Lange Topic & Alfredo Melly Cava (2002) Catequil: The Archaeology, Ethnohistory, and Ethnography of a Major Provincial Huaca, in William H. Isbell & Helaine Silverman (eds) *Andean Archaeology 1, Variations in Sociopolitical Organization*. New York: Plenum.

Topic, Theresa Lange & John Topic (2010) Contextualizing the Wari-Huamachucho Relationship, in Justin Jennings (ed.) *Beyond Wari Walls: Regional Perspectives on Middle Horizon Peru*. Albuquerque: University of New Mexico Press.

Torres, Constantino Manuel (1998) Psychoactive Substances in the Archaeology of Northern Chile and NW Argentina: A Comparative Review of the Evidence. *Chungará*, 30 (1): 49–63.

——(2006) *Anadenanthera: Visionary Plant of Ancient South America*. New York: Haworth Herbal Press.

Toshihara, Kayoko (2002) *The Cupisnique Culture in the Formative Period World of the Central Andes, Peru* (2 volumes). Doctoral Dissertation, University of Illinois and Urbana-Champaign.

Tripcevich, Nicholas (2008) *Llama Caravan Transport: A Study of Mobility with a Contemporary Andean Salt Caravan*. Presentation at the 73rd Annual Meeting of the Society for American Archaeology, Vancouver, B.C., Canada.

Tschauner, Hartmut (2003) Honco Pampa: Arquitectura de Elite del Horizonte Medio del Callejon de Huaylas, in Bebel Ibarra (ed.) *Arqueolgia de la Sierra de Ancash: Propuestas y Perspectivas*. Lima: Instituto Cultural Runa.

Tung, Tiffiny A. (2007) Trauma and Violence in the Wari Empire of the Peruvian Andes: Warfare, Raids, and Ritual Fights. *American Journal of Physical Anthropology* 133: 941–956.

——(2012) *Violence, Ritual, and the Wari Empire*. Gainesville: University of Florida Press.

Tung, Tiffiny A. & Kelly J. Knudson (2008) Social Identities and Geographical Origins of Huari Trophy Heads from Conchopata, Peru, in William H. Isbell & Helaine Silverman (eds) *Andean Archaeology III: North and South*. New York: Plenum.

Ubbelohde-Doering, Heinrich (1967) *On the Royal Highways of the Inca: Archaeological Treasure of Ancient Peru*. New York: Praeger.

Ubelaker, Douglas H. (2003) Health issues in the Early Formative of Ecuador: skeletal biology of Real Alto, in J. Scott Raymond & Richard L. Burger (eds) *Archaeology of Formative Ecuador*. Washington, D.C.: Dumbarton Oaks Research Library and Collection.

Uceda, Santiago (2001) Investigations at Huaca de la Luna, Moche Valley: An Example of Moche Religious Architecture, in Joanne Pillsbury (ed.) *Moche Art and Archaeology in Ancient Peru*. New Haven: Yale University Press and the National Gallery of Art.

Uhle, Max (1913) *Die Ruinen von Moche*. Mâcon, France: Protat Frères.

——(1991 [1903]) *Pachacamac: A reprint of the 1903 edition of Max Uhle*. Izumi Shimada (ed.). Philadelphia: The University Museum.

Urteaga, Horacio H. (1978) El Arte de Navegar Entre Los Antiguos Peruanos, in Rogger Ravines (ed.) *Tecnología Andina*. Lima: Instituto de Estudios Peruanos.

Urton, Gary (1988) At the Crossroads of the Earth and the Sky: An Andean Cosmology. *Latin American Monographs*, 55 (reprint of the 1981 edn.). Austin: University of Texas Press.

——(1990) *The History of a Myth: Pacariqtambo and the Origin of the Inkas*. Austin: University of Texas Press.

——(2003) *Signs of the Inca Khipu: Binary Coding in the Andean Knotted-String Records*. Austin: University of Texas Press.

——(2008) The Body of Meaning in Chavín Art, in William J. Conklin & Jeffrey Quilter (eds) *Chavín: Art, Architecture and Culture*. Cotsen Institute of Archaeology Monograph 61. Los Angeles: Cotsen Institute of Archaeology Press, University of California.

Valdez, Francisco (2008) Inter-zonal Relationships in Ecuador, in Helaine Silverman and William H. Isbell (eds) *Handbook of South American Archaeology*. New York, NY: Springer.

Valdez, Francisco, Jean Guffroy, Geoffroy de Saulieu, Julio Hurtado & Alexandra Yepes (2005) Découverte d'un Site Cérémoniel Formatif sur le Versant Oriental des Andes. *Comptes Rendu Paleovol* 4: 369–374.

Valencia Zegarra, Alfredo (2005) Wari Hydraulic Works in the Lucre Basin, in Gordon F. McEwan (ed.) *Pikillacta: The Wari Empire in Cuzco*. Iowa City: University of Iowa Press.

Van Buren, Mary (1996) Rethinking the Vertical Archipelago: Ethnicity, Exchange, and History in the South Central Andes. *American Anthropologist* 98 (2): 338–351.

Van Gijseghem, Hendrik (2004) *Migration, Agency and Social Change on a Prehistoric Frontier: The Paracas-Nasca Transition in the Southern Nasca Drainage, Peru*. Doctoral dissertation. Department of Anthropology, University of California, Santa Barbara.

——(2006) A Frontier Perspective on Paracas Society and Nasca Ethnogenesis. *Latin American Antiquity* 17 (4): 419–444.

Vaughn, Kevin J. (2005) Crafts and the Materialization of Chiefly Power in Nasca, in Kevin J. Vaughn, Dennis E. Ogburn, Christina A. Conlee (eds) *The Foundations of Power in the Prehispanic Andes*. Archaeological Papers of the American Anthropological Association, 14. Berkeley, CA: Published by the University of California Press for the American Archaeological Association.

——(2009) *The Ancient Andean Village*. Tucson, AZ: University of Arizona Press.

Vega, María del Carmen (2012) *Paleoepidemiología de Huaca 20, una Población de la Época Lima Tardío del Valle de Rímac*. Paper presented at Arqueología y Patrimonio de la Cultura Lima. 14–16 August at the Museo de Arte de Lima (MALI), Lima, Peru.

Velarde, D. María Inés & Pamela Castro de la Mata G. (2007) Tecnología Metalúrgica Pashash. *Acta Microscopia* 16 (1–2; Supp.2): 287–288.

Verano, John (1986) A Mass Burial of Mutilated Individuals at Pacatnamu, in Christopher B. Donnan & Guillermo A. Cock (eds) *The Pacatnamu Papers*, Volume 1. Los Angeles: Fowler Museum of Culture History, University of California.

——(2001) War and Death in the Moche World: Osteological Evidence and Visual Discourse, in Joanne Pillsbury (ed.) *Moche Art and Archaeology in Ancient Peru*. New Haven: Yale University Press and the National Gallery of Art.

——(2008) Trophy Head Taking and Human Sacrifice in Andean South America, in Helaine Silverman & William H. Isbell (eds) *Handbook of South American Archaeology*. New York: Springer.

Villalba, Marcelo (1988) *Cotocollao: Una Aldea Formativa del Valle de Quito*. Serie Monográfica 2. Miscelánea Antropológica Ecuatoriana. Quito: Museos del Banco Central del Ecuador.

Vogel, Melissa A. (2012) *Frontier Life in Ancient Peru: The Archaeology of Cerro la Cruz*. Gainesville: University Press of Florida.

Von Humboldt, Alexander (2006, 1907) *Personal Narrative of Travels to the Equinoctial Regions of America During the Year 1799–1804*, Volume 1. Charleston, SC: Bibliobazaar.

Vranich, Alexi (2001) The Akapana Pyramid: Reconsidering Tiwanaku's Monumental Center. *Boletín de Arqueología PUCP* 5: 295–308.

Vreeland, James M. (1993) Naturally Colored and Organically Grown Cottons: Anthropological and Historical Perspective. *Proceedings of the 1993 Beltwide Cotton Conferences*. Memphis, TN: National Cotton Council of America.

——(1999) The Revival of Colored Cotton. *Scientific American* 280 (4): 112–118.

Walker, Charles F. (2008) *Shaky Colonialism: The 1746 Earthquake-Tsunami in Lima, Peru, and Its Long Aftermath*. Durham, NC: Duke University Press.

Wallace, Dwight T. (1962) Cerrillos: An Early Paracas Site in Ica, Peru. *American Antiquity* 27 (3): 303–314.

——(1991) A Technical and Iconographic Analysis of Carhua Painted Textiles, in Anne Paul (ed.) *Paracas: Art and Architecture*. Iowa City: University of Iowa Press.

Watanabe, Shinya (2001) Wari y Cajamarca In Huari y Tiwanaku: Modelos vs. Evidencias, Segunda Parte. *Boletín de Arqueología PUCP* No. 5, Peter Kaulicke & William H. Isbell (eds). Lima: Fondo Editorial de la Pontificia Universidad Católica del Perú.

Wayne, Robert K., Jennifer A. Leonard & Carles Vilà (2006) Genetic Analysis of Dog Domestication, in Melinda A. Zeder, Daniel G. Bardley, Eve Emshwiller & Bruce D. Smith (eds) *Documenting Domestication: New Genetic and Archaeological Paradigms*. Berkeley: University of California Press.

Webb, Hillary S. (2012) *Yanantín and Masintín in the Andean World: Complementary Dualism in Modern Peru*. Albuquerque: University of New Mexico Press.

Webb, S. David (ed.) (2005) *First Floridians and Last Mastodons: The Page-Ladson Site in the Aucilla River*. Dordrecht, The Netherlands: Springer.

Weismantel, Mary (2004) Moche Sex Pots: Reproduction and Temporality in Ancient South America. *American Anthropologist* 106 (3): 495–505.

——(2006) The Ayllu, Real and Imagined: The Romance of Community in the Andes, in Gerald Creed (ed.) *The Seductions of Community: Emancipations, Oppressions, Quandries*. Santa Fe: School of American Research Press.

Wendt, W. (1964) Die Präkeramische Siedlung am Rio Seco, Perú. *Baessler-Archiv*, n.f. 11 (2): 225–275.

West, M. (1970) Community Settlement Patterns at Chan Chan. *American Antiquity* 35: 74–86.

Wester de La Torre, Carlos (2012) *Sacerdotista Lambayeque de Chornancap: Mistério y História*. Lima: Ministerio de Cultura.

Wheeler, Jane C. (1984) On the Origin and Early Development of Camelid Pastoralism in the Andes, in Juliet Clutton-Brock & Caroline Grigson (eds) *Animals and Archaeology, Volume 3: Early Herders and their Flocks*. BAR International Series, 202. Oxford, UK: British Archaeological Reports.

——(1985) De la Chasse à l'Elevage, in Daniel Lavallée, Michèle Julien, Jane C. Wheeler & Claudine Karlin (eds) *Telarmachay: Chasseurs et Pasteurs Préhistoriques des Andes I*. Paris: Editions Recherches sur les Civilisations, ADPF.

——(1999) Patrones Prehistóricos de Utilización de los Camélidos Sudamericanos, in Peter Kaulicke (ed.) El Periodo Araico en el Perú: Hacia una Definición de los Orígenes. *Boletín de Arqueología PUCP* 3: 297–305. Lima, Peru: Fondo Editorial Pontificia Universidad Católica del Perú.

Willey, Gordon R. (1943) Excavations in the Chancay Valley, in William D. Strong, Gordon R. Willey & J. M. Corbette (eds) *Columbia Studies in Archaeology and Ethnology* 1(3). New York.

Willey, Gordon R. & Jeremy A. Sabloff (1993) *A History of American Archaeology*. 3rd edition. New York: W. H. Freeman and Company.

Williams, Carlos (1985) A Scheme for the Early Monumental Architecture of the Central Coast of Peru, in Christopher P. Donnan (ed.) *Early Ceremonial Architecture in the Andes*. Washington, D.C.: Dumbarton Oaks Research Library and Collection.

Wing, Elizabeth S. (1972) Utilization of Animal Resources in the Peruvian Andes, in Seiichi Izumi & Kazuo Terada (eds) *Andes 4: Excavations at Kotosh, Peru, 1963 and 1964*. Tokyo: University of Tokyo Press.

Yaroslav, Kuzmin, V. (2006) Chronology of the Earliest Pottery in East Asia: Progress and Pitfalls. *Antiquity* 80(308): 362–371.

Young-Sánchez, Margaret (ed.) (2004) *Tiwanaku: Ancestors of the Inca*. Lincoln: University of Nebraska Press.

Zeidler, James A. (1988) Feline imagery, stone mortars, and Formative Period interaction spheres in the northern Andean area. *Journal of Latin American Lore* 14 (2): 243–283.

——(2003) Appendix A: Formative Period Chronology for the Coast and Western Lowlands of Ecuador, in J. Scott Raymond & Richard L. Burger (eds) *Archaeology of Formative Ecuador*. Washington, D.C.: Dumbarton Oaks Research Library and Collection.

——(2008) The Ecuadorian Formative, in Helaine Silverman & William H. Isbell (eds) *Handbook of South American Archaeology*. New York: Springer.

Zeidler, James A. & John S. Isaacson (2003) Settlement Process and Historical Contingency in the Western Ecuadorian Formative, in J. Scott Raymond & Richard L. Burger (eds) *Archaeology of Formative Ecuador*. Washington, D.C.: Dumbarton Oaks Research Library and Collection.

Zeidler, James A. & Deborah M. Pearsall (eds) (1994) *Regional Archaeology in Northern Manabí, Volume 1: Environment, Cultural Chronology, and Prehistoric Subsistence in the Jama River Valley*. University of Pittsburgh Memoirs in Latin American Archaeology No. 8. Pittsburgh and Quito: University of Pittsburgh and Libri Mundi.

Zuidema, R. Tom (1964) The Ceque System of Cuzco (trans. by Eva M. Hooykaas). *International Archives of Ethnography* Supplement to Volume 30. Leiden, The Netherlands: E. J. Brill.

——(1990a) Dynastic Structures in Andean Cultures, in Michael E. Moseley & Alana Cordy-Collins (eds) *The Northern Dynasties: Kinship and Statecraft in Chimor*. Washington, D.C.: Dumbarton Oaks Research Library and Collection.

——(1990b) *Inca Civilization in Cuzco*. Austin: University of Texas Press.

INDEX

Numbers in **bold** indicate figures

n = note